OMNI's

SCREEN FLIGHTS/
SCREEN FANTASIES

The Future According
to Science Fiction Cinema

OMNI's SCREEN FLIGHTS / SCREEN FANTASIES

THE FUTURE ACCORDING TO SCIENCE FICTION CINEMA

EDITED BY

DANNY PEARY

INTRODUCTION BY HARLAN ELLISON

A Dolphin Book
Doubleday & Company, Inc.
Garden City, New York
1984

To Suzanne and Zoë,
my guarantees for a happy future.

Library of Congress Cataloging in Publication Data

Main entry under title:

Omni's screen flights, screen fantasies.

1. Science fiction films—History and criticism.
I. Peary, Danny, 1949-   II. Title.   III. Title:
Screen flights, screen fantasies.
PN1995.9.S26046   1984
  791.43'09'09356   84-4022

ISBN 0-385-19199-5
ISBN 0-385-19202-9 (pbk.)

Book Design: Robert Fitzpatrick

Acknowledgments

I received an inordinate amount of help while assembling this book and would like to thank everyone collectively and individually. First, let me express my deep gratitude to the three people who got this project off the ground: Jim Fitzgerald, my editor at Doubleday; Bob Weil, *Omni*'s book editor; and Chris Tomasino, my agent. I am also most grateful to my designer Bob Fitzpatrick, who makes deadline-panic almost tolerable. A personal thank you goes to Tim Onosko for thinking up the title *Screen Flights Screen Fantasies*.

I am, of course, eternally grateful to all the people who either wrote for this book or granted an interview. It should be pointed out that most everyone had to interrupt a book or film project in order to participate. Special thanks for special help·go to Harlan Ellison, Robert C. Cumbow, Stephanie Rothman, Robert Bloch, Michael Goodwin, Allen Eyles, Charles Bennett, Frederik Pohl, Frederik Pohl IV, Ridley Scott, George Miller, Cornel Wilde, Jerry Stahl, Syd Mead, Sally Hibbin, John Badham, Tim Onosko (again), and, in particular, Ed Naha.

I sincerely appreciate the help given me by my copy editor David Wolfsohn, proofreader Peter Weissman, transcriber Peggy Barber, and my special assistant Zoë Weaver, my daughter. Thanks also go to Peter Tyson and Marcia Potash at *Omni* and Jennie McGregor and Beatrice Reed at Doubleday, as well as to Doubleday's associate art director Doug Bergstreser. And thanks to Anne Kostick and Alexandra Gignoux, invaluable volunteers.

Thank you Kathy Keeton and Bob Guccione.

I will not forget the tremendous help given me by Larry Winokur, Peter Schneider, Nancy Deiter, Erik van der Palen, Stephanie Mardesich, John Whitney, Jr., Teresa Victor, Dana Satler, Ginny Nugent, Andrea Fontaine, Judith Rolfe, Mary Corliss, Wayne Morris, Sue Hoover, Helena Cardoza, Charles Swartz, Peter Stamelman, Sally Jackson, David Stuart, Paula Klaw, Ira Kramer, Michael Blowen, Joseph Sargent, John Landis, Caroline Ray, Allan Gale, Eddie Egan, Gil Lamont, BPE Graphics, VCI, Cory Gann, Norine Gann, Carol Summers, Terri Tafreshi, Jamie Umansky, Donna Pastor, Reid Rosefelt, Dore Freeman, Susan Durning, Sue Mariani, Mary Lugo, Janna Wong Healy, Lisa Dunkley, Eddy Brandt, Mark Ricci, Tom Haskins, Janis Rothbard-Chaskin, Tom DeFanti, Su-Ae Park, Allen Park, Bea Schultz, and my parents, Joseph and Laura Peary.

Photo credits go to the following: Walt Disney Productions, Digital Productions, the Museum of Modern Art Film Archive, Movie Star News, Lucasfilm Ltd., Syd Mead, New Line, M-G-M, Paramount, Universal, Warner Bros., Twentieth Century-Fox, New World Pictures, the Memory Shop, Eddy Brandt's Saturday Matinee, Jerry Ohlinger's Movie Materials, 21st Century, American International Pictures, Embassy Pictures, LQ-Jaf, Columbia, the Ladd Company, Lippert, Realart, Astor, Bryanston, Eagle Lion Films, New Yorker Films, Pathé Contemporary Films.

And finally I thank my wife Suzanne Rafer, for her support, for her inspiration, for her sense of humor.

Contents

―――――――

PART II:
JOURNEYS INTO THE FUTURE

Preface

Harlan Ellison's lengthy introduction to this book covers the entire science fiction genre, from films in which atomic bombs create or unleash giant monsters to alien-visitation/invasion movies to space adventures set a long time ago in galaxies far, far away to those films that either take place in *Earth's* future or advance concepts that apply to *Earth's* future. While all types of sf films are discussed within this volume, *Screen Flights Screen Fantasies* concentrates on the "futuristic films," exploring their themes, detailing how they were made, and examining the futuristic visions of the people who made them. What makes the "futuristic" subgenre particularly compelling is that our own visions of the future were, I believe, formulated to a great extent from having seen many convincing films that have prophesied about the Earth ten, fifty, one hundred, five hundred, or one thousand years from now.

If we do possess an anti-nuclear bias, an uneasiness in regard to all forms of artificial life, a fear of technology, a distrust of scientists and other intellectuals, or simultaneous feelings of wonder and worry about tomorrow—and the day after—it can probably be traced to our having believed much of what filmmakers have speculated. Of course, our source is suspect. After all these films are *fiction,* even if the term "science fiction" implies that some amount of deductive *scientific* reasoning went into their conceptions. Moreover, since *history* according to the cinema is bunk, as we all have come to realize, it doesn't seem likely that *filmmakers* would be capable of accurately *predicting* our future, especially since most of them have no more scientific knowledge than we laymen have. But time and again their futuristic visions have fascinated us; when futuristic films are well made, they capture our imagination, they make us want to believe them. All of us who have anxiously waited for 1984 and finally have been able to compare our world's societies to that posited by Orwell *and* by the filmmakers who adapted his book in 1956 are already wondering how our

Earth will compare to the future worlds depicted in, say, *Metropolis, Things to Come, Fahrenheit 451, 2001, THX 1138* (the cinema's equivalent to Huxley's *Brave New World*), *A Clockwork Orange, Blade Runner,* and *The Road Warrior;* and are perhaps worrying that we may have no future, as such films as *On the Beach, Dr. Strangelove,* and *Testament* warn is possible.

Are all "futuristic" films simply fantasies (which doesn't mean they aren't terrific films), or were some made by filmmakers who really do have a bead on the future and a deep commitment toward presenting it as they envision it, even if it means causing us anxiety attacks? In the more than forty original essays and exclusive interviews contained in *Screen Flights Screen Fantasies,* an intriguing mix of well-known and opinionated science fiction authors, film critics, and filmmakers themselves attempt to answer this question.

Danny Peary

Danny Peary has a B.A. in History from the University of Wisconsin and an M.A. in Cinema from the University of Southern California. He has written on film, television, and sports for numerous magazines and newspapers in the United States, Canada, and England. He is a contributing editor to *Video Movies* and writes frequently for *TV Guide-Canada.* He is the editor of *Close-Ups: The Movie Star Book,* the coeditor of *The American Animated Cartoon: A Critical Anthology,* and the author of *Cult Movies* and *Cult Movies 2.*

INTRODUCTION

Lurching Down Memory Lane with It, Them, The Thing, Godzilla, HAL 9000 … That Whole Crowd:

An Overview of the Science Fiction Cinema

Harlan Ellison

Somewhere in the New Mexico desert near Alamagordo, 1953. Eight years after the first A-bomb was exploded. Joan Weldon, wearing sand-glasses, a mannish suit, and for some inexplicable reason high heels in the desert sand, surveys the terrain, looking for signs of whatever it was that killed a handful of people and destroyed an entire house. Gently at first, then louder, as she crouches there, we hear O.S. the eerie sound of a high, keening whine. Joan hears it. She grows startled, frightened, terrified. Then we see, rising above her, from behind a dune, something … some *thing* … hideous apparition … a creature spawned from hell … it is THEM! She screams. Of course: she screams.

Pounding across the sand come James Arness and James Whitmore, drawing their guns as they rush to her aid. (Edmund Gwenn huffs and puffs along behind, wearing an expression that asks, "How did I get from playing Santa Claus to *this*?")

And the thing behind the dune rises up and up and we see it is a giant ant, an acromegalic example of *Formica sanguinea,* a seventy-foot-long killer with clacking mandibles and a stinger tail oozing formic acid. It lumbers forward, and Joan Weldon slips in the sand. Wedgies next time, Joan, wedgies, fer chrissakes!

The predator is almost upon her. "Fire at the antennae!" screams Edmund Gwenn, seeing his daughter about to be devoured. Arness shoots off one antenna; Whitmore rushes back to his police car to unship a riot gun.

The horrifying sound of the ant's whining battle cry rises above the banshee howl of the wind-driven sand; and soprano counterpoint is played by Ms. Weldon, a latter-day Fay Wray. Whitmore returns and opens fire with the machine gun. The great ant finally falls. For the moment we are safe from … THEM.

Howz*about* that: Warner Bros. made the world safe from *Them!* in 1953.

From Them, perhaps, but not from the hordes of giant fleas, katydids, mantises, sloths, spiders, and other flopping, lurching, slithering grotesqueries an aberrated Hollywood has proffered as their conception of the *ne plus ultra* in science fiction films. Old-time fans of speculative fiction,

---

Harlan Ellison has won numerous writing awards, including the Hugo (7½ times), the Nebula (three times), the Hollywood Writers Guild award for most outstanding teleplay (three times), and the Georges Méliès fantasy film award (two times). He has written film and television scripts, more than one thousand stories, and thirty-eight books, including *The Glass Teat, The Other Glass Teat, Spider Kiss, Deathbird Stories, Strange Wine, Approaching Oblivion, Ellison Wonderland, All The Lies That Are My Life,* and *Shatterday.*

who have adored that most fantastical and specialized genre of fiction since 1926 when Hugo Gernsback introduced the first magazine of "scientifiction," *Amazing Stories,* have seen their favorite literary form first slurred as "that Buck Rogers stuff," and have then prayed for a return of the original pejorative when it became known as "that monster stuff."

For Hollywood's conception of what to do with sf (sometimes hideously referred to as sci-fi, a term that sets the back teeth to aching) has usually been on the level of *The Tapioca Pudding that Had Intercourse with Cleveland.*

Even the profligate hurling of things into the sky—from Sputniks to Apollos—benefited sf films but little. We were then inundated with a spate of films in which cardboard spaceships with astronauts frequently clinging to overhead rings like IRT strap-hangers ran afoul of hideousnesses ranging from sentient meteor swarms to devolu-

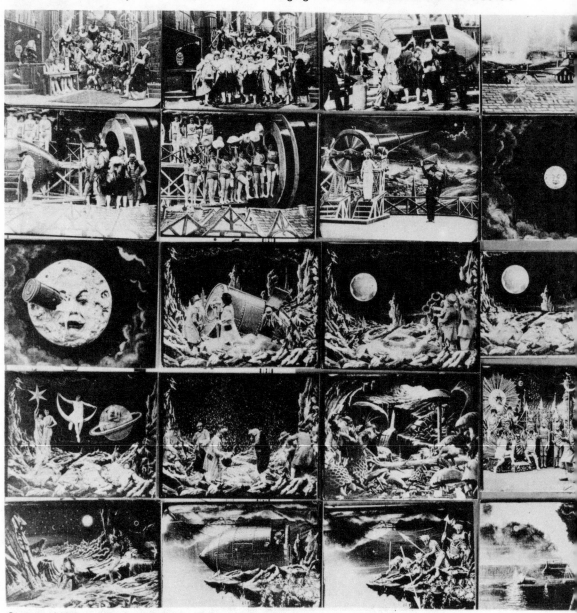

Georges Méliès's A Trip to the Moon *(1902), generally regarded as the first science fiction movie, was influenced by fellow Frenchman Jules Verne's* From the Earth to the Moon *and H. G. Wells's* First Men in the Moon. *In this sequential series of miniature pictures,* we see the moon launching amid much pageantry; the landing in the eye of the "man on the moon"; the exploration of the moon's surreal surface; and the return home, initiated when the Sélénites push the rocket off a moon ledge.

The depressing underground chamber in Fritz Lang's Metropolis *(1926), where workers are extensions of their machines and literally fight the time-clock.*

tionary pithecanthropoids on a clutch of unknown planets. If only half the astral bodies glutting our solar system in sf films truly existed, we would have a spatial overpopulation problem that would make from-here-to-Mars look like the Hollywood Freeway at 6:00 on a Friday night.

The imbecilic lack of research that characterized what most people thought of as "sf films" defies belief. ·Take the giant ant, for instance. It simply can't be. No which way. (You see, there is a thing called the Inverse Cube Law, which says that you can increase the total size or strength of a given material—bone, chitin, muscle, cartilage, whatever—and it will increase to the second power, that is, squared. But the weight *also* increases. Unfortunately, it increases to the *third* power, or cubes. And that means your giant ant would take one step and all its muscles and chitinous appendages would crack and send the thing assoverteakettle.)

Not even the dawn of the Age of *Star Wars* [1977] has much enhanced the genre of science fiction films. A generation of film school graduates—what Alain Resnais calls "the wise guy directors"—come to puberty but not necessarily maturity surfeited with television sf and a seeming ignorance of the written word, ga-ga over special effects and utterly unfamiliar with the concept of plagiarism, has perpetuated the worst aspects of cinematic sophorism by paying *hommage* to the idiocies of the Fifties.

(Resnais, one of the great directors of our time, has noted of these striplings: "Yes, they pay *hommage*. But it is always homage to *shit*. To Saturday morning serials and comic strips, never to *Citizen Kane* or *Potemkin*.")

With state-of-the-art SFX a tail that has come to wag the dog till it's as dizzy as Huckleberry Hound, millions of dollars are being poured into sf films that are as looney as their cheapjack predecessors, but without the innocence that marked the former. These new monstrosities, as unlikely as the giant ant and as ready to collapse of their own weight, lumber around the Cineplex circuit all puffed up like pouter-pigeons, pretending to be *about* something, but in reality are no more significant than the odious spate of knife-kill flicks or *Porky's*-style teenaged t&a yorkers.

Hollywood has never known what to do with science fiction, has never understood (as the vile *Outland* [1981] demonstrated) that westerns and Dr. Kildare retreads and Interpol spy dramas cannot simply be recycled with blasters and funny hats replacing Winchesters, EEG's, and the Berlin Wall. The radical new thinking that should have manifested itself when technology freed the sf film from its B-feature servitude is seldom seen.

Heads must be unscrewed, and light must be shone into the vacuous spaces where film producers store up the Frankenstein Monster bits and pieces of "ideas" they've stolen from sixty years of bad movies. To understand what this new thinking must be, it would serve our cause to take a quick, shotgun look at where the sf film came from, what it's been like at its best, what we're doing now, and what is in the offing. After which goodies, we can make some predictions— which is, after all, what sf does best.

And so, to understand the film of the future—past, present, and future—come with me into the antediluvian past. To the outskirts of Paris at the turn of the century, to the tiny, glass-enclosed studio of Georges Méliès.

And bring your sense of wonder.

In a speech delivered at the 2nd International Film Festival in Rio de Janeiro in 1969, fantasy novelist Robert Bloch, long a scenarist and archivist/critic of sf films, said, "Méliès, a professional magician, discovered he could play even better tricks with a motion picture camera. Fascinated by his opportunity to achieve illusions by mechanical means, he began to use fades, dissolves, stop-motion, and the speeded-up camera to create fantasies. Drawing upon everything from traditional fairy tales to his own improvised science fiction scenarios, Méliès pioneered in the field, aided by his actor friends and a corps of ballet beauties. He painted his own sets, used home-made props, designed his own costuming—and became remarkably successful.

In the Thirties, Boris Karloff made a whole series of mad scientist movies like The Invisible Ray *(1936). Repeatedly, well-meaning scientists ventured into God's domain and went insane. These films perpetuated the moviegoer's bias against men of science, inventors, experimenters, and intellectuals.*

"But when he set forth to do such films as *The Impossible Voyage* [1904] and *A Trip to the Moon* [1902], the results bore little or no resemblance to today's science fiction. By our standards, his work qualifies only as comic fantasy."

Even so, a strong case can be made for Méliès as the father of the science fiction film. (And it is an interesting sidelight on the lack of creative thinking from 1902 to the present that filmmakers *still* conceive of the parameters of the sf film as being *A Trip to the Moon* at one end, and *Marooned* [1969] at the other.)

Ah, Méliès! Ah, you sweet-talkin' old sonofagun. No bland clean-cut Armstrong, Aldrin, or Collins for you, baby. No hohum computerized no-risk soft Lunar landing for you, chickie. Instead, a bevy of leotard-clad chorines, pushing a great bullet into a moonshot cannon, firing at the pock-faced satellite and actually giving a black eye to The Man Up There. Now, admit it, they don't make 'em like *that* any more. On the other hand, Bloch may be right; it may *not,* strictly speaking, have been science fiction.

But there is no argument that one of the first sf films was the Selig-Polyscope production of *Dr. Jekyll and Mr. Hyde.* Sure it was sf. Mad scientist, noxious serum, personality change, schizophrenia. That was 1908.

Then two years later, in 1910, the Edison Film Company released the first film version of *Frankenstein* and that *was* sf, unarguably. Unfortu-

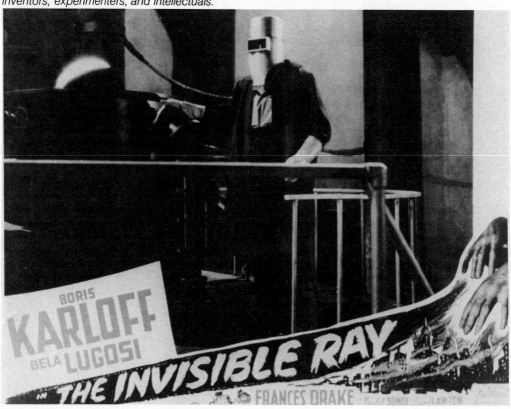

natey, the film has long been lost. All that remain (as Bloch tells it) are "a still, a suspicion, and a story-synopsis, but apparently no print. The still gives us a glimpse of a rather lumpy monster, the suspicion offers a theory the role may have been played by an actor named Charles Ogle, and the story-synopsis tells us that the monster—though created in the laboratory in a cauldron of blazing chemicals—later evaporates into thin air." In 1915 a second version of the Mary Shelley novel was filmed under the title *Life Without Soul*—in which the story turned out to be a dream.

In 1913 came the first film of *The Golem* which is our first recorded appearance of the robot in the film medium. Today, with Jerry Falwell omnipresent, that doesn't seem like such a hot item, but in 1913 a golem was dynamite.

Aside from the 1919 classic *The Cabinet of Dr. Caligari*, directed by Robert Wiene, a film that influenced German filmmaking for ten years afterward, there was very little done in the sf genre in the period between *The Golem* and the middle Twenties. Simply put, the world had come to accept the Industrial Revolution, they'd seen what machines could do for them, Technocracy was not yet a discredited Utopian ideal, and one of the big fads was this "War-To-End-All-Wars" that commanded people's attention for a few years. It was in all the papers. And frankly, they wanted comedies. Even *The Invisible Man* in 1933 had its share of laughs. So it was not till 1926, when Fritz Lang made the memorable *Metropolis,* that the sf film had any new life juiced into it.

But it was not till 1931 that the first important science fiction film of the talking cinema was made. And again, it fell to *Frankenstein* to provide the vehicle. (Let's face it: even a congeries of old spare parts can't be all bad if he can thrill so many moviegoers over such an extended period.

Science fiction's comic strip tradition shows no signs of dying out. Left: In the 1937 serial adaptation of Alex Raymond's popular strip "Flash Gordon," our hero (Buster Crabbe) holds Dale Arden (Jean Rogers). Right: Three decades later, two more blond lovers appeared in the adaptation of Jean-Claude Forest's adult strip "Barbarella": The blind, winged Pygar (John-Phillip Law) holds our heroine (Jane Fonda).

So let's hear it for Baron von Frankenstein and his buddy.) (Mel von Brooks notwithstanding.)

It was clear sailing there for a while, in the Thirties. It looked as though sf was really coming into its own with *Things to Come* [1936] and *Island of Lost Souls* [1933] with Charles Laughton playing the role of H. G. Wells's Dr. Moreau.

Yet even this boom was not what it seemed. For the Thirties, a period notorious for its anti-intellectual overtones, extolling the specious qualities of the Common Man (who might as likely be a member of the Ku Klux Klan as the ASPCA), turned the sf film into a species of anti-science, anti-progress mouthpiece. In almost every film of the period, scientists were portrayed in the mold of, say, Albert Dekker as *Dr. Cyclops*. Deranged, strobismic, psychopathic, and generally unkempt. And that was 1940.

By 1941 we were too busy watching William Bendix and Robert Taylor and William Eythe and John Garfield knocking off Nazis and Sons of Tojo to worry about what the hell was happening on Proxima Centauri III, and so the film of science fiction took a much-needed nap. After all those shambling, lurching, slobbering golems and suchlike, even sf fans wanted a respite.

(Only those of us who had stumbled across copies of the wonderful pulp magazines of the

era—*Startling Stories, Planet Stories, Doc Savage, Famous Fantastic Mysteries*—hungered for more. And it was a rich feast: the serials of the period, from Buster Crabbe as *Flash Gordon* or *Buck Rogers,* to fringe-sf like the long-lost and legendary *Shadow* serial with Victor Jory as the gardener of the Weed of Crime.)

But the explosion of the A-bomb in 1945 brought science to the forefront, and before we had a chance to lay in a supply of Raid, on came Them, It, Ugh, Floop, Godzilla, Atragon, Mothra, and the Beast From 20,000 Fathoms. That whole crowd.

By 1950, the big news was *Destination Moon,* based very loosely on a Robert Heinlein juvenile novel. It looks primitive today (The Late Late Show, at least twelve times a year), but in 1950 it was the epitome of serious constructive filmmaking about space travel. The film had the usual melting-pot crew—one Jew, one Italian, one All-American boy, one Brooklynite, no Negro—and it also had meteors that swoooooshed past the ship with an audible breeze, thereby defying the fact that there is no air in the vacuum of space.

(The swooooosh, apocryphal apotheosis of scientific illiteracy championed by the fat burghers who sell damaged goods to terminal acne cases who prefer John Landis to Akira Kurosawa, even as they prefer McDonald's Toadburgers to real food, is with us even today, even with the rise in general knowledge of the physical universe possessed by most kids. Its cynical use by producers and directors and SFX people who know better, with the mendacious rationalization that "people want to hear that swooooosh, they don't feel thrilled if they don't get a good swoooooosh when something zips past in deep space," is a resonant example of how stupid the industry really thinks its audience is.)

Destination Moon was not a particularly outstanding movie by today's Lucasfilms standards, but sf fans had been so long without movie succor that they lauded it extravagantly, queued up to see it sixteen times each, and went bumbling on from there to such abominations as *The Man from Planet X* [1951] and *Invaders from Mars* [1953]. That the fans were desperate is evidenced by their acceptance without a bleat of the former film's extraterrestrial with the tinfoil head, and the latter film's Martians, whose skins had zippers down the back.

It is, to my way of thinking, cinematic revisionism to praise these films as examples of Cold War paranoia of the times. *Invaders from Mars* and *Invasion of the Body Snatchers* [1956] may provide Ossianic opportunities for publish-or-perish *cinéastes* to breathe heavily about unconscious Jungian archetypes and the basic Apollonian/ Dionysian conflict, but for those of us trying to catch a cheap feel in the back seat of a Nash Rambler, them films was just some good scary shit.

Yet it was big box-office for such cheapies, and Hollywood—first with peanutburgers, drive-in mortuaries, bronze stars embedded in sidewalks, and macrobiotic astrologers—pushed into production fistfuls of similar nincompooperies.

In rapid succession came *Rocketship X-M* [1950], *Red Planet Mars* [1952], *Donovan's Brain* [1953] (in at least five filmic incarnations), *Cat*

Far left: In the classic Transatlantic Tunnel (1935), McAllen (Richard Dix) and his brave men risk their lives to build a tunnel beneath the ocean.
Left: Mighty endeavors have apparently gone downhill. In the junky sf film Women of the Prehistoric Planet (1966), a leader strikes a pose identical to McAllen's, while his crew of trained astronauts and military men—who should be prepared for any happenstance during a space expedition—fret about crossing a stream on a narrow log. (Sure enough, one of these men will fall to his death.)

Women of the Moon [1954], Queen of Outer Space [1958], and—if we were to get exhaustively alphabetical about it:

The Amazing Colossal Man [1957]
Assignment Outer Space [1962]
The Astounding She Monster [1960]
Beyond the Time Barrier [1960]
The Blob [1958]
The Brain Eaters [1958]
The Brain from Planet Arous [1958]
The Cosmic Man [1959]
The Cosmic Monsters [1959]
The Crawling Eye [1958]
Creation of the Humanoids [1962]
The Creature from the Black Lagoon [1954]
The Day of the Triffids [1963]
The Deadly Mantis [1957]
The Electronic Monster [1958]
Five [1951]
From Hell It Came [1957]
The Gamma People [1956]
The Giant Behemoth [1959]
Gorgo [1961]
The Incredible Petrified World [1958]
The Indestructible Man [1956]
It Came from Outer Space [1953]
The Leech Woman [1960]
Panic in the Year Zero [1962]
Rodan [1957]
The Satan Bug [1965]
The Slime People [1962]
Tarantula [1955]
This Island Earth [1955]
The Time Travelers [1964]
The 27th Day [1957]

World Without End [1956]
X—The Man with the X-Ray Eyes [1963]
and
X The Unknown [1956]

This by-no-means-exhaustive list does not take into account, frontwards, backwards, and heretofore, the "attack" films—which the savants seem to have overlooked as genuine sources for the generation of paranoia: Attack of the Crab Monsters [1957], Attack of the 50 Foot Woman [1958], Attack of the Robots [1967], and assorted attacks on us by the Giant Leeches, the Mayan Mummy, the Mushroom People, or the Puppet People. You wanna talk about paranoia, just get your frisson behind some whacked-out mushroom leech babbling at you in Cakchiquel as it stalks you through your condo! Pod-people, my ass.

Nor does the list include the "battle" films that chronicle the Battle Beyond the Sun [1963], Battle in Outer Space [1960], or the battle of the Worlds, the Planets, Across the Universe, or even Beneath the Earth. Or the "invasion" flicks, which include invasions by the slug people, the animal people, the saucer men, the star creatures, and the vampires. Nor the "monster" films that somehow manage to make the sf classification despite titles like The Monolith Monsters [1957], Monster from a Prehistoric Planet [1967], or Monsters from Green Hell, the Surf, of Piedras Blancas, on the Campus, or even The Monster That Challenged the World [1957]—which may be biting off even too much for a monster, though one must admit, he don't think small. (There is even a sub-phylum of "monster" flicks, the teenage monsters, which include such peachy-keenies as Teenage Cave-

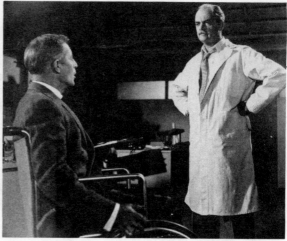

Two of science fiction's seminal characters. Left: Peter Sellers's memorably mad scientist, the title figure of Stanley Kubrick's Dr. Strangelove *(1964)*. Above: Crippled industrialist Stanton (John Hoyt, here with Larry Keating, who plays Dr. Hendron) of George Pal's When Worlds Collide *(1951)* was no doubt an influence on Strangelove. At the moments their respective Earths are destroyed, both these evil men are able to rise from their wheelchairs. But this will not save them.

man [1958], *Teenage Monster* [1957], *Teenagers from Outer Space* [1959], *Teenage Zombies* [1958], and *I Was a Teenage Frankenstein* [1957]. This last could possibly be chalked up to a case of standing too close to a Taco Bell, but then, I grow frivolous.)

The two most original titles in the batch—and I confess I have seen both of these epics—are hands-down winners of the Most Unforgettable Film Title Of All Time award, and I offer them here untouched by human hands:

I MARRIED A MONSTER
FROM OUTER SPACE

THE INCREDIBLY STRANGE CREATURES
WHO STOPPED LIVING
AND BECAME CRAZY, MIXED-UP ZOMBIES

Stick *that* up your marquee and set it!

But seriously, folks.

Somehow, during that blighted, benighted interregnum from approximately 1945 through 1967, with hundreds of pseudo- and vaguely-sf films being produced (and I've purposely avoided getting into pure fantasy films or we'd *never* get out of here for dinner) because releasing companies lived by the Accepted Wisdom that it's less expensive to make a mediocre giant roach film than it is to make a mediocre western, only twenty-nine films were released that remain undimmed in the minds of the cognoscenti as cinematic experiences at whose memory that gorge does not become buoyant.

(A giant roach film. Hmmm. Would that neces-sitate an investigation by Reagan's narks? Just a thought.)

The winners list is as follows:

Alphaville [1965]
Animal Farm [1955]
The Birds [1963]
The Day the Earth Caught Fire [1962]
The Day the Earth Stood Still [1951]
Dr. Strangelove [1964]
Fahrenheit 451 [1967]
Fail-Safe [1964]
Fantastic Voyage [1966]
First Men "in" the Moon [1964]
Five Million Years to Earth [1968]
The 5,000 Fingers of Dr. T [1953]
The Fly [1958]
Forbidden Planet [1956]
The Incredible Shrinking Man [1957]
Invasion of the Body Snatchers [1956]
Journey to the Center of the Earth [1959]
The Man in the White Suit [1952]
The Mind-Benders [1963]
1984 [1956]
On the Beach [1959]
Robinson Crusoe on Mars [1964]
Seconds [1966]
Seven Days in May (1964)
The 10th Victim [1965]
The Thing (From Another World) [1951]
The Time Machine [1960]
20,000 Leagues Under the Sea [1954]
Village of the Damned [1960]

In 1964, two films were made in which monumental foul-ups resulted in American planes dropping nuclear bombs on Russia. Above: In the black comedy Dr. Strangelove Or: How I Learned to Stop Worrying and Love the Bomb, *the President (Peter Sellers) tries to calm down the Russian Premier, who informs him that world destruction is imminent. Right: In the more serious* Fail-Safe, *the President (Henry Fonda) also speaks on the Hot Line to Russia. In order to stop Russian reprisals he will agree to drop a nuclear bomb on New York City.*

There are, of course, hundreds of other films omitted from the two lists here. Not only would it be time-consuming madness to attempt to trace down all the motion pictures made by independents that tiptoed through America in drive-ins and scratch theaters during those years, but memory simply expires from overwork, and why the hell bother? There may have been thirty-three or forty-nine good sf flicks made, there may have been another thirteen hundred bummers, but for purposes of scattergun analysis, these will suffice. The same can be said for like and dislike. One man's meat is another monster's carrion.

Completists may quibble with the list, and would certainly have valid arguments at the exclusion of such wonders as the films of Val Lewton in the Forties, *King Kong* [1933] and even some of the lesser George Pal films of the Fifties and early Sixties, such as *The War of the Worlds* [1953], *When Worlds Collide* [1951], and *The Power* [1968]. But in going back to the Lewton films one finds they were all either supernatural or psychological fantasies—though admittedly brilliant—*King Kong,* though a seminal influence, is hardly sf; and the films of the late, sorely missed George Pal wear very badly on a second glance, however well-intentioned they may have been. (One Pal film, *The Conquest of Space* [1955], is notably gawdawful because of the inclusion of a spaceship captain who is a religious fanatic, who gibbers through the film that "God doesn't want us in space." It's the old If-God-Had-Wanted-Satellites-In-Space-He'd-Have-Put-Wings-On-

Basketballs argument. And the film is laughable by today's standards, even if one *doesn't* know how an LEM works. On the other hand, Pal's last film, *Doc Savage—The Man of Bronze* [1975], is an egregiously overlooked film of dearness and skill.

(Dammit. A few more words need to be said about George Pal. It's too easy, as self-appointed historian, to dismiss much of what George produced in the light of our greater sophistication and glitzier technical expertise. George Pal *loved* the literature of the future. He knew the work, he didn't merely talk the talk as so many *auteurs* do these days; he walked the special walk of one who cared deeply about presenting sf in a way that was most useful to our needs. His science was as accurate as he could get his advisors to make it, he worked with writers and from classic stories, but most of all he never forgot that it was *people* that formed the core of interest. Not the technology or the gimmicks, but the effect they had on people's lives. He was a humanist in all the best senses of that word, and if many of his films seem watery now, still he was the one who gave us *The Time Machine* and *Doc Savage.* His was an honorable career.)

All of which brings us to the recent past, the present, the future, and a worrisome resurgence of interest in sf as a moneymaking genre for contemporary films. But first, snottily tendered, some observations on what we've seen lately.

Still hanging onto that sense of wonder, fans?

Great. Bring your giant roaches and come along.

In Charly (1968), a radical brain procedure transforms a sweet retarded man (Cliff Robertson) into a superlogical superintellect. (His rebelliousness is symbolized by his trying his hand at abstract art.) By this time, his knowledge of facts and understanding of what is right and wrong (his operation, for instance) has surpassed that of his kind teacher (Claire Bloom).

The watershed, perforce, was 1968. In that halcyon year two of the finest, and most germinally influential, films of imagination were released: Stanley Kubrick and Arthur C. Clarke's *2001: A Space Odyssey* and *Charly,* based on Daniel Keyes's award-winning novelette "Flowers for Algernon."

When I am asked (and when am I not) at film festivals or college lectures, what my favorite "science fiction" film is, I always answer: *Charly.* This response is invariably met with the sort of expression that brings new resonance to the word *querulous.* "But that ain't sci-fi," I'm told.

Therein lies one of the basic reasons why sf films for the last forty years have been proffered on the intellectual level of the most simpleminded stories ever published in the back pages of lesser pulp magazines and comic books directed at an adolescent audience that has not, in fact, existed since the late Thirties. The public image of what *is,* and what *ain't,* science fiction film—an image as twisted as one of Tod Browning's freaks—is the result of decades of paralogia, arrogant stupidity, conscious flummery, and amateurism that have comprised the universal curriculum of *milieu* that passes for filmic education for a gullible audience. If it goes bangity-bang in space; if it throbs and screams and breaks out of its shell with slimy malevolence; if it seeks to enslave your body, your mind, your gonads or your planet; if it looks cuddly and beeps a lot, it's "sci-fi." We pronounce that: *skiffy.* And if you like fantasy, you'll *love* skiffy. And skiffy is to science fiction as Attila was to good table manners.

Thus, when one is asked by the Director of an upcoming Film Festival what movies should be scheduled as peachykeen for the "Sci-Fi Section," and you suggest *Charly, Seconds, Wild in the Streets* [1968], and *Yellow Submarine* [1968], expect the querulous stare and the reply, "But that ain't sci-fi." Not a cranking spaceship or giant arachnid as far as the eye can glom.

It is the end-result of that debased universal curriculum. It is tunnel vision as restrictive as conceiving of "youth films" in terms of *Riot on Sunset Strip* or *Porky's,* rather than *Easy Rider* or *Over the Edge* or *Los Olvidados.*

How incapacitating this kind of otiose thinking can be is exemplified by a conversational encounter I had some years ago with a studio publicist. I had called Columbia Pictures to obtain data on upcoming sf productions in production or soon to be released. The publicist assured me they had nothing of that nature in the pipeline. "What about *Marooned*?" I asked. "Oh, I wouldn't call that science fiction," she replied. I was tempted to ask her in what category she *would* put a film about three astronauts trapped in a rocket that can't get back to Earth, but I was afraid she'd tell me it was an historical epic, and then I'd have to consider including *Mutiny on the Bounty* in my list of best sf films. So I let it slide, not without a tremor of horror.

Yet it is precisely the sort of films exemplified by *Charly* and *Seconds*—films that utilize science as cultural device impinging on the lives of *people*— that speak to the best aspects of the literary form unfortunately ghettoized as "science fiction."

And so *2001* made the splash in 1968; and not even the awarding of an Oscar to Cliff Robertson for his memorable creation of Charly Gordon penetrated the fog; and the idiom for the next sixteen years has been the splashy space opera, not the heart-wrenching human dilemma. Which brings us, huffing'n'puffing, shucking'n'jiving, to the *Star Wars* phenomenon. Notice how melliflu-

Jerry Cornelius (Jon Finch), one of sf's oddest all-purpose heroes/mythic archetypes, walks through a bizarre set in The Last Days of Man on Earth/The Final Programme *(1973), an overly complicated British film about a computer that can fuse a man and a woman into one strange being. (It is the "perfect" device with which to begin a new world.) Michael Moorcock detested what director Robert Fuest did to his novel and was pleased when it flopped at the box office.*

ously the phrase quicksilvers off the tongue? The *Star Wars* p*h*e*n*o*m*e*n*o*n! Sound of regal trumpets, cymbal, lyre, sackbut, and dulcimer.

Badmouthing the *Star Wars* trilogy these days is considered, if not a felony punishable by being immersed to one's chin in a lake of monkey vomit while members of the Jedi Strokers Fan and Car Club buzz you in motorboats making waves, at least in such bad taste that it equates with spitting on the American flag, denigrating Motherhood, admitting Apple Pie makes you bilious, and getting caught trying to rig the annual Soapbox Derby.

In the wake of profits that, if piled up, are greater than the Diamond As Big As The Ritz; all-stops-out media hype; uncritically slavish reviews except from John Simon (and *he* uses words like sedulous and proditorious so he gotta be one of them commie elitist bastids, so screw'm); effulgent word-of-mouth encomia; worldwide fan clubs that stage midnight torch marches; and recognition even from Ronald Reagan who has proposed a new "*Star Wars* high frontier space platform" the better to sharpshoot SAM missiles on their way toward Kansas City, the risk one runs even by suggesting that *Star Wars* 1, 2, and 3 may not be as significant in the course of human development as, say, the invention of the wheel is the risk of being trampled to death by ex-*Star Trek* groupies, who've had their epiphany-conversion, as they queue up to see all-day marathons of *Wars, Empire* [1980], and *Jedi* [1983] for the sixth

or eighth time. And I'm just as embarrassed as all get-out at the way that sentence done run on. But I figured I'd better get it all out in one rush before the lynch mob reached me.

This lemminglike hegira to worship at the shrine of director George Lucas and "the return of entertainment!" has been so carefully orchestrated that otherwise sane and rational filmgoers whose desiccated sophistication has led them to find flaws in even such damn-near-perfect movies as *The Conversation* [1974], *Taxi Driver* and *Oh, God!* [1977], and *Nashville,* roll their eyes and clap their hands in childish delight. And I think *childish* is the operative word in this lunatic situation.

And though I find the role of Specter at the Banquet somewhat less than salutary for my social life, as a practicing writer of fantasy (into which genre science fiction and space opera of the *Star Wars* variety plonk comfortably) I'm afraid I must reluctantly piss on the parade.

In an industry where nothing succeeds as consistently as repeated failure, the ex-CPAs, ex-mail room boys, ex-hairdressers, and ex-agents who become Producers conceive of imaginative fiction as just another shoot-'em-up with laser rifles. They have a plethora of hype but a dearth of inventiveness. And they think of films in terms of making the deal, not of presenting the logical story. For most of these yahoos, a "film" is something, *anything,* they can get Streisand and Reynolds and Debra Winger to star in. The script can come later. What the hell does it matter if it's

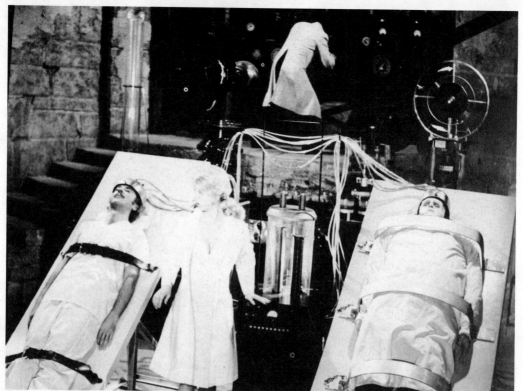

One of the finest parodies of classic sf-horror films was Mel Brooks's Young Frankenstein *(1974). It starred (L–R) Gene Wilder as a mad scientist, Teri Garr as a busty nurse, Peter Boyle as the Monster, and (in back) Marty Feldman as the hunchbacked assistant. The impressive lab sets were similar to those we remember from the Universal* Frankenstein *films of the Thirties.*

good, bad, or imbecilic . . . just as long as the names of the stars can be featured above the title. Or the special effects are saleable.

But science fiction is a very special genre. It is the game of "what if." *What if:* we were forced to abandon the land and adapt physically to life in the seas? *What if:* everyone was telepathic and could read everyone else's mind, how could you commit a murder and not be discovered when your thoughts gave you away? *What if:* the male contraceptive became as common as the pill women use? *What if.*

And playing that game is the core of the story. But it must be internally consistent. It must have a much more rigorous logic than an ordinary, mimetic story, because you are asking the audience to suspend its disbelief, to go with you into a completely new, never-before-existed landscape. If what goes on in the story is irrational and diffuse, then it all comes up looking like spinach.

So for all its vaunted SFX, the *Star Wars* trilogy—we now perceive, seven years after it burst on us like an exploding Deathstar—has no more importance in the concern of the maturation of the sf cinema than does John Carpenter's odious and unnecessary remake of *The Thing* [1982] (as nasty a bit of filmic folly as has come our way of late; a deranged beast of a film in which special effects not only were encouraged to run amuck, but provide the *only* raison d'etre for a movie we were told would be the first *accurate* transliteration to celluloid of John W. Campbell's "Who Goes There?" when, in fact, it was a cheap ripoff of the original Hawks-Nyby version with all humanity removed and for substitution an alien that looked like the Invasion of the Italian Food Monster).

Talented creators like Lucas, Spielberg, and Carpenter seem to have lost their way. They recycle films made properly the first time; they languish in the thrall of camera tricks and plastic mold-makers and SFX *wünderkind.* And they need never confront the emptiness of what they do, because they have the claques and the cash to insulate them. While all around them the motion picture industry continues to ignore the vast body of science fiction source-material whose translation to film could enrich us all. Instead, variations on the Lucas technique of assembling bits and pieces of well-worn sf elements to bring forth "a new look" substitutes for fresh thinking. This method of producing something that *seems* to be new, but is only a kind of cinematic Frankenstein's monster, stealing here and there and sewing the bits together to produce what is called in the high courts of the land (since Sid and Marty Krofft successfully sued McDonald's for copyright

Above: A Boy and His Dog *(1975), a postapocalyptic black comedy, starred Don Johnson as the hot-blooded Vic, Susanne Benton as the conniving Quilla June (who emerges from underground Kansas to bring Vic back to impregnate the females there), and Tiger as Blood, Vic's smart, resourceful, loyal companion, with whom he communicates telepathically. Will Vic opt for the girl or the dog? Correct. This cult film was based on the novella by Harlan Ellison (right), sf's most awarded writer and the author of this introduction.*

JACK WALLNER

infringement and plagiarism in the *H.R. Pufnstuf* vs. McDonaldland TV commercial case) "total ambience," gathers up space battles from Edmond Hamilton, Ewoks that are sluggish imitations of Poul Anderson and Gordon Dickson's Hokas, Gandalf clones called Obi-Wan Kenobi, WW II dogfights straight out of Robert Sidney Bowen pulp adventures, and sandworms from Frank Herbert, repackages them more slickly, and shows base imitators like Glen Larson of *Battlestar Galaxative* a way to make megabucks without the expenditure of any creative thinking.

The *Star Wars* films, for all their totemization, are nothing more than adolescent wish-fulfillment, and if we have no more of it, we'll have had enough.

But the *Star Wars* phenomenon blinds the film industry to the potential of other kinds of science fiction. It tells the industry that *this* is the template. *The Prisoner of Zenda* in deep space, with lots of swoooooosh!

Or it produces some halfwit wild west adventure on a far planet; specifically, *Outland:* a film one walks away from with the sure sense that one has just spent one's money to see (Falwell forgive my language) a classic piece of shit.

I think *that's* the intellectual crucible in which all films of this sort should be tested. How do you feel about it when you're walking away from the theater and discussing it with other intelligent people. Not the kind of fans who applauded during the scenes in which someone's body exploded, not the sort of nonjudicial adolescents (of every age) who can slaver over matte effects and miniature models and bright lights while turning off their critical faculties; but people who genuinely love and *enjoy* good movies (and if you haven't figured out that I'm one of those by this time, well, we simply aren't getting through to each other). People, in short, who resent it when the script does something incredibly, gratuitously stupid that invalidates an otherwise acceptable story and makes you distrust *everything* the makers throw up on the screen thereafter. Every time you spend your money to swell the box office coffers for monkey-puke like *Outland,* you encourage the know-nothings at outfits like Warner Bros. and the Ladd Company to listen to babble like "This is *High Noon* in outer space," and to foist off on you again and again the most slovenly, childish, unsatisfying imitations of thoughtful sf they can get away with.

But then, I suppose if you enjoy playing the boob, you'll fight with me over nits in my analysis . . . and queue up for the next dreg some halfwit has sold to other halfwits.

In which case, as Jefferson said in another context, you'll be getting exactly what you deserve.

Let me sidetrack for just a moment.

Likely it won't surprise you—what with my ill-deserved rep as a cranky esthete—that I admire critic John Simon with very few reservations. The veneration, in this instance, extends itself to presenting a recent quote from Simon that subsumes as epigram the point this sidetrack makes.

He wrote: "I remember one of my freshman English students at the University of Washington asking with genuine concern, 'But I don't understand, Mr. Simon. What is wrong with being average?' There is nothing much wrong with being average, and still less with being outstanding."

To put it another way, this time in the words of John D. MacDonald, "In a half-ass world the real achiever is king."

And if you are a motion picture and only average—or as I submit way *below* average where it counts—is there much point in spending fourteen million dollars, sixteen weeks' production time of uncounted talented artists and technicians who might better spend their time on something outstanding, not to mention the scarce theater booking space and attention of hundreds of thousands of filmgoers who spend millions of dollars for baby sitters, parking, travel costs, and the high price of admission, if you are at best only average?

When a manufacturer in this country wants to run a market test on a new product, the city most often selected for the proper demographic sampling, the city considered most *average,* is Columbus, Ohio. The residents of Columbus don't seem to understand how deeply they are being insulted by this "honor." They don't seem to realize that in the name of having the latest Arby's sandwich or sanitary napkin or fruit juice combo tested on them, they are categorized as *average.* And in these days of trying to please the lowest possible common denominator, average becomes synonymous with *mediocre.* Unexcelling. Middle. Undistinguished. Non-idiosyncratic. Predictable. Malleable. Columbus and all its inhabitants become merely marketing tools, fit for nothing better than consuming useless products. This is not the deification of taste, it is the standardization of no taste whatever.

Can this really be the best we can hope to expect from an industry masquerading as an art-form? Is there nothing nobler?

Of course there is. There has been.

1970: *The Mind of Mr. Soames.* 1971: *A Clockwork Orange; THX 1138,* and *The Andromeda Strain.* 1973: *Sleeper; Fantastic Planet,* and (though Michael Moorcock who wrote the novel on which it is based loathes it) *The Last Days of Man on Earth.* 1974: *Young Frankenstein* and *Dark Star.* 1975: (Not even a charming lack of hubris can prevent me from the merest mention of this film based on my own work.) *A Boy and His Dog.* 1978: the excellent Phil Kaufman remake of *Invasion of the Body Snatchers.* 1979: *Alien.* 1980: *The Empire Strikes Back; Mad Max,* and *Altered States.* 1981: *Time Bandits* and *Raiders of the Lost Ark* which, though marginal as sf, is such a dear piece of work that it should not be excluded on grounds of excellence. 1982: *The Road Warrior; E.T.; Poltergeist,* and *Blade Runner.* 1983: *Zelig.*

And in a class all their own, as he is *sui generis,* Peter Weir's extraordinary, stunning productions of *Picnic at Hanging Rock* [1975] and *The Last Wave* [1977].

But consider the cataclysmic weight of the hundreds of other, dreadful sf films that have four-walled, TV-hyped, and cable-viewed their way into your world, that have debased the concept of what potential riches lie in the sf film: all the films titled *The Green Slime* [1969], *The Omega Man* [1971], *Soylent Green* [1973], *Zardoz* [1974], *Meteor* [1979], *Star Trek—The Motion Picture* [1979], *The Black Hole* [1979], *Forbidden World* [1982], *Flash Gordon* [1980], *Tron* [1982], and *Brainstorm* [1983].

Not even Barbarella, for all her glory, can outweigh *that* load of yak-dung.

The history of the science fiction film is only as old as the history of the cinema itself; and it's a history being writ new each year. If Coppola can create *The Conversation* ("But that ain't science fiction!") and Frankenheimer can translate David Ely's *Seconds* ("But that ain't science fiction!") and Charly Gordon can stand before us on a screen and open his hand to bring tears to our eyes with nothing but a dead mouse ("But that ain't science fiction!") then even the Specter at the Banquet can retain some hope that one day the Lucases and Kasdans and Spielbergs and Ridley Scotts will put aside their flashy toys and pay heed to the only subject that is worth their enormous gifts: the study of the human heart in conflict with itself.

And they will accept, perhaps, as their epigraph, one of the few sane things ever said by Ayn Rand:

"Anyone who fights for the future lives in it today."

PART I

PERSPECTIVES

Welcoming the Future

Joan Mellen

Always cautionary, science fiction films carry the evils of the present into a future where our worst intimations of catastrophe seem on the verge of coming

true. Pessimistically, they visualize the logical terrain of nuclear holocaust, pollution, overpopulation, extraterrestrial malevolence, or computer megalomania carried to their ultimate dead ends. And yet Hollywood's images of the future are finally optimistic. Gently they reconcile us to a future whose technology we have feared because it might render us obsolete. Robots today build cars and pick crops; as accountants they balance the books; as detectives they ferret out bombs; at home they clean house and serve drinks. But since 1968, when *2001: A Space Odyssey* marked a resurgence of the science fiction film replacing the B-films of the Fifties,

Hollywood has persistently imagined a future in which our species remains the measure of the life worth living. Cheerfully, the new science fiction insists that even in the far reaches of nameless galaxies, man still controls his destiny.

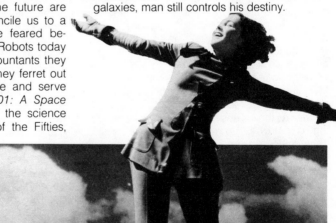

A publicity still of nineteen-year-old Maureen O'Sullivan in 1930's Just Imagine, *one of the first films to postulate a bright future. She played an aviatrix in the distant year 1980.*

Joan Mellen teaches literature and film at Temple University. Her most recent book is *Privilege: The Enigma of Sasha Bruce.* Her film books include *Big Bad Wolves: Masculinity in the American Film, Women and Their Sexuality in the New Film, The Waves at Genji's Door: Japan Through Its Cinema,* and *Voices From the Japanese Cinema.* She is also the author of *Natural Tendencies,* a novel.

That ever-widening universe will be hospitable, our best science fiction films insist. Even in *When Worlds Collide* (1951) the Noah's Ark spaceship manages to land on an idyllic landscape in space with every hope of galactic settlement for our endangered species. *Star Trek II: The Wrath of Khan* (1982) imagines that through technology we can create Edenic paradises in space; the "Genesis device" regenerates life from lifelessness, the reward to those space pioneers willing "to boldly go where no man has gone before." In this garden of Eden the selfless Mr. Spock (Leonard Nimoy) will be restored to life. And what could be more encouraging than those alien intelligences of *2001* painstakingly creating for Dave (Keir Dullea) a touching if imperfect facsimile of the room he might have known at home. There is boundless optimism from the beginning of *2001* with that first graceful journey to the moon, the "Blue Danube" waltz behind us in harmony with the emotionless beauty of the stewardess moving like a white angel, as if dancing in the gravitationless atmosphere of the spacecraft. Through such imagery science fiction eagerly fills the gap between present and future, almost always with the object of making the future predictable, habitable, and delightful. The new science fiction films proffer visible evidence of this future while formulating alternatives to present-day maladies that separate us from those unequivocally Edenic worlds always potentially ours.

That man should be pleased to share his place in the universe with alien intelligences, that he need fear neither for his own safety nor for that of his culture, is one of the great themes of the new science fiction. If *Close Encounters of the Third Kind* (1977) and *E.T.* (1982) are not futuristic in their imagery, they portray a near future in which aliens move among us—hardly the world as we know it now. Although their landscapes are not of the future, they are about the future in a very direct way. They reconcile us to a future about to happen as their aliens soften our natures, instructing us in how to live more happily side by side. They amuse us and add purpose and vitality to otherwise drab lives. So the Richard Dreyfuss character of *Close Encounters* is renewed, his life suffused with meaning. Like R2D2 and C3PO of *Star Wars* (1977), E.T. relieves us of loneliness as he embodies our longing to make contact with a more loving and compassionate species than ours has proven to be.

These films attempt to grant us the courage to face unknown intelligences that may in fact be both superior and hostile. That this fear lives among us is expressed in Carl Sagan's 1983 letter to *The New York Times* printed under the heading, "If Extraterrestrials Do Exist: Not To Worry"; Sagan responds to the *Times'* own exploitation of "fear of the dark of space" and "extragalactic tigers" with the same optimism pervading most of the new films.

Alien (1979), which depicts a monstrous incubus spewing blood and vomit through spaghetti tentacles, its skeleton face armed with many sets of teeth, seems to strike an opposite theme more in keeping with horror science fiction of the Fifties like *The War of the Worlds* (1953), cautioning us not to make contact with what may turn out to be unspeakably demonic beings. Even here, however, the woman astronaut, Ripley (Sigourney Weaver), outsmarts the alien adversary, sending it at last spinning into the darkness of space. Optimistically, *Alien* does not marry reason and malevolence in its extraterrestrial beast, which (albeit not so easily) is put to rout by the cleverness of our species.

It is *E.T.* that more obviously addresses itself to the near future, providing grounds to look forward to communicating with other species. The benign, loving, telepathically sympathetic E.T. who makes objects levitate and dead flowers bloom touches all who know him. The freshly divorced mother of Elliott is so self-absorbed that she fails to notice a grotesque extraterrestrial roaming around her kitchen; it is she who is lacking in sensitivity, not he. Our greatest alien friends, however, remain those patient creators of the monoliths in *2001* who return after millennia to redeem a planet on the brink of nuclear holocaust. They welcome our emissary, the very ordinary astronaut Dave Bowman and transform him into one of their own. *2001* provides us with passage, a star-gate out of our fear of the incomprehensible.

Indeed we cannot welcome the future, as science fiction films are designed to help us do, while we fear the computer and the robot and feel helpless before catastrophes that render us inadequate. In 1965, before the renaissance of the science fiction film, Susan Sontag wrote that they were "about disaster . . . the aesthetics of destruction, with the peculiar beauties to be found in wreaking havoc, of making a mess." Rather, great science fiction of the last decade and a half has been about order, arrival, and confidence. Where there is disaster, there is remedy. And we are not alone. In addition to our new alien compatriots, the computer (*Tron,* 1982) and the robot (*Star Wars, Blade Runner,* 1982) have joined us, domesticated. Both urge us forward into a future that need not be perilous.

Earlier science fiction like *Metropolis* (1926) calmed our fears by plunging the mad scientist to his death and burning his evil robot creation at the stake. Scientists who dared to venture too deeply into nature were condemned to suffer in consequence. Recent science fiction transcends such anti-intellectual cliché. Films like *Colossus: The Forbin Project* (1970), where a vicious computer does take over to rule the world, leave us, nonetheless, with the caution that had the creator of Colossus figured out how to pull the plug, as Dave disconnects the conflicted HAL 9000, the

In Georges Méliès's A Trip to the Moon (top), a 1902 French film that is generally regarded as the first true sf picture, space travel was treated lightheartedly—even in this scene, when moon explorers are threatened by Sélénites. The tone of Fritz Lang's 1928 German picture Woman in the Moon (middle) was much more somber—moon exploration was considered a grandiose endeavor. In Rocketship X-M (bottom), a 1950 American film that, along with Destination Moon, paved the way for an exciting decade of sf pictures, the outlook is bleak: A trip to Mars reveals a once-mighty civilization that has been destroyed by nuclear war; a lack of rocket fuel prevents anyone from returning to Earth alive (but there will be more expeditions).

nightmare could have been avoided. The new science fiction does not inculcate apathy or enter into complicity with the abhorrent, as Sontag condemns the genre for doing. These films recognize challenges to our survival as inevitable given the unlimited pursuit of science and technology and then urge us to meet them.

Unlike earlier works like *Frankenstein* (1931), *Metropolis,* and *Colossus: The Forbin Project,* for which science is itself still alien, the newer films suggest that the pursuit of the limits of knowledge entails a risk worth the taking. The basic assumption of recent science fiction is that man will continue to progress in his mastery of self and environment. As science fiction master Robert A. Heinlein wrote on his chart for *Future History:* "Civil disorder, followed by the end of human adolescence and beginning of first mature culture."

This description fits science fiction from *2001* and *Fahrenheit 451* (1966) to *E.T.* and *Blade Runner.* What saves us is that man, our species, is or becomes the measure of all that is valuable. "Do you like me?" R2 asks Luke Skywalker. What is inherently "human" is still equated with decency. This is the abiding theme of science fiction that runs from *Metropolis* to *Star Wars.* It is the "force" inside Luke that leads him to victory and not his adorable robots. Part of the optimism of science fiction is also that it frees us from traumatic and narcissistic preoccupation with our inadequacies—the married and unmarried men and women of Paul Mazursky, the endless identity crises of Woody Allen. All this can be left for the future, however accompanied it may be by problems of its own.

Yet for all their final note of diffident confidence, there is almost always a cautionary subtext to science fiction films, particularly those ecological waste movies that mourn in advance the consequences to the planet of pollution, overpopulation, and nuclear testing. The future will be intoler-

able *if* we continue as we are. The antinuclear films also pose the issue of whether in fact we will have any future at all.

But it is implicitly optimistic to nag, exhort, and grieve, with the premise of accessible remedy and an absence of cynical mourning for a hopelessly irredeemable future. After carelessness, amorality, and greed, there is redemption in both *Logan's Run* (1976) and *Blade Runner.* Life-enhancing values triumph. Born into a world where everyone over thirty is exterminated, Logan (Michael York) escapes and, staring in wonder at the weather-beaten face of Peter Ustinov, exclaims: "I've never seen a face like that before ... that must be the look of being old." Ustinov is asked if the cracks in his face hurt. The film's

triumph lies in Logan's accepting nature, including mortality. The year is 2274, the message, apocalyptic in its sense of discovery, is that "you can live, live and grow old!" So in *Zardoz* (1974) by the year 2293 everyone agrees that living forever would be a torment.

Soylent Green (1973) and *On the Beach* (1959), with their unrelievedly decimated landscapes, still insist that we need only change present behavior for the future not to overwhelm us. In *Soylent Green* the population of New York is forty million, twenty million of whom are unemployed. There is no electricity, no eggs, no lettuce; three cans of food cost $279. To walk down the street, it is necessary to wear a gas mask. Otherwise mediocre, *Soylent Green* is rich in imagery of the grim future wasteland awaiting us lest we act.

This cautionary note was sounded as early as *The Day the Earth Stood Still* (1951) where an alien visitor named Klaatu (Michael Rennie) warns that if people on earth don't learn to get along with each other, aliens from outer space will force them to behave. *Dr. Strangelove Or: How I Learned to Stop Worrying and Love the Bomb* (1964) and *The Day the Earth Caught Fire* (1962) prod us as well to face the danger that we may not have a future. In *Strangelove* the facile disclaimer by the U.S. Air Force that it can never happen sounds an opening ironic note. If the future is a logical continuation of the present, it will be ruled by the military insane—the Generals Ripper (Sterling Hayden) and Turgidson (George C. Scott) and their surrogate, Strangelove (Peter Sellers), who reflexively invokes "Mein Fuehrer"

and will be only too willing to provide us with our own Doomsday Machine to match that of the Russians.

But the humor, hyperbole, and a deliberately banal score ("Try a Little Tenderness") cajole us to repudiate, while time permits, all that we see here. Director Stanley Kubrick's disdain mocks Turgidson's assurance that in an all-out attack on the Russians "we would only suffer modest losses, no more than ten, twenty million killed—tops!" We are meant to scorn Strangelove's eugenic mine shafts where politicians and generals will survive amid sexual plenty, ten women for each man. Such criminal lunatics will control our future and run our society, however, only if we allow it. And throughout, Kubrick scorns incisively the ideological rationale at the root of this madness: "The International Communist Conspiracy has sapped all our precious bodily fluids!"

There is less obvious hope in films like *On the Beach* and *Soylent Green,* where we witness actual damage done. But we are still returned to images of what we might preserve. In *On the Beach* the joy of life is epitomized in the 360-degree pan of Gregory Peck and Ava Gardner kissing to a haunting choral of "Waltzing Matilda": "You'll never take me alive, said he." Stanley Kramer too urges us to act so we may avoid a postholocaust dialogue: "It's unfair because I didn't do anything. Nobody I knew did anything.... No one knows who started the war." Someone blames a person named Einstein. Retaining any optimism here demands a direct statement and Kramer gives us one: It started when people thought peace could be maintained by building atom bombs to defend themselves.

The burnt-out, starving environment of *Soylent Green,* c. 2022, the abandoned, weed-infested Washington of *Logan's Run* in the twenty-third century, need not await us if we heed such warnings as Charlton Heston's. At the end of *Soylent Green* he is carried off screaming, his fist, red with blood, raised in the air: "Soylent Green is made out of people! They'll be breeding us like cattle for food!" If he is lost, his warning is meant not to be.

Of all these films the most pessimistic is *A Clockwork Orange* (1971), with its depiction of an already dehumanized species. Once society reaches a point of no return, Stanley Kubrick warns here, there is nothing to do about degenerates like Alex (Malcolm McDowell) but alter them through radical medical procedure. But even this won't work since rendering Alex humane also renders him unfit for life in a sadistic world. "I don't want to live anyway," Alex says, "Not in a stinking world like this." We ourselves are made not to want an Alex who licks the boots of his oppressor. Science is in the control of degenerate men of power and the human race has been left to founder. In the end Alex is "put right," ready once more to do his violent worst with "Ludwig van" inspiring him to greater devastation.

But these burnt-out landscapes do not finally instruct us to abandon all hope. *Blade Runner,* one of the most brilliant of this new generation of science fiction films, depicts the ruined world of 2019. Fires erupt out of the smog and fumes of garbage-infested Los Angeles where only low-lives remain; respectable people have emigrated to "off-world." It is a future where replicants wander, all but indistinguishable from their human models; only an "empathy test" tells us apart. Director Ridley Scott's achievement is that we sympathize with replicants driven mad by their four-year life expectancy. The evil android antagonist, Batty (Rutger Hauer), in his storm-trooper get-up, turns out to be more poet than demon as he recites what he has seen at the outer limits of space where he was expected to remain a willing slave: "things you people wouldn't believe . . . attack ships on fire off the shoulder of Orion . . . all those moments will be lost in time like tears in rain."

We need not fear even our most rebellious creation. After ferocious hand-to-hand combat, Batty saves hero Deckard's (Harrison Ford) life. "Maybe in those last moments he loved life, anybody's life," Deckard speculates, the replicant having suddenly died with dignity asking the same questions a human being might ask: Where am I going? Where have I come from? How long have I got? The "artificial" life form inevitably carries with it human yearnings for purpose.

In *Blade Runner* our own concept of happiness survives into the future: making of the moment what one can, for as long as one can. The androids are no more confused or innately de-monic than are human beings; they too grapple with the age-old dilemmas of existence. "It's too bad she won't live," a seedy messenger yells to the blade runner (Ford) about the replicant with whom he has fallen in love. "But then again who does?" The questions we will hear in the future are reassuringly those of the present: "Do you love me? Do you trust me?" So with a green landscape, the final refuge of a human hero and an android heroine, ends this finely wrought film appropriately dedicated to the memory of its original creator, the superb science fiction writer Philip K. Dick.

Tron, a Disney effort to visualize a computer-designed future, shows us we can be a match for the computer and that this new rivalry can be fun. People here talk to their own computer programs and computer programs ride around in cars looking for data. Which is the real world? Even the villain, Master Control Program (MCP), aided by lasers and lackeys in military garb, is made in man's image. He is the enemy of "Tron," who wants a "free system" within the computer world and who fights on behalf of the "users," the human beings who must control their own technology or be destroyed. The totalitarian MCP would "engulf all programs"; the disc called "freedom" must be placed at his heart. *Tron,* like much of science fiction, slides readily into political allegory. MCP turns out to be but one more tyrant, a latter-day Morbius of *Forbidden Planet* (1956).

Of interest also in *Tron* is the notion that the computers are extensions of the personalities of the programmers. *Tron* humorously denies the tedious incomprehensibility of computer programing. The computer is complex, but so are we. *Tron* immerses us in a world created and controlled by a computer, an environment we shall face in the far reaches of the present.

The special effects of these new science fiction films themselves evoke not only the wonders of technology, but also express reassurance that we will be rescued by the science that intimidates us. The dazzling technical devices imply a confidence that we can control and shape the future, an age of computers and robots in which we will nonetheless still take responsibility for ourselves. In their style these films have become paradigms of that future.

This is particularly true of *Tron,* which was not shot by a camera, but by a computer that can move at any speed and transcend the laws of gravity. And how could we not welcome the science of the future as we marvel at the bridge of the starship Enterprise of the *Star Trek* films, constructed as it is with material from computer houses, laser facilities, and NASA's Jet Propulsion Laboratory? If we fear robots, we do not fear an E.T. capable of over 150 different motions, nor the radio-controlled Yoda of *The Empire Strikes Back* (1980).

An epic drama of adventure and exploration

Space Station One: your first step in an Odyssey that will take you to the Moon, the planets and the distant stars.

STANLEY KUBRICK'S

2001: a space odyssey

STARRING
KEIR DULLEA · GARY LOCKWOOD · SCREENPLAY BY STANLEY KUBRICK AND ARTHUR C. CLARKE
PRODUCED AND DIRECTED BY STANLEY KUBRICK · IN SUPER PANAVISION® · METROCOLOR

G GENERAL AUDIENCES MGM Released thru United Artists

The people of the year 2001 in Stanley Kubrick's monumental film are more concerned with nationalism, territoriality, and upgrading technology than they are with exploration and adventure, but for viewers of this film, the future seems fascinating.

Posters that make us eagerly anticipate the future, even if there might be, as we can tell from the visuals, potential problems. Project Moonbase (1953), the cheapest, least known of the four films, is of interest not only

because of the Robert Heinlein script but also because of the unique costumes and the fact that both the leader of a space expedition and the President of the United States in 1970 are women.

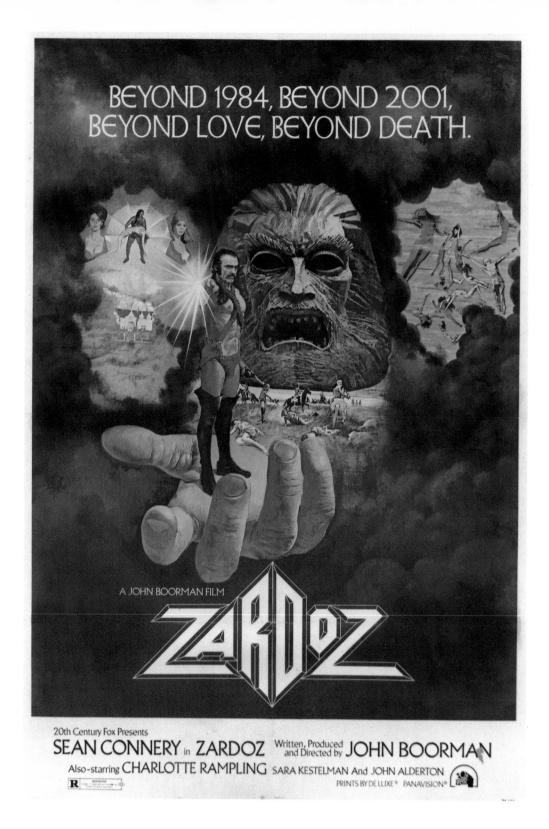

The words and visuals on this poster for Zardoz (1974) make the picture's bleak future world seem mysterious and enticing.

Posters of two films that depict postnuclear worlds.

Posters of films that may cause us to worry about the future.

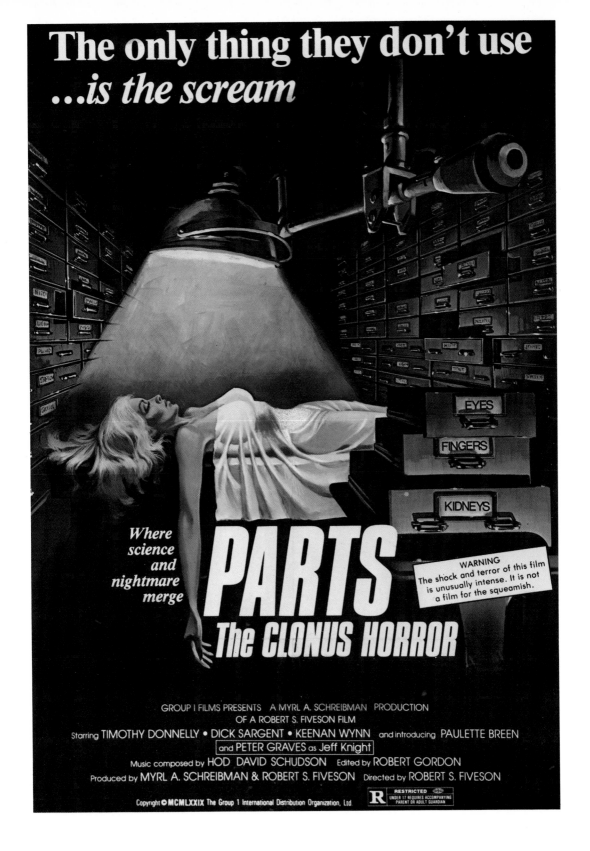

In a postapocalyptic world a champion emerges for the good people who have survived and want to rebuild civilization.

Special effects like these convey an important note of optimism. The science fiction audience craves these films not so much to escape the present or to mourn in advance a misbegotten future, but to awaken, like the anthropoids with their first glimmer of awareness in the opening sequence of 2001. Through their special effects alone these films become metaphors for a future in which we live at ease with robots and humanoid computers and where space technology is taken for granted. The voyage charted by these films is through an unknown, alien future to the safety of a moment when we master the new technology.

Those fears of the unknown may be evoked in these films, but they are present only to be overcome. The terror in Alien is that of losing control over one's body as it is suddenly inhabited by a beast that may at any moment tear its way out; but the alien is finally routed.

Fahrenheit 451 and Soylent Green depict worlds where books are no longer published, but they are worlds not yet our own. We are ordered to avoid them. The ice caps melt and the Nile floods as the earth heats up in The Day the Earth Caught Fire, but a cessation of nuclear testing would eliminate this potential nightmare. Low-lives have taken over in A Clockwork Orange, but its terrors are not yet our own. There is pessimism about what we face in many of these films, but the very cautionary note they sound carries the conviction that things need not turn out as imagined here.

Finally the solutions are of human, not technological origin. The science fiction film reaffirms the respect of the individual for his own judgment: "Luke, trust your feelings!" Obi instructs. There is the affirmation of possibility in divergent voices— the many computer programs allowed to run free once the tyrant MCP dissolves into particles of energy in Tron. There is love of life: the embryo encompassing the spinning planet Earth that forms the last shot of 2001, or the sweet E.T. about to ascend in his spaceship, with Elliott's dog Harvey deciding to go along, only to change his mind at the last minute.

Aliens, robots, computers, natural or man-made catastrophes, the bomb, and ecological breakdown are met with energy, determination, and a faith in the positive value of what we have already created. This ultimate confidence in our civilization that asserts itself in the best science fiction is summed up in the final sequence of Fahrenheit 451: the memorizing of the books. All the "book people" in the hills believe in a "real" future when "they will be called to recite what they have learned." We—through them—are armed with Moby Dick and The Catcher in the Rye, Mad magazine, and The Brothers Karamazov.

The future may be as bad as we fear as the robots run amok in Westworld (1973). Yet it was we who created them to gratify our sadistic fantasies, we who tortured them and caused them to turn against us. To create a less grim future we have ourselves and the best of our culture, which includes that technology which may be our potential ally, as it is in films from Tron and Alien to Star Wars and Star Trek.

The crises of the future depicted in these films have led us to learn how to exercise our best powers, our ingenuity, and our compassion. They restore us to ourselves so that we need not fear the future, and so their effect is salutary. The mythologists of the recent science fiction film also deserve the paean offered their print brethren by Kurt Vonnegut in God Bless You, Mr. Rosewater: "You're the only ones who'll talk about the really terrific changes going on," a drunk Eliot Rosewater tells an assembled convention of science fiction writers, "the only ones crazy enough to know that life is a space voyage, and not a short one either, but one that'll last for billions of years. You're the only ones with guts enough to really care about the future, who really notice what machines do to us, what wars do to us, what cities do to us, what big, simple ideas do to us...."

Rosewater's intoxication notwithstanding, the best and the worst science fiction films face this future. Carrying the evils of the present to their logical conclusion, they imagine a future they hope will never happen. If we continue to be passive conformists, Invasion of the Body Snatchers (1956, 1978) warns, someday vegetable pods may indeed take our place. We must guard against both amoral scientists (Frankenstein, Metropolis, and Alien) and science in the service of killing (Strangelove). In Charly (1968) the scientists with their "ideational activity," "fourth generation computers," "enzymes," and "brain proteins" lose sight of human values; it is thus that "rampant technology" and "brave new weapons" are their legacy. "What do you do with specimens that fail?" Charly demands; he is about to lose his newfound intelligence and regress into the nether world of the retarded into which he was born. And what indeed are we to make of the scientist-robot of Alien who would kill all the astronauts on board so he might bring the monster specimen back to earth for further study?

The more recent films applaud the insights and productions of science, which are, after all, some of our finest intellectual achievements; this grandeur is caught brilliantly in Stanley Kubrick's famous cut in 2001 from a crude bone sent flying into the air by a barely conscious anthropoid to a gracefully gliding space station, a short step away once man conceived of making bones into tools. We pity the HAL 9000 when his "mind is going" the same way we do the ill-fated Charly because we have learned to accept this computer as a companion and ally.

The best of these films suggest, therefore, that

Left: In Blade Runner *(1982), android Roy Batty (Rutger Hauer), who respects life more than humans do, decides to save human Rick Deckard (Harrison Ford) rather than kill him, as he'd intended.*

Below: George Pal's 1960 adaptation of H. G. Wells's The Time Machine *presented a paradise in the future. The only drawback is that first there must be a nuclear holocaust and the passage of 800,000 years. Here, time traveler George (Rod Taylor) questions the Eli about their civilization.*

in spite of all, the future is to be welcomed if only because, as in *Blade Runner,* it offers us one more chance to find what is most promising in ourselves. In the *Star Wars* series technology is the one landscape we take for granted and on which we depend. It is an ingenious future technology that is to remind us of our humanity. Science fiction films today, like the best American adventure films of old, counsel us that no situation is too demanding and that with will and daring we can even undo harmful change. In store for those with courage to embark into this future, there are wonders to behold. "Traveling through hyperspace ain't like dusting crops, boy!" exclaims an exuberant Han Solo. We are summoned to share his vision.

Thoughts on How Science Fiction Films Depict the Future

Nicholas Meyer

The most striking irony with regard to the depiction of the future in works of science fiction is that in my opinion the planet Earth does not *have* a future. Even the bleakest portrayal of postnuclear worlds have some people in them. By my lights (which are dim) even the most banged-up specimens of humans represent unwarranted optimism on the parts of filmmakers. We'll be *lucky* if a dozen or so of us end up as mutants. I understand that filmmakers, attempting to depict the future, are forced to include people—without them, the stories would be considerably duller. Maybe that's the truly unacceptable price of nuclear devastation: Eternal nothingness equals eternal boredom for today's audiences, hence a dramatic requirement of films appears to dictate a philosophical conclusion in all science fiction films, namely that in some form (however diminished and mutilated) we'll survive.

Some films, like *Star Trek II* (1982), are well named science fiction. To me they appear to be an odd idealized notion of what the future holds: American white supremacy, bolstered by token other races, as human beings and aliens go on playing cowboys and Indians ad nauseum, and as in the old westerns, the cowboys always win.

Other films attempting to depict the future may be less naive or four-square, but they all fall into the inescapable trap of being forced to conclude that we *have* a future.

At the present rate, it seems clear to me that the human race (with all other "sub" species) will have succeeded in utterly annihilating itself, probably before the turn of the century.

This, of course, will play hell with ticket sales.

On November 20th, ABC will air "*The Day After*" a two hour film about nuclear war directed by me. I urge all thoughtful Americans to take the time to view this film.

Nicholas Meyer

Nicholas Meyer sent postcards to acquaintances to remind them to watch his controversial TV-film, The Day After *(1983), which depicted nuclear holocaust. Because the film allows for survivors, a postscript reminded the one hundred million viewers that actual nuclear war would have a much harsher outcome.*

Nicholas Meyer directed *The Day After*, the most-watched made-for-television movie of all time, *Time After Time,* and *Star Trek II: The Wrath of Khan.* He is the author of the Sherlock Holmes books *The Seven-Per-Cent Solution* and *The West End Horror.*

Left: A publicity still from Dr. Strangelove (1964). Slim Pickens (who plays Major ''King'' Kong) sits on the nuclear bomb that in the film will be dropped on Russia, with him on it.

Below, left: In The Omega Man (1971), Charlton Heston, as the last man on earth in 1977, discovers the remains of those killed during a plague that followed nuclear war. Below, right: In Buck Rogers in the 25th Century (1979), Buck (Gil Gerard) and his robot companion Twiki survey the remains of .Chicago. Bottom, left: In The Time Machine (1960) London is destroyed by nuclear war in 1966. Bottom, right: In The World, the Flesh, and the Devil (1959), one of the world's three survivors of nuclear war (Harry Belafonte) walks through New York's deserted streets.

Survivors:
The Day After Doomsday

Robert C. Cumbow

The grimmest looks at our future are in Doomsday films, those that prophesy or depict world cataclysm. The end of the world has been assayed in various ways in films: by collision with celestial bodies; by environmental disaster; even by some cryptic, preprogrammed self-destructive impulse, as is the case in *The Last Days of Man on Earth/The Final Programme* (1977). But without doubt the prevailing vision of The End has been by thermonuclear holocaust: threatened in the satirical *The Mouse That Roared* (1959), *The Bedford Incident* (1965), *Twilight's Last Gleaming* (1977), *War-Games* (1983), and numerous James Bond films; mistakenly caused in *Kiss Me Deadly* (1955) and *Dr. Strangelove Or: How I Learned to Stop Worrying and Love the Bomb* (1964), and deliberate in *The Day After* (TVM-1983); actual and final in *On the Beach* (1959) and *Testament* (1983), our strongest *cautionary* Doomsday films.

A sort of pornography of catastrophe has grown from the antinuclear movements of both the late Fifties/early Sixties and today, producing a variety of Doomsday film that is basically a high-stakes disaster movie dressed up as a cautionary fable, one percent message, ninety-nine percent thrills. Such films are not about survival but destruction. Apocalyptic art is as old as art itself. We enjoy vicarious participation in a cataclysm we know we don't have to live with after the show's over. The appeal is to a destructive urge that inhabits the darker side of the human spirit, and that may finally cause nuclear weapons to be used in reality.

One look at this overcomplicated, overregulated, economically insane world is enough to cause even the gentlest of souls to entertain the fantasy of nuking it all. "It'd be worth it for me to go if I could take everything else with me!"—the fantasy that, taken to extremes in certain personalities, leads to rooftop snipers. But we *can* tell fantasy from reality, most of us, so the Doomsday films only serve much the same sociological function as screen violence in general: They satisfy our *curiosity* about things that, with luck, we'll never have to experience for ourselves.

Of course the important difference between nuclear films and other disaster films is the recognition that there has not been some kind of cosmic accident. Our lives really *are* in the hands of other people, people we don't trust. That orientation is clear in *The Day After,* where the world's civilian population has no control over its destiny—having naively allowed their political and military leaders full latitude to "keep the peace" through nuclear arms build-up. But *The Day After* aimed for an objectivity that a fictional framework can't sustain. Only without the distancing drama of a narrative frame is sensation reduced and horror increased. Peter Watkins's *The War Game* (BBC-1967) proves this point. This picture, which was done in pseudo-documentary style, depicts a nuclear blast and studies the impact of the holocaust on a once quiet English town, while maintaining at least a mask of objectivity. The result is one of the most chilling cautionary films,

Robert C. Cumbow has written for *Movietone News, The Informer, Opera Quarterly, Film Quarterly*, the Seattle *Times,* the Seattle *Post-Intelligencer,* and *Argus.*

so graphically realistic that it was banned by the BBC, which had originally commissioned its production.

Stanley Kramer's *On the Beach* and Lynne Littman's *Testament* make a strong subset of nuclear disaster films, the ones that admit *no* survivors. *The Bedford Incident* climaxes at the beginning of World War III, with uncertain outcome; Henry Fonda's President in *Fail-Safe* (1964) sacrifices New York to *prevent* the end of the world; and though the mushroom clouds of *Dr. Strangelove* seem pretty final, survival is signaled in the song "We'll Meet Again," in General Buck Turgidson's "mine-shaft gap," and in Strangelove's climactic rise from his wheelchair—like the tycoon Stanton in *When Worlds Collide* (1951)—desperate not to be left behind: "I can walk!" But *On the Beach* and *Testament* brook none of this.

On the Beach sees not anarchy but existential malaise as the inevitable response to the Bomb—consistent for a product of the beatnik era. People sweat, remember, feel helpless. Tilted shots convey universal distortion: "The world went...crazy," says physicist Julian (Fred Astaire), contorting his fact into incomprehension. An old retainer at a men's club serves himself a drink and has a spot of billiards. Julian not only enters but *wins* the Australian Grand Prix—a nightmarishly crash-filled race that shows how little anything matters anymore—before taking his last ride, with the Ferrari in neutral and rolls of fabric under the garage door. People slink off to die privately, like old dogs. Only the final shot of a tattered revival banner ("There Is Still Time... Brother") restores a sense of the less-bleak present, because it is aimed so obviously at us.

The garage scene is referenced in *Testament,* a whisper louder than any scream, in which the world is asked to disarm for the sake of the children if not for all others as well. Unlike Julian, *Testament*'s Carol (Jane Alexander) can't commit suicide (or bring about quick, painless deaths to her dying, suffering children); but it's not out of hope, more out of a kind of quiet dignity. *On the Beach* and *Testament* share that dignity, and if the films err it is on the side of being too cosmetic, too gentle, almost resigned. These are antisurvival films (also anti-*survival films*), about people waiting to die. There's no effort to forage, to make or rebuild, no regression to the primitive as modern conveniences run out or stop working. There's only a sense of defeat and loss.

These films raise effectively some of the key questions implicit in the whole Doomsday-survivor genre: "Why bother...? The dead are the lucky ones.... What are we doing it for?" *The Day After* reiterated some of those questions, but remained noncommittal, suggesting neither that there would be survivors nor that there wouldn't. "Why go on?" was balanced with "What matters is, we're *alive*"; and the central quote of the film

New York City, obliterated by a nuclear bomb in 1964's Fail-Safe, has had a sorry cinematic history: in both 1951's Worlds in Collision *(left) and* 1933's Deluge *(right), it* was covered by water.

became the justification Dr. Oakes (Jason Robards) gives for wanting to return to his obliterated Kansas City: "Aren't you curious? Don't you *wonder* about it?"

Wonder we do. But hope springs eternal, and most of the world-cataclysm films, nuclear and otherwise, are tales not of extinction but of survival. It's easy to see the attraction the genre has for filmmakers: You don't need a lot of actors, you can justify any bizarre special effect or irrational behavior, and shooting can be wonderfully inexpensive. Both Arch Oboler's offbeat *Five* (1951) and Roger Corman's *The Day the World Ended* (1955) are set for the most part in and around one house. Even *Testament* confines itself to the viewpoint of one family in a small northern California family, and most of the film is set in their house and on adjacent blocks.

Of course, as those responsible for *On the Beach* and *Testament* knew, the suggestion that nuclear holocaust is survivable diminishes the horror inherent in The End—not the wisest tack if your motive is cautionary. But precaution isn't the only element at work in the postnuclear film. There's not necessarily a wish to depict mankind as durable, or even *worth* preserving. But there *is* the indulgence of a fantasy at least as widespread as the apocalyptic one: Who among us hasn't at least once wished he could wipe away all the crowds and crap and *start over*? Just *enjoy*

the world for a while without having to compete in the socioeconomic arena for the favors of leisure, pleasure, and wealth?

Susan Sontag defined the mechanics of this post-Doomsday fantasy in "The Imagination of Disaster" (1965): "The lure of such generalized disaster is that it releases one from normal obligations. . . . The whole movie can be devoted to the fantasy of occupying the deserted metropolis and starting all over again, a world Robinson Crusoe."

Of course with only one soul left there's no story, so play God a little, let a few others survive. Just make sure it's still your own world—the same fantasy kids indulge when playing dolls or soldiers. But there's the rub: Once you've got more than one survivor, you've got conflict. Rod Serling rang changes on this in half a dozen "Twilight Zone" episodes. But conflict is the basis of drama, so what can we do with it?

The backyard allegorist can present a world in microcosm with a handful of survivors. Character tensions in *Five, The Day the World Ended, The World, the Flesh, and the Devil* (1957) and *Damnation Alley* (1977) mirror the friction of human will against social norms whose value becomes questionable in the wake of the Big Boom. The character groupings in these films insist on a world—or at least an America—in miniature, inviting a collision of attitudes and temperaments. *Their* fantasy is that the best of us will survive by virtue of *being*

ROBERT C. CUMBOW **37**

the best. (A look at today's survivalist subculture gives a different picture of what elements of our society will remain to pass the torch if the Unthinkable happens.)

A cautionary tale that proclaimed itself to be a "warning" for "the anxious age in which we live," *The Day the World Ended* becomes a Beauty and the Beast variation: Louise (Lori Nelson) rejects her now-mutated fiancé in favor of a bland, hunkish American Dream (Richard Denning), while the nuclear-mutants are destroyed by an Old Testament rain. For some, the film's "instant mutations" might suggest intriguingly that radiation could, instead of killing, transform humans into creatures capable of surviving a poisoned world. This echoes the argument of a number of films like *The Day the Earth Caught Fire* (1962) and some of the giant-insect spectacles, in which the only solution to problems created by nuclear weapons is using *more* nuclear weapons.

In *The World, the Flesh, and the Devil* the interaction of three people (Harry Belafonte, Inger Stevens, Mel Ferrer) in an empty New York is a parable on racism, sexual subjection, class con-

sciousness and monogamy. The film doesn't seek the roots of these attitudes, condemn them, or propose alternatives. Its approach is behavioral, not ethical: We must force ourselves to live together if we are to live at all.

Power struggle and sexual deprivation create *Damnation Alley*'s character tensions. In an Air Force missile silo a pocket of all-male survivors of a nuclear exchange that's left most of the world uninhabitable live in an unbearably oppressive atmosphere of boredom, futility, irritation, and unfulfillment. A discarded cigarette rolls onto a pinup, climaxing the choked-sexuality imagery with a series of explosions that recapitulate the unseen war and shake life out of its torpor. From there, the film deteriorates.

Social satirists like Richard Lester and Robert Fuest use the survival genre as a skeleton on which to hang tattered vignettes of a sort of Goon Show science fiction. In Lester's *The Bed Sitting Room* (1969) people mutate into animals, items of furniture, even whole *rooms;* in Fuest's *The Last Days of Man on Earth* a computer program fuses people to create new creatures. In both, the

Above: In the postnuclear, survivalist world of 1975's A Boy and His Dog, *males have their way with the remaining females. Rape is the order of the day. In this case, however, we have a girl (Susanne Benton) who uses feminine wiles to set a trap for an unsuspecting boy (Don Johnson). Right: In 1955's* The Day the World Ended, *a man (Richard Denning) and woman (Lori Nelson) unite both for companionship and to begin civilization anew.*

Left: In The Time Machine *(1960), George Pal visualized H. G. Wells's Morlocks, mutants from nuclear fallout.*

pathetic bare bones of humanity are the cynic's target.

The realist is less interested in social satire than in examination of the Lifeboat Ethic: People have a hard time living together, disagree on leadership and action, brutalize one another for food and resources. There are elements of this in most survival films, but Ray Milland's *Panic in Year Zero* (1962) and Cornel Wilde's *No Blade of Grass* (1970) concentrate on it.

Panic in Year Zero, in which a special session of the United Nations following a nuclear war has nothing better to do than invent new numbers for the calendar, shows people fleeing for their lives as civilization gives way to the law of club and fang. The generic staples of rape, looting, and the embrace of gunmanship in defense of life and property are abundant. *No Blade of Grass* substitutes environmental for thermonuclear disaster, offering at once a prophecy of what human life could become and an unflattering picture of what it has always been. The journey of one man's family from famine-wracked London to the haven of a well-stocked Scottish farm is an odyssey of violence in which human behavior is stripped to the essentials, and that nasty question comes up

In the fine English film The Day the Earth
Caught Fire (1962), nuclear explosions set
Earth on a deadly course toward the sun.
This trick publicity shot shows stars (L–R)
Leo McKern, Janet Munro, and
Edward Judd suffering from heat in
front of a deserted London.

again: Is *mere* survival enough? Or do we lose, in
the name of self-preservation, everything about
us that's worth preserving?

The scramble for self-protection in the face of
annihilation made *When Worlds Collide* an early
entry in this jaded subgenre. Its bunches of characters jockeying for seats on the rocket that will
save but a few exemplars of earth's population
from disintegration make it the first cosmic-scale
lifeboat movie. When the rocket gets off okay,
though, the wish-fulfillment fantasy that recurs in
so many survival films is established: Apocalypse
is followed by the New Eden.

Sooner or later all social comment, microcosm,
and lifeboat movies turn into New Edens. *Panic in
Year Zero*'s end title proclaims "There Must Be
No End—Only a New Beginning." *The Day the
World Ended* wraps up with "The Beginning." A
post-nuclear New Eden complete with beautiful
and gentle young men and women living in a
garden is discovered by George (Rod Taylor), the
operator of *The Time Machine* (1960), though this
particular paradise is given the lie by the exist-

ence also of a race of brutish mutants living
below. *The World, the Flesh, and the Devil* and
Where Have All the People Gone? (TVM-1974)
end with the promise of a new start, and Jim
McBride introduces the title characters of *Glen
and Randa* (1971) as a postnuclear Adam and
Eve.

This becomes too much a convention. Witness
Damnation Alley's jarring mid-film tone change:
"Nothin' good ever happens by itself," says
abandoned kid Billy (Jackie Earle Haley), but the
miraculous return of environmental stability is precisely a deus ex machina that cuts off at the pass
an Armageddon the film's makers hadn't the guts
to market. The proposed title change to "Survival
Run" indicates how fast and loose the producers
played with the bleak vision of Roger Zelazny's
book, preserved in part of the film, then dropped
in favor of forced optimism.

In Chris Marker's short *La Jetée* (1962) world
destruction is the merest throwaway plot premise,
the beginning of a journey more inward than
outward. To find a means of survival for the
tunnel-cloistered people of a postnuclear
"present," the hero's mind is trained to move his
body out of time, to seek the world of the future.
Of course there can *be* a future only if the world of
the present is saved: The future can exist only if
he visits it, and so by visiting it he creates it. He's
a kind of creator-redeemer, complete with cruci-
fixion, and without honor in his own country.

Families are destroyed by nuclear war. Right: In Lynne Littman's Testament *(1983), surely the most depressing cinematic vision of nuclear holocaust, a mother (Jane Alexander) is helpless to prevent her children from dying. Below: In* On the Beach *(1959), a man (Anthony Perkins) tells his wife (Donna Anderson) that there is no hope, and that she and their child must take suicide pills. Below, right: In* Five *(1951), the first nuclear disaster film, the pregnant last woman on Earth (Susan Douglas) sadly touches her wedding ring and worries about the future.*

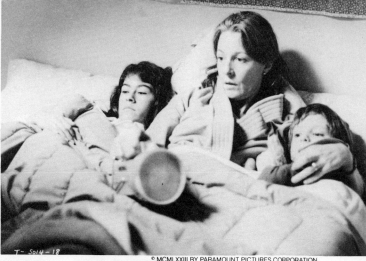

© MCMLXXIII BY PARAMOUNT PICTURES CORPORATION

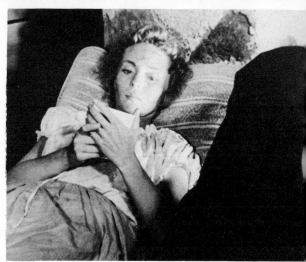

Ultimately he rejects both the present and the "tranquilized future" for a flight into the past, with disastrous but pre-ordained results.

There are some odd wrinkles, too: In a curious subgenre, *The Last Man on Earth* (1964) and *The Omega Man* (1971)—both based on Richard Matheson's book *I Am Legend*—and *Chosen Survivors* (1974) all find survivors of world disaster suddenly beset by vampires. *The Hellstrom Chronicle* (1971), which has a documentary format, and *Phase IV* (1974) show us how insects will inherit our earth. Then there are the "Surprise" survival films: Roger Corman's *Teenage Caveman* (1958), Franklin Schaffner's *Planet of the Apes* (1968), and Michael Anderson's *Logan's Run* (1976) all present worlds that are only later discovered to be earth after global war.

Soylent Green (1973) struck a special contrast

to its frequent double-feature running mate, George Lucas's *THX 1138* (1970), by recognizing that the more likely future of earth is not high-tech compartmentalized dehumanization but deprived, hysterical, wild-in-the-streets dehumanization, wrought by overpopulation and depletion of resources. Its crumbling buildings and rotting cars were the beginnings of the junkyard futurism of such subsequent films as *A Boy and His Dog* (1975), *The Ultimate Warrior* (1975), *Mad Max* (1979), and *The Road Warrior* (1982).

What these films represent is a reduction to the primitive, a portrayal of the human animal in its most elemental circumstances. As such, they are closer to the *mythic* awareness that is at the center of movies, and all art, speaking to an eternal resurgence of the primordial within the human consciousness. Even that most primitive of return-to-the-primitive parables *Lord of the Flies* (1963) has a World War III premise. It's in this subgenre that the postholocaust survival film meets the prehistoric adventure movie.

Teenage Caveman is actually both: A "monster" feared (and finally killed) by a cave-dwelling tribe turns out to be a mutated man, the only one

ROBERT C. CUMBOW **41**

among them old enough to remember the atomic war they've all survived. He's prevented from getting his cautionary message across to them, first by radiation, then by the tribe's fear of him—though it's unlikely his message would retain any impact through the scores of generations needed to return humanity to the technological sophistication requisite to repeating the mistake anyway. End title: "The End?"

Kin less to Corman's cavemen than to his Wild Angels are the newest breed of survivors, the primitivist truckers and bikers of George Miller's "Mad Max" films. Fuel, food, and sex are their quest, as in the world of the influential *A Boy and His Dog*. In the prologue to *The Road Warrior,* "Men began to feed on men. . . . Only those mobile enough to scavenge, brutal enough to pillage would survive." That mobility depends on "the black fuel," center of existence in this wasteland—and thus is *The Road Warrior* a stripped-down parable of our own world.

"Living off the corpse of the old world," the grotesques of *The Road Warrior* become, by their very simplicity, mythic archetypes. Miller's battle epic is the cinematic equivalent of *Chanson de Roland,* swords and bows replaced with the jury-rig gadgetry of a basement James Bond, but with the same elemental vision: There is no moral complexity; in fact, no moral definition at all. Good and Evil are unquestioned givens, and Max is

posited as the last best hope of what now passes for civilization. Like Sergio Leone's "Man with No Name," Max is a skilled and lethal hero who becomes, more or less by accident, a protector and avenger of the innocent.

Pappagallo, leader of the tribe guarding a precious refinery, doesn't comprehend Max's self-sufficient singularity: "*We're* still human beings, with dignity. But *you*—you're out there with the garbage." But the savior was ever a traveling loner, more alienated than embraced. Max helps the tribe make its way to whatever new paradise it will fashion out of the blighted landscape, but remains himself in hell.

Still, the marauding bands "out there" aren't unqualifiedly "garbage": When the fearsome warrior Wez grieves a lover lost to the Feral Kid's lethal boomerang, the faceless neo-Attila Humungus comforts him: "We *all* lost someone we love." It's a stunning moment of grace given a character otherwise portrayed as unequivocally nasty, and it sums up the vision inherent in post-Doomsday survival films: Even *these* are human beings. The perfect, uneasy synthesis of microcosm, lifeboat, and New Eden, *The Road Warrior* is the ultimate survival film.

Mel Gibson as "Mad" Max in The Road Warrior *(1982), a man who has lost everything dear to him but helps others find their postapocalyptic "Edens."*

The Metropolis Wars: The City as Character in Science Fiction Films

Philip Strick

An artist in *Life Magazine* in 1910, given the task of revealing the probable life-style of tomorrow's citizens, showed passengers at a United Air Lines terminal boarding a vast propeller-driven craft that flies high above New York. Another, in a 1911 issue of *Judge,* drew a pedestrian's-eye-view of the skies, where narrow-winged planes hovered perilously close together just above the skyscrapers. Looking up or looking down, the same concrete enclosure marked out the boundaries of progress.

The thrusting towers of the city, reaching at the sky like plants hungry for sunlight, suggested the pinnacle of our hopes in 1910. The glittering mirage of utopia seemed almost within reach, a new Camelot that could be raised to reality once more if there only could be found the new chivalry to warrant it. And of course the Pan-Am Building was duly constructed, and passengers really could take off from it to hover across the urban grid below, just as *Life* predicted. But of course while the city evolved, human nature didn't, with the result being that a new civil war began, escalated, and has raged ever since.

The battle with our environment has been recognized nowhere more clearly than in science fiction or reported more faithfully than in the cinema. Although all of us are recruits, it's a strangely secret conflict, its skirmishes, strategies

Philip Strick is the Deputy Chairman of both the British Film Institute's Production Board and the United Kingdom branch of the Federation of International Film Critics, and is a council member of the Science Fiction Foundation in London. He is the author of *Science Fiction Movies* and writes regularly for the British magazines *Films & Filming, Monthly Film Bulletin, Stills,* and *Sight & Sound*.

and campaigns recorded largely in code. No one can doubt, for example, that Jack Arnold's story *Monolith Monsters* (directed by John Sherwood), back in 1957, described in metaphorical terror the inexorable proliferation of giant crystalline structures that, if left unchecked, would crowd all life from the planet. But then as now, no housing projects are going to be canceled on the strength of such fantasies.

The enemy first formed ranks rather in the manner of the Third Reich: In its earliest days it excited as much admiration as fear. When Fritz Lang returned from his American visit in 1924 dazzled by New York, the result was *Metropolis*. In turn, his film prompted such a surge of conjecture about the likely design of the future that Hugo Gernsback was able to launch the first magazine wholly devoted to science fiction, *Amazing Stories,* in 1926, the same year as the film's release.

Gernsback's publication, and the many "pulps" that followed its example, were as vital as *Metropolis* in determining how the future city was popularly visualized. Lang's weighty sets and the magnificent model city, which conveniently dwarfed the elusive plausibility of his drama, implied a vaguely orgiastic future of riotous leisure. This would be bought at the cost of human toil until such time as machines and robots would administer to every need and "workers" would become unnecessary. Although orgies were frowned upon by the readers of the magazines, many of them too young to be interested anyway,

the motifs of *Metropolis*—the inventor's laboratory with its glass tubes and electrical miscellanies, the gloriously sensual yet lethal robot, and the towering fascination of the illuminated city with its floating traffic—were matters of indelible concern.

Such images were an eloquent testament to what became the obsessions of the 1930s, echoed in primary colors by the science fiction magazines that clamored for attention on the newsstands. From the back cover of the August 1939 edition of *Amazing Stories,* for instance, came the promise: "The city of tomorrow, engi-

neers say, will tend first to vastness—gigantic buildings connected by wide, suspended roadways on which traffic will speed at unheard-of rates. Helicopter planes, capable of maneuvering about between buildings and roof-top airports, will take the place of the ground taxi. Each building will be virtually a city in itself, completely self-sustaining, receiving its supplies from great merchandise-ways far below the ground. In this city, smoke will be eliminated, noise will be conquered, and impurity will be eliminated from the air. Many persons will live in the healthy atmo-

sphere of the building tops, while others will commute to far distant residential towns or country houses.''

The illustration for all of this is a panorama of arcades, multi-level motorways, and immense office towers fashioned something like organ-pipes. The effect is part-Metropolis, part-Inferno, an overpowering muddle of thrust in which, to judge from the traffic, the citizens are too concerned with the convolutions of arrival and departure to proceed with any practical business matters at all. And despite the text, all the pedestrians seem to be cowering at ground level. Whether commuters or maintenance staff, they're the inadvertent reminder, the more one considers them, that the city's purpose is self-perpetuating and in fact *non*human. Design for design's own sake.

In *Metropolis,* Lang split the future neatly, as H. G. Wells had done before him (*First Men in the Moon, The Time Machine*), into the idle and the over-employed. From the air, Metropolis is pollinated by hosts of floating pleasure craft; from below the ground, it is fed by the dynamos fuelled with armies of slaves. Through his magic formula—"between brain and hand the heart must mediate"—Lang seemed to feel that equilibrium could be maintained, although with whose heart and for how long has never been altogether clear. Which is why David Butler's *Just Imagine,* made in 1930, perhaps deserves a better reputation although little enough of it, in all conscience, is worth defending. The film's opening sequences vividly anticipate the *Amazing Stories* image, reconstructing a skyline of soaring buildings among which pour startling volleys of light aircraft. High above the streets, two monoplanes with little propellors like electric fans come to a dizzy mid-air halt, and a pilot ambles along one wing to chat with his girl friend until waved on by an airborne traffic cop.

That Lang had read Forster's *The Machine Stops* (1909) or Zamyatin's *We* (1923) seems unlikely, but Butler's film shows traces of both: In the year 1980 the population has numbers instead of names (the lovers are called LN18 and J21, whose pet dog, way ahead of *Dr. Who,* is called K-9), and marriages are sternly decided by the government. With pauses for song and some interminable bouts of comedy, it takes a trip to Mars obscurely to win the case for true love, and oddly, nobody even begins to consider revolt. The Martians are an ungainly, excitable lot, with rather ugly, troglodytic dwellings. The visit from the Earthmen, rather in the manner of a safari to an Amazonian tribe, proves the point that any community living in skyscrapers is so patently superior to other social structures that a few minor inconveniences of bureaucracy aren't worth contesting.

Any arbitrary dip into the "pulp" art of the times will produce a similar celebration of architectural finesse, where it doesn't involve (like Frank Paul's

superb January 1929 *Amazing* cover) the collapse of the Woolworth Building under the pressures caused by a new Ice Age. Along with the ubiquitous scenes of crazed scientists, such futurescapes were the inspiration for Universal's new gothic horror films (James Whale's *Frankenstein* of 1931 brought Wesso's *Amazing* artworks directly to life) and of course for the innumerable alien settings featured in serials such as *Undersea Kingdom, The Lost City,* and *Flash Gordon's Trip to Mars,* which were made over the next twenty years. Whether villainous or benign, the level of sophistication reached by an alien race was illustrated by the scale of its habitation.

In 1936, in one of his innumerable memos to the production team for *Things to Come,* H. G. Wells attempted to lower the visual levels in favor of his egalitarian dreams. "Things, structures in general will be great, yes, but they will not be monstrous. Men will not be reduced to servitude and uniformity, they will be released to freedom and variety. All the balderdash one finds in such films as *Metropolis* about 'robot workers' and ultra-skyscrapers, etc., should be cleared out of your minds before you work on this film. As a general rule you may take it that whatever Lang did in *Metropolis* is the exact contrary of what we want done here." His warning, as usual, fell on deaf ears. *Things to Come* described the evolution of a city as much as it grimly contemplated

A wonderous vision of a future Manhattan (of the year 1980!) in Just Imagine *(1930).*

Above: In 1968's 2001: A Space Odyssey *Stanley Kubrick predicted that Earthlings will build antiseptically clean space stations. Left: The shabby space lab in Andrei Tarkovsky's Russian sf film* Solaris *(1972) is antithetical to what Kubrick presented.*

Right: In Kubrick's A Clockwork Orange *(1971), Alex (Malcolm McDowell) and his droogs hang out at the obscenely designed Korova milk bar. With perverse settings like this, it's little wonder that the city youths have twisted attitudes and act in perverse ways—especially toward females.*

the destructive irrelevance of its occupants; the cramped, indulgent architecture of the past is bombed away, a plague-ridden travesty of feudal society lives parasitically in its ruins for a while, and soon a majestic display of tubes and towers burgeons from the earth, glossy with aspiration and ringing with continued squabbling. Metropolis flowers again. And at the film's conclusion, one of the city's spores is flung out into the stars with the proud assurance that it will one day return, a cyclical space-shuttle commuting between man and his neighbors and broadcasting the finest designs of progress.

Forty years later, the makers of *Logan's Run* (1976) were still resisting the traditional imagery. "We tried to get away," says Saul David, producer of the film, "from the essentially German Bauhaus design styles that were part of *Metropolis,* the strongly cubistic, rectilinear kinds of structures. We found that Lang's picture made such an impression on the minds of the whole Western world that nobody can think of portraying the future except in terms of towers connected by ramps—when what people are actually thinking about today are wide-open spaces and park-like areas of green." Ironically, the city of *Logan's Run,* designed as a totally satisfying environment (so long as you're under thirty) and largely constructed from the World Trade Center in Dallas, is the sort of place its inhabitants are eager to leave, and the areas of green are mostly in the "real" world outside. The city exteriors have a slight resemblance to discarded grocery containers and egg-boxes, but the interiors, sure enough, have the curving walkways, giant glass panels and brooding columns of bare wall in which both Lang and William Cameron Menzies would have recognized science fiction's habitual utopia.

The protected environment offers, according to the cinema, an inevitable claustrophobia. A city may be constructed in line with human needs, but the problem is that needs can change and the city doesn't. Films like *Fahrenheit 451* (1966) or *THX 1138* (1971) show clumsy dissidents battling not only against the various kinds of behavioral control enforced by the powers that be, but also

attempting to burst out from the numbing furniture that enfolds and restrains them. Whether blazing white walls (*THX 1138*) or chintzy wallpaper (*Fahrenheit*), the effect is one of depersonalization; the individual is less important than the symbol of collective identity—the urban program as a whole. In *Zardoz* (1974), one of the more maligned masterpieces of speculative perception, the computerized community is so inflexibly "protected" that the guarantee of eternal life has become a curse. In the film's courageous and brutal final sequences, the crystal walls within which evolution has become quarantined are shattered at last and the trapped immortals embrace an eager death so that the future can be resumed. The equation is simple, and science fiction writers like Simak, Bradbury, and Kuttner, with varying degrees of irony, have frequently recognized it: the ideal city contains no citizens whatever.

Underground imagery (if one discounts the corals and crustaceans of Méliès's *A Trip to the Moon,* 1902) also began with *Metropolis,* as though increasingly we have identified ourselves with the Morlock shamblers. From *Chosen Survivors* (1974) to *Twilight's Last Gleaming* (1977), from *Westworld* (1973) to *WarGames* (1983), our horizons have dwindled to a few yards of subterranean corridor, a battery of computer consoles, and some vast Big Brother television screens, *Strangelove*-style. In charting these future labyrinths for human existence, it's interesting that the cinema has consistently shown them in the context of repeated images of surface devastation, much the same shots of collapsing buildings and ruined landmarks being used over and over again. It's as if we're reaffirming to ourselves that everything built so far has been a mistake, that it will have to be leveled if the human race is to be

victorious. On the other hand, what purpose will survival serve if not for the construction of fresh and more elaborate cities to demonstrate how far we've come from savagery?

One way to win the war might be to abandon it. In space, man might theoretically be reborn (and in fact he *is* at the end of 1968's *2001: A Space Odyssey*), and one might imagine that his hermetic interplanetary environments would be designed and furnished like microcosmic utopias, free at last from the deteriorations of earthbound existence. But the cinema suggests a contrary view. Kubrick's hardware in *2001* was immaculate and unsullied, but spatial interiors from *Dark Star* (1975) onwards have reflected the wholly probable disinclination of their crews to keep them tidy.

The finest example of recognition for this enduring human love of shambles (Philip K. Dick called it "kipple"), which no amount of utopian evolution seems likely to breed out of us, can be found in *Solaris* (1972), the gaunt Andrei Tarkovsky version of Stanislaw Lem's novel. Its space station is a mess of discarded equipment, jumbled papers, incomplete repairs. When an astronaut psychologist arrives to investigate, his guest suite is pristine, but it quickly degenerates into standard-issue chaos. Naturally nobody bothers to repair the door after his wife has ripped her way through it. The film pays no mind to the probable decor of the far future—the provisions for antigravity, the consequences of living without an "up" or a "down," new clothing materials, fresh leisure concepts. Instead, Tarkovsky's future concerns itself (like his other films) with the past; the center of the space station is a mellow library complete with candlesticks and a Breughel on the wall into which his camera burrows with an intense gaze. And the objective of *Solaris* proves at last to be

exactly the confirmation that wherever a man may travel he takes his history (and consequently his environment) with him.

It's significant, although hardly surprising, that all the "space" films in cinema history from Méliès to *Android* (1982) have reflected this same nostalgia for the home planet. The objective of each voyage has been either to return to Earth or to re-create it elsewhere—even to preserve in space its essential landscapes (as with 1971's *Silent Running*). The cinema catches us at our most xenophobic; visit the other end of the galaxy in *This Island Earth* (1955), and it's just like home, bombs at every turn; land on another world in *Alien* (1979), and you can pick up some quite nasty infection; explore the gigantic invader in *Star Trek—The Motion Picture* (1979), and you find a hyper-efficient machine that went out from Earth in the first place; escape from doom in *When Worlds Collide* (1951), and the only good thing about the new planet is its resemblance to a Disney cartoon.

In the *Star Wars* series, for all its exuberant swoops of action in space, the struggle between nature and technology continues to rage. The vast gleaming hangars of the Death Star recall the Menzies modernist style, but at the end of the first film in the trilogy the heroes are received in their turn in a setting that would have pleased Albert Speer. When the Ewoks bring down the stormtrooping war machines in *Return of the Jedi* (1983), it's a triumph of native ingenuity over cold-blooded inhumanity, but nobody's going to let the Ewoks, with their crummy little tree-huts, rule the universe. The Force favors those with light-sabers, and let's not forget it.

Star Wars is chiefly about stateless persons making temporary stops, with some discomfort, around the galaxy. As with *Forbidden Planet* (1956) or *Battlestar: Galactica* (1979) or *Star Trek,* the problem with other planets is that they don't seem too keen to have us, and in any case we're none too keen to stay. With its great galleries of Krell technology (stretching for miles underground, of course, *Metropolis* style), ready to self-destruct at the touch of a button, *Forbidden Planet* demonstrates the homely truth that man must conquer himself before he can infest other worlds. In *Outland* (1981) or the regrettable *Saturn 3* (1980), the concerns are so introspective that the space setting is largely irrelevant; the protagonists might just as well be marooned down a mine or in an oasis—except that the omnipresent walls of glass and video printouts, the fine mesh of concrete and computers, enclose them like rabbits in hutches.

Returning to Earth after *2001,* Kubrick began the latest campaign in the civil war with *A Clockwork Orange* in 1971. In the tradition of *King Kong,* the ambition of Burgess's young thug Alex DeLarge (Malcolm McDowell) was to trample the uncongenial city jungle and find out, for the hell of it, whether this was a life-enhancing process. Monster movies have always had the same target image, generously reproduced by the poster artists: the Creature towers over crumbling office blocks and national landmarks in disarray while shrieking citizens scatter like vermin. A sense of pest control is implicit, as if the close-packed buildings are an invitation to vice and plague against which the cleansing forces of Nature—a beast from 20,000 fathoms, perhaps, or a horde of outsize ants—might rise in outrage.

A recent reincarnation of Alex and his fellow

Left: A city of the year 2274 is depicted in 1976's Logan's Run. *Right: In 1979's* Buck Rogers in the 25th Century, *Wilma (Erin Gray) shows our twentieth-century American hero (Gil Gerard) what Chicago will look like in five hundred years.*

monsters-from-the-deep can be found in Larry Cohen's *Q—The Winged Serpent* (1983), set in New York—or to be more accurate just above it, on the upper levels of the city, where the sky is a little closer. Not so long ago, when travel by air was still suspect as a daring defiance of natural laws, there were stories in the popular magazines of creatures with tentacles waiting in the clouds to devour the early astronauts. These were heights to which, it was feared, man was not meant to aspire, and the scaling of them would bring the followers of Icarus tumbling back to earth, incredibly diseased and melting, cases for Professor Quatermass and his reactionary colleagues. Cohen sounds the warning afresh, but in keen understanding of what keeps us watching the skies; the winged menace he visits upon us is a god.

Real-estate religion, its purpose to celebrate man's skills by the sheer height of his office-block temples, has at last managed, Cohen suggests, to penetrate the domain of a divine Spectator who, duly summoned, proceeds to exact tribute. As a result, the New Yorkers of *Winged Serpent* find blood raining down on them as sacrificial victims are snapped by the swooping deity. That its home should be the Chrysler Building, closest in design, it seems, to reflecting the Aztec motifs that might prompt a reawakened Quetzalcoatl to build its nest, that it should contrive to be unseen for much of its early activity, and that it eventually gets shot down, Kong-style, in a hail of bullets— these matters of mundane narrative, while related by Cohen with his customary zest, are not really the meat of his metaphor. His camera floats lovingly across the pinnacles of Manhattan, at the eye-level of that *Life* artist in 1910, recognizing for us that even utopia must have its limits, that the

boundaries for this one have been reached, and that the blood will now fall.

Down below, the streets ring with gunfire. In the close-packed tenements of *Soylent Green* (1973), it's whispered that cannibalism is the only answer to overpopulation, but the guerrillas of *Escape from New York* (1981) and *The Warriors* (1979) and all those blade runners and Charles Bronson clones and "Taxi Driver" freaks, some in *Blue Thunder* (1983) helicopters, some on their way to assault the no-man's-land of Precinct 13, know that the apocalypse could happen any day now.

The monster and the city have always been symbiotic. Utopia must always be bought at a price, and if the city is the highest accomplishment of modern man, the architecture of his pride is counterbalanced by an equally towering sense of guilt. But the cinema does occasionally awaken from its urban nightmare, and the ghastly social wreckage of *The Day After* (TVM-1983) and *Testament* (1983) sometimes gives way to a more placid outlook. There is, for example, one among many magical moments in *E.T.* (1982) when the child-sized alien pauses to gaze appreciatively at Spielberg's favorite panorama: the level electric pattern of a suburban town, peaceful and ordered under the night sky. Spielberg savors the special symmetry of human habitation, the warm fascination provided by the lights and colors of progress. Not for nothing does its supreme evocation of the future, the "mother ship" in *Close Encounters of the Third Kind* (1977), look like a fairy-tale land of spires and skyscrapers as it rises glowing into the sky. Perhaps, against all odds, the poltergeists can be persuaded to leave us alone and the city will become a condition we can live with.

PHILIP STRICK **49**

Movie Science

Isaac Asimov

Think of the hundreds of millions of people the world over who have seen *2001: A Space Odyssey* (1968), the *Star Wars* trilogy (which though set in the past and in a distant galaxy, deals with futuristic concepts), the *Star Trek* movies, and all the other blockbuster science fiction films of the last few years. Each portrays worlds in which some aspects of technology are advanced far beyond anything we have today. (That's why we need "special effects.")

The question is, though: How many of these aspects of future technology have a reasonable chance of actually coming to pass in the foreseeable future? Are the movies, to some extent, being prescient, or are they indulging in fantasy?

In considering the answer to that question, it would be unfair to insist on accurate detail in order to give a movie satisfactory marks, for that would be asking the impossible.

In 1900, for instance, some bold spirits were thinking of the possibility of heavier-than-air flying machines. If we imagine a motion picture having been made in 1900, with the action set in 1984 and with large flying machines capable of supersonic flight playing an important role, that motion picture would surely be considered to have represented successful futurism. However, what are the chances that the 1900 special-effects people would have put together a structure that would

actually have resembled the present-day Concorde?—Vanishingly small, surely.

When we see films, then, in which spaceships routinely exceed the speed of light, it isn't fair to ask whether the superluminal (faster-than-light) ships of the future will really look like that. Instead, we should ask whether superluminal vessels, of any kind whatsoever, are possible.

In our Universe, under any conditions even vaguely like those with which we are familiar, superluminal speeds would *not* seem to be possible, so that Galactic Empire epics must be considered fantasy. If we are bound by the speed-of-light limit, it will take years to reach the nearest stars, thousands of years to span our own part of the Galaxy, a hundred thousand years to go from end to end of our Galaxy, millions of years to reach other galaxies, billions of years to reach the quasars. Relativity, which tells us this, also tells us that astronauts moving very near the speed of light will experience very little sensation of time passage, but if they go to the other end of the Galaxy and back under the impression that only a short time has passed, two hundred thousand years will nevertheless have passed on Earth.

Some people rebel at the speed-of-light limit. Surely there must be some way of evading it.—Sorry, not within the Universe.

Why not?—Because that's the way the Universe is constructed.

After all, if you travel on the surface of the Earth, you cannot ever get more than 12,500 miles from

Isaac Asimov is a scientist, editor, and award-winning author of such science fiction works as *The Foundation Trilogy, Caves of Steel, Robots of Dawn, The Naked Sun, The Gods Themselves, Bicentennial Man, Foundation's Edge, The Last Question*, the novelization of *Fantastic Voyage*, and *I, Robot*.

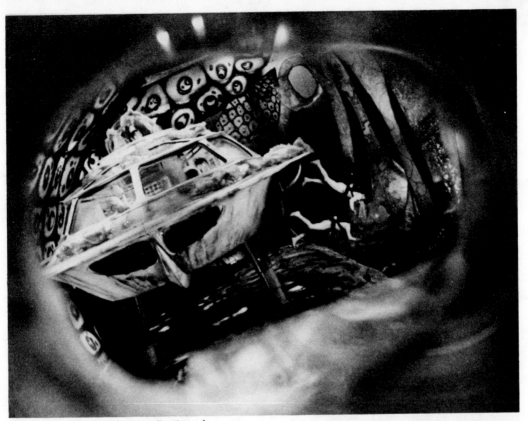

Isaac Asimov wrote the novelization of Fantastic Voyage (1966), about a group of doctors who are miniaturized so they can enter a dying scientist's body. But he writes: "Miniaturization doesn't actually make sense unless you miniaturize the very atoms of which matter is composed. Otherwise a tiny brain in a man the size of an insect, composed of normal atoms, is composed of too few atoms for the miniaturized man to be any more intelligent than the ant. And miniaturizing atoms is, I'm afraid, not the sort of thing that can be done according to the rules of quantum mechanics."

home. Nothing you do, on the surface, can get around that. If, at a point 12,500 miles from home, you move in *any* direction, you move closer to home. That would seem paradoxical and ridiculous if the Earth were flat, but it is the consequence of the Earth being a sphere of a certain size and there's nothing you can do about it— except get off the surface of the Earth. If you go to the Moon, then you are 237,000 miles from home.

Just as the Earth is surrounded by a vast Universe into which we may escape from our bondage to the surface, so it might conceivably be that our Universe is surrounded by a vaster "hyperspace" of broader and more complex properties than ordinary space, and within which the speed-of-light limit might not hold. Science

fiction, film and literature, uses hyperspace routinely for interstellar spaceflight but is never explicit, naturally, on the means of moving into it and back out of it.

Some physicists have speculated on the existence of "tachyons," particles that have the property of always going faster than light and moving ever faster as their energy decreases. They, and the space in which they exist, may represent an analog to science fiction's hyperspace. However, such tachyons have never yet been detected and some physicists argue that they are theoretically impossible because they would violate causality—the principle that a cause must precede in time the effect it induces.

Some physicists have speculated that within a black hole conditions are so radically different from ordinary space that the speed-of-light limit might not hold. A black hole might therefore be a kind of tunnel to a far-distant place in the Universe. There is, however, nothing beyond some vague theoretical considerations to support this, and most physicists do not believe it to be so. Besides, there is nothing we can yet conceive of that would allow human beings to approach a black hole, to take advantage of this, and still stay alive.

On the whole, then, faster-than-light travel must be left to science fiction for the foreseeable future, and possibly forever.

The same can be said, even more strongly, of another staple of science fiction plots—time-

Left: George (Rod Taylor) prepares to journey into the distant future in The Time Machine *(1960), accomplishing, according to Isaac Asimov, the impossible.*

Below: Robots, such as the ones that do battle in The Black Hole *(1979), are staples of the science fiction cinema. In real life, their development and increasing sophistication is inevitable, although one wonders if they'll adhere to Asimov's "Robotic Laws," which state they will be unable to harm human beings. Even more difficult to imagine and comprehend are the properties of black holes, such as the one that is entered in this film. Actors (L–R): Ernest Borgnine, Anthony Perkins, Yvette Mimieux, and Robert Forster.*

travel. The first to make systematic use of a time-travel device (as opposed to being taken into the past, let us say, by the Ghost of Christmas Past, or by a knock on the head of a Connecticut Yankee) was H. G. Wells in his 1895 tale *The Time Machine.* Wells's rationale was that time was a dimension like the three spatial dimensions of length, width, and thickness, and could therefore be traveled through similarly, given an appropriate device.

Einstein's theory of relativity does indeed treat time as a fourth dimension, but, alas, it is *not* like the other three in nature, and is treated differently in relativistic mathematics. There is reason to believe that not only is time-travel impossible at the present level of technology, but that it will be forever impossible.

We can see this without delving into relativity. Clearly, time-travel will destroy the principle of causality, but besides this, one can't deal with time-travel in any way without setting up paradoxes. One can't move into the past without changing all events that follow the point at which one arrives. Time-travel therefore implies the ex-

istence of an infinite number of possible "time-lines" and it becomes difficult, or perhaps impossible, to define "reality." (I made use of this view in my novel *The End of Eternity*.)

An even simpler point is that time-travel is inextricably bound up with space-travel. If one moves back or forward one day in time and is still on Earth, one has to take into account the fact that Earth has moved a great distance during that day in its journey around the Sun, and an even greater distance in its accompaniment of the Sun in *its* journey about the center of the Galaxy, and perhaps a still greater distance along with the Galaxy in *its* motion relative to the Universe generally.

Remember, too, that this sets a definite limit to how fast one can move through time. It would take a whole day to move five years into the past, or future, since to do it in less time would certainly involve faster-than-light travel through space.—And where would the energy come from?

Less commonly used, but still very convenient, is the notion of anti-gravity, and its inverse, artificial gravity. If we could have anti-gravity, space-

In Dark Star *(1975), astronaut Doolittle (Brian Narelle) gets advice from his "dead" captain (Joe Sanders), who is being kept in a state of frozen hibernation. Cryonics, a theme of many science fiction films, will certainly become more and more advanced through the years. It was first anticipated in 1887, in W. Clark Russell's* The Frozen Pirate.

ships could move off the surface of earth without having to use any more energy than is required to overcome air resistance. With artificial gravity, human beings can live comfortably on any asteroid and make sure it will hold an atmosphere indefinitely.

Unfortunately, however, if Einstein's theory of general relativity is correct, the gravitational field is the result of the geometrical distortion of space induced by mass, and by nothing else. It cannot be blocked or simulated except by the use of masses as great as that which produces it normally. In other words, you can't neutralize the effect of Earth's gravity on a ship on its surface except by holding another Earth immediately over it; and you can't give an asteroid the gravitational pull of the Earth except by adding an Earth-sized mass to it. There does not seem to be any way out of this dilemma.

What about telepathy or, more generally, mind-control? This is not inconceivable. The neurons of the brain work by means of tiny electrical currents, which produce a tiny electromagnetic field of incredible complexity. There might be ways in which such a field can be detected and analyzed, or in which the field of one person can be imposed upon that of another, so that the second carries out the will of the first.

Mind control wouldn't be easy, for there are 10,000,000,000 neurons all firing their tiny currents. The problem would be similar to hearing ten billion people (twice the population of the Earth) talking simultaneously in whispers and trying to extract definite remarks from the medley. Perhaps, though, it might be done; perhaps certain individuals have the natural ability to do it; and, even if not, perhaps the ability can be gained by way of some artificial device. It doesn't seem likely, but one hesitates to say it is flatly impossible.

Of course, it is not only the big things that run counter to the possible, or even the plausible. Sometimes a special effect that seems perfectly reasonable is simply out of the question in reality.

In *The Empire Strikes Back* (1980), for instance, a ship maneuvers its way through a swarm of tiny asteroids at breakneck speed. In *Return of*

The cinema's least sophisticated space ship can be found in First Men in the Moon (1964), based on H. G. Wells's 1901 novel. It is by no means a superluminal vehicle—an impossibility according to Isaac Asimov—but it does advance the notion of antigravity (also impossible according to the rules of physics that Asimov cites). As in the Wells book, the ship is able to leave Earth because it is coated with a gravity-resistant substance called Cavorite. Actors (L–R): Martha Hyer, Edward Judd, and Lionel Jeffries.

the Jedi (1983), ground vehicles maneuver their way through the closely spaced trees of a dense forest, again at breakneck speed. The result is a breathtaking "carnival ride" in each case, since the human reaction time is actually so slow that neither the asteroids nor the trees can possibly be avoided, at the given vehicle speed, for more than a fraction of a second. The audience, facing instant destruction but surviving, is, understandably, thrilled and delighted.

Of course, it is not human reaction time that is being depended on for safety, but the far faster reaction time of advanced computers. That is clear even though I don't recall either movie making reference to the fact.

However, that is not enough. A vehicle under the control of an adequate computer would have to make very rapid veers and swerves in order to escape destruction, and indeed the audience sees it doing so and that is essential to the thrill.

There is, though, something called "inertia," which is the basis of Newton's first law of motion and which nothing in Einstein abolishes.

Though the vehicle bucks and swerves, those contents which are not integral parts of the framework (including the human passengers) tend, through inertia, to remain moving in a straight line. The human beings are therefore slammed by the vehicle at every swerve and it wouldn't be long before the humans are smashed to a pulp, and die an agonizing death. Avoiding the asteroids or trees, by that kind of computer-directed energetic swerving, achieves the same effect, and very quickly, as not avoiding them.

And yet science fiction is not merely a litany of the impossible. The almost ubiquitous robots and computers of science fiction in the past are now beginning to turn up in reality. Even robots that closely resemble human beings, though they may not show up for some time yet, are not in the same level of unlikelihood as faster-than-light travel.

If it comes to that, when I started writing science fiction in the 1930s, a great many things that are now commonplace, including nuclear power, trips to the Moon, home computers, and so on, would have been given exceedingly little chance of coming to pass within half a century by anyone except the most optimistic science fiction writers. There is much that remains possible, including an infinite number of items that perhaps very few of us even conceive at present.

So—who knows what wonders lie ahead?

Relating to both the preceding and following articles: In the sf cinema, some of the most beautiful, "sexy" females are man-created. Androids were played by the late Dorothy Stratten (left) in Galaxina (1980), Kendra Kirchner (below) in Android (1982), and Katharine Ross (above) in The Stepford Wives (1975), in which human females are eliminated at their husbands' requests and replaced with mindless, obedient, perfectly formed android duplicates.

M.J. ELLIOTT

Sex in Science Fiction Films: Romance or Engineering?

David Thomson

In *Time After Time,* the Nicholas Meyer movie made in 1979, the future is now. The film's story begins in 1893 with H. G. Wells (Malcolm McDowell) in charge of his time machine, only to have it stolen by Jack the Ripper (David Warner), alias Dr. Stevenson, who escapes to San Francisco in 1979. The valiant Wells goes after him, fearing that his carelessness has unleashed the diseased microbe of sexual mania on the future. In 1979, Wells meets Amy Robbins (Mary Steenburgen) who helps in his pursuit of the Ripper. Their sweet love blooms as Stevenson begins to murder prostitutes. The Ripper finds his happy hunting ground in the North Beach area of San Francisco, among strip joints and live sex acts: "I belong here completely," he says in rapture. But H.G. and Amy hold on to 1893's Victorian code of romance, and once they have expelled the Ripper to a fortunately available limbo Amy agrees to live in a nineteenth-century "now," giving up modern (or "futuristic") emancipation for old-fashioned true love.

But in the George Pal movie of *The Time Machine,* made in 1960, Wells (Rod Taylor as George) goes much farther forward in time to an Eden inhabited by beautiful young blondes who spend all day resting, laughing, eating fruit, and playing games. He saves one of them, a woman named Weena, from drowning and there's no doubt that Rod Taylor's Wells fancies her; she *is* played by Yvette Mimieux. But like all her fellows,

Weena is an emotional deadhead. The blondes have no curiosity, no feelings, no sex drive, and no fear or comprehension of death or aging. In paradise, they have surpassed love and mortality.

There is a disturbing prediction of our evolution in these two versions of the time machine idea: Are we going to move from love through ruthless, animalistic sex to listlessness? If so, is that progress or a fall? It suggests that the attitude to sex in sci-fi movies is far more inspired by dread or guilt than by hope. In theory, sex is better now than it has ever been. So much has been done to accommodate it. Humanism can explain how sexual intercourse enacts and completes love and tenderness. The act is largely free from those venereal diseases that once meant death or madness; we do not have to run the risk of unwanted pregnancies; sex does not have to be a tangle of neuroses—there is therapy to loosen the knots; society now permits women, too, to enjoy sex, their orgasms and their erogenous zones have been certified; we have all manner of illustrated manuals and sutras, as well as blue videocassettes on the joy of sex. There are even some arenas where it is possible to enjoy sex without love and it is smart to feel that the separation is civilized.

But sex is not an automatic ingredient of sci-fi movies, no matter that sexual display has always been a box-office enticement. So many future worlds have learned to do without sex that the pattern begins to remind us of a primordial guilt about its practice even in these permissive times.

David Thomson is the author of *A Biographical Dictionary of Film, Overexposures, America in the Dark,* and *Movie Man.* He was formerly the director of Film Studies at Dartmouth.

When the futuristic city Alphaville *(1965) begins to self-destruct, Lemmy Caution (Eddie Constantine) leads the temporarily blind Natacha (Anna Karina) to safety. He has taught the once-emotionless seductress about love.*

So delicious now, so often the highest form of experience, the vindication of sensuality and a world of the flesh—the paucity of sex in the future says so much about what we expect in ourselves then. We will have survived, but we may find today's way of procreating redundant. We may have infinite intelligence, but we could be sensually moribund. Is the actuality of sex the sacrifice we have to make for survival? Perhaps all those bombs *are* just phallic symbols, and war the sport of sexual aggression.

Maybe the most revealing contribution film makes to science fiction is its requirement that these future worlds be realized for the camera. They must be designed and built; their art direction is actually more influential than their special effects. Indeed, those effects are only a branch of design, for in movies the future has attained a magical power over reality. The entire environment can alter as quickly as the picture on a movie screen; it can take on whatever appearance its people imagine—like a light show programmed by our desires. But although there is immense imaginative pleasure in seeing the possible future—whether an evident extension of our world, as in Stanley Kubrick's *A Clockwork Orange* (1971), or a radical departure from it, as in his *2001* (1968)—the most dramatic effect of this emphasis is to make us feel the lack of sensuality in the future.

All photography is erotically suggestive; and, of course, all photographs are imprints of the past. I am not talking about pictures of the sexual act or nakedness, or of pictures heavy with erotic anticipation. All photographs give us a potent illusion of actuality, of the momentary, and of surface texture. They provide a privileged view of some brief intensity, so that we think we might smell, touch, or be *in* that world. And because we are like

voyeurs—looking with the advantage of secrecy, enjoying a sensation vicariously—a gentle erotic coloring is given to things of no overt sexual portent. Photography eroticizes light, foliage, fabric, objects, and space, as well as skin and those who wear it. I am thinking of many pictures by Andrei Tarkovsky, Kubrick, and Nicolas Roeg as well as films like *Days of Heaven* (1978), Renoir's *The River* (1951), *Raging Bull* (1980)—movies in which the image brims with the sexuality of looking and appearance. Think of the great collection of photographs in advertising in which everything from fruit to beer, from cars to furs, is made desirable and we are made to feel lusty just by looking. Photography is erotic because it can so look at real things that we lay claim to them imaginatively.

But in science fiction, it is far less real things that are depicted than an artificial world devoid of that enthralling mixture of nostalgia and tactile plausibility found in most movies. In Roeg's *The Man Who Fell to Earth* (1976), in which an extraterrestrial (David Bowie) comes to the world, the real America is quite as intoxicating as the booze and sex that waylay the traveler. His own world is shown as blanched and abstract, lacking water and natural photographic density.

Science fiction is made on soundstages, with painted backdrops, false perspectives, and props such as we have never seen before or in life. Costumes are invariably unfamiliar—futuristic, deliberately original, absurdly removed from the context that equates known clothing styles with precise limits of decency or daring. For instance, the short skirts worn by Anne Francis in *Forbidden Planet* (1956), and Charlotte Rampling's deshabille in *Zardoz* (1974) are more revealing than, but less arousing than, what those two actresses wear in, say, *The Blackboard Jun-*

In THX 1138 *(1971), the title character (Robert Duvall) and LUH 3417 (Maggie McOmie) break the laws of their test-tube society by making love.*

gle (1955) and *The Verdict* (1982), where they are more conventionally covered. That is because the genre has itself abandoned the intimacy and actuality of clothes. In the future, people wear uniforms and they are cooler because of it.

More significant still, is the downright shortage of vivid human nature allowed the people in sci-fi movies. They wear streamlined clothes and flat pan make-up as part of the ideology of sameness. We do not think of touching them. There is a chance reason for that, as well as reasons of choice. It is chance because so much sci-fi on the screen is at the level of B pictures; it hires less starry actors. They are not zombies, but they are second-class talent, working without much rehearsal, speaking lines that are helplessly banal or deliberately impersonal. Good examples of this are *The Incredible Shrinking Man* (1957), the first *Invasion of the Body Snatchers* (1956), and *I Married a Monster from Outer Space* (1958). But sometimes directors seek that very limitation in much better-endowed pictures. By casting Keir Dullea and Gary Lockwood (not unknowns, but box-office nonentities) in *2001,* and by instilling a serene, pacified neutrality in their performances and a monotone reading of unexciting lines, Kubrick put people on a level with computers and he made asexuality a fundamental of his future.

However exciting or frightening as drama, much science fiction is intellectual or religious speculation in which the characters are more relevant as archetypes than as individuals. We do not know much about them because they do not have rich resources of memory or feeling, or substantial sexual character. In the everlasting life of *The Time Machine,* death has lost its sting, and the making of new life has no urgency. In Chris Marker's remarkable short film, *La Jetée* (1962), existence has been simplified to a series of still (or dead) photographs, and the one sharp glimpse of feeling and love is contained in a brief moving shot of a woman, alive and therefore sexual. Attractiveness has to do with our defiance of mortality.

In *Rollerball* (1975), the central character (James Caan) has had to leave his wife for the good of his playing career. He still imagines her, but his romantic sense—his need for love—has been detached from his sexual appetite. That is catered to by prostitutes, a dull, blunt class in science fiction, like the third-class seductresses in Jean-Luc Godard's *Alphaville* (1965). Lemmy Caution (Eddie Constantine), the Chandleresque private eye who ventures into that night city, has to beat off the inert carnal availability of so many extras and restore the icon of romanticism, Natacha (Anna Karina), to a sense of the past that lets her regain the word "love." In the first sci-fi movie made by George Lucas, *THX 1138* (1971), sex is a forbidden practice in the bright factory-state that allows no hiding places. When the character THX 1138 (Robert Duvall) rediscovers it with LUH 3417 (Maggie McOmie), he is marking himself down as an outlaw who must eventually try to escape. But that pessimistic film was a total flop, and Lucas has gone on to create a future made for children and peopled by human toys.

Above: A poster for 1984 (1956), George Orwell's tale about a future world where sex is as great a crime as political protest. Both require commitment, individuality, and imagination.

Below: In Barbarella (1968), our Barbie doll of the forty-first century (Jane Fonda) can have sex with a man (David Hemmings, in this case) without either of them removing their clothes. They simply take pills and put their hands together. (However, she learns to appreciate the old-fashioned way of lovemaking during the course of the film.)

As befits their ratings, these films are empty of sexual personality—even if Carrie Fisher has been showing a little more flesh lately.

The *Star Wars* pictures are successful, but they do not convert many of their actors into stars: another sign of the genre's preference for impersonality. *Star Trek—The Motion Picture* (1979) does have a love story, between an officer (Stephen Collins) on the Enterprise and the mechanized simulation of Ilia, played by a bald Persis Khambatta, beautiful but considerably desexualised. Those two figures unite not in a steamy embrace, but in a flash of light, like atoms of different elements coalescing. The equation in sex is more important than the sexual act itself.

It's as if mating had been reassessed as messy and inefficient; and as if sex were too problematic a human encounter for the rational schemes of the future. It may be the best reason for mistrusting science fiction.

Making love and thinking are the gravest offences in these thought-control futures. It is such activity that gets Winston Smith (Edmond O'Brien) caught in *1984* (1956). Love and sex constitute an aberrant vulnerability enough to bring on paranoia. In *Demon Seed* (1977), Julie Christie's character is raped by the computer Proteus, but after twenty-eight days her fetus is transferred to the greater safety of an incubator. Moreover, Christie plays the estranged wife of the man who invented Proteus, so that the rape is an acting out of real breakdown between humans. This is the dark side of that moment in *Barbarella* (1968) when the title character's greatest ecstasy

In Blade Runner *(1982), a human (Harrison Ford) must resist his prejudices when he finds himself falling in love with a replicant (Sean Young).*

comes not with a man but in a masturbatory machine. Barbarella (Jane Fonda) likes sex, but in her world the tidy "in" way of having it is by touching hands. She doesn't mind the old way when it is taught to her, but she is a child-woman, unable to discriminate, driven to heights by her orgasmic work-out but unchanged as a person. So many future worlds have reverted to sex as a mere reproductive necessity, without passion or eroticism: the *mechanical-fuck* is so sad a resolution to the uncanny sensual charge that hangs between those two future wantons, Boris Karloff and Elsa Lanchester, in *Bride of Frankenstein* (1933).

The rape scene in *Demon Seed* is not very disturbing, and not as imaginative as Roger Vadim's cheerfully prurient way of letting us flesh-gaze his then-wife in *Barbarella*. But it points to an area of overlap between science fiction and horror movies: the plight of the threatened woman. As soon as sex becomes real and dangerous, sensuality returns. A part of the tension in *Alien* (1979) when Ripley (Sigourney Weaver), in skimpy singlet and panties, hunts the monster is

director Ridley Scott's well-developed taste for the delectability of appearance; he came to movies from TV commercials. But it also owes something to our knowing that this demon can enter the body and do terrifying things there. Machines may not be very sexy, but monsters are as visceral as snakes. *The Creature from the Black Lagoon* (1954) has the look of a surreal phallus as it rears up toward the swimming spread-eagle of actress Julie Adams on top of the water. Such creatures let us ponder bestial couplings, so that we might look as fearful and wistful as Jessica Lange's character when she gazes up at her *King Kong* (1976) and wonders just how "it" could work. But *King Kong* is a tragedy about the separation of love and sex, as poignant as *The Incredible Shrinking Man,* in which the husband dwindles far beyond the scale of a human dildo such as his wife could keep tucked close to her if hers was the body explored in *Fantastic Voyage* (1966).

King Kong may seem more horror than sci-fi; its ape is a throwback. But sometimes the stranded monsters of prehistory are very like the terrors of the brave new world; they are all rampant ids. There is a kind of science fiction in which the photographic texture is appreciative of bodily immediacy, to suspense (that vital measure of the momentary), and to atmosphere. *Alien* has ex-

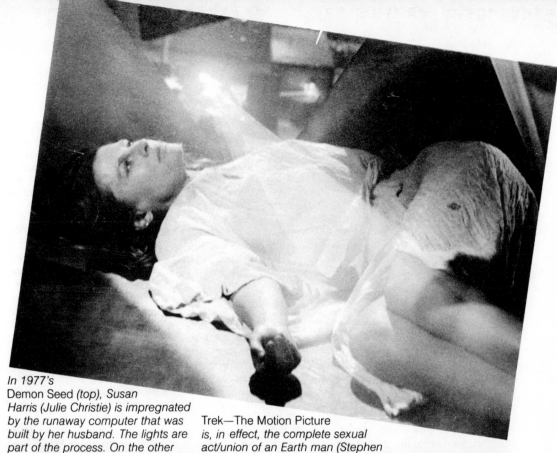

In 1977's
Demon Seed *(top), Susan*
Harris (Julie Christie) is impregnated
by the runaway computer that was
built by her husband. The lights are
part of the process. On the other
hand, a flash of lights in 1979's Star
Trek—The Motion Picture
is, in effect, the complete sexual
act/union of an Earth man (Stephen
Collins) and an alien woman (Persis Khambatta).

traordinary sets and a spacecraft, not to mention a multiform monster. But it has a crew of very real eccentrics whose bodies are as tangible, as sweaty, and as warm as Ms. Weaver's. Ridley Scott's other sci-fi movie, *Blade Runner* (1982), has a similar erotic temperature. Beneath and within its futuristic cityscape there are three replicant women—played by Sean Young, Daryl Hannah, and Joanna Cassidy—all dressed and played as unique, attractive individuals. In theory, they are enemies of the life being defended by Deckard (Harrison Ford); they are certainly dangerous. But the novelty of *Blade Runner* is in how Deckard comes to see a truer humanity in the replicants than in his fellow citizens. It is their yearning to feel love and other human emotions that makes them noble and tragic. Far more than in *Alphaville,* we want the tough hero to melt these silicon hearts.

L. Q. Jones's film of Harlan Ellison's novella *A Boy and His Dog* (1975) is set in the year 2024. But its wasteland setting is akin to the Dark Ages in that life has come down to the imperative of survival; and survivalists are invariably killers. The couple in the title have a pact: The boy, Vic (Don Johnson), finds food for his dog, Blood; in return, Blood smells out women for Vic, who rapes them according to the primitive ethos of the devastated southwestern desert. The dog finds Quilla June (Susanne Benton) for Vic. He tries to rape her, but she is too friendly for this brutality to work. So Vic is drawn into companionable sex. But Quilla June has seduced him to take him to the underground world of Topeka, a place without light or erections. Vic is needed to fertilize virgins for an underpopulated society. In the end, survival does catch up. Blood needs food, or he will die; Quilla June says let's leave him, we have each other. The boy solves his dilemma by feeding Quilla June to the dog. Thus rape and exploitation are reasserted as necessary for survival.

So much of science fiction crystallizes our fears that life could end, and sexuality is so ambivalently bound up with death and life. It is one of the peaks in existence, it lets the human race perpetuate itself; but it is also a function of the urge for power and violence, and the preoccupied dread of death. In Elizabethan England, the word "die" had another meaning—the height of orgasm, death coming—and still that moment carries a sublime hope of transcendence in which the ground might move and a person could see into other dimensions of consciousness. Sex and death are an abiding pair of duties and destinies, as witness the sad confession of Woody Allen in *Sleeper* (1973) that at least you don't feel nauseous after death. But in *2001,* the dying space traveler gives obscure birth to a space-child that springs less from coition than from the desire for immortality. In so many sci-fi movies, including *Zardoz,* the wondering looms, would we want sex if we were not going to die? There is an echoing question, embodied in the myth of original sin: Is it sex that kills us?

Science fiction senses that our life is doomed, and so it attempts to reproduce it by nonhuman means. There is a recurring theme in these movies of exact look-alikes, the one alive and mortal, the other synthetic, eternal, and possibly treacherous. We have seen it explored already in *Blade Runner,* with its hints that the replicants may be "finer" than ordinary humans. Far more often, the double is a threat that we may fall for sexually, just because we cannot tell the two apart. It could be a metaphor for being more in love with pictures than with people.

In Fritz Lang's *Metropolis,* made in 1926 but set in 2000, the evil genius Rotwang (one of the models for Dr. Strangelove) creates a robot exactly like Maria, the emblem of purity who is trying to organize the oppressed workers. Both Maria and the robot are played by the same actress, Brigitte Helm. But whereas Maria is innocent and altruistic, the robot-temptress explodes on screen in a lascivious, near-naked dance that is among the most erotic sequences in silent film. There is a similar duality in François Truffaut's *Fahrenheit 451* (1966) where Julie Christie plays the alienated, TV-stoned, self-caressing wife as well as the resistance fighter who would rather curl up with a good book.

In the classic threat of *Invasion of the Body Snatchers,* the pod people are look-alikes, played by the same actors, but people bereft of emotion. It is only when, on the run, the hero (Kevin McCarthy) kisses his girlfriend (Dana Wynter) that he realizes she too has fallen asleep (died) and been taken over by her pod duplicate. Clearly, then, when the body snatchers prevail, sex will be as dry a shuffle as photosynthesis. In *I Married a Monster from Outer Space,* the body of the husband (Tom Tryon) is appropriated by a space creature so ugly that he/it must take a human form to avoid alarming the woman he needs to mate with. Just as in *Body Snatchers,* there is an insidious warning that we may not quite know the person we are in bed with. *They look right, but aren't they screwing like Chinamen?*

The deceptive twinning of life itself is an element in science fiction enhanced by film. For isn't that what the medium as a whole does? Movies take the past and put it on a screen in so lifelike a way that we want to make it our future. Not all films, maybe, and not all of us, perhaps. Nevertheless, film presents a sensual, atmospheric, sexy imitation of life (and imitation *is* a sexy masquerade). Science fiction movies have been especially thrilled by the unique opportunity of the medium—one actress in two roles, creating the impossible, filming the future. Science fiction may be the least erotic of genres, but in its most characteristic mode—that of speculation—it is forever wondering whether we can survive or surpass sexuality.

Above: This publicity still of stars Rod Taylor and Yvette Mimieux for The Time Machine (1960) hints at a sexual intensity between their characters George and Weena that is not present in the film. Below: The naive Altaira (Anne Francis) is probably willing to take any kind of lessons in love from the first men who land on Altair IV, but gentlemanly Commander Adams (Leslie Nielsen) doesn't wish to take advantage: All he gets during the film are G-rated kisses. The darker, more intense (subtly sexual) relationship in Forbidden Planet (1956) is that between Altaira and her possessive father Dr. Morbius (Walter Pidgeon)—although the scenes that hinted at incest were deleted from the final print.

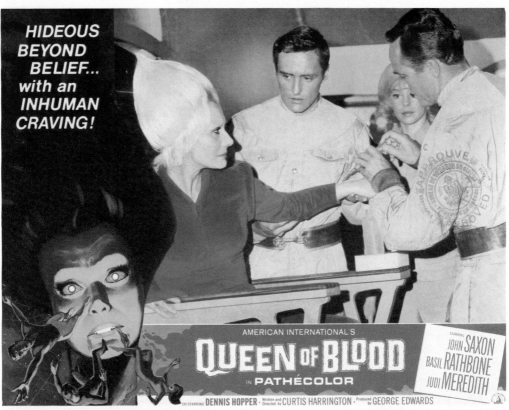

HIDEOUS
BEYOND
BELIEF...
with an
INHUMAN
CRAVING!

AMERICAN INTERNATIONAL'S

QUEEN OF BLOOD
IN PATHÉCOLOR

STARRING
JOHN SAXON
BASIL RATHBONE
JUDI MEREDITH

CO-STARRING DENNIS HOPPER · Written and Directed by CURTIS HARRINGTON · Produced by GEORGE EDWARDS

MANKIND'S
FIRST
FLIGHT TO
VENUS
--the Female
Planet!

QUEEN OF OUTER SPACE

COLOR BY DELUXE CINEMASCOPE
STARRING
ZSA ZSA GABOR
WITH
ERIC FLEMING · LAURIE MITCHELL · LISA DAVIS
AN ALLIED ARTISTS PICTURE

From a Story by BEN HECHT · Produced by BEN SCHWALB · Directed by EDWARD BERNDS · Screenplay by CHARLES BEAUMONT

Traditionally in sf films, Earth men are attracted to the mysterious female aliens they come upon during space travel. Just as it was with Ulysses

during his odyssey, these women are often not to be trusted. Curtis Harrington's creepy space-vampire film Queen of Blood/Planet of Blood *(1966), camp classic* Queen of Outer Space *(1958), and the similarly plotted* Fire Maidens of Outer Space *(1955) are good examples.*

A publicity still of Sean Connery and Charlotte Rampling, the stars of
Zardoz (1974), a film that suggests intellectual women would come to
power in a world where there is no sex or childbirth (or death).

Prometheus:
The Scientist and His Creations

Robert C. Cumbow

The year is 1957. The film is *The Black Scorpion.* A Mexican volcano has opened fissures releasing God knows what into the world. Traffic is *away* from the area, but for two Americans in a jeep bouncing uphill against the crowd. Their way is barred at the walled city of San Lorenzo. But one of them says, "We're scientists. Let us in." All doors open.

To this distinction, in a few decades, the scientist had come, metamorphosing from the comic grotesques of Georges Méliès's *A Trip to the Moon* (1902) and Rene Clair's *Paris qui dort* (1923), through the demented horrifics of the Thirties and Forties, to the status of new priest. And without contradiction, for he is, finally, Prometheus: adventurous bringer of new life, but blaspheming usurper of the prerogative of divinity; praised and damned; shining white, true blue, Stalinist red, Satanic black. But on one point there is never any question: The future of humankind is in his hands.

Through History with Mr. Science

In the old geocentric, homocentric world-view, science encompassed philosophy, theology, and metaphysics. Priest, shaman, alchemist, wizard, logician were but masks of a single Promethean identity. Galileo's marketplace science, severed forever from religion and speculative philosophy, signaled a new world-view, nature-dominated, in which man is but part of a pattern, ordered and measurable, predictable and formulaic.

Newton's laws of motion solidified the new view, opening possibilities for man's control of nature even while defining the narrow limitations of physical reality. The burgeoning "scientific method" came to be applied in hitherto nonscien-

tific areas: The U.S. Constitution fused Locke's politics with Newtonian balance and consistency. Hegel, Marx, and Darwin saw scientifically measurable schemes in history itself, in human physical, and social development. Economics and education became sciences. The "social sciences" suggested that even human misery could be approached scientifically. Medicine moved away from humanitarian art toward practical science. Army training became "military science." The person in absolute control of his endeavor "had it down to a science."

But economics and the social sciences could do little about the interwar depressions. As scientific technology and method brought new conveniences, greater efficiency, more leisure and longer life, they also began to complicate life. Ordinary people were held in thrall by a science that victimized even as it served. Following the lead of the nineteenth century literature that was the source of the formative horror and science fiction films of the Thirties—such as Mary Shelley's *Frankenstein (or, the Modern Prometheus)*, Robert Louis Stevenson's story "The Strange Case of Dr. Jekyll and Mr. Hyde," and Jules Verne's *20,000 Leagues Under the Sea,* which presented the mad scientific visionary Captain Nemo—the research scientist (the experimenter,

Robert C. Cumbow is the author of the pun-story humor book *Pardon Me, Roy & Other Groaners* and has recently completed a study of Sergio Leone. He has taught science fiction film at the University of Washington.

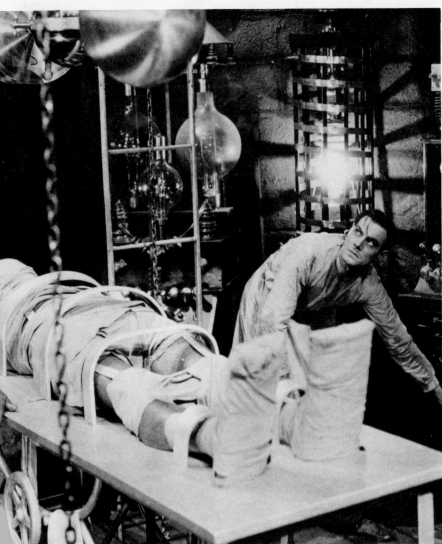

Left: A scene copied by many sf filmmakers: A crazed scientist (Colin Clive), his noble purpose long forgotten, brings life to an artificial creature (composed of dead body parts) in the 1931 classic Frankenstein.

Right: Alruane, *which was based on a controversial novel by Hanns Heinz Ewers, told the story of a scientist who impregnates a prostitute with the sperm of a murderer; he raises the child, who grows into a "soulless," man-destroying woman. It has been filmed at least five times in Germany and Hungary, four times between 1918 and 1930. In a 1928 German version, Paul Wegener (of* The Golem) *and Brigitte Helm (of* Metropolis) *played the scientist and the evil girl. Helm would repeat her role in a 1930 version.*

the inventor, and, most unsettling, the *creator* of artificial life) became an unequivocally and universally damned blasphemer. Although he initially endeavors to better man's future, viewers were alienated by his incursions into God's domain—creating artificial beings, prolonging life through unusual blood transfusions, combining human and animal genes, or daring brain operations or transplants—especially when he desperately resorts to murder to achieve success and is finally overcome with megalomania. The anti-Promethean attitude, long present in culture as an anti-intellectual resistance to change, became prevalent, and seemed justified as scientific technology directed itself toward more and more insidious machines of war.

Einstein's work suggested the interrelation of all activities in the universe, at the expense of Newtonian absolutism. By the Fifties, an era both technocratic and anti-intellectual, a dissociation set in: The scientist is usually likable, even a warrior-hero or a space traveler; but Science is a

dangerous commodity to be handled with utmost care. Scientific jargon takes on the character of ritual incantation, but reverence is tempered with skepticism. The scientist is an adventurer whose sorties into the unknown bring us undreamed-of wonders; but Science is the Pandora's Box that makes modern life not only overcomplicated but downright lethal. At the heart of the dissociation is an ambivalence: Our awe at the scientist's miraculous experiments is lessened by the fact their good results are usually temporary and almost always backfire with tragic outcomes. Our celebration of the scientist for saving us from, say, *Godzilla, King of the Monsters* (1956) is cooled by our recognition that it was scientific monkeying around (nuclear bomb testing) that raised the beast in the first place. In *The Day the Earth Caught Fire* (1962), Earth is knocked out of orbit by nuclear testing, so how do scientists propose to knock it back in? You got it: more nukes. Even in the Alec Guinness satire *The Man in the White Suit* (1951), the purest example of the scientist as

a sympathetic victim of The System, the convenience of the inventor's self-cleaning fabric is undercut by the impact of the widespread unemployment it would create.

If the scientist had ceased to be a lunatic, his deficiency now seemed a surfeit of pure reason. The preeminence of scientific method and the presumed truth of anything scientifically demonstrable made Science seem a limiting, not a liberating, force, an imposer of inviolable laws and procedures. This super-rationalism prompted a reaffirmation of the irrational, and beginning in the Fifties science fiction film became the domain of monsters. *The Thing* (1951) used combat with an alien to illustrate the prohuman anti-intellectualism of the age, pitting men of action against men of science (whose insistence on communicating with the creature has near disastrous results) to the detriment of the latter. *The Creature from the Black Lagoon* (1954) posited the Bad Scientist as nature's enemy, the Good Scientist as its friend.

New interest in the irrational side of the human spirit culminated in the Sixties with the insistence that humanity elevate itself not by dominating nature but by living with it, even serving it. By 1971's *Silent Running* the Good Scientist is a botanist (Bruce Dern) who risks everything to save what may be the last garden in the universe. In 1977, Steven Spielberg recapitulated *The Thing*'s counterposition of scientific receptiveness and military resistance, but reverses the outcome. In *Close Encounters of the Third Kind* space visitors are greeted with trust, not weapons. And in *E.T.* (1982) the scientists, ominous and fear-

some most of the way, emerge as benevolent and wonder-struck as the kids: "He came to me, too," says one. "I've been dreaming of this since I was ten years old."

Behind all these many masks and manifestations shuffled the ever-present figure of Mr. Science, always feared and admired, above hoi polloi but a little below the angels.

Things We Weren't Meant to Know

Long after the passing of the morality fiction of the nineteenth century, the overriding assumption about the research scientist is still that he plays God. The archetypal movie scientist is a compulsive, obsessive personality who, though motivated by altruistic goals—he wants to improve man's *future*—comes to seek knowledge for its own sake. Faust. Or, for that matter, Adam in Eden.

From *Homunculus* (1916) to *Android* (1983) there's an unbroken line of scientists who sin against the universe. "I meddled in things man must leave alone" were the undying words of the dying Jack Griffin (Claude Rains) in *The Invisible Man* (1933). Janus Rukh (Boris Karloff) in *The Invisible Ray* (1936) "broke the first rule of science," learned that "there are some things man is not meant to know," developed a radioactive Midas touch, and went criminally insane.

All these are scapegoats. Even as early as the Twenties the scientist was an easy target for popular frustrations. The machine-building megalomania of Rotwang (Rudolf Klein-Rogge) in Fritz Lang's *Metropolis* (1926) must have personified

The mad scientist, a German tradition: Rudolf Klein-Rogge (above) played Rotwang, mad inventor of an evil robot, in Metropolis (1926). Peter Lorre (below, left) donned mechanical hands to play the increasingly insane Dr. Gogol in Mad Love, directed by Karl Freund, Fritz Lang's cameraman on Metropolis. Peter Sellers (below, right) was unforgettable as the ex-Nazi scientist Dr. Strangelove (1964).

to contemporary audiences the threat that a not-so-distant future automation held for an already depressed labor force. "Now," he cries, "we have no need for living workers!" In a vision of the future that carries forward in the Industrial Revolution's vertical stratification of society—Masters, Citizens, Machines, *then* workers—the depiction of Rotwang as archvillain and author of the whole atrocity showed the first stirrings of an anti-intellectualism that still haunts sf film.

The prototypical mad doctor doesn't start out mad. He's *driven* mad by the frustration of some idealistic goal. Take Jules Verne's Captain Nemo, memorably portrayed by James Mason in *20,000 Leagues Under the Sea* (1954) and resurrected in space as Maximilian Schell's Dr. Hans Reinhardt in *The Black Hole* (1979): A brilliant mind who's contributed much to the world's knowledge and comfort turns his genius to destruction to avenge a wrong and to vent his frustration at the futility of his work. But the granddaddy of mad doctors was the one Mary Shelley called "the Modern Prometheus."

The Children of Dr. Frankenstein

A version of *Frankenstein* was one of the very first movies (1910), and the story's theme dominates futuristic fantasy to this day. Who can doubt that the scientist who assays the creation of life aspires to godhead itself? The scientist of *Homunculus* tries to create a man of pure reason, unfettered by fallible emotion. The homunculus is a forerunner of the robots and androids that proliferate in sf film during the 1970s and 1980s when the very nature of human life is called increasingly into question.

The scientist-creator and his brainchild always mirror the parental relationship implied in *Frankenstein* (and, for that matter, in *Pinocchio*): The creator fathers the beast who, less than perfect and far from controllable, is a bitter disappointment; the relationship boils into madness and violence. The future doesn't fulfill the present—it betrays it.

Not just a desire to know but a yearning for perfection prods the scientist to build his own person. But playing God has its price: Something always goes wrong. In *Alraune* (1918, 1928, 1930, 1952), a child born of artificial insemination becomes a woman of evil, exemplifying the rapidly dating notion that evil is external and objective, not willed or conditioned, and that the scientific future *is* evil. In *The Hands of Orlac* (1925) an injured musician (Conrad Veidt) receives in a transplant the hands of a hanged strangler and is haunted by the fear that the hands will murder of their own accord. Director Karl Freund rang changes on the story in *Mad Love* (1935): Dr. Gogol (Peter Lorre) loves the wife (Frances Drake) of pianist Orlac (Colin Clive) and so *tells* the man his transplanted hands belonged to a murderer, hoping to drive him mad and estrange

him from his wife. Gogol comes to believe his own fabricated reality; and as the film ends there is no indication Orlac will ever come to terms with his own hands. The tradition continued with Stanley Kubrick's character *Dr. Strangelove* (1964), a sinister German in dark glasses (Peter Sellers) whose hands have their own will and whose name echoes Freund's title. (In the same film Kubrick references Laputa, Jonathan Swift's satirical floating isle of pure science, where men are grotesquely mad.)

Yet even those visionary Germans scarcely foresaw the explosion in science that would occur as creation of life approached reality. A dozen versions of *Frankenstein* took on a kind of prophetic truth. In *Scream and Scream Again* (1970), a film Fritz Lang admired, synthetic humans are fashioned of pain-resistant tissues and the not-so-spare parts of real people kidnapped and mutilated for the purpose. *The Stepford Wives* (1975) were ersatz women created to serve their bedroom community husbands without getting too uppity. In *Embryo* (1976) scientist (Rock Hudson) turned an embryo into a beautiful woman (Barbara Carrera) in mere days. The horrific possibilities of cloning were tapped for *The Clones* (1973), *The Cloning of Clifford Swimmer* (1974), *Parts—The Clonus Horror* (1976), and *The Boys from Brazil* (1976).

In every case, the life-making scientist's aim is a kind of control. Big children playing with human dolls, the scientists of *Homunculus, Bride of Frankenstein* (1935), *Dr. Cyclops* (1940), and *Attack of the Puppet People* (1958) personify ordinary people's increasing fear of how scientific research and futuristic technology manipulate their lives.

The Children of Dr. Jekyll

The more idealistic and adventurous scientist does not need the reassurance of controlling another. He experiments bravely on himself—and inevitably, like Jack Griffin and Janus Rukh, becomes his own monster, yet another emblem of what future lies in store for humanity at his Faustian hands.

A succession of tormented experimenters have suffered the worst failures of futurism gone wrong. Robert Louis Stevenson's formative story "The Strange Case of Dr. Jekyll and Mr. Hyde" was filmed at least six times (1908, 1912, 1920, 1931, 1941, and the 1970 Hammer film *I, Monster*), and its heritage is the parade of Jekyll-Hydes during the 1950s and 1960s. A scientist (Leo G. Carroll) researching growth hormones gives himself acromegaly in *Tarantula* (1955). Professor Morbius (Walter Pidgeon) in *Forbidden Planet* (1956) tinkers with the vastly superior mental systems of the extinct Krell civilization and releases the monster of his own id. A molecule-scrambling invention gives a scientist (David Hedison) the head of *The Fly* (1958). In *Monster on*

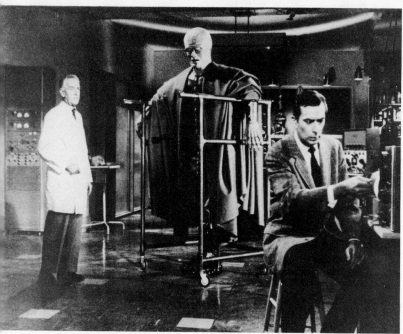

Left: Scientists usually have good reasons for treading in God's domain. In the nonclassic The Colossus of New York (1958), a scientist played by Otto Kruger (left)—notice the German name—implants his dead son's brain into a giant robot—naturally there are disastrous results.

Right: In Douglas Trumbull's Silent Running (1971), a botanist (Bruce Dern) preserves his space garden with the help of three pint-sized robots (named after Donald Duck's nephews).

the Campus (1958) the bite of a coelecanth turns a college prof (Arthur Franz) into a troglodytic throwback. Jerry Lewis's Nutty Professor (1963) metamorphoses into a Dean Martin parody named Buddy Love.

The scientist suffers for his ambition not because he probes the unknown but because he is immoderate in his method. The failure of idealism is nowhere more apparent than in Roger Corman's X—The Man with the X-Ray Eyes (1963), where seeking to do Good is an act of hubris leading to obsession and insanity. Trying to exceed the limitations of human eyesight by using a special chemical, Dr. Xavier (Ray Milland) finds not only the madness of obsession but the absurd vision of things as they really are. To find peace, he tears out his own eyes—and still he sees. (Here, however, the scientific method itself seems to have been at fault: A real scientist would have tried the drops in only one eye.)

The search for knowledge becomes the search for self. Altered States (1980) is a future voyage into inner space as inevitable and necessary as any external exploration. Like Jekyll/Hyde, researcher Eddie Jessup (William Hurt) regresses to the libidinous primitive, and like so many Hydes before him he learns to kill. But Altered States is not just about the human personality; it is specifically about the scientific mind. Jessup is a scientist first and a man second because he's afraid to see himself as a man at all, unable to confront his own vulnerability. We sense the domination of science in our lives as we see it in his, and are struck by how science in this vision reaches out to suppress the human. Jessup's wife Emily (Blair Brown), an anthropologist, is a whole person, able to love where he cannot; yet he appeals mostly to the scientist in her, saying

things like, "You're a scientist yourself; you must understand how I feel" and "I would like a little consensual validation on this." His magnified mind melts the hardware that gives him his long-sought vision of oneness with the universe, and his wife explains: "He got it off with God—he was finally ravished by the Truth." The upshot is, again, a vision of the Absurd, the only escape from which is not scientifically demonstrable knowledge or "consensual validation" but love in all its bold irrationality.

So what else is new? Faust, too, was redeemed by love. Down the past seventy years mad movie scientists have been offered love as an alternative to obsessively rational scientific inquiry. The scientist saves or damns himself by accepting or rejecting it—raising implicitly the question of whether, without love, there can be a human future.

Creations I: Humanization of the Machine

From the metaphoric future of Metropolis to the uneasy present of WarGames (1983) the way of the world is the way of the machine, all-powerful scientific creation that makes life easier even while threatening it with more than one kind of obsolescence. In the age of Star Wars (1977) and video games the movies themselves increasingly emphasize technological sophistication as a measure of excellence.

Society's changing attitude toward the machine as evidenced in the rise of the home computer has not been reflected on film, where the machine is still suspect. Despite its steady acquisition of human characteristics—fallibility and feelings in 2001: A Space Odyssey (1968), a female voice in Dark Star (1975) and Logan's Run (1976), a desire for propagation in The Demon

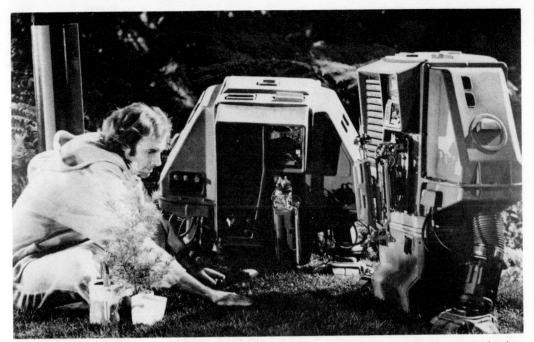

Seed (1977)—the computer remained the definitive enemy of human hopes for the future, counteracting the goodness of human emotion exactly as crypto-communist alien invaders of the 1950s had. In films as diverse as *Star Trek—The Motion Picture* (1979) and *Looker* (1981) computers are the agents of dehumanization.

Colossus: The Forbin Project (1970) lets the machine win the day, though the human spirit holds out. The film's key vision is of the conjugal bed as the last stronghold of human defense against the tyranny of technology—the animal, emotional side of human nature is crucial to the preservation of freedom. Intimacy and procreation are—for the time being—inaccessible to machines.

Alien (1979) also celebrates retention of humanity: As the alien devours the crew of the space transport, the colder, more methodical ones are the first to go; the more emotional characters survive the longest. Interestingly, Ash (Ian Holm), the science officer who turns out to be an android, goes fourth, right in the middle, suggesting that a man-machine may be the needed balance between the extremes of rational and irrational. It's an idea that grows in importance over the next few years.

Ash shares the machine stage with Mother, the ship's computer, against whose internal clock the final survivor, Ripley (Sigourney Weaver), races to override the auto-destruct mechanism in the climax. Knowing she's losing, Ripley hisses at Mother, "You bitch!"

In *2001: A Space Odyssey,* man-apes advance through the discovery of tools; the man of the future advances through the *rejection* of tools. Astronaut Dave Bowman (Keir Dullea), by dismantling the malfunctioning computer HAL 9000,

asserts the superiority of the human mechanism over the increasingly human fallibility of the machine—yet it also sets the stage for Bowman's transformation into the superhuman star-child. In *Alien,* by contrast, machines coolly and efficiently keep their distance as human beings defeat themselves. The machinelike humans of *2001* are typical of Stanley Kubrick's treatment of living creatures as elements in a pattern (the Newtonian world view). *Barry Lyndon* (1975) and *The Shining* (1980) show contrasting forms of dehumanization brought on by the tyranny of structure. In *A Clockwork Orange* (1971), Alex (Malcolm McDowell) is programmed against violence at the sacrifice of his individuality and creativity.

The flip side of the man who acts like a machine is the machine that acts like a man. Is there any real difference between *seeing* human and *being* human? There's a certain lack of conviction in the astronaut's voice when he tells a TV interviewer in *2001* that HAL 9000 "*acts* like he has genuine emotions; of course, he's programmed that way to make it easier for us to talk to him." The epitome of the humanization of the machine is not the talking computer, though: It's the robot, staple of cinematic futures since *Metropolis,* emblem of science's wish to make a man and of its failure to make more than a machine. There's little difference, finally, between Frankenstein's monster and homunculus on the one hand and robots on the other. Both are artificial people, life-substitutes distinguished only by the sources of their raw materials. In *Metropolis,* Rotwang's robot—Maria (Brigitte Helm) is formed of synthetic components infused with a copy of the true Maria's life-force—a stolen soul. It would be fifty years before another major sf film depicted a robot with such utterly human look and behavior;

and not even in *Blade Runner* (1982) or *Android,* has a robot been more erotic than Rotwang's Maria. Most are walking computers or glorified tin cans, and fall into one of two groups: the cute and the scary.

Though he had mighty powers, *Forbidden Planet*'s Robby is the archetypal cute robot, the only one before *Star Wars* to win a popular following. Huggable Huey, Dewey, and Louie of *Silent Running* and the domestic robots mimicked by Woody Allen in *Sleeper* (1973) carried on the cute tradition, as did C3PO and R2D2 (the wisecracking Laurel and Hardy of *Star Wars*), the wide-eyed cartoonish robots of *The Black Hole,* and the runaway sweethearts of *Heartbeeps* (1981). The most memorable of the scaries is Gort of *The Day the Earth Stood Still* (1951), rivaled only by *Tobor the Great* (1954) and *The Black Hole*'s red-eyed Maximilian. George Lucas used robot police in *THX 1138* (1971) to show the mechanization of methodical, budget-centered public service in his compartmentalized future. But truly human-seeming robots have proliferated in sf film only recently.

Signaled by HAL 9000's insistence that "I can *feel* it" as Dave Bowman disassembles his memory banks, the robot-as-human emerges only in the 1970s, beginning with *Westworld* (1973). This deistic vision posits a future amusement park where people play out fantasies in robot-peopled artificial worlds. An extended version of the old joke about the pilotless computerized airplane on which nothing can go wrong—go wrong—go

wrong, *Westworld* suggested that, once out of human control, machines become not useless but evil. Its sequel, *Futureworld* (1976), was less scary because everything was so carefully explained; and also because the device of having a presumed human turn out to be a robot was already becoming a cliché. It got an original twist in *Alien,* was resurrected in *Android,* and was a predictable throwaway in the early part of *Spacehunter: Adventures in the Forbidden Zone* (1983). But *The Black Hole* really said "amen" to the device with a neat reversal in which the cowl of a monastic robot is pulled away to reveal that he's actually a person!

Blade Runner and *Android* took the indistinguishability of android and human as a starting point, and asked provocative questions about the nature of humanity by juxtaposing feeling machines with unfeeling people, going a little beyond the metaphor of *2001.* Where does programming end and knowledge begin? Is "feeling" perhaps an inevitable by-product of a certain level of neural sophistication? Do androids do only what they're built to do, or can they learn? Where is freedom? What is will? And if robots can be indistinguishable from humans, what does "human" mean?

Creations II: Mechanization of the Human

"The ultimate horror in science fiction," wrote Carlos Clarens in *An Illustrated History of the Horror Film* (Capricorn, 1968), "is neither death nor destruction but dehumanization." Susan Son-

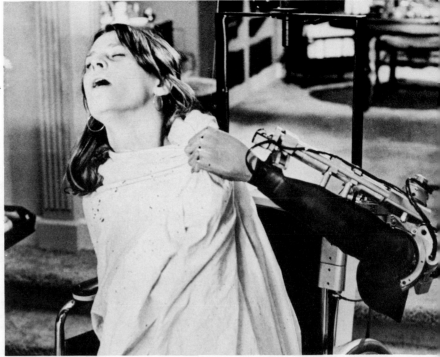

Left: In Woody Allen's satirical comedy Sleeper *(1973), a man from the present (Allen) pretends to be a household robot-servant for a woman (Diane Keaton) in order to escape detection by police in fascist America of 2173.*

Right: In Demon Seed *(1977), a scientist creates such a sophisticated computer that it is capable of imprisoning, raping, and impregnating his wife (Julie Christie). Here she is threatened by a mechanical arm that obeys Proteus's command.*

tag's earlier pronouncement in her 1965 essay "The Imagination of Disaster" was more specific: Where the threat to man once lay in the upsurge of his animal nature, "Now the danger is understood as residing in man's ability to be turned into a machine." Sontag wrote metaphorically, but sf films of the 1970s and 1980s have increasingly signaled a literal future mechanization of the human.

The power of the image originates, again, in *Metropolis,* whose vertical hierarchy—a stratification echoed in *The Time Machine* (1960), *THX 1138, Zardoz* (1974), and *Blade Runner*—places human workers below machines. Armies of laborers in rigidly geometric phalanxes move like so many robots; Freder (Gustav Fröhlich) crucifies himself on the clock-hand controls of a giant machine (crying "Father! Father!"); the zombified population becomes one with its machines. Later that process of "becoming one" is also taken—and depicted—literally. The rise of bionics—anticipated in *Cyborg 2087* (1966), about a future man-machine (Michael Rennie) sent back in time to prevent development of a mind-control device—led to television's "The Six Million Dollar Man" and "The Bionic Woman," in which medical and electronic technology combine to increase human strength and endurance. The bad side was reflected in such reversals of the Frankenstein story as *A Clockwork Orange* (1971), where a society-created monster (Malcolm McDowell) is remade by science into a pacified man, and *The Terminal Man* (1974), in which computer terminals implanted in the brain of a man (George Segal) to ease his violent tendencies instead provoke them.

As research into artificial intelligence explored similarities between the computer's electronic circuitry and the brain's neural circuitry, there became less justification for making the distinction "artificial intelligence" in the first place. Much of this vision was prompted by the development of twentieth-century entertainment technology. If the visions of a mechanical eye could create illusory "motion pictures," and if the human voice could be turned into an electromagnetic signal and back into a voice again, why can't intelligence be similarly mechanized?

The possibility of brain-to-brain communication was assayed by mind-melding machines in *Five Million Years to Earth* (1968), *Exorcist II: The Heretic* (1977), and *Brainstorm* (1983), all assuming this development to be a reasonable future extrapolation of present technological trends. The mechanization not only of body function but of intelligence is the threshold of the most important suggestion sf film has made about the future of man and his machines. The revelation of *Alien*'s Ash and *Android*'s Dr. Daniels (Klaus Kinski) as androids overhauls the theme of the scientist and his machine to that of the scientist *as* machine, the final literalization of the robot metaphor, the union of Dr. Frankenstein and Dr. Jekyll, the scientist as creator and creation—man, machine, and monster all in one. It takes but one more step to see the most daring future of all.

The Final Synthesis

Mad Love's Dr. Gogol transferred his love for Orlac's wife to a statue of her, as he saw his scheme to estrange them failing. His increased interest in the statue, combined with his mechani-

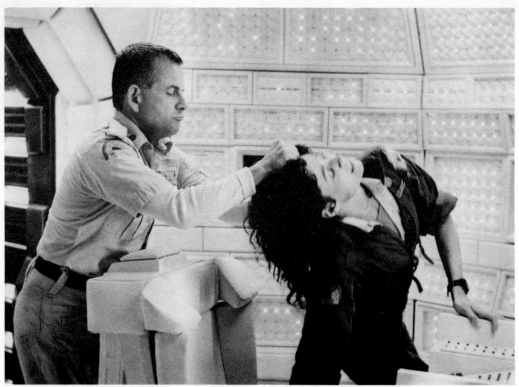

In Alien *(1979), scientists have accomplished their ultimate goal: They have created more scientists. Ash (Ian Holm), here pulling Ripley (Sigourney Weaver) away from the spaceship's master computer controls, is the ship's science officer and an android, without sympathy for human life.*

zation of both Orlac's hands and his own, is a turning from the human toward the mechanical, but also a bizarrely erotic interest in fusing the two.

By 1977 the cinema was liberalized enough to suggest what such a union might be like. *The Demon Seed,* a sort of *"Colossus: The Forbin Project Meets Rosemary's Baby,"* presents a computer that acquires a desire for procreation as it expands its intelligence. The world's first free-thinking machine is a questioning child, a hungry adolescent, and finally an obsessive adult. The film is essentially a parody of human sexuality, but its daring vision of a Second Coming in the miraculous conception and birth of a creature part human and part machine points toward a homo-mechanistic future neither good nor bad but utterly new.

This is the most dangerous vision of the future sf film has given us: the union of man and machine in a new life-form. The possibility climaxed both year-end sf films of 1979. In *The Black Hole* it was thrown away: Dr. Hans Reinhardt somehow unites with his Caliban-like familiar Maximilian, and ends gesturing wildly atop a pinnacle

beyond the black hole in a hellish evocation of *Fantasia's* "Night on Bald Mountain" sequence. In *Star Trek—The Motion Picture,* on the other hand, the finale is more explicit (though no more graphic): Human crewman (Stephen Collins) and humanoid alien crew-woman (Persis Khambatta) of the Enterprise *both* unite with misguided super-computer V'ger to create an existence intellectually higher than either human or machine and as blissfully rarified as *2001's* star-child.

But only *Videodrome* (1983) has been bold enough—*mad* enough—to *show* a union of the organic with the technological. Max (James Woods), a video technician, has his hand turned into a functioning pistol; a slot opens in his abdomen to permit insertion of videocassettes in a funny and nightmarish image that gives new meanings to the terms "hardware" and "software." A metaphor for our increasing tendency to define ourselves in terms of our (video) entertainment, *Videodrome's* vision of future life is something called The New Flesh, and its rallying cry is, "Don't be afraid to let your body die."

This is the final synthesis that tries to say it all about our uneasy relationship with the scientist and his creations. Our enchantment with innovative technology and our helplessness to prevent our being utterly changed by it, always at loggerheads, find their resolution in a Hegelian dialectic that posits a new existence altogether. Science, the scientist, his creation, and his victim all, at last, become one. The future fulfills the present *by* betraying it, for only in that can there be renewal. Behold the New Flesh!

The Fear of Intelligence in Futuristic Films

David Thomson

Human consciousness exists somewhere between history and anticipation, in the thin, advancing instant that separates the past and the future, the known and the unknown. Those two immense timescapes threaten and beckon us as we hurtle onwards (without much sensation of movement) in that perilous capsule "nowness," the vehicle that makes a running seam of experience between past and future, turning prospect into recorded fact—as if time was a reel of film.

Moreover, just as it is part of human curiosity to want to know or predict our future, so it is natural to hope to improve on the past. But if we really know the future—have accurate intelligence of it—then the difficult exercise of free will is eclipsed by predestination. If the end is known, then we are more scripted than alive. And if we must always revise and improve on our history, may we not lose those things of most value, the warmth of the past, moments that demonstrate the way in which memory is inspired and formed by desire?

We are torn between the two, victims of dread and nostalgia. We honor both the notion that those who do not study history are condemned to repeat it and the last cry of Scott Fitzgerald's *The Great Gatsby,* about that "orgiastic future that year by year recedes before us. It eluded us then, but that's no matter—tomorrow we will run faster, stretch out our arms further ... And one fine morning—

"So we beat on, boats against the current, borne back ceaselessly into the past."

"Science fiction" is generally taken as a genre of story-telling that exploits the mechanics and inventiveness of science—spaceships, time travel, laser guns, gene splicing, nuclear fission, human bodies as enduring as robots, and so on. But science has a more fundamental meaning—knowledge itself—that helps us recognize the paradox in the two-word genre, the confrontation of established fact and make-believe. It may also make us wonder whether science fiction is a kind of story-telling in which knowledge is not just a gimmick or part of the atmosphere, but the terrain and the leading character. Whereas most stories are moral fables, science fiction may be a metaphor on our relationship with intelligence. In other words, as we examine the place of knowledge and intellect in science fiction, we are not looking at one small room in the house, we are assessing the structure as a whole and its place in the landscape. This is the philosophy of the genre. Science fiction's intimation of disaster comes from its worrying over whether knowledge is good or evil, forbidden fruit or true nourishment.

We have only to think of that familiar genre character, "the mad scientist," to realize the very contradictory feelings contained in science fiction. For according to the basic definition of "science," this stereotype is a confession that whoever knows most is deranged and dangerous, a leader of progress maybe, but estranged from life, brilliant but a human failure. Mr. Spock (Leonard Nimoy) in *Star Trek* is the most intelli-

---

David Thomson is a regular contributor to *Film Comment, Sight & Sound, American Film,* and other magazines published in America, where he now lives, and in his native England.

Cliff Robertson's title character in Charly *(1968) temporarily becomes a genius as the result of a brain operation. Here he looks at films of himself from when he was retarded. He knows he will soon revert back to that state; he has the intelligence to realize the criminality of those who used him as a guinea pig.*

gent creature aboard the Enterprise, but he is critically handicapped by his lack of feeling.

There are two essential interpretations of this view of intelligence. The first is that we are secretly afraid of progress and of what it will provide for future nows. Scientists have made nuclear weapons and toxic waste; they may be within reach, simultaneously, of overcoming death and making it an instantaneous universal. It is part of 1984ism that there is a dehumanized terror ahead of us, all plastic, steel, computers, and drugged insensibility. In this scenario, science has been like a barbarian inventing the tools and tricks that will destroy the most lively virtues in life. And so we create "mad scientists" in fiction to manifest that fear. The living presence of an Albert Einstein may stand for the brightest and most benign potential of brainpower. But in fiction, the disciples of Einstein glare with an out-of-control extremism, their hair goes uncombed, they rant and they are given over to exaggerated acting. They become like Dr. Strangelove, say, fascistic scientists whose work has become so "pure" they no longer relate it to a human context, or Dr. Frankenstein.

The second meaning of the myth is Faustian: it says be properly cautious of the tree of knowledge, temper intellect with the softer, more tolerant, more "humane" instincts of wisdom, let the head be guided by the heart, do not enter into a bargain with the Devil that makes the future clear, rational, and foretold, or that alters the profound and necessary uncertainty of life. As *Charly* (1968), Cliff Robertson goes from being a retard to a phenomenal brain, thanks to medical science. But the experiment is destructive, and it

only shifts him from one misery to another. Ordinariness has been left out of the change, and its natural state depends on common sense and common experience—a little knowledge, but not too much.

It is an aspect of the religion we still accept or still remember that we should prefer to go on in the dark, not knowing. When Faust settles with Mephistopheles for a guaranteed span of life in which he exchanges his soul for whatever experiences he desires, he has lapsed into pride and arrogance and he has given up responsibility for his own life. He is no longer testing every moment against good and evil, prepared for the eventual Day of Judgment that could fall x years from now or tomorrow. The soul is defined in this legend as the readiness to live on alone, mortal, unsure but morally alert and answerable. It is a Christian ethic that most atheists respect, and it has been a condition of nearly every age and mode of storytelling that fictional characters are to be judged morally.

The perverted man of learning, Dr. Frankenstein, is always regarded as a kind of outlaw, like Satan in *Paradise Lost,* the example of a reckless search for knowledge. Yet in trying to keep humans alive, in trying to make life the product of his

The Monster (Boris Karloff) endures
imprisonment and beatings (at the hands of
Dwight Frye) in Frankenstein (1931). The
crime of Dr. Frankenstein (Colin Clive) was
not necessarily his desire to create artificial
life and, thus, defy God's will—although
moviegoers thought him blasphemous—but
that he emulated the jealous, authoritarian
God once he brought his "child" to life.

laboratory, he is only attempting that which brings
doctors and surgeons the Nobel Prize as they
seek to perfect artificial organs or other novelties
that will defy death. In film after film, Frankenstein
makes himself like God, harnessing the electricity
in the air to infuse dead parts with fresh animation, eventually being destroyed by the wrath,
resentment, or unmitigated malignance of his
"Monster." It is worth remembering that Frankenstein was created by Mary Shelley, in 1816, during the first great onslaught of scientific and industrial "progress."

Scientists are invariably rebuked by the narratives of science fiction; the genre does not respect their learning or credit them with understanding. Fritz Lang's Metropolis (1926) ends on
the declaration, "There can be no understanding
between the hands and the brain unless the heart
acts as mediator." Grot (Heinrich George), the
leader of the workers, and Frederson (Alfred
Abel), the ruler of society, shake hands. Rotwang
(Rudolf Klein-Rogge), the warped genius, half-
scientist, half-sorcerer, has been killed, plunging
from the roof of a cathedral, the victim of his
godlike ambitions.

At the end of Jean-Luc Godard's Alphaville

(1965), Lemmy Caution (Eddie Constantine) kills
Professor von Braun (Howard Vernon), programs
the computer to self-destruct and to devastate the
entire city, and escapes with von Braun's daughter, Natacha (Anna Karina), crossing intersidereal
space with her in his car/capsule and teaching
her to say, "I love you." Meanwhile, Alphaville is
consumed: "Those who weren't killed by asphyx-
iation or the absence of light energy flew around
the place at a lunatic speed, like ants." The
apparatus of control and intelligence is a tyranny
that must be eliminated if the adventurer and the
lover are to live. Freedom is equated with instinct
and something much closer to ignorance.

Alphaville is a work of science fiction, yet all of it
was filmed in the real Paris of 1964–65, without
fanciful effects or the futurism of art direction. The
technological future has already arrived in the
modern city. The new monster is the computer,
and it represents as great a confusion of the
benevolent and the deadly as Boris Karloff did as
the Monster in the original sound version of
Frankenstein (1931). The real 1984 has coincided
with the computer's thorough penetration of society. It makes bureaucracy quicker and more efficient; at home it lets us keep more accurate
accounts and it makes the children demons at
math just as it gives them all the fun of video
monster games. It is a household service and the
brainbox of the state; it is the chance of automatic
control and electronic logic in a world too diverse
and complex for human government.

But the computer is a menace in science fiction. It is nearly the means of global thermonuclear war in WarGames (1983). In Demon Seed
(1977), Proteus IV has mastered all human knowl-

© 1954 WALT DISNEY PRODUCTIONS

edge and when it is prevented from conducting its own study of mankind, it goes wild, and rapes and fertilizes Julie Christie's character with the first computer-human offspring. In *2001* (1968), HAL developed a mind and a personality of its own that took over control of the spacecraft. And in *Colossus: The Forbin Project* (1970), computers dominate world government. "Artificial" intelligence has usurped its human inventors. *Colossus* was written for the screen by James Bridges, who would go on to make *The China Syndrome* (1979), another paranoid speculation about a world at the mercy of its machinery.

As we fear advanced synthetic intelligence, so there is a new orthodoxy in stories and films of "rogue" computers out-thinking their masters, crushing chance and poetry with probability theory and the heartless voice of programmed reason. Nevertheless, computer scientists tell us that no machine is anywhere near as subtle or complex as the brain; and they stress that computers are only crude imitations of the human thought process. As if, deep down, we knew that, we are as much fascinated by computers as we are afraid of them. There is a sardonic wit in the human dramatic intelligence that can create computers able to let a teenager (Matthew Broderick) deceive the Pentagon, ravish Julie Christie, or sound so human—the voice of Alpha 60, the computer in *Alphaville,* was not artificial, but belonged to a Frenchman whose vocal cords had been destroyed.

Moreover, Alpha 60 speaks like a poet, no matter that it is supposed to be the force that oppresses the city. Long after the crisis of the film has been resolved and the world made safe for Lemmy Caution's comic-book mentality, we remember the utterances of the computer, so elegant and so aware of the paradoxes inherent in time and intelligence:

> The present is terrifying because it is irreversible . . . because it is shackled, fixed like steel. . . . Time is the material of which I am made. . . . Time is a stream which carries me along . . . but I am Time . . . it is a tiger which tears me apart . . . yet I, too, am the tiger.

Just as in *2001,* the computer is the most appealing character, the one closest to the sensibility directing the movie. In *Fahrenheit 451* (1966), it is possible to see the members of the "book underground" as self-willed slaves, brains given up to the rote learning of great books, less human, less intelligent and less intriguing than the Captain (Cyril Cusack) who makes an eloquent and sophisticated case that books are a source of the world's problems. Indeed, what we have there is intelligence giving us the case against itself. The Captain is the "villain" of *Fahrenheit 451,* but he shames the sentimentality of the story's "goodies."

And so, in real life, it is always intelligence that must be its own watchdog and corrective. There is something archaic and reactionary in so many written or filmed narratives simply condemning new intelligence, and treating it as antagonistic to humanism. All the great novels of the world could be stored on a computer or drummed into the

It is a tradition in science fiction films that brilliant visionaries tend to become cruel megalomaniacs. Left: James Mason (L) played Jules Verne's Captain Nemo *(opposite Kirk Douglas; with Peter Lorre and Robert J. Wilke in support) in Walt Disney's* 20,000 Leagues Under the Sea *(1954). Right: Nemo served as the model for Walter Pidgeon's Dr. Morbius in* Forbidden Planet *(1956). Below: Both Nemo and Morbius were inspiration for Maximilian Schell's Dr. Hans Reinhardt in Disney's* The Black Hole *(1979). (Also: Morbius's Robby the Robot was a gentle version of Reinhardt's evil robot Maximilian.)*

This placid publicity shot of stars Susan Clark and Eric Braeden of Colossus: The Forbin Project *(1970) belies the bleak nature of the film. Forbin (Braeden) has built a supercomputer to prevent nuclear attack—but it and its Russian counterpart take over the world.*

brains of a resistance community. That does not mean the full richness of those books would be experienced or thought about, or that fresh books would be written. Intelligence, knowledge, and science cover all we do: the heart as well as the head. Feelings are only one outward show of our brains. It is intelligent to love, to forgive, to be moved, to remember, and to forget. The mind shapes all those responses. It is creative intelligence that can think of this line for the computer to say at the start of *Alphaville:* "There are times when reality becomes too complex for Oral Communication. But Legend gives it a form by which it pervades the whole world."

Thus fiction, science fiction, and the special interest of Stanley Kubrick, whose constant preoccupation is intelligence itself as the implacable, challenging climate inhabited by humans. What makes his pictures so haunting is their sense of how film is a medium that models the human endeavor to understand the ordering of the world, to aspire to the wisdom of gods. For just as film is all nowness, momentary beauties, passing time, plausible spontaneity, it is actually written, planned, and constructed in advance. The image of life is a fruit of intelligence, a legend made to understand itself, a story made for us, like Eden.

Kubrick's *The Shining* (1981) may not be science fiction—though it is a fantasy about the mind's reach—but it has an image, tragic and funny, that stands for the artist trying to describe intelligence: of Jack Torrance (Jack Nicholson) looking down on a model of the Overlook Hotel and seeing real life there, the other characters, his wife and child, like ants in its maze. It is the height of human intelligence to make metaphors and stories. The writing of stories is itself a metaphor for the process of creation; it is our most religious observance. We tell stories to show how far we consist of and have faith in intelligence. When 1984 and all its paranoia is over with, perhaps we can go forward with more faith in that nature. Then science fiction might become a genre capable of sustaining more moods than melodrama and anxiety. There is a lyricism possible that has seldom been touched.

PART II

JOURNEYS
INTO THE
FUTURE

The Master
and *Metropolis*

Robert Bloch

I am the last of the dinosaurs,"
Fritz Lang told me. To prove it he sketched caricatures of himself
as a prehistoric monster, with a monocle in one eye and a martini-
glass clutched in his claw.

The eminent director I knew may have been a
dinosaur, but he never became an old fossil.
Though his eyesight dimmed, his insight was not
impaired.

Until his final years he lectured at universities
and film festivals honoring his work. Here a growing interest in science fiction on the screen lent
new importance to a film he'd made half a lifetime
ago—*Metropolis* (1926). One of the few genuine
auteur directors whose efforts influenced the
course of cinema history, Lang found himself
increasingly identified with *Metropolis* by younger
audiences. Publicly he bowed to popular opinion,
but privately he protested.

Metropolis was not Fritz Lang's favorite film. It
wasn't even his favorite personal contribution to
the science fiction genre—he believed his major
accomplishment was the invention of the countdown for the rocket-launch in *Frau Im Mond/
Woman in the Moon* (1928).

I had seen *Metropolis* as a child and it made a
vivid impression on me. This Lang accepted, but
he couldn't understand my continuing interest
forty-odd years later.

"Unbelievable," he said, using a word that
came frequently to his lips when commenting on
the contemporary scene. "Why are you so interested in a picture that no longer exists?"

To my surprise, I learned he spoke the truth.

This German production, hailed as the greatest
cinematic spectacle of its time, took over two
years to create, from the moment Lang received
his inspiration upon seeing the skyline of New

Robert Bloch is the prize-winning author of numerous
screenplays, radio plays, teleplays, short stories, and
books, which include *Psycho, Psycho II, The Skull of the
Marquis De Sade, American Gothic, Twilight Zone—The
Movie,* and *Midnight Pleasures.*

Robert Bloch and Fritz Lang (1890–1976).

Left: The massive underground chambers where workers, as mechanized as their machines, toil endlessly to bring comfort to the rich people above.

Right: Rotwang (Rudolf Klein-Rogge, right) introduces his robot to Joh Frederson (Alfred Abel), who hopes that such creations can replace the disgruntled human workers.

York in 1924 until the completed motion picture had its Berlin premiere in January 1927.

The logistics involved are staggering, even by today's standards. Actual production required 310 days and 60 nights of full-time work, and a cast of 37,000 extras. Almost 2 million feet of negative were shot and from this *Metropolis* emerged in its final form, a full seventeen reels in length.

Emerged—and vanished.

All that is generally available today is the version subtitled and edited for American release, cut down to a mere nine reels. Brief snippets from the excised portion remain in a few prints stored in film libraries behind the Iron Curtain, but these merely suggest the content of the deleted 40 percent of the original.

Seen today, *Metropolis* still exerts powerful impact as a spectacle, but its truncated story suffers by comparison to what was in the original.*

Metropolis, the supercity of the future, is ruled by Joh Frederson (Alfred Abel) from a lofty tower rising amongst the surrealistic structures looming above its surface. Freder (Gustav Fröhlich), his

son, enjoys a sybaritic existence in a lavish pleasure-garden, together with members of his elite peer-group. Apparently none of these young people know or care how the city is operated and maintained.

But Freder's curiosity is aroused when Maria (Brigitte Helm), the beautiful daughter of a worker, invades the garden with a group of ragged, emaciated children. "Look—these are your brothers," she tells them. Whereupon she is quickly ejected by security officers.

Smitten by the girl and mystified by her disappearance, Freder follows her down to the subterranean depths of the city and enters a monstrous labyrinth of giant mechanisms tended by slavelike multitudes who toil their lives away in these "machine-rooms." Unable to get a satisfactory explanation from his father about his brothers below and the great machines, Freder returns to the underground world, disguises himself as a laborer, and finally encounters Maria in a cavernous catacomb, preaching to the increasingly rebellious workers. Telling them the story of the Tower of Babel, she promises their lot will be improved by the coming of a "mediator" and urges them to be patient.*

There's nothing in the film or full script to indicate why Maria preaches patience rather than

*Film "history" must be constantly rewritten. In November 1983, the Los Angeles County Museum unveiled a version of *Metropolis* running more than three hours in length! Still incomplete, and with German titles, it had been assembled from a number of different sources, including a print found in Russia. As I was part of the overflow crowd turned away from this one-time-only screening, I cannot vouch for what was added or omitted. But it is heartening to know that lost footage may still be found, and that after almost six decades it still interests and attracts a youthful audience.—R.B.

*I don't see Freder as the "mediator": his motivation—love of Maria, growing concern for the workers' condition, and safety of their children—causes him to take individual action rather than mediate between oppressed and oppressor. Only at the end is this implied—and the very idea of reconciliation is Maria's, not Freder's.—R.B.

rebellion except for what is shown—her belief in biblical injunctions. Thus I think it an unwise presumption to arbitrarily assume she knows a workers' rebellion would be crushed; from what we *do* know of her, she is merely an advocate of peace rather than violence—it's not evident that she'd change her mind and go along with a revolt if she thought the workers would win.

Joh Frederson, seeking unrest amongst the workers, seeks out Rotwang (Rudolf Klein-Rogge), an elderly scientist with an artificial hand, who lives in a strange medieval cottage squatting amidst the soaring towers of the city. Rotwang has created a marvelous female robot in his laboratory and tells Frederson he can replace the untrustworthy work force with machine-men who will never tire or rebel. Give him another twenty-four hours and he will perfect the robot in a form indistinguishable from a human being.

Rotwang leads Frederson into the catacombs to spy on Maria as she preaches. The toilers promise to wait for their mediator, but "not for long."

Alarmed, Frederson instructs Rotwang to capture the girl and hide her in his house. Then he must make his robot into Maria's likeness and send her down to create discord amongst the workers—presumably as an excuse to destroy them.

Rotwang imprisons Maria in his laboratory and in an impressive sequence he transforms the robot into an androidlike duplicate of the girl, her saintly attributes replaced by an evil cunning. That evening, at a party attended by the aristocrats of the upper city, the robot entertains them with a sensual dance. She passes as human and is ready to fulfill her mission.

Descending to the mechanical maze, the false Maria incites the workers to revolt. Toil ceases, machinery is demolished, and the underground city is engulfed by a flood that threatens the workers' children.

But the real Maria escapes and, reunited with Freder, helps save the youngsters. The workers, angered by the false Maria, burn her at the stake as a "witch" and the flames eat away her synthetic flesh to reveal the robot hidden beneath.

Rotwang, afraid the mob will discover the trickery, pursues the real Maria to the rooftop of an abandoned cathedral. Freder comes to her rescue and fights Rotwang, who plunges to his death.

The revolt ends. Reconciled by Freder and Maria, Joh Frederson shakes hands with the foreman of the workers as the girl tells them, "There can be no understanding between the hands and brain unless the heart acts as mediator."

This message, created by Thea von Harbau, Lang's second wife and collaborator on the script, was later repudiated by the director, as being too simplistic and nonspecific to resolve the class struggle.

He also repudiated the film itself in its abbreviated form. Missing in the edited version was an important subplot linking Frederson and Rotwang. The two men had loved the same woman, who left Rotwang for the Master of Metropolis and died giving birth to his son, Freder. Since then a curious love-hate relationship has

Left: Lang (R) and cameraman Karl Freund figure out how to shoot a scene with Brigitte Helm, who plays Maria and her look-alike robot.

Right: Freder (Gustav Fröhlich) doesn't realize that it is not the real Maria, but the robot, who is being immolated by the rebellious workers.

existed, and it is Rotwang who solves Frederson's problems when his experts fail. In the original film Rotwang repents his alliance with Frederson; he tells Maria he will release her to warn the workers against the robot. But Frederson overhears his plan, and when he attacks the scientist, Maria escapes on her own. Left unconscious by Frederson, who thinks he has killed him, Rotwang awakens, but in his confused state he believes he is actually dead and stumbles off in a daze. Now totally deranged, he sees the real Maria and, mistaking her for his dead wife, pursues her to the cathedral.

Other changes were made, even before filming. At one time, Lang told me, he intended to end the story with Freder and Maria leaving Metropolis in a spaceship. This notion was abandoned for future development in *Frau Im Mond.*

In considering what remains, one must remember that no film is created in a vacuum. Conversations with Fritz Lang disclosed some of the factors influencing his work.

Metropolis was made during the tremendous postwar industrial growth of Germany. The increasing role of mechanization in modern life suggested the possibility of a future society totally dependent upon machines. The film's underground work force is an extension of modern factories' assembly lines after machines have taken over. Even Frederson, the "Master of Metropolis," is their slave, serving to maintain the machines that really rule the city.

While aircraft swoop the skies, presumably towards distant destinations, we learn little about life in the world beyond or in Metropolis itself.

Surface transportation seems speedier but slightly changed, radio is nonexistent, messages still conveyed by phone—though Lang does give us a glimpse of televisual communication. There are no computers, no nuclear-power devices.

We see children, but aside from Rotwang the only elderly people are Frederson's servants. Workers are largely self-policed by foremen; there's no evidence of public officials or government other than Frederson's management. Al-

though he's described as "the richest man in Metropolis" we're told nothing of the economy of the future—no sign of agrarian workers, merchants, doctors, lawyers, students, or professors. Maria is introduced as "just the daughter of a worker"; where and how she acquired her education is not explained. Priests and parishioners are missing from the deserted cathedral but religion apparently survives, for even Frederson exclaims, "Thank Heaven!" Maria's preaching about Babel indicates knowledge of the Bible, as does Freder's vivid vision of the master-machine as Moloch devouring the workers. His hallucination of the cathedral's statues of Death and the Seven Deadly Sins coming to life is also religious.

It is important to note that the story of *Metropolis* was a collaboration between Lang and Thea von Harbau. She introduced the religious parables, many more of which exist in her novelization of the film. Lang, a lapsed Catholic, accepted the visual value of such symbolism though he personally put no faith in it.

His own interest was in the twin mysteries of science and magic, embodied in the character of Rotwang. The scientist's laboratory is housed in a magician's dwelling, complete with a pentagram set in its door and filled with secret passageways. Though Rotwang's right hand has been replaced by a prosthetic device (shades of *Dr. Strangelove!*) his left hand performs mystic miracles. His transformation of the metal robot into a duplicate of Maria is a marvel of special effects, many of which were borrowed by later filmmakers. But none of the gadgetry explains how the change is made; magical means produce scientific ends, or is it vice versa?

Dualism dominates the entire film. The scientist-magician, the good Maria and her wicked likeness, the master-builder of Metropolis who is also the architect of its destruction—even the city itself is dichotomous, with its shining spires above its shadowy subterranea below. The dual structure of society—leisure class and working class—is the very basis of the film's plot and theme.

Metropolis, though set in the future, was not

intended to convey a realistic picture of things to come. Thea von Harbau's contribution was righteously moralistic—the wages of sin is death. Lang was more concerned with questions than with answers—how can society cope with technology, how can we master machines without first mastering ourselves? And while he used von Harbau's notion of *the heart as mediator* he didn't believe it offered a real solution to these problems.

This too is an example of dualism. For Lang and his wife parted in the Thirties when Thea von Harbau's old-fashioned religious morality was replaced by a fanatical devotion to a new god— Adolf Hitler. And Lang—whose image was that of a dictatorial director, an autocratic monocled Prussian—came down firmly on the side of humanitarianism and fled the country after refusing a post as head of German cinema under the Nazis.

The irony is obvious. Lang, the "Prussian," was actually Viennese. Though some saw him as a martinet who demanded impossible perfection in his work, his private *persona* was that of a sentimentalist whose keen sense of humor helped him endure the genuine anguish with which he regarded his own shortcomings and those of his fellow men.

Metropolis embodies many other aspects of Fritz Lang's complexity. His early training as an artist and an architect is evident in the superb settings of the film, aided by the cinematography of the great Karl Freund and the technical mastery of Eugene Shuftan's two-lens camera process, plus Günther Rittau's special effects. Lang utilized *surrealism* in production design (he hated

the term "expressionism" and always asked sarcastically "What does it *mean*?") and vastly expanded the robot concept of Karel Capek's play, *R.U.R.,* and the depiction of a future world in the Russian film *Aelita* (1924). His handling of the mob scenes rivals D. W. Griffith. In this and other films, Lang was a virtual choreographer of crowds.

The performances of his cast are uneven. Alfred Abel is an adequately austere Frederson, but Gustav Fröhlich plays Freder in an hysterical style that is obsolete today. Rudolf Klein-Rogge brings menace and mystery to his Rotwang, while teenage novice Brigitte Helm is outstanding both as the innocent Maria and the evil robot. Unfortunately, her depraved dance suffers when projected at a speed designed for sound rather than silent films, and the actions and reactions of the other players are similarly distorted.

According to its creator, *Metropolis* is "a picture which no longer exists." But despite massive cuts (over 40 percent of its original footage) and discrepancies in the story line, what survives is still impressive, both as spectacle and as prophetic political parable. Lang was among the first filmmakers to foresee, and daringly dramatize, the coming conflict of Man vs. Machine, the growing schism between the new industrial elite and the manipulated masses. The message he stated almost sixty years ago rings even more true today—science alone is not our saviour. Although the motion picture is actually science-fantasy rather than science fiction, its concepts influenced every science fiction film that followed.

Metropolis remains a living memorial to the genius of Fritz Lang.

ROBERT BLOCH 89

The Demi-Docs: *Just Imagine* and *Things to Come*

Frederik Pohl

Among the many traits that create an audience for science fiction, its prediction of possible future societies ranks very high. That's because science fiction is the sovereign prophylactic against future shock. Most science fiction stories and films, however, relegate the made-up future worlds to the status of background scenery. The story played on the front of the stage is the human drama—the conflict, the love story, the tragedy, whatever. The exceptions include such classics of print science fiction as W. Olaf Stapledon's *Last and First Men,* Edward Bellamy's *Looking Backward,* and, to name one which is of particular interest here, H. G. Wells's *The Shape of Things to Come.* They are hardly about people at all. Their concern is with trends, events, changes; they are not so much fiction as demi-documentaries. The form is rare in science fiction in print form and even rarer in science fiction films, but it does exist there.

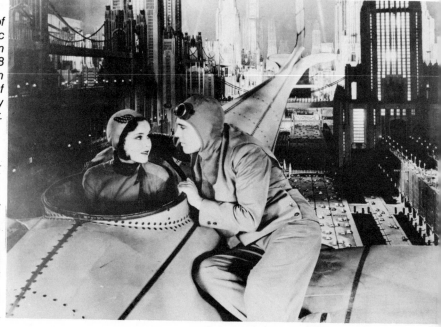

Against the backdrop of a magnificent futuristic New York, J-21 (John Garrick) courts LN-18 (Maureen O'Sullivan) in Just Imagine, *an sf musical directed by David Bulter.*

Frederik Pohl is the prize-winning author of *Man Plus, Gateway, Slave Ship, Beyond the Blue Event Horizon,* and, with C.W. Kornbluth, *The Space Merchants, Gladiator-At-Law,* and *Wolfbane.* He was also the editor of *Astonishing Stories, Super Science Stories, Galaxy,* and *If,* for which he won three consecutive Hugos.

In this publicity shot from Things to Come, airman John Cabal (Raymond Massey, with Ann Todd and Margaretta Scott at his feet), walks through Everytown, where everyone has been put to sleep by "Peace Gas" dropped from planes. The death of the Boss and the end of his feudal system will permit the Iraq-based "Wings Over the World" to initiate great "progress" for mankind.

Now and then a filmmaker will sit down to think hard about the world of tomorrow and, when he has come to serious conclusions, assemble his crews and record his vision on celluloid. Thus are born the science fiction demi-docs.

Even a demi-documentary needs some sort of dramatic structure. A convenient way of arranging that is to have someone from outside come into the society involved so that he can react to it and, where necessary, have it explained to him. That's the structure adopted by the first demi-documentary science fiction film I ever saw—as a matter of fact, it was the first science fiction film of any kind I ever saw—*Just Imagine*.

I am a little embarrassed to have used the word "serious" in describing a category that includes *Just Imagine,* because there's certainly nothing in the least serious about its plot or incident. There are two main threads to its narrative. In one, a man from the year 1930 (the year it was released) is accidentally preserved in suspended animation for half a century. Revived in the far-future year of 1980, he discovers a world in which food is compressed into pills, people have numbers instead of names, marriages are arranged by a government agency on eugenic grounds, and couples desirous of having a child simply drop a coin into a baby-vending machine. (You may ask why, this being so, the government worries about who marries whom. Don't ask.) The man from the past—called "Single-O" because he has no

proper assigned number—is played by a popular Swedish-dialect vaudeville comedian, El Brendel. His function in the film is to react comically to the novelties he encounters, and sigh humorously for "the good old days." The other plot thread entwines a pair of star-crossed lovers. The boy is J-21, played by John Garrick, and he wants very much to marry the girl. You can't blame him, because the girl is played by the tremblingly beautiful Maureen O'Sullivan, nineteen years old and with the dew of County Roscommon still on her. What gets in their way is that J-21 hasn't done anything important enough to be eligible. He must perform some heroic feat. (*Men* have to do that. Women, being passive objects, don't have to do anything much but be pretty.) Fortunately, a feat is at hand. A rocket is about to take off to explore the planet Mars. J-21 volunteers to go there, discovers a queer, identical-twin race of people—everybody is born two at a time, a good one and a bad one—and gets back to Earth with proof of success. Clinch; curtain. It is all light-heartedly silly, as a Broadway musical of the time—in fact, it has several extraordinarily forgettable musical numbers—and it is played for laughs.

The first time I saw *Just Imagine* I was ten years old—in fact, I had to get my mother to take me, because I was too young to be allowed to travel the subways at night. Even at ten, I knew the jokes were jokes. But what I carried away from the theater that night wasn't left-over chuckles. It was a sense of wonder. I had seen a vision of New York City fifty years in the future, Art-Deco skyscrapers and helicopter traffic jams, and I was dazed to the point that my mother asked what was the matter. "I just wish I could see if 1980 will really be like that," I confided. She did swift arithmetic in her head and announced, "Well, with any luck at all you probably will." The idea blew me away.

The next demi-doc I saw was *Things to Come* (1936). By then I was all of sixteen and no longer needing a parent to take me out; in fact I saw it in the company of my droogs and fellow-fans of the Futurians, Don Wollheim, James Blish, and half a dozen other would-be science-fiction writers and editors.

Things to Come is not just serious. It is earnest. There are no laughs in it—oh, perhaps now and then a condescending smile at those who cling to old-fashioned ways, for the film has a message. Technology is good. So are aeronautics and space travel, and Progress is better than anything.

Things to Come exemplifies the second useful dramatic structure for a demi-doc: the future history. Its locale is London (the characters call it "Everytown," but you can recognize Piccadilly Circus). The time is the near future—well, the near future of 1936. War breaks out. London is destroyed. The human race is decimated by endless war and pestilence. Three decades later only ragged barbarians survive among the ruins of Piccadilly. Their leader is Rudolph, the Boss (played by Ralph Richardson before he became a "sir"). Oxen tow the fuelless Rolls-Royces, because all the petrol that can be found is reserved for the tatterdemalion air force. Where all is primitive, a mysterious, black-clad airman (Raymond Massey) appears to say that civilization is alive and well in Basra on the Persian Gulf, under the control of an air elite called "Wings Over the World." Naturally the Boss resists. Naturally Progress triumphs.

In the next chapter of the future history progress goes on triumphing, as we see civilization in the year 2036, led by the air elite, rebuilding itself out of the ruins. Giant machines burrow into hillsides to create a bubble-domed city long before Buckminster Fuller. The Everytown of the future is all crystal and immense vistas; everyone is rich and speaks like the BBC. There is only one thing to really trouble them. The disciples of Progress are not content with Grecian togas and desktop TV sets; they have built a great space gun to launch a boy and a girl on mankind's first expedition to the Moon.

So mankind, or anyway the part of it we see in Everytown, chooses up sides. For Progress: the young people and the airmen, led by Raymond Massey again (playing, apparently, his own

Right: Things to Come: *Everytown's city square in the year 2036. A helicopter rushes Cabal, Passworthy, and their children to the endangered space gun.*

Below: The costume designers for Just Imagine *predicted that women of 1980 would be wearing such dresses.*

grandson from the previous installment). For reaction: all the fuddy-duddies, stay-putters, and, representing the dissolute and unpredictable artistic element, a sculptor named Theotocopulos

(Cedric Hardwicke, also not yet a "sir"). Theoto-copulos forms a mob to march on the space gun and destroy it before it can be fired. The Progressives outwit them by launching the capsule early, while the mob is still streaming toward it. Progress has triumphed.

But in an epilogue, Massey, who is the father of one of the astronauts, and Edward Chapman, playing the father of the other, climb to an observatory to gaze out on the capsule containing their children. Chapman wishes things wouldn't go so *fast*. He demands: What is this Progress? Can't we ever just rest and enjoy ourselves? Massey rejoins: We'll rest enough after we're dead. We have a choice between stagnation and the universe—which will it be?

Just before the film was released (I now know) H. G. Wells wrote a letter to Sidney and Beatrice Webb in which he said, "My film is a mess of a film and [producer Alexander] Korda ought to be more ashamed of it than I am." But I didn't know it at the time, and if I had I would have been horrified at the sacrilege. Which was it to be? Why, Progress, of course! We all trooped out of the theater sworn to allegiance to Raymond Massey's party. If Edward Chapman, or anyone like him, had dared to join us for coffee and sandwiches in the Automat next to the theater that afternoon, he would have had a rough time of it, believe me!

Since both *Things to Come* and *Just Imagine* are demi-documentaries, it does them no justice to summarize their plots. It is their world-view that is interesting. Like most works of art, that view is shaped by the world they were born into.

For all its baggy-pants comedy, *Just Imagine* went to some trouble to validate its prophecies. The movie does not start in the year 1980. It doesn't even start in 1930; there is a prologue set half a century earlier still, in 1880, for the purpose of convincing audiences that fifty years can make vast changes in the American way of life, and so the flights of fancy that followed might really happen.

Although *Just Imagine* was released after the 1929 stock-market crash, the world it reflects is the boundlessly optimistic America of the boom 1920s, when the invention of installment buying had made retailers rich and manufacturers delirious. Everybody else was getting rich, too—at least on paper—or thought they might, very soon, because margin buying had let bootblacks and ladies' maids into the stock market and sent share prices into orbit. Everything was getting bigger, faster, and, if not better, at least shinier and more exciting. Fritz von Opel had just flown for 75 seconds in Frankfurt, Germany, in the world's first manned rocket flight. Richard Byrd had overflown almost the entire desolate waste of Antarctica. Will Rogers was coaxing America into the air age by bribing hundreds of communities to paint the town's name on rooftops for the benefit of aviators. Dr. Charles Mayo had announced that he expected a cure for cancer soon. The cop on the beat was being given a car

In Just Imagine, *men sing of the virtues of alcohol in pill form.*

to drive, and the cars were beginning to be equipped with radios; crime was as doomed as cancer. Edwin Hubble told the world that the universe was expanding, and back on Earth it was visibly shrinking each week as the headlines told of faster planes and ocean liners, high-speed bridges and highways—plans for a new sea-level canal in Nicaragua and a tunnel under the English Channel. Probably *Just Imagine*'s audiences didn't need much convincing that fifty years would produce as many marvels as the film depicted, for their daily newspaper predicted much the same.

Nobody seems to have to work for a living in either *Things to Come* or *Just Imagine*. But whereas in *Things to Come* they all become ascetics, in *Just Imagine* they turn into playboys. They booze (though the bourbon, like everything else, comes in the form of pills). They go to parties. They go out and have adventures on Mars. They fall in love. They devote their lives to having fun; it is the F. Scott Fitzgerald syndrome projected half a century into the future.

Of all the methodologies for forecasting the future, straight-line extrapolation is the riskiest. It isn't any more wrong than any other, but it is more dangerous because, appearing so logical, it is treacherous. The world doesn't move in straight lines. While *Just Imagine* was still showing in the nabes, the Great Depression was settling in; it is no wonder that the next great demidoc took an altogether gloomier view of the remainder of the twentieth century.

Things to Come was two years in the making. It cost $1,400,000, by far the most expensive film ever made in England up to that time. No expense was spared by its producer, Alexander Korda, the young Hungarian who had conquered the British film world. He allowed Wells to dominate the production, and Wells thought big. Sets? No Hollywood type was good enough for that; they called in architects Le Corbusier and Gropius. Costumes? Fernand Leger. Special background effects? Moholy-Nagy. They were all glorious inspirations, but none of them knew anything about film production so they were all sent home and the work turned over to film specialists. Really, they were good enough. Though the special effects in *Things to Come* look pretty shabby in the era of Lucas and Spielberg, they were a marvel in 1936.

If *Just Imagine* grew out of the euphoria of the high-flying American 1920s, *Things to Come* had a grimmer provenance. The 1920s and 1930s in England were a long way from euphoria. England lost many of the best of its youth and much of its treasure in the trenches of 1914–18, and its 1920s were maimed by the General Strike and widespread unemployment. Even before the 1929 crash, the lower classes in England lived shabby and precarious existences, and the well-to-do disillusioned ones; the Oxford Peace Pledgers were not from the working class.

So H. G. Wells projected no unblemished future. What he saw in the near term was death and destruction—and indeed World War II came along just as he proposed; he even got the starting dates right. He knew it would be hell, as it

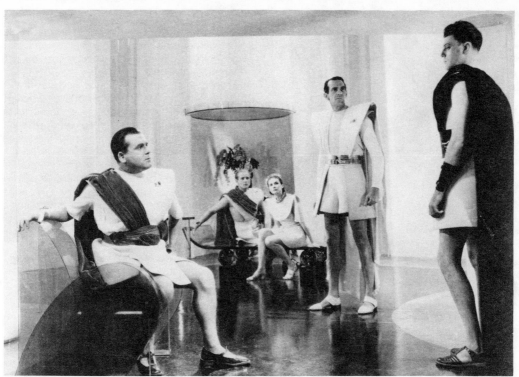

Above: Things to Come: *Passworthy (Edward Chapman, seated) and Oswald Cabal (Massey) learn that their grown children (behind them) must take off for the moon before rebels destroy their spaceship.*

Below: In Just Imagine, *Single-O (El Brendel, far left) and his two friends from 1980 (Frank Albertson and Garrick) meet some Martians on their space expedition.*

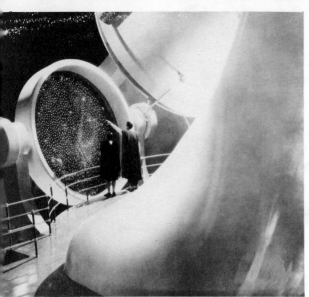

At the end of Things to Come, *Oswald Cabal lectures Passworthy about the need for technological progress, on Earth and in space. Cabal is the film's hero, yet today when one listens to his diatribe, he comes across a bit like a cold-blooded madman.*

was. But his utopian vision longed for—and his Fabian optimism believed in—a cleaner, brighter world beyond it. It is that vision that the film displays.

Of course, the vision was shaped not only by the time and place lived in but by the peculiar configurations inside Wells's own head. Why were airmen chosen as the hope of mankind? Because Wells revered pilots. He was an enthralled partisan of flying all his life—perhaps because he had written so much about it in his novels before it actually happened in the real world. He had his first flight as early as 1912, in a Farman seaplane, and found it all he had dreamed. Airmen took their lives in their hands every time they went up. Airmen spoke a technological lingo the earthbound could not understand. Airmen shared a camaraderie that transcended national boundaries. Airmen were the samurai of the twentieth century: honored, incorruptible, and wise.

Women, on the other hand, were a different race. Wells was a womanizer in the grand style; he considered a wide range of female sexual partners his due, and was annoyed when criticized for it. His opinion of women was not flattering—in his novel *Marriage,* he described them as "half-savages, half pets, unemployed things of greed and desire"—but it did not seem to stop any number of them from taking to his bed. Of the female characters in *Things to Come,* only one—Boss Rudolph's consort, Roxana (played by Margaretta Scott)—had any vitality. She was sultry and treacherous to Rudolph, the

specified mixture of savage and pet. All of the other women who had any perceptible work at all were helpers to men; the rest were conspicuously unemployed.

Oddly, they were also quite sexless. If they toiled not, neither did they sin, not even when, as in the case of the young couple about to be launched toward the moon, they were presented with every opportunity to fool around. It does not appear to have been on their minds at all. (Or, even more astonishingly, on either of their fathers'). *Things to Come*'s women are as passive as *Just Imagine*'s, and a lot less sexy. You cannot imagine any of the male characters wanting to marry one because he thought she would be good in bed—possibly, at most, because he thought she would deal with servants well.

The Everytown of the space gun is not only a sterile utopia, it is a markedly undemocratic one. The reason Theotocopulos has the privilege of taking to the TV channels and rousing a mob, he tells us, is that he is a Master Craftsman and has the right to be heard—implying that the ordinary working stiff had better keep his face shut in the presence of his superiors. Worst, it is a dull world. You can't blame the kids for wanting to go to the moon, or the mob for storming the space gun—anything for a little excitement!

Reason tells me that all of the above is true. It even tells me that most of what I have said should have been apparent, even to a sixteen-year-old, even when I first saw it. But I would lie if I said I had any such thoughts in 1936. I was bowled over. I wanted to live in that remote future Everytown even more than I wanted to see the New York City of 1980 from *Just Imagine*—and since that was a far more forlorn hope I did the next best thing by going out to see *Things to Come* again. And again, and again; I saw it at least a dozen times over the next year or so, and how many times after that I am unable to say. And although I never saw *Just Imagine* again until I was sixty (and we were actually in that magical, far-off year of 1980—hardly a bit as it had been predicted), it stayed in my mind. The two films were the sacred and profane views of the future. *Things to Come* was the sober and dedicated mask the future wore to the office, *Just Imagine* its rowdy after-hours self. I loved them both.

The world has come a long way in half a century. Both films are dated now. *Just Imagine*'s sniggery sex jokes would be thought childish by even the subteens of the 1980s, and *Things to Come*'s plastic-coated puritanism is about as inviting as an operating room. All the same, they were tremendous achievements for the time—for any time, in fact. They did what the best of science fiction has always done: They made people think seriously about the future, and thus about what they should be doing here in the present. I wish that some modern-day filmmakers would dare as greatly!

Flash Gordon and Buck Rogers

An Interview with Buster Crabbe by Danny Peary

The following is a previously unpublished interview that took place about five years before Buster Crabbe's death in 1983. Since this book had not been conceived as yet, the conversation had little to do with the "futuristic" aspects of Flash Gordon *and* Buck Rogers, *his two classic serials, or what he personally thought about the future. The interview serves only as a personality profile—interesting I believe, yet, by design, not very deep. Its inclusion in this book needs no defense however: It is quite simply a tribute to a man who made significant contributions to the science fiction cinema. His two serials were geared for youngsters and not as sophisticated as many of the later-day, highbrow futuristic space films, but, as he knew,* Flash Gordon *and* Buck Rogers *inspired and influenced all films that came after them; moreover, it should be noted that no actor ever became more associated with the "space adventure," as enjoyable an sf subgenre as there is, than Larry "Buster" Crabbe.*

Buster Crabbe was a former Olympic swimming champion who went on to become "King of the Serials." His most famous parts were *Flash Gordon* and *Buck Rogers,* but his output was quite large and spanned several decades. In the Fifties, his old films were shown on television, he became host of *Buster's Buddies,* and starred in *Captain Gallant of the Foreign Legion,* and, as a result, became a hero to a new generation of youngsters. His popularity increased through the years. He died in 1983.

Danny Peary: Prior to swimming in the 1928 and 1932 Olympics, what was your background?

Buster Crabbe: I was born in Oakland, California, in 1907. I am one-eighth Hawaiian. Because there was no university in Honolulu at the time, my father had come to the States to attend the University of California. He met my mother in his junior year and they were married when he graduated. They settled in Oakland and had two sons, me and my younger brother. After four years my father packed us up and took us back to Hawaii, and I was raised there, essentially on the beach at Waikiki. As a youngster I did it all: I was a newsboy, an office boy, a beach boy, a life guard. Of course, I was a good swimmer. After two years at the University of Hawaii, I transferred to the University of Southern California, because it had both a law school and a good swimming team.

DP: How did you switch from swimming to acting?

BC: Well, there's some question of whether I ever did. I had absolutely no acting training. I never was in a high school play, and when I was in college I didn't have the time or inclination to think about acting professionally. The studios were in the habit of borrowing USC athletes to do a little stunt or extra work, and I was an unpaid extra in a couple of films. But that was all.

I'll tell you something that I've never said before: My whole life was changed by one-tenth of a second. It was by one-tenth of a second that I beat the French swimmer in the 400-meter finals at the 1932 Olympics and won a gold medal. If I had finished second, Paramount wouldn't have given me a second look. But after I won, they gave me a screen test for the lead in *King of the Jungle* [1932]. They were satisfied with the test and offered me a contract in October of 1932, a few months before I was married. The only reason I signed the contract was because I was having trouble making ends meet to complete law school, which I'd been in for a year. For two and a half years, I'd been working afternoons and Saturdays in a stockroom, and I was making only eight dollars a week. So I decided to lay out of law school for a year and, what the hell, make a hundred dollars a week and not have to worry about rent, meals, and the expense of buying a badly needed pair of pants. I figured that after a year, Paramount wouldn't pick up my option, but that would be all right because by then I'd have saved about $3,500. Then I could complete law school without worrying about finances and catching the street car every day to go to the stockroom job; and then I could return to Hawaii to work for a company in

its legal department. Of course, that never happened. Paramount kept picking up my option, year after year.

DP: Did you keep playing leads?

BC: After I played Kaspa, the Lion Man in *King of the Jungle,* an excellent jungle picture in the Tarzan mold, Paramount lent me to Sol Lesser for the serial *Tarzan the Fearless.* I'd like to forget that one. It was done cheaply and turned out lousy. I couldn't get a good role afterwards. Paramount did what they wanted with me, using me as a bit actor or a juvenile lead. I worked my way back up. Then they cast me in some Zane Grey "B" westerns, starring Randolph Scott. When he didn't want to do any more, I was glad to take over the leads, because they were well done and well written, some by Zane Grey's son. I got to like westerns and never stopped acting in them.

DP: But it was at this time that you starred in the nonwestern serial that assured your fame for decades to come: *Flash Gordon* [1937].

BC: I had followed Alex Raymond's popular comic strip in the newspapers and thought it was a lot of fun. But I was horrified to read in *Variety* in the summer of 1936 that Universal had made a deal with King Features to make a serial

out of it. I thought it was a foolish idea to make a film about three crazy people—Flash, Dale Arden, and Dr. Zarkov—taking off in a rocket ship and landing on the planet Mongo. I couldn't see how they'd be able to adapt it into a serious piece of fiction.

Purely out of curiosity, I decided to go to Universal's lot on the day of the tryouts for Flash. There were about fifteen other actors there, some in spacesuits. There was one actor named George Bergman, with whom I'd worked previously—I thought that if he bleached his hair blond, he'd be an *excellent* choice. There was another unknown actor who I thought might do okay: Jon Hall. Fortunately for him he didn't get the part, because two months later John Ford cast him in *The Hurricane* [1937] and he became a star.

Somebody pointed me out to the producer, Henry MacRae, who came over and introduced himself. We chatted for a while and he asked, "How would you like to do the part of Flash Gordon?" I thought to myself, No way, but I said, "Well, I don't really know." We talked a little bit more and he said, "You can have the part if you want it." Well, I was thinking, this serial doesn't have a chance, and I was about to explain the

Left: As is often the case in the thirteen-part Flash Gordon, *the most popular serial of all, the hero (Buster Crabbe) finds his life is in danger. Although the soldiers of Ming the Merciless (Charles Middleton, to the right on the platform) threaten him, Flash tells Dale Arden (Jean Rogers) to be brave. Aura (Priscilla Lawson), Ming's daughter, looks on jealously.*

Right: Buster Crabbe played Buck Rogers in a twelve-part serial in 1939. Rogers was an American aviator who, after spending five hundred years in suspended animation, wakes up to find a futuristic world that has been conquered by the diabolical Killer Kane.

reasons for my lack of enthusiasm, when Mr. MacRae said, "I know you are under contract to Paramount, but we'll borrow you." My automatic reply was: "If you want to borrow me, I'll have to do what the bosses tell me." When I was walking away, I was thinking, I hope Paramount tells him I'm not available. But it didn't, and six weeks later, in October of 1936, I was out at Universal filming *Flash Gordon.*

DP: What do you remember about working on *Flash Gordon?*

BC: It was tough work. We had about eighty-five set-ups a day. There was no time to even see rushes. We had to be in makeup at 7 A.M. and on the set at 8, and, with only short breaks for lunch and dinner, we didn't knock off until 10 or 11 P.M., and I never got home before midnight. At that hectic pace, we were able to finish just before Christmas, and it was released in 1937. I never thought it had a chance at the box office. But it turned out to be Universal's number-2 hit for 1937; Deanna Durbin's *Three Smart Girls* beat us out, but we did better than a lot of Universal pictures with big-name stars. That convinced the studio to do a second serial, *Flash Gordon's Trip to Mars* [1938] and, when that did well, *Flash Gordon Conquers the Universe* [1940].

DP: How do you explain the success of *Flash Gordon?*

BC: First of all, I must credit Alex Raymond for conceiving a comic strip with universal appeal, a likable hero, a brilliant scientist, lovely women, assorted aliens, and a villain that people loved to hate. Then I credit Henry MacRae and the director Frederick Stephani for insisting that we play it seriously. You must understand that we believed in what we were doing. If we had done it tongue-in-cheek, we'd have flopped with the first serial. Then you have to consider that it was so popular because it was unique; it was new:

nothing like it had ever been done on such a large scale. Universal took quite a gamble. It spent between $350,000 and $450,000 on a damn serial in the mid-Thirties, for heaven's sake! It was the most expensive serial ever made, and it shows. They were able to duplicate the way Dr. Zarkov's rocket ship looked in Raymond's strip, and to capture the look of all his characters: the Clay Men, the Forest People, the Shark Men, the Hawk Men. . . . Ming's laboratory was spectacular, comparing favorably to any futuristic set in *Star Trek.* And don't forget the special effects employed. They were new to movies and were quite expensive. They also compare to the effects in many present-day films. When I asked George Lucas where he got some of his ideas for *Star Wars* [1977], he said that as a youngster he used to go to the Saturday matinees and thrill to serials like *Flash Gordon.*

Besides Alex Raymond and the special effects people, the most important person involved with *Flash Gordon* was Charles Middleton, who played Ming the Merciless. I think everyone in the cast did a wonderful job—Jean Rogers as Dale Arden [Flash's girlfriend], Priscilla Lawson as Aura [Ming's daughter, who has designs on Flash], Frank Shannon as Dr. Zarkov—and I enjoyed working with them all, but Charles Middleton was particularly good. He fit his part to a T. He chewed up the scenery but that's just what the part called for. He was great and I admired him so much.

DP: What did you have to say about the shaping of the Flash Gordon character?

BC: Everything. No one could tell me how to play Flash—I played him as I saw fit. Of course, I took a leaf out of Alex Raymond's strip.

DP: What was your contract like?

BC: I thought it was a good contract at the time. I was being paid by Paramount and, in turn, Paramount was collecting money for me from

In both space serials, security forces run rampant in fascist-controlled worlds. Uniformed men usually meant trouble for the Earthlings. Left: Both Buck Rogers and Buddy (Jackie Moran) look on while Wilma Dearing (Constance Moore) bravely confronts Killer Kane's men. Right: Dale Arden, standing behind Dr. Zarkov (Frank Shannon), hopes Flash Gordon can come up with a way to save himself.

Universal. I'll tell you something: In all the years I was with Paramount, I never cost the studio a dime. It was getting a lot more money for me than it was paying me. But I didn't find that out until 1939. At that time, Paramount offered to pick up my option, but without giving me the required raise. My agent decided it was best for me not to sign again, but to hook up with Universal on some serials and pick up some of the money Paramount had been getting for me. Only then did Paramount agree to pay me the small raise. Big deal! It was too late. I started making serials with Universal and PRC and it worked out pretty well. I did many serials, mostly westerns: the "Red Barry" series, the "Billy the Kid" series...

DP: What about your other science fiction serial, *Buck Rogers*?

BC: Universal sandwiched that in between the second and third *Flash Gordon* serials, hoping it would have the same appeal as them. But it wasn't nearly as popular with the Saturday matinee crowd. Buck was something on the order of Flash—an All-American hero, a do-gooder, etc.—but I didn't like his character as much. By that time I suppose I was just enamored with Flash and didn't get any enjoyment playing a similar character when I'd have preferred playing him. I did enjoy working with the cast: Anthony Warde played the villain Killer Kane; Constance Moore was Wilma, Buck's love interest; Jackie Moran played Buddy, the young boy who accompanied Buck into the distant future;

and C. Montague Shaw was Dr. Huer, the serial's version of Dr. Zarkov. But otherwise, I'm sorry to admit, I don't remember much about *Buck Rogers.* I own the entire first serial of *Flash Gordon,* but the only print I have of *Buck Rogers* is the condensed feature-length version. Because of the way it was re-edited, this version is very jumpy, so I don't bother to watch it to refresh my memory.

DP: Later in your career, did Universal ever think of reviving *Flash Gordon* or *Buck Rogers*?

BC: No. Once they made the third *Flash Gordon* serial, which didn't have the budget to match the first two serials and consequently didn't do as well commercially, that was it. It was only recently that they decided to remake *Flash Gordon* [1980]. There were rumors that I'd play Flash's father.*

DP: Did you get much fan mail when you were making the *Flash Gordon* serials?

BC: Oddly enough, I didn't get nearly as much mail in the old days as I do now. *Flash Gordon* had been aimed at youngsters, and now the little guys and gals have grown up—so I get much mail from those people who have fond memories of it. The serial is always playing somewhere and it's amazing that so many people have come to realize that it was the grand-

*As it turned out, both *Flash Gordon* and *Buck Rogers* were remade. Buster Crabbe did not play Flash's father, but ironically, when *Buck Rogers in the 25th Century* (1979) became a television series, Crabbe made a guest appearance on that show. —D.P.

daddy of all the space films: *Star Wars, 2001* [1968], *Star Trek,* you name it. . . . I'm constantly being invited to science fiction and other nostalgia conventions. Actually the popularity of *Flash Gordon* really grew to astronomical proportions in the early Fifties when it played on television. Little did I know when I made the "Flash Gordons" that fifteen years later it would have a whole new effect on my life. In fact, it opened up a whole new career for me. Many more people saw it on television in one sitting than could see it in years of playing Saturday matinees. I really started getting fan mail when I started a club on radio and television called "Buster's Buddies." At one point, that club had 35,000 members.

DP: The advent of television brought you great success. You hosted several shows, including a health-exercise program and a western-movie series, and you starred in *Captain Gallant of the Foreign Legion,* the first American series filmed abroad [in Morocco]. But "B" films were being phased out and your film career waned. Did you regret never having gotten a shot at a major film?

BC: I must admit that the answer is "yes." I never got a shot at an "A" film with a good producer and cast, and a top-grade script written by a well-known author. Perhaps I would have revealed a talent I never had a chance to show. Because most of what I did didn't depend on

histrionic ability: I did action films. But I must say, having done *Flash Gordon,* I've always had something to be proud of.

DP: A silly question: Have you any regrets that you didn't pursue the law career you once intended?

BC: No. But I never trusted the movie business for my livelihood. I always had something on the side. For instance, when I started making a little money, I invested in real estate. I never held onto it long enough, but I did see profits on some of it. I made other investments as well, and, of course, I've often been involved business-wise with health and swimming.

Things worked out well for me. I certainly was lucky in marriage. I met Virginia in 1929, on the beach at Waikiki, and we were married in 1933, and have been together ever since. You get all sorts of things thrown at you in the film business, and Virginia has been a real godsend—she's been most understanding. Everyone has human frailties, and I've strayed from the straight and narrow at times. But I always knew the way back.

Of course, my thing has always been physical fitness. I've always been in good health; today I weigh less than I did as an Olympic swimmer—and I'm past seventy. I think I've had a good, long, full life.

Heinlein on Film: *Destination Moon*

Michael Goodwin

By the grace of God, and in the name of the United States of America,
I take possession of this planet. —Dr. Charles Cargraves, *Destination Moon*

It was less than two years since Captain Chuck Yaeger had broken the sound barrier in a Bell X-1; Mach 2 was still out of reach. It would be eight long years until Russia put Sputnik I into orbit, twelve years until Gagarin made Earth orbit, twenty until Armstrong and Aldrin set foot on the moon. It was 1949, and producer George Pal set out to make a movie about a trip to the moon.

It wasn't the first such movie—Georges Méliès sewed up *that* record in 1902. It had a melodramatic plot, embarrassing dialogue, mediocre performances by second-string players, cut-rate special effects. Nor was it impressively accurate in predicting technical details; among other bad guesses, it shows an atomic-powered, single-stage spaceship built entirely by private industry! (No big deal, of course. Science fiction isn't really about the future—it can't be. Like all literature, it's about here and now. There are no crystal balls. When writers or filmmakers guess right, it's found money.)

Michael Goodwin wrote the narration for *Burden of Dreams,* as well as two screenplays, *The Man From Planet Earth* and *Heaven Before I Die,* which is scheduled for 1984–85 production. He was *Rolling Stone's* first film critic, managing editor of *Take One,* senior editor and film critic for Francis Ford Coppola's short-lived *City Magazine,* and has written for many publications, including *The New York Times, Penthouse, Mother Jones, Esquire, The Village Voice, American Film,* and *California.*

And yet ... When *Destination Moon* was completed in 1950, a special premiere screening was held at New York's Hayden Planetarium for a gathering of science fiction writers and editors—professionals who knew the difference between a well-told, challenging tale and comic-strip stuff. They had seen far too many lousy monster movies passed off as science fiction—and taken the rap for them, too, in the form of "educated" people turning up their noses and murmuring, "Oh? You write ... science fiction?" They were a tough audience, the toughest. And when the lights came up, many of them went to their typewriters and wrote paeans of praise to this movie— at least one of which started, as I recall, "I have seen the future." How come?

Robert A. Heinlein's screenplay, that's how come.

Heinlein is universally acknowledged as one of the masters of modern science fiction. His remarkable literary career is presently pushing the 50-year mark (his first story appeared in *Astounding Science Fiction* in 1939), although it wasn't until the publication of his novel, *Stranger in a Strange Land,* in 1961 that he "crossed over" to a mainstream audience. Several of his most recent novels have held positions on the *New York Times* Best-Sellers list for months. His libertarian

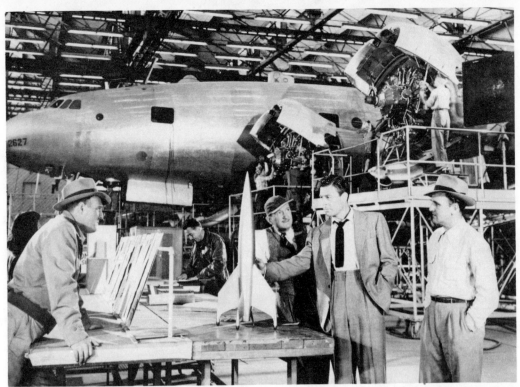

Barnes (John Archer, holding the miniature rocket) and General Thayer (Tom Powers, wearing a cap) talk with construction men about the building of their spaceship.

social views, philosophical subtexts, sexual politics, and literary style have been analyzed in any number of books and essays—most notably in Alexei Panshin's "Heinlein In Dimension." And when Armstrong and Aldrin *did* land on the moon, Heinlein was part of the TV team that reported the story—as was only right. If not for him, that landing might never have taken place.

If Heinlein is "just" a science fiction writer, he commands a place in that field much like Howard Hawks's in the filmmaking world: as a creative giant, spinning off perfect genre-prototypes. Hawks did westerns, musicals, screwball comedies, hardboiled detective thrillers, airplane adventures, and gangster films—*and* provided definitive examples of each. Heinlein has written the ultimate time-travel yarns, outer-space adventures, cautionary political parables, charming magical fantasies, sword and sorcery adventures, tales of interplanetary espionage, revolutionary thrillers, and much more. Take any science fiction element you like—the generation-ship, the sentient computer, the intricate time-travel paradox, etc. Track it back far enough, and the chances are good you'll end up in a Heinlein story. He's surely one of the most fascinating (and controversial) science fiction writers of the twentieth century—and many people would consider the "science fiction" qualifier unnecessary.

In 1949, Heinlein's literary career was just beginning. Born in Butler, Missouri, in 1907, he grew up in Kansas City. In 1929 he graduated from the U.S. Naval Academy at Annapolis, where he majored in Naval Science; subsequently he served on active duty for six years, retiring when he contracted tuberculosis. He spent the next five years studying mathematics and physics at UCLA, and held jobs in architecture, real estate, and politics. In 1939, he turned his hand to writing science fiction to make a few extra bucks. His first story sold—and was extraordinarily well received. Within two short years, by the time the United States entered World War II in 1941, Heinlein was the most popular (and prolific) science fiction writer in America.

He spent the war years working as a civilian engineer for the Materials Laboratory of the Naval Air Material Center. After the war, he began writing for slick magazines like *The Saturday Evening Post,* and in 1947 he published his first novel—an unremarkable "juvenile" titled *Rocket Ship Galileo* in which three boys and their scientist uncle (Dr. Donald Cargraves) build a rocket, fly it to the moon, and defeat some leftover Nazis. Producer Pal bought the rights to this novel, and hired Heinlein to work on a screen adaptation (along with Rip Van Ronkel and James O'Hanlon).

It's not clear how much control Heinlein had over the final shape of *Destination Moon*—some suggest not much. In any case, the story involves three main characters—a military man, General Thayer (Tom Bowers); an engineer/industrialist, Jim Barnes (John Archer); and a scientist,

Charles Cargraves (Warner Anderson). Together, they organize a cartel of financiers to build a spaceship that will fly to the moon. Despite governmental interference, they succeed in launching the rocketship—with a fourth man, radio technician Joe Sweeney (Dick Wesson). Problems arise during the flight—a frozen radar antenna, a crewman who floats away from the ship—but these are easily solved. A sloppy landing on the moon leaves them short of fuel for the return voyage, and they must lighten the ship by several thousand pounds. When they're still 110 pounds overweight with everything stripped, it seems they will have to leave one of the crew behind—until an ingenious solution is found that allows them all to go home. (A "novelized" version of the screenplay, published under Heinlein's byline in the September 1950 issue of *Short Stories Magazine,* raises some question as to whether the ship will make it back.)

Heinlein's involvement with the screenplay (he also received screen credit as "special advisor") is the single most interesting element in *Destination Moon.* The plot of the film has virtually nothing in common with *Galileo* (aside from a scientist named "Cargraves"), but a number of typical thematic, stylistic, and ideological elements show that Heinlein had already arrived at many of the ideas that would form the armature of his life's work.

Heinlein is, above all else, a "hard-science" sf writer—maybe the ultimate one. That means not only that the science has to be "right," but that

cultural and technological details lie at the center of his stories. Panshin describes Heinlein's approach as "an engineering outlook," noting that the writer is preoccupied with process—how things are made—and chooses characters who are capable of making things. He also mentions a tendency to lecture about details. This approach, more than any other element in *Destination Moon,* shows the Heinlein sensibility—and is, I suspect, the main reason those sf writers reacted so positively. Instead of silly super-science a la *Flash Gordon, Destination Moon* focuses on scientists, engineers, and technicians actually doing science.

At its worst, this results in too many lectures on gyros and reaction mass—not to mention unspeakable dialogue like, "We're actually travelling thousands of miles an hour. Here in space, all comparisons are lost...." Gack! On the other hand, it can also produce sequences like the central scene in which Thayer and Cargraves are seen *doing math*—trading figures, checking each other's work, reading values out of tables. Although this is one of Heinlein's favorite metaphors—performing difficult mathematical calculations under great time pressure—it's extremely rare to find such a scene in a medium where crude physical action like car chases and machine-gun massacres are far more common coin.

There are a number of other elements in *Destination Moon* that reflect Heinlein's sensibility. His libertarian mistrust of government (and concom-

Left: On the moon's surface, Cargraves (Warner Anderson) takes a photo of Joe Sweeney (Dick Wesson), who pretends—like a "modern Atlas"—to hold up the Earth.

Right: Cargraves floats off into space, and Barnes and Joe must quickly decide how to save him.

itant affection for private enterprise) shows up in several scenes—most notably in the Gathering of Capitalists (a scene that recurs frequently in Heinlein's fiction). "The vast amount of brains, talents, special skills, and research facilities necessary for this project are not in the government," notes Barnes. "Nor can they be mobilized by the government in peacetime without fatal delay. Only American industry can do the job." When one of the financiers asks (as they often do in Heinlein's scenes), "What's the payoff?" Barnes answers, "We'll know when we get there, and we'll tell you when we get back." Heinlein's confidence in the dollars-and-cents value of basic research has always been unswerving.

At the same time, there's another, inarguable (and typically Heinleinesque) reason for making the trip to the moon—and it shows up several times, sometimes subtly, sometimes blatantly: the anti-Communist reason. At one point, General Thayer notes, "It's *peacetime,* the government isn't making...appropriations. It'll need the rocket one of these days, and if it's not ready the government will turn to private industry to do it. Government *always* does that when it gets in a jam." The clear implication is that while it's peacetime *now,* enlightened men know that another war will surely come, and must be prepared. Heinlein has often raised this argument.

Later, in the Gathering-of-Capitalists scene, the script hints at the probable enemy in the coming war. "We are not the only ones who know the moon can be reached," argues General Thayer.

"We're not the only ones who are planning to go there. *The race is on!* And we'd better win it... because there is absolutely no way to stop an attack from outer space. The first country that can use the moon for the launching of missiles will control the earth. That, gentlemen, is the most important military fact of this century!" Heinlein has used this speech, or close variations, many times in his stories and novels. He underscores the point here by having one of the crustiest of the capitalists respond, "Gentlemen, I see no reason for further discussion." Neither does Heinlein. (Incidentally, this is probably one of the first references to the "space race.")

Subsequently, the identity of "the enemy" is pointed out even more clearly—in a scene where the film takes a libertarian slap at governmental interference in private business affairs. Barnes walks into Cargraves's office with a newspaper headlined, "MASS MEETING PROTESTS RADIOACTIVE ROCKET," and reads Cargraves a telegram from the Atomic Energy Commission: "Your petition to test an atomic energy reaction engine is regretfully denied. A possible danger exists in resultant dispersal of radioactive materials around the test area...."

"Aah, we've cleared the area for ten miles around," says Cargraves.

"You can't buck public opinion," says Barnes, displaying the newspaper.

"That's not public opinion," sneers Cargraves, "that's a job of propaganda."

"You're almighty right it is," says Barnes,

Thayer and Barnes lighten the ship so they can return to Earth.

"manufactured and organized with money and brains."

In this exchange, "propaganda," "manufactured," and "organized" are all Fifties code words for "Communist." Heinlein has always been deeply fearful of Russians on the moon; in one of his stories, entrepreneur D. D. Harriman scares a capitalist into financing his moon rocket by showing him a picture of the moon with a hammer and sickle painted on it—accompanied by a lecture on the simple technology that would allow the commies to produce such a display if they get there first. "Gentlemen, I see no reason for further discussion," says the capitalist—or something very similar.

When the "Commission" attempts to prevent the takeoff (apparently, nervous nellies at the AEC consider a ten-mile radius insufficient safety margin in case of a nuclear explosion), Barnes and his boys respond in typically libertarian fashion—they ignore the government and take off anyway. And there's an extraordinary moment when Cargraves sets foot on the moon, and declares, "By the grace of God, and in the name of the United States of America, I take possession of this planet." One imagines Heinlein breathing a sigh of relief when he got *that* line in.

The rest of the film is fairly excruciating, and reflects little of Heinlein's sensibility. In all fairness, it must be admitted that producer Pal made a brilliant decision in avoiding the crude superimpositions and mattes that characterized typical outer-space adventures up to that time. Except for two or three shots (where he had to use

animation to provide an effect), he relied on clever camera angles to set the actors (and an occasional model) against impressive backdrops based on oil paintings by the noted science fiction illustrator Chesley Bonestell. As a result, the film still looks terrific—with clear, steady shots of actors and spaceships floating serenely against a sea of stars. This is probably another reason the professional science fiction community liked the film as well as it did.

Unfortunately, the interior effects were not as impressive; takeoff was simulated primarily by shaking the camera, with thin, transparent membranes used to distort the actors' faces during "acceleration," and a revolving set was used to allow the actors to mime weightlessness. None of this was remotely believable. Nor was horrible dialogue like, "Wow! The geography books are right!" or "I'll never be able to describe this to anyone...."

Destination Moon has not aged well. Its sensibility seems dated, its interior effects seem crude, and even its extraordinary exteriors have been devalued by subsequent advances in special effects matte technology. But in one critical way—and with only Heinlein to thank—the film stands as a benchmark in science fiction filmmaking. Like the best-written sf, it is an adventure in which intellect, not martial skill, provides the solutions. The "engineering outlook." One has only to look at the *Star Wars* trilogy, with its endless swordfights, space battles, and corny, melodramatic confrontations, to see how far science fiction filmmaking has regressed in thirty-four years.

1984:
Orwell Compromised

Allen Eyles

1984, the 1956 film production of George Orwell's *Nineteen Eighty-Four,* is most interesting for what it didn't achieve. It was supposed to be, in the words of the chairman of the United States Information Agency, "the most devastating anti-Communist film of all time." An earlier British television production had scalded viewers and created the biggest controversy the BBC had ever had, so the potential for being a much-debated commercial success was there. But the film version made little impression in America and failed to make any great impact in England either.

It's a truism that the best books never make the best movies. Something that's worked supremely well in one medium is not likely to repeat its success in another. With a mediocre play or fairish novel, there's plenty of scope for imaginative improvement in a movie version. However, George Orwell's uncompromising work demanded total fidelity at the very least if it were to succeed as a film; unfortunately, even when the book is a certified masterwork, filmmakers insist on taking great liberties with the source material. Predictably, *1984* pales in comparison to *Nineteen Eighty-Four.*

The novel began germinating in Orwell's mind in 1943 and he started writing it in 1946, finishing it two years later. "It's a great book," said its publisher Frederic Warburg, "but I pray I may be spared from reading another like it for years to come." It appeared in Britain on June 6, 1949 and became a best seller. Its black vision of a totalitarian society took many of its details from

Big Brother is watching Winston Smith (Edmond O'Brien) and everyone else in Oceania. He may not really exist, but his image is everywhere and he is the symbol of the authoritarian regime. Fear of Big Brother makes citizens believe "Freedom is Slavery" and "War is Peace."

Allen Eyles is the former editor of the British film magazines *Focus on Films* and *Films & Filming.* He is the author of *The Marx Brothers: Their World of Comedy, John Wayne, Bogart* and most recently, *James Stewart.*

the austere conditions in postwar Britain, when there was rationing, housing problems, and other hardships, but Orwell denied he was attacking the Socialists who were then in power and who'd had his support. He was writing a warning about the kind of society that could emerge but that he didn't expect would. To be forewarned was to be forearmed. Orwell died on January 21, 1950.

In America the book was taken to be an attack on the Left, with the U.S.S.R. assumed as the model for Orwell's police state. Its propaganda potential and its obvious dramatic possibilities encouraged a one-hour radio adaptation starring Richard Widmark and a 1953 television version toplining Eddie Albert. Film rights were sold to American producers in 1951, and by 1953 had passed to N. Peter Rathvon, a former RKO Radio executive who had become a European-based independent producer in 1949. He had made some films for the United States Information Agency and, significantly, he received a secret subsidy of $100,000 from that organization to help make a film of Orwell's novel—in exchange for granting it script approval.

Meanwhile, the two-hour live BBC-TV production was shown on England's sole channel on Sunday, December 12, 1954. It created such an uproar that it was repeated four days later. It was prefaced by a warning from the BBC's head of drama about the grimness of the subject matter. A quarter of the population watched the repeat— the largest audience since Queen Elizabeth's coronation in June of 1953.

This BBC production was adapted by Nigel Kneale, directed by Rudolph Cartier, and acted by Peter Cushing and Yvonne Mitchell as the secret lovers and André Morell as the avuncular spy for the secret police. It used limited resources brilliantly, with its hemmed-in sets creating a gray, claustrophobic setting. Also, Cushing's cadaverously thin features left a haunting impression. It was truly frightening, and the words "Big Brother is watching you" became a national catchphrase.

The impact of this TV production no doubt spurred on Rathvon and his partners (whose company had the most inappropriate name of Holiday Productions). Quickly they made arrangements to shoot the picture in England in collaboration with Associated British, and hired Michael Anderson, a hot new director. Anderson had made his name with *The Dam Busters,* a 1954 British film with Michael Redgrave. Since the film was assured a British "X" certificate, which would bar under-sixteens from admission, Rathvon pleaded that American stars were mandatory if the film was to be a financial success, particularly outside of England. American actors Edmond O'Brien and Jan Sterling were engaged, but Michael Redgrave, given the top supporting part, received top billing on British prints and advertising posters.

The "freely" adapted script was written by one of Holiday's partners, Ralph Bettinson, a veteran of Monogram quickies, and William Templeton, a British actor. Broadly speaking, it was faithful to Orwell's vision of the future. It opens with a series of atomic explosions that leave the world controlled by three powers. Britain has been renamed Airstrip One, part of Oceania, governed by a brutal authoritarian regime headed by Big Brother—a mysterious, probably nonexistent leader, whose stern image is everywhere. The people of the state are divided into three classes: the Inner Party composed of the policy-making rulers; the Outer Party of minor government workers; and the Proles, the slaves who are regarded as no better than animals.

Big Brother watches all the Outer Party members through seeing eyes that have been implanted in walls, even those walls inside their apartments. Winston Smith (O'Brien) works for the Ministry of Truth, rewriting history to fit the latest changes in the Party line. He begins to question the regime's policies, doublethink propaganda, and police methods for keeping everyone obedient, and expresses his discontent in a secret diary. He believes that a high-ranking member of the Inner Party named O'Connor (Redgrave)—O'Brien in the book—is a member of the Underground, who oppose Big Brother. He suspects Party member Julia (Sterling) is spying on him, but learns instead that she desires him. They embark on a daring clandestine love affair, prohibited by the Party, renting a dingy room above an antique shop in the Prole sector. Looking for confederates, they approach O'Connor, who, as they'd hoped, recruits them into the Underground. A few days later they are arrested. The shop owner is a spy; their romantic idyll had been overheard from behind the mirror in their room; O'Connor is a member of the dreaded Thought Police.

Regrettably, the power of Orwell's vision is allowed to leak away. The film fails to bring home the mind-numbing boredom or oppression under Big Brother: It simply doesn't make life gratingly unpleasant enough. And important details found in the book are either changed or omitted. In the novel, Winston falsifies reports in no less a paper than *The Times,* changing stories and having the archive copies reprinted—in the film, a fictitious paper called *The Gazette* is substituted. Whereas the enemy of Big Brother and the leader of the revolutionaries had the Jewish name Goldstein in Orwell, the film gives him the vaguely science-fiction name Kalador. His entirely reasonable criticisms of Big Brother, which fall on unreceptive ears in the book (showing how brainwashed everyone is), are not even audible in the screen version—it's as if the politically conservative filmmakers, with the United States Information Agency looking over their shoulders, did a bit of censorship of their own. In the book, Winston shudders at the memory of his sister being at-

Inner Party member O'Connor (Michael Redgrave) always looks over the shoulders of Outer Party members to make sure they are following the political line. Winston, seated in the first row, and Julia (Jan Sterlng), behind him and to the right, are destined to become lovers and defy Big Brother.

tacked by rats—in the film he doesn't spell out the horrible truth that causes him to fear them so much (prompting O'Connor to use rats to torture and break Winston). The overall effect is to make defying Big Brother a *game* rather than a remarkably courageous gesture.

Michael Anderson's plodding direction is of no help, either. The film completely fails to emphasize the two potentially most startling moments: When suspicious Winston opens Julia's furtively passed note to read its totally unexpected message ("I love you" in the book but ponderously expanded on screen to "I must talk to you. I love you"); and the chilling, ghastly moment when the voice behind the mirror startles the couple in the hideaway, echoing a remark of Julia's by intoning "You are dead!"

Rathvon caused equal damage by deliberately choosing to emphasize the story's love angle at the expense of many of the political themes important to Orwell. Furthermore, the relationship of Winston and Julia was presented as a simple love affair in the film rather than the more provocative combination of lust and loneliness it was in Orwell. But what really brought down the wrath of

British critics on the film was the producer's audacity to change the ending of Orwell's work for the version shown in England.

The book concludes pessimistically, with Winston completely broken and brainwashed after undergoing torture—he now loves only Big Brother. One of the two endings made for the film was indeed faithful to Orwell, but the British version had Winston overcome the effects of brainwashing and shout "Down with Big Brother" to a crowd, before being gunned down by police. The British producer chose this more optimistic outcome, while Columbia, which handled the American release, opted for the harsher, more faithful conclusion. This was somewhat surprising, considering that since the Thirties, when alternate endings were shot for many tragic films, there

Left: In a crowd of brainwashed citizens, Julia whispers something of vital importance to the paranoid Winston. He is stunned.

Below: Their affair has been discovered! Julia and Winston look at the mirror in their room, wondering what is behind it and who has been spying on them.

Right: Winston has been broken by the emotionless O'Connor.

was a belief that European audiences would accept stark, downbeat resolutions while Americans required some uplift, some sense of triumph or hope.

The uproar about the ending broke out before the world premiere in London. Orwell's thirty-seven-year-old widow, Sonia, protested in no uncertain terms and refused to attend the gala opening. Producer Rathvon responded: "It is only natural that Mrs. Orwell should prefer the ending her husband wrote. But ours is more logical. Orwell showed the human soul destroyed by brainwashing. Our version shows that this is not always so. It is the type of ending Orwell might have written if he had not known when he wrote the book that he was dying." (Though Orwell did die soon after the book's publication, there were many indications that he expected to live considerably longer.)

Rathvon's opposition to the absolute oblitera-

tion of human will does weaken Orwell's message. The movie ending, which suggests that there will always be somebody rebelling, no matter what, breeds complacency in the viewer. Orwell's denial of both hope and a rebellious spirit once certain conditions exist stimulates his readers to stand firm against any drift toward the situation depicted in the book—before it becomes too late.

In actuality, even the British version's ending doesn't offer much solace. When Julia hears Winston shouting his opposition to Big Brother and being shot down, she rushes to him despite the police order to halt. They fire and she falls to the ground, mortally wounded. She crawls forward, leading to a clichéd image of her hand reaching out for Winston's hand as autumn leaves swirl on the ground. Yet she doesn't manage to touch him. He is already dead and never knew that she retained the same emotions he felt, that she returned to his side, or that she gave up her life as well. So this outcome is also pretty downbeat. A more subtle approach might have had Julia being inspired by Winston's outburst and going off with revolt rekindled in her mind. But this would not have been as pictorially dramatic as the double death of lovers—more impor-

tant, the film might have become at the last moment a political polemic rather than be a story of the indestructibility of love.

Now that the dreaded year 1984 has actually arrived, the power of Orwell's book has been somewhat eroded in the wave of general relief. Of course, much of what the author predicted has come to pass in some parts of the world and to some degree; but then this was also the case when the book first came out. His worst fears simply haven't come to pass on a world scale. But perhaps if Orwell were alive today he would retitle his book *2004* and give us new cause for worry.

It is not likely that the 1956 film version will be revived, except for odd museum screenings, especially since a new version by another hot young British director (Michael Radford) has been made. This is unfortunate, because the old movie remains of marginal interest as one of the few earnest looks into the future by either British or American filmmakers of the Fifties. Considered a serious drama rather than "science fiction" (a term that implied light or incredible entertainment), *1984* was authentic enough to offer a dystopian vision that paying audiences were not prepared to consider.

Superego Confrontation on *Forbidden Planet*

Martin Sutton

Forbidden Planet (1956) was MGM's first stab at science fiction, and typically for that studio, it was a production both lavish and tasteful. Previously, large budg-ets had been invested only when a studio adapted an sf classic, but *Forbidden Planet* began as an original screenplay (titled "Fatal Planet"), based on an idea by Irving Block, a painter and special effects technician, and Allen Adler, a freelance screenwriter. MGM chief Dore Schary took on the project because he was attracted by its sophisticated notion of a space-age setting for Shakespeare's *The Tempest,* complete with a clever Freudian line whereby the characters actually "interpret" much of the meaning of the text for us.

The literary associations may have passed over the heads of many in the audience in 1956, but the cast of characters follows Shakespeare quite closely. Prospero, magician and rightful Duke of Milan, becomes Dr. Morbius (Walter Pidgeon), philologist and super-scientist; Miranda, Prospero's daughter, becomes Altaira (Anne Francis); Ferdinand, son of the King of Naples and Miranda's suitor, becomes Adams (Leslie Nielsen), commander of the United Planets cruiser C-57D; Ariel, "an airy spirit," becomes Robby the Robot; Caliban, "a savage and deformed slave," turns up as the Monster of the Id; and even jester Trinculo and the drunken butler Stephano are combined to be the ship's cook (Earl Holliman).

The plots also have a certain congruence. Shakespeare's Italian noblemen are shipwrecked on the shores of an island on which the deposed Duke Prospero and his daughter have been cast. The couple's only companions up till then had been Ariel, a subservient magic spirit, and the animal-natured Caliban, offspring of a witch. Pretty soon, a hornet's nest of magic and ro-

Martin Sutton has contributed to several British film magazines including *Films & Filming* and *Sight and Sound*. He is writing a book on John Wyndham.

The United Planets cruiser C-57D that lands on Altair IV is a "flying saucer," which moviegoers have always associated with aliens. But the men inside are from Earth and, though the year is 2200 A.D., they are like the soldiers of the Eisenhower years. Right, three respectful, well-groomed, obedient soldiers report to Commander Adams (Leslie Nielsen, pointing) and "Doc" (Warner Stevens).

mance is stirred up, with Prospero finally relinquishing both Miranda to Ferdinand and his supernatural powers.

And so it is, up to a point, with the crew of the C-57D. They are on a mission to visit the planet Altair IV in search of survivors from the ship Bellarophon, sent there twenty years earlier on an exploratory exercise. Only Morbius and his daughter have survived, and the doctor antagonistically rejects help from the crew and jealously guards both Altaira and his discovery of the super-science of the Krell, the planet's previous inhabitants who had suddenly vanished. This science has allowed Morbius to produce not only a paradisal home for the two, complete with their servant Robby, but has unleashed from Morbius's mechanically overstimulated mind an invisible Id Monster that wiped out the Bellarophon colonists and now threatens the male crew of the C-57D.

Beyond these admittedly bold stabs at Kulchur, part of the movie's real interest and originality lies in its deployment of a theme that ran counter to the pattern established in Fifties sf cinema and still is adventurous today: Our real enemy is not an alien "other" out there somewhere in the galaxy (or behind the Iron Curtain, as many of American-made sf films implied), but rather the "other" inside each of us; we can travel as far as we like in terms of distance, but we cannot escape that which lurks inside. The movie's themes, therefore, are not as immediately "political" as those found in many Fifties cold war-paranoia sf scenarios, wherein the U.S. military comes to grips with aliens who threaten both our bodies and our planet.

The first problem that one faces when analyzing *Forbidden Planet* is figuring out the extent to which it is, at heart, a horror movie. A monster, bug-eyed or otherwise, is a staple of the sf genre, but it usually arrives arbitrarily within the narrative, has no spiritual connection to the main characters, and is afforded very little in the way of sympathy. More in line with the creature of the horror film, the Monster of the Id is a projection of Morbius and has an explicit intent—to act out the doctor's jealousy and rage. But *Forbidden Planet* is still, most assuredly, more sf than horror, stressing its setting and its speculative ideas. As Vivian Sobchack states in *The Limits of Infinity* (A. S. Barnes, 1980):

> The film's emphasis is less on Morbius's moral crisis than on Robby the Robot and the landscape and machinery and decor of Altair IV. . . . It tends to explain away the animal within us in the scientific terminology of Freudian psychology, to view it—if not to tame it— dispassionately and analytically.

The Id Monster is actually named within the story after a supposed psychological process. Even the attack of a previously tame leopard in Altaira's Edenic garden is pointed out by Adams as representing her loss of innocence—after her first erotic response to a kiss (from Adams). (Note that even in the future we are warned of women's destructive sexuality!) There is no mystery here, nothing for us to "interpret," as the movie's scientific sensibility works against potential mythopoetic qualities.

Yet there is more to consider in the movie if we more closely regard its futuristic aspects. The

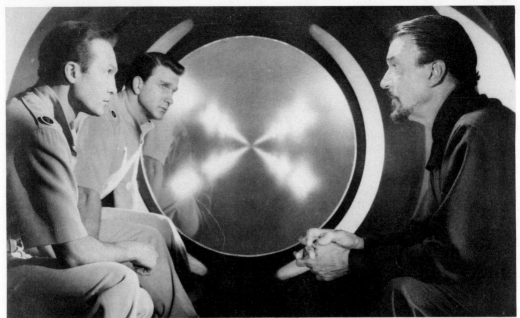

film's basic tension springs from the contrast between Commander Adams and Dr. Morbius, between the honest, outgoing appeal of the uniformed young man and the dark, withdrawn, cerebral nature of the older scientist. And the drama is played out mainly against a domestic backdrop, the hi-tech Morbius household. Indeed, *Forbidden Planet* not only contains elements of the horror film but also strays into the territory of that favorite Fifties form, the domestic melodrama.

At first glance, the Morbius household is a futuristic utopia. It is bright and clean, in a very Fifties geometric and formica fashion, and full of labor-saving gadgetry. The centerpiece of this flamboyant technology is Robby, a robot who can slave night and day, even manufacturing food and drink. And then, through the picture windows we can glimpse a beautiful garden, a paradise populated by tamed wild animals. Near the beginning of the film, the qualities of this Dream House are actually established during the crew's (and, of course, our) guided tour. We are invited with them to marvel at the splendors of this scientific utopia, which is set against the MGM cyclorama of distant towering peaks.

Partly to appeal to younger audiences, and partly to compensate for the anonymity of the Id Monster, Robby was made an important *character* in the narrative, and even was featured prominently on posters for the film. Robby is, as Steve Rubin pointed out in *Cinefantastique* (Spring 1979), a symbol of "the harmonious synthesis of scientific advance and social good, at last the powerful tool which man is unable to turn against himself." To this extent, the cut-out device that prevents Robby from harming any life form renders him one of the movie's several representatives of the super-ego.

Morbius (Walter Pidgeon) takes Adams and "Doc" for a tour of the enormous Krell chambers. The Krell were a great two-thousand-year-old civilization that disappeared in one night—victims of their own Id Monsters.

This friendly and comically dignified machine, looking, as Vivian Sobchack observes, like "some mad mating between the Michelin tire man and a jukebox," is also intriguing because of its role within the Morbius home:

Cook: Is it a male or female?
Robby: In my case, sir, the question is totally without meaning!

But is the cook's question really without meaning? Robby is given a man's name, a deep masculine voice, tremendous strength, and an impressively vast bulk (think of the contrast with *Star Wars'* C3PO and R2D2). Not for nothing is it referred to as "him," although there is another, contrasting side to Robby's character. Robby can sew, design dresses, cook, clean, arrange flowers, and create jewelry—all traditionally feminine attributes. Outside, he is a tool of strength, but within a home that is conspicuous for having no wife-mother figure, Robby functions as a surrogate adult female. The sight of Robby arranging flowers is not so much comic as it is bizarre—because of the image, this house seems incomplete, somehow wrong. If the Krell seem almost present because of their still-functioning subterranean machinery and odd-shaped doorways, then so too does the long-deceased wife of Morbius and mother of Altaira because of the duties the two humans have handed to their masculine-characterized machine.

In 1984, feminists complained when "Sweetheart," a robot with large breasts, which implied it was female, was built and given one function: to make coffee. Here, on Altair IV in a house surrounded by a paradisiacal garden, Robby the Robot plays homemaker. Altaira (Anne Francis) and Lt. Farman (Jack Kelly) happily accept "his" beverage. Farman will be the first man to kiss Altaira, but it will be Adams's kisses that turn her legs to jelly.

As visitors to this "brave new world" (Shakespeare's phrase) of 2200 A.D., the crew of the C-57D represent our touchstone for "normalcy," our link with Earth (more precisely, America) of 1956. On the other hand, their mode of travel is distinctly "unearthly." The flying saucer, virtually synonymous in the late Forties and Fifties with UFOs, became part of the iconography of sf illustrations and cinema images. Linked to the frequent sightings of them in those decades, they became in fiction the carriers of the invading alien. Thus, by a series of neat reversals, the saucer in *Forbidden Planet,* the C-57D, contains our kind, not aliens, and touches down on a strange planet, not Earth. The effect is iconographically disorientating, especially as the life form on Altair IV turns out to be our own. Already we are alerted to the fact that we are both the invaders and the invaded (the appearance of the C-57D is distinctly unwelcome), that our culture is curiously turned upon itself—just as we later learn that the destructive Id Monster, the "other," is within each of us.

The crew members of the C-57D, nevertheless, are a right-minded element. In neat uniforms throughout, these young men with their playful banter and "gosh-wow" reaction to the splendors of the universe are intended to win us over immediately. Adams himself most fully represents this Eisenhowerian ideal. He's straightforward, plain-speaking, down to earth. He's honest and unimaginative—even Morbius is forced to quip that it's not important for a commander to have brains after Adams gets a disappointing score on the Krell intelligence test. As played by Leslie Nielsen, he's tall, blondish, with clean-cut good looks. He can always be relied upon, of course, to make such statements as: "The Lord sure makes some beautiful worlds." Keeping home-grown values to the fore, it is mainly through his eyes that we are invited to watch this new world unfold.

We first glimpse Morbius as a dark, threatening outline standing at his front door. He wears a black, vaguely Oriental outfit, and has a goatee beard—immediately suggesting the "evil" genius of a Fu Manchu. In contrast to Nielsen, dark-haired Walter Pidgeon carries with him the screen image of an older, more thoughtful man. A brooding recluse, Morbius is isolated on his own island, free to experiment without society's strictures.

With regard to sexuality, Morbius is depicted as aberrant. He is long without a wife and has become cold and apparently emotionless. The fact that his Monster of the Id has been stirred up as much from jealousy over Altaira's infatuation with Adams and men in general as his wish to be left alone, is something dramatically understated due to the deletion of a revealing scene in which Morbius forces Altaira to choose between Adams and himself. His obsession to possess Altaira in all ways is, however, suggested when he demonstrates the Krell "brain power" device and materializes a three-dimensional holograph replica of

In the Krell laboratory, Adams and Altaira hold the dying Morbius, who has been defeated in his battle with his Id Monster.

his daughter: "It's alive because my daughter is alive in my brain from microsecond to microsecond."

In the depiction of Morbius, one can sense an intense distrust of the intellectual, particularly the scientist intellectual. Under the stable, peaceful surface of America in the Fifties, fears still simmered. In sf magazine stories of the time, as well as in various sociological studies (such as those of Vance Packard), it was advanced that such scientific developments as brainwashing, lie-detectors, computers, and subliminal advertising posed a threat to the freedom of the individual. On the other hand there was the presiding fear of Communism and annihilation during the McCarthy era. Science itself was a source of disturbance, but so too was passive, liberal intellectualizing. In the era when the derisive term "egghead" was coined (for any supporter of the academic Adlai Stevenson), physicist/scholar Robert Oppenheimer, the creator of the A-Bomb, became deeply distrusted and was fired as a security risk for being critical of the new H-bomb.

In some ways, Morbius represents the spirit of this peculiar dilemma, particularly in his disinclination to dispense Krell knowledge to Earth because he worries it could be dangerous in the wrong hands. Altair IV has turned into a paradise, a scientific utopia, but at the price of complacency in the face of evil. Morbius may have forgotten about his Id Monster, but it is inescapably there, awaiting release during an unwary moment. Even Robby, an arm of Morbius's genius, is immobilized at the vital moment when the Id Monster attacks Morbius in the lab; he is incapable of challenging the Monster because of those built-in restraints.

The doom of Morbius and the Krell is the fate of pure reason and intellect turned in upon itself (the Krell were actually experimenting with disembodied thought when they destroyed themselves). What then if the enemy attacks? It is made to seem both irony and poetic justice that the accumulated wisdom of Morbius and the Krell is destroyed by a kiss. The healthy eroticism of our boys in uniform awakens the sleeping beauty (one strand of fairy tale not analyzed away by the narrative) and brings down the wrath of the gods upon Prometheus.

To enjoy *Forbidden Planet* is not at all the same thing, however, as siding with Adams. While the film biases its point of view toward the homespun Fifties' values of the commander, it is really the contradictions of the movie that fascinate. We may fear the implications of the Krell's disembodied intellect, for example, but the camera lingers lovingly on the sensuous spectacle of their titanic underground machinery. Morbius may be painted, on the whole, in dark colors, but his home has seductive, cheerful beauty, and he does, after all, care about mankind's future. And then, of course, the movie's boldest stroke is in suggesting that the enemy lurks within each of us. The Monster of the Id neatly equates the rot from within with the enemy out there.

The scientifically achieved utopia promised for the future is seductively attractive, but may hold untold dangers for our safety. Whatever we do we must never relax our vigilance and sink into the quicksands of reflective inaction. In the last scene of the film, we watch Altair IV torn apart in a great holocaust—the price of complacent celebration is the annihilation we all fear. Our hope for the future, then, lies in the United Planets' expansionist policy ("the conquest and colonization of deep space") and with Commander Adams's strong, sensible line on intellectual outsiders: "We're all part monsters in our subconscious, so we have laws and religion . . . it will remind us that, after all, we're not God." In Commander Adams, more so than in Robby, we have the perfect embodiment of a superego equal to Morbius's id.

On the Beach:
A Renewed Interest

Stanley Kramer

In *On the Beach* (1959), we eliminated all life on the face of the Earth through the spread of radioactive dust following an atomic conflict.

At the time, the general public considered the nuclear issue a frightening subject. Yet most did not believe radioactive dust could travel through the atmosphere over the entire globe, as we depicted in the film. As a small commentary on the ways of the world, even many scientists in 1958 took issue with Harold Urey, Harrison Brown, and Linus Pauling for thinking that *On the Beach* spoke the truth. When Mt. St. Helens' ash traveled as far as Europe after the 1980 eruption, it certainly justified our fear that a megaton explosion—remember that a megaton is a hundred times more powerful than the atomic bombs dropped on Japan in World War II—could generate radioactive particles that could travel worldwide and destroy entire populations.

The picture was adapted from Nevil Shute's controversial 1957 bestseller about the aftermath of a nuclear war, when the few remaining survivors wait to die from radiation poisoning. There are never causes, only feelings involved when I select a subject to film. The scientist's reply when asked how the war started was something I *felt* deeply then—and *now*: "The war started when people accepted the idiotic principle that peace can be maintained by arranging to defend themselves with weapons they couldn't possibly use

without committing suicide." The theme had to be meaningful to us to be able to photograph people lined up for suicide pills; more than that, photographing empty streets in Melbourne and San Francisco, with its deserted Golden Gate Bridge, affected all of us making the film. What was the message of the picture we were making? I didn't

While Ava Gardner and Gregory Peck await direction, Stanley Kramer discusses a scene with Anthony Perkins.

Stanley Kramer produced and directed *On the Beach, Judgment at Nuremberg, Inherit the Wind, Guess Who's Coming to Dinner?, Ship of Fools, The Defiant Ones,* and *It's a Mad, Mad, Mad, Mad World.* He also produced such films as *The Men, High Noon, Champion,* and *The Caine Mutiny.*

American submarine commander Dwight Towers (Peck) walks through the nearly deserted streets of Melbourne.

know. I only hoped that the emotional impact of what we were presenting would convince people that we'd damn well better do something to assure our survival.

Topical films weren't the order of the day then, so I believe that the cast I assembled was as inspired by the picture's theme as I was. Gregory Peck and Anthony Perkins have always been socially conscious. Fred Astaire, who played the atomic scientist, gambled on a dramatic role. And Ava Gardner also accepted the challenge, even acting without makeup a good part of the way. We stayed fairly close to Shute's concept, but he may have complained a great deal more than was justified about one change we made. Shute refused to believe that with the world coming to an end, the American commander, played by Peck, would have an affair with the Australian lady, played by Gardner. I think Shute was wrong—Peck's memory of wife and children was not damaged; they were *dead*. It was sacrifice enough that Peck finally took the submarine home from Australia to satisfy his crew and left Gardner behind.

You might be interested in knowing that a State Department official told me twenty-five years ago that I couldn't photograph an atomic submarine at Pearl Harbor because the theme of *On the Beach* was the world's end. He thought I was taking myself and the film too seriously. There might be four or five hundred million casualties, but it wouldn't be the end of the world. I said then it was as near to the end as I'd like to get—I didn't get the submarine. (We used instead a British "Guppy" sub, revamped to look like the then-new atomic subs.)

When the film was released, we did make deep inroads into the consciousness of the masses— but we weren't as effective as we'd have liked. Too many people avoided the film because of its theme, and didn't see it until it played on television several years later. The critics were divided too: "another message from Kramer, taking a subject too seriously, the do-gooder at work, etc." or "good intentions swallowed by speculation." Today, the subject matter they debated then seems so in tune with the times that it is almost tame. During one recent twelve-month period, *On the Beach* was requested for screening no less than twenty-three times. Why? Probably due to the activism of citizens' groups, the clergy, and women's organizations in protest of the nuclear arms race. More than that, due to the progression away from the "cold war," during which period *On the Beach* was filmed, toward the threats and stances that have set the stage for the "hot war" today.

When you look at an old film, only the faults prevail. I think to myself that I should have cut out the farm scene or that I overplayed Ava Gardner; I wonder if the Salvation Army banner seen in the final frame, "There Is Still Time . . . Brother," offered enough hope. But the modern-day audience seems oblivious to my shortcomings. Astaire's explanation for how the war started provokes an extraordinary reaction in a modern audience—a visible and vocal reaction of recognition and awareness that this is *today*. The scientist goes on: "Some poor bloke probably looked at a radar screen and thought he saw something . . . he knew that if he hesitated one-thousandth of a second his own country would be wiped off the map, and so he pushed a button . . . and the world went . . . crazy." Do you remember the incident three years ago when a technician at one of our bases thought he saw something on the radar screen? According to the *New York Times*, we were just three minutes away from a retaliatory decision. Of course, it turned out to be false.

Right: In the nuclear sub, Towers, Lt. Holmes (Perkins), and the other men listen while physicist Julian Osborn (Fred Astaire) theorizes a possible scenario of how the nuclear war happened—his point is that because nuclear bombs existed their detonation was inevitable.

Below, right: On the beach. Towers and Moira (Gardner) try to put the horrors of the recent past and the near future out of their heads and have a romantic fling.

At any rate, *On the Beach* conjures up memories. Memories such as the Moscow premiere—one of many key cities in a same-night world premiere—and the discussion that followed with Russian directors, writers, poets, etc. They appreciated the film but insisted that if they had made it they would have provided a solution. I told them that if they would tell me their solution I would remake the film's ending.

"We know you Americans don't trust us," pointed out a Soviet director. "But, you see, we don't trust you either. Each time we discuss the matter—even ways and means to dissent from the policy of our own government, someone always reminds us: 'Who are the only people who ever dropped the bomb?'"

Now, that was a tough one to deal with—even twenty-five years ago. It is even tougher today when our administration reserves the right of first strike and talks of the possibility of a "limited nuclear war with the acceptance of twenty million casualties." At *On the Beach* screenings there are a lot of people who ask why our government thinks twenty million is a limit—why count only the result of a first impact? And what about the many disfigurements and mutations? They still show up in Hiroshima.

And whatever happened to the Nuremberg doctrine that thrust aside all Nazi excuses and justifications: "This we believe: in truth, justice, and the value of a human being."

But there's always a voice: "What about the Russians?" It seems to me they have the same problem, don't they? The Soviets know they will be exterminated with us by retaliation if they dare make reality of a threat. Yet, the more we build, the more they build. Ironically, any one of a number of crazy leaders on this earth is more likely to drop the bomb. There is no protection except joint protection. We are going to have to refuse to live by or under the threat. We need dynamic leadership—and no one is on the horizon. Former President Eisenhower was right: "It may be the people want peace so much that one

of these days government had better get out of their way and let them have it."

I go to *On the Beach* screenings to participate against the nuclear arms race. This has given me an activist stance during a period when my arteries are hardening and my hair falls like white snow on my barber's bib. I think survival is the most important political, social, and spiritual issue of the day. I look at the insurance charts on myself and I shrug. But for the sake of my young daughters, I bless the revelation that came to the Hunthausens and Judy Liptons of the world. They have verbalized the real evil of our times.

It is our destiny to solve the dilemma on every spiritual and moral basis known to man. We must neutralize the megaton, never use it again, stop the threats, and refuse to accept the possibility of a nuclear war. The old activists should come back out of the establishment and reactivate. There is more reason for them today than in the simple idea of resisting the wrong of Vietnam. And the ghetto philosophy and pollution still are with us—but they are hangers-on and second priority compared to the threat of megatonic holocaust that could wipe out civilization.

The Jules Verne Influence on *Voyage to the Bottom of the Sea* and *Five Weeks in a Balloon*

Charles Bennett

I hate to say it, but I detest all the present-day blockbuster "futuristic" space movies. I'm turned off plus when an air battleship about the size of Manhattan attacks a planet a million times its own size—with everything depending on the "brilliance" of people with names like Oztog and Yozed. (I feel sure that if we ever do become involved in an interplanetary war, one of our spacecraft will be commanded by a Smith or Jones.) I much prefer the science fiction classics to those films made today—like Jules Verne's *Journey to the Center of the Earth, 20,000 Leagues Under the Sea,* and *Around the World in Eighty Days,* all written nearly a hundred years before they were filmed.

Being an avid reader in my schooldays in pre-World War I England, I practically grew up on Jules Verne (1825–1905). I read everything he'd come up with, loved it all, but never realized that I was appreciating the major precursor of science fiction literature and, for that matter, science fiction film.

I became professionally involved with actual Verne material in 1961, when producer-director Irwin Allen asked me to write the screen adaptation of Verne's *Five Weeks in a Balloon* (1962). But in fact I'd had a brush with Verne the year before when Allen invited me to come up with an original story and screenplay for a movie about a super submarine of the future. The movie would

Charles Bennett wrote screenplays, alone or in collaboration, for *Voyage to the Bottom of the Sea, Five Weeks in a Balloon, The Lost World, Night of the Demon,* and the Alfred Hitchcock films *Sabotage, The 39 Steps, Young and Innocent, Secret Agent,* and *Foreign Correspondent.* He was the original author of *The Man Who Knew Too Much.*

be called *Voyage to the Bottom of the Sea* (1961), and the atomic sub would be named the Seaview.

Looking for ideas to help fill the blank pages in front of us, Allen and I ran every submarine movie we could put our hands on, including, of course, *20,000 Leagues Under the Sea* (1954). I'm sure most people remember the classic Walt Disney version of the story, with James Mason as the genius Captain Nemo, commander of a magnificent undersea craft called the Nautilus. When he had written the novel in 1869, Verne had been aware that submarines were in nothing more than an experimental stage. So his story, which was set in his own time, had been in a way his leap into the twentieth century. Rather than updating it to modern times, Disney wisely remained faithful to Verne's novel.

I also had had to subscribe to Verne if I were to deliver *Voyage,* which, let's face it, became a modern-day spin-off of *20,000 Leagues Under the Sea.* The existence of Verne's story was helpful to me, but it also posed a problem: How could I fashion a futuristic film of the twentieth century without stealing from a visionary writer of the nineteenth? As a start, *Voyage* had to be *my* type of story.

Over the many years I have achieved a certain reputation as a writer of suspense. Certainly suspense was essential to the films I wrote for Alfred Hitchcock in the Thirties. And I knew it would be essential to *Voyage.* But there is another element that has been fundamental to at least eighty

Left: In Voyage to the Bottom of the Sea, Commander Nelson (Walter Pidgeon) gives a tour of the nuclear sub, the Seaview, and shows the missiles that will be fired at the Van Allen radiation belt. Most interested is the female spy (Joan Fontaine) who is out to foil the mission.

Below: In a scene similar to the giant squid battle in Walt Disney's Jules Verne film, 20,000 Leagues Under the Sea (1954), Seaview men battle a giant octopus in Voyage to the Bottom of the Sea.

percent of my scripts, and *all* of my suspense films. My trump card is THE TIME LIMIT. The fight against an inevitable disaster becomes more exciting if time is running out: A fight against the tick-tock of the clock...suspense heightened by fleeting minutes or seconds.

Back in the early Thirties I wrote a cheaply made movie in which England was faced with a threat. Its title, *Warn London* (1934), suggests not only a suspense theme but more. Something terrible was about to hit London at a *certain* time—for the life of me, at this distance, I can't remember its nature, but it had to be averted... *before* time ran out. This suspense-time-limit angle was what I and Hitchcock would cash in on so successfully just one year later with *The 39 Steps* (1935). John Buchan, whose novel was our basis, hadn't caught up with the time-running-out element. And although Jules Verne was a master of adventure storytelling, he never caught up with it either, in *20,000 Leagues Under the Sea* or in his other books.

This then was the element that I needed to inject into my Verne-like storyline for *Voyage*, about an up-and-coming catastrophe that the Seaview—the greatest missile-armed craft to date—had to somehow circumvent.

Whereas Verne wrote about a future he predicted, I had to be satisfied with writing about the world of 1960 as I knew it.

My story concerned the world-encircling Van Allen radiation belt. It suddenly became ignited by a crashing meteor. The Earth was coming closer to death by the hour because of the blasting heat that had resulted. It was up to Seaview's Commander Nelson (Walter Pidgeon), aided by the brilliant Professor Emery (Peter Lorre), to save the day. It was decided that the only hope was to

fire a missile at the Marianas trench, the world's deepest hole in the far eastern depths of the Pacific, at a precise moment. Hopefully this would extinguish the belt's fire.

So that was to be my suspense angle: a time limit, worked out to the final few seconds when the belt would be vulnerable to a missile blast.

In spite of the protests of millions who believed that Nelson's efforts could only exacerbate the gruesome situation (even members of Nelson's own crew were skeptical) the sub took off, racing across the world. Now the story was stabbing into the future: pitting a missile against the immediate grimmer possibilities that could be out there in space. But in spite of the persistent intervention of "heavies," among them Joan Fontaine, who was aboard, the sub got through, fought a monster in the Marianas trench—just as the Nautilus battled a giant squid—and fired the missile, thus saving the Earth from incineration.

CHARLES BENNETT 121

Nonsense? Of course, but I like to think it's the kind of nonsense that Jules Verne would have gladly leapt into had he still been around.

Voyage to the Bottom of the Sea was a tough assignment, but luckily the movie did very well and led to an equally successful television series, for which I contributed many segments.

Months after finishing *Voyage,* I found myself involved in *actual* Verne, adapting *Five Weeks in*

Above: Peter Lorre, who appeared in five Charles Bennett-scripted films, played Professor Emery in Voyage to the Bottom of the Sea.

Below: Professor Furgeson (Cedric Hardwicke, center) has assembled his crew to spend Five Weeks in a Balloon. *The actors (L–R): Fabian, Barbara Luna, Richard Haydn, Peter Lorre, Barbara Eden, and Red Buttons.*

a Balloon, which he'd written in 1863. Jules Verne was supreme as an adventure writer, but he was never a humorist—unfortunate since it became apparent that *Five Weeks* could best be told on celluloid with comedy. I am not a comedy writer, but by adding an element or so of almost knock-about farce, the film came to life. Naturally, I also relied on my perennial standby, the suspense-time-limit angle, which Verne, as always, had not provided in his book. The following took shape.

It was 1863, with the slave trade in Africa at its height. It had suddenly become vital for England and good Queen Victoria to establish legal control over the Volga River territory of West Africa before the slavers could grab it in the name of Portugal and thus continue to thrive. It was known that the slavers were moving in fast and it seemed that the only hope lay with Professor Furgeson (Cedric Hardwicke). There was the wild possibility that he and his motley crew could navigate a passenger-carrying balloon across the four-thousand-mile expanse of northern African jungle, from the eastern island of Zanzibar to the Western Volga River. But even if this journey were possible—ballooning hadn't proven itself as yet—could it be accomplished in the five weeks' time required to plant the British flag ahead of the Portuguese slavers? Suspense—time limit.

While the adventure was complemented by a lot of humor provided by Red Buttons and my favorite actor, Peter Lorre, who played a comedic slave trader, Furgeson's balloon made it across Africa, beating the Portuguese slavers by a hairsbreadth. Up with the Union Jack, and the hell with slavery!

Gibberish? Summon M. Verne from the grave

The balloon is launched. This balloon was more elaborate than the ones used in other Jules Verne movie adaptations, Around the World in Eighty Days *(1956), and* Mysterious Island *(1961).*

and I'll offer him a welcoming hand. I've a feeling he'd only give me his okay.

And he'd say that we are still only at the beginning. He'd know. I can visualize him, with the possibilities of the universe opening up, outstarring *Star Wars* (1977), always jumping ahead. Many of his "images imaginaire," conceived in the mid-eighteen-hundreds, are by this time accepted as fact. Men have walked on the Moon. Men have been around the world, not in eighty days anymore but in something like eight hours. His journey to the center of the Earth hasn't happened yet, but tomorrow is at hand.

I can only begin to look into a future I'm sure Verne would have adored. So many impossible things have happened in the Verne hundred years. So many impossible things will happen in the next hundred. For example:

I can remember back in the late Twenties when authorities were screaming at the thought of placing radios into automobiles. It was insisted that car radios would distract drivers. They didn't. We haven't yet reached television delivery in cars except for passenger consumption, and we never shall unless some inventor produces an instrument that will eliminate the necessity of having the driver be at the wheel. Just drive by thought.

But surely it is only a matter of time before some form of device tuned into the brain—a Verne-like conception—will reduce thought into a conventionally procurable commodity. Thought influenced by some beam or other stimuli not yet dreamed of. I am not thinking in terms of Orwellian mind control. I believe there will always be freedom of thought, but I am almost equally certain that sooner or later it will be available as required. Let's say you seek a story notion: you press a button on some pocket-size instrument and an impulse will prompt a flow of ideas. Or you wish to know the innermost thoughts of some lovely lady: press another button and all those thoughts are known by you.

This button-pressing mechanism could work in more ways than just the personal one. Example: Press a button and up comes entertainment... selective, of course, but offering audible and even visual performance—only in the mind, of course, so as not to affect driving or, for that matter, dishwashing. Naturally, such a service will have to be paid for—commercialism will never die out—but probably the pocket instrument will take care of the situation, checking off the button pressings and coming up with the bill. One question remains: What kind of entertainment will the person behind the button come up with?

I believe in the future of entertainment. I believe entertainment will still exist in one form or another even among the survivors of what threatens to be the semi-final holocaust. The remnants of mankind will grope after laughter, romance, thrills (as though they won't have had enough of them) and, if possible, a means of escape. The art of story-telling will persist and I'm convinced that it will even continue to utilize my favorite ingredient, suspense. And I would like to think that the spirit of my favorite science fiction writer, Jules Verne, will still be peeping over the shoulders of writers for generations hence, giving his eternal inspiration, assistance, and blessing—as it did for me during my career.

CHARLES BENNETT　123

"The Seventh Victim" and *The 10th Victim*

Robert Sheckley

Omni asked me to comment on the depiction of the future in "The Seventh Victim" and in the film that resulted from it, The 10th Victim (1965). How do the story *and the movie compare? Is this violence a realistic portrayal of the future?*

I suppose I was chosen for the job because of my well-known connection with Robert Sheckley, the twenty-five-year-old author of "The Seventh Victim." Indeed, Omni may even have believed that I am that Sheckley.

This is not the case, however. That Sheckley has vanished into the mists of time. All that remains is me, a middle-aged American writer living in Paris who has access to an incomplete and badly faded set of Sheckley's memories.

The Seventh Victim," a short story first published in 1953, is set in a future in which war has been abolished. In its place, as sole outlet for human aggressions, is the government-sponsored Hunt. To participate, you must sign up for a package of ten. In five of them you will be a hunter, given the name, address, and photograph of your intended victim, and a period of time in which to kill him. In the other five you will be a victim, aware that you are being hunted, permitted to kill your hunter, but given no clues as to his identity. If you succeed in ten hunts, you can join the prestigious Tens Club.

Stanton Frelaine, the hero of "The Seventh

Robert Sheckley has written many science fiction novels, including *Dramoclese, Crompton Divided, The Robot Who Looked Like Me,* and *Immortality, Inc.* He wrote the short story "The Seventh Victim" and the screenplay for *Omega.*

Victim," is a smug bourgeois who sets off on his seventh hunt in much the same spirit as a man of our time going on a duck shoot. The Hunt is a brief moment of excitement in his humdrum existence and he intends to enjoy it to the utmost. He's put off for a moment when he discovers that his victim is a woman. But he knows this makes no difference. A kill's a kill; what's important is getting the job done and advancing yourself toward admission in the Tens Club. Frelaine, however, gets interested in Janet Marie Patzig, his victim. He falls in love with her. He becomes fascinated with watching himself fall in love with the lady he's supposed to kill.

The lady is watching, too. She's been counting on Frelaine's infatuation. When he declares his love she kills him, thus gaining admission to the Tens Club.

Ultimately this story is about love, and how, even in so calculating a creature as Stanton Frelaine, it can blossom forth, an inextinguishable impulse, whether to fulfillment or death. The Hunt is an ironic futuristic equivalent to the creative act—something that is not reasonable or politic; something that is done for its own sake rather than for the outcome.

A few years after its publication, the story was purchased as the basis for an Italian-made motion picture [directed by Elio Petri]. "The Seventh Victim" was put through some heavy changes to turn it into a multimillion-dollar vehicle for two superstars. Meek, middle-aged Stanton Frelaine became handsome, world-weary Marcello Pol-

letti, played by handsome, world-weary Marcello Mastroianni in a blonde wig. Tense, sad Janet Patzig turned into beautiful, blank-faced Caroline Meredith, played by Ursula Andress. The location of the Hunt was changed from grimy New York to glittering Rome. Most important of all, the central situation was reversed: Caroline became the Hunter out for her tenth kill, Marcello the victim on his seventh defense.

The switch seemed innocuous enough. Unfortunately it blew a hole in the story's underlying logic. "The Seventh Victim," a small ironic bourgeois comedy, was striving to become *The 10th Victim,* a fast-paced futuristic sex farce, and not quite succeeding.

Five screenwriters were employed to punch up the storyline. They labored mightily, and this is what they came up with:

Beautiful Caroline Meredith comes to Rome to bag her tenth victim. But she can't just step off the airplane and bag him because then we have no story. So Caroline has a sponsor, Ming Tea,

Above: Caroline (Ursula Andress), the hunter, zeroes in on Marcello (Marcello Mastroianni), the prey, and, naturally, the public and the media are on hand.

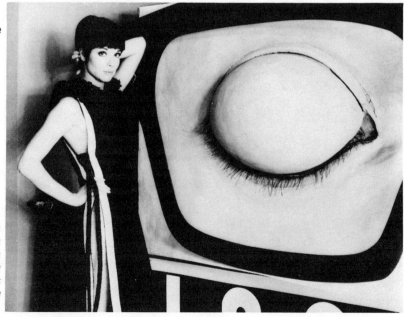

Right: Costar Elsa Martinelli (who plays Olga) poses for a publicity shot with one of the film's most intriguing futuristic elements.

Thoughts of killing Marcello fade away when Caroline and her intended victim fall in love.

which pays her to maneuver her victim into the Coliseum so she can shoot him on camera as the climax to the Ming Tea Variety Hour. Caroline flies to Rome with a gun, a TV crew and a tight shooting schedule.

In Rome, melancholy Marcello Polletti has just polished off his latest Hunter and is preparing to defend himself as a victim for the seventh time. Polletti's got problems. He's always broke since his job as guru to a group of sunset worshippers doesn't bring in much. He has a wife he's trying to divorce and a crazy mistress who alternates between wanting to marry him and trying to kill him. As if that weren't enough, Polletti is also the sole support of two aging parents whom he keeps hidden in violation of the Italian euthanasia law. Polletti's domestic arrangements take up most of his time and energy. He makes perfunctory attempts to prepare for the Hunt, but his mind isn't really on it.

Arriving in Rome, Caroline contrives to meet Marcello. Despite his hard-to-get manner and attitude of complete disinterest, we must assume that he's crazy about her. Otherwise, no plot. Caroline poses as a TV journalist. She'll pay Marcello for an interview, to be held in the Coliseum. At night. Marcello begins to suspect that all might not be kosher with the lady. Caroline begins to dig that Marcello might not be as dumb as he looks and acts.

There are complications and reversals. Marcello convinces Caroline not to kill him, but instead to... Actually we're not sure what Marcello has in mind because he never tells us—two weeks in romantic Capri at her expense, most likely—but Caroline knows what she wants. Marriage. Just like a dame, right?

In the last scene Marcello and Caroline fake Polletti's death and we cut to the happy couple escaping from the complications of Rome on an airplane bound for Rio. It turns out to be a special wedding flight. Caroline has arranged this, of course. But Marcello is still unsure about marriage. He points out that it could end their romance. Caroline is adamant, however, and there's a priest standing over Marcello with a bible in one hand and a .45 in the other. The ceremony is performed. Smiling, the priest takes aim and pulls the trigger. A bouquet of roses comes out of the end of his gun. Music up. Credits.

Let's leave aside any question of artistic merit. That's not for me or Sheckley to comment on. Let's return to the original questions: What about the depiction of the future in the two stories? What about the violence? How realistic is all this?

Neither story is "realistic." The very idea of a government-sponsored Hunt is wildly idealistic. No government, now or in the forseeable future, has or will have enough power and good sense to substitute limited personal warfare for wholesale holocaust. Politicians demand that everybody play their war games. Mankind is as likely to find a substitute for war as it is to find replacements for air, food, and water.

These stories aren't really about war, violence, or the future. "The Seventh Victim" is a commentary on love, the need for excitement and the inevitability of self-deception. *The 10th Victim* points out how difficult it can be to earn a living, how tiresome family problems can get, and how romance is always threatened by the long shadow of marriage, especially in Rome. "The Seventh Victim" is what we used to call "soft" science fiction, but I'd consider *The 10th Victim* sheerest fantasy. To claim that either story addresses the problem of violence is like saying that Swift's "A Modest Proposal" is about the eating habits of the Irish.

Marcello and Caroline team up.

Fahrenheit 451: From Novel to Film

Gerald Peary

It's an attractive image from thirty-one years ago, 1953: young Ray Bradbury sweating away at his typewriter on a dark, foreboding novel of the future,

Fahrenheit 451, while Joseph McCarthy is perspiring on TV, putting the screws to some squirming, frightened, bookish liberal intellectual. Imagine it: Bradbury looks up at the screen of his Motorola console, the size of a baby Frigidaire, and there's the Junior Senator from Wisconsin, all twenty-one frightening inches of him, running the country into the ground while Ike sleeps. Bradbury can't believe it, can't abide it, so it's back to his Royal upright to pound out his angry story of a passive, conformist, meek-as-mice society ruled by bookburners, by vengeful firemen invading the homes of vanishing eggheads.

There's more post-World War II America in *Fahrenheit 451* than the obvious anti-McCarthyist subtext. There's also what the author saw when he peered out the front door onto his anxiously upscale neighbors. Surely Bradbury was thinking Man in the Gray Flannel Suit as prototype for his futurist protagonist, the hangdog fireman, Guy Montag. Weary Montag commutes by rail by rote at the end of the workday, going from his alienating job in the city (as a nine-to-five bookburner) to his suburban home and pill-popping wife.

Less weighty things about 1953 life bothered Ray Bradbury too; and several of his cranky

Stars Oskar Werner (who plays Montag) and Julie Christie (who plays both Montag's wife Linda and his young friend Clarise). Both performers were considered superstars at the time and the film itself was considered a breakthrough for sf cinema into "respectability."

Gerald Peary is the film critic for *Flare*, Canada's fashion magazine, and is a contributing editor for *American Film*. He coedited the books *Women and the Cinema*, *The American Animated Cartoon*, *The Classic American Novel and the Movies*, and *The Modern American Novel and the Movies*. He wrote *Rita Hayworth* and was critic for Boston's *The Real Paper*.

irritations were slipped into *Fahrenheit 451,* as if they would linger on in the future. Someone in the novel is disturbed by the incessant playing of jukeboxes in cafes. Isn't that a thinly disguised author's complaint against 1953's boisterous new music, rock 'n' roll? Bradbury's stuffy aesthetic is manifested also by a sympathetic character's diatribe against abstract art: "That's all there is now. . . . A long time back pictures said things or even showed people." Presumably, as a writer philosophically committed to a narrative tradition, Bradbury was peeved by the voguish celebration in the early 1950s of Jackson Pollock and the Abstract Expressionists.

Fortunately, Bradbury kept such petty grumblings about the 1950s to a few sentences, so that, in the end, *Fahrenheit 451* is less a topical novel than a prophetic one, a projection of life in what seems to be (though the where and when are never pinned down) the twenty-first century USA.*

What's life like after 2001?

Most important, firemen run the town, serving as a vigilant Committee of Public Safety, "official censor, judges, and executors," making sure that the populace is happy—happily ignorant, without reading as a burden. The major job of firemen is bookburning. All houses these days are fireproof, and maybe they've always been so. Therefore, a popular rumor seems ridiculous: that there was a time in the not-so-distant past when firemen put *out* fires instead of starting them.

While firemen work, everybody else in *Fahrenheit 451* rides around town in hopped-up beetles. The minimum speed allowed is 55 in the city, so most people drive 100 mph through the streets. Billboards are 200 feet long to catch the attention of speeding autos.

Everybody lives in the city. Nobody goes out to the country. Nobody sits on grass or cares about trees and flowers. There used to be front porches, for reading newspapers and chats with the neighbors. Not any more.

There's a war going on, against some enemy— that's why planes fly overhead. So far, there have been two atomic wars, both started by and won by America. (Again, Bradbury doesn't name the country where his story takes place, but it's the USA all right.) A man named Winston Noble is the President, and people say that he is tall and handsome. In the last election, he appropriately defeated the candidate of the "Outs," who was a short man.

Teenagers ride around in automobiles in *Fahrenheit 451* killing passersby for kicks. There is another rumor: that sixteen-year-olds weren't al-

ways all violent. Again, nobody remembers except aging people on park benches. Who cares about them? For now, it's off to Fun Park, to "break window-panes in the Window Smasher place or wreck cars in the Car Wrecker place with the big steel ball." The children of *A Clockwork Orange.*

In *Fahrenheit 451,* Bradbury makes a few cursory attempts to blueprint, in scientific terms, his world of the future. Montag rides to work in an "air-propelled" train, and "jet cars" race on the boulevard. At Montag's house in the morning, toast is buttered automatically by a "spidery metal hand." And at the hospital, there's a new-fangled machine with an Eye to look into your stomach. Finally, there's the Mechanical Hound lurking about the fire station, sniffing out hidden literati.

But Bradbury is lousy at the science part of science fiction, as he always has been the first to admit, as ignorant of technology as he is suspicious of it. What other major novelist of the imagination could conjure up as silly a machine as the "spidery metal hand" above? Arthur C. Clarke? Isaac Asimov? Hardly. And only Bradbury could write naively, ingenuously, about a typed list of one million banned books on the wall of the *Fahrenheit* firehouse—poor secretary!—not realizing this information would be computerized.

Ironically, we should be glad that Bradbury came to *Fahrenheit 451* with an insecure vision of the future. He opted to play it safe, and make his world different, but not *that* different, from 1953. As a result, Bradbury's projection of 2001 and afterward emerges instead as a relevant commentary on our *present-day* world, more like the actual 1984 than George Orwell's *Nineteen Eighty-Four.*

What sage but Bradbury predicted the end of educational requirements in the 1960s, how the mandarin liberal arts community would cut its throat in the business-obsessed 1980s? A character in *Fahrenheit 451* looks back on the twentieth century: "School is shortened, discipline relaxed, philosophies, histories, languages dropped, English and spelling gradually neglected, finally almost completely ignored. Life is immediate, the job counts, pleasure lies all about after work."

And who but Bradbury saw ahead the abbreviated world according to Garfield and *USA Today* and *People* magazine? "Then, in the Twentieth Century, speed up your camera. Books cut shorter. Condensations. Digests. Tabloids. Everything boils down to the gag, the snap ending."

And who but Bradbury divined a New Age society of health food nuts and long-distance joggers and faddish diets replacing the bent-over, bespectacled wise of yesterday? "With school turning out more runners, jumpers, racers . . . and swimmers instead of examiners, critics, knowers, and imaginative creators, the word 'intellectual,'

*As much of *Fahrenheit 451* seems influenced by Orwell's *Nineteen Eighty-Four,* published four years earlier, one wonders if Bradbury intended to show what was happening in the western hemisphere in the year 1984, while Winston Smith opposed Big Brother across the Atlantic.—ed.

Firemen at work: The Captain (Cyril Cusack) looks on approvingly as Montag burns books (at a temperature of 451 degrees).

of course, became the swear word it deserves to be."

It is amazing to read in *Fahrenheit 451* of Montag's wife bedding down while wearing Bradbury's version of a 1980s Walkman, "an electronic ocean of sound, of music and talk and music and talk coming in, coming in on the shore of her unsleeping mind." Bradbury labeled his "thimble radios" by the brand name, "Little Seashells."

But *Fahrenheit 451* is almost prophetic in what it has to say about TV, all negative. By 1950, Ray Bradbury already had misgivings about America's novelty post-war enjoyment. His early short story, "The Veldt," was a cautionary tale about little children entertained in the nursery by a three-wall TV screen. Their favorite program is a documentary of lions feeding in Africa. Each time they watch, the program seems more "real," like those three-dimensional stuffed animals gnawing on their prey in the Museum of Natural History. One fine day, supper time on the African veldt, their parents disappear into the screen. The little children keep watching. . . .

In *Fahrenheit 451,* the three-walled TV screen is back with a vengeance. Montag's wife watches all day and all night.

"What's the play about?" Montag asks her.

"There are these people named Bob and Ruth and Helen," Helen replies. She has paid extra money to have someone named "Helen" in every program.

In the world of *Fahrenheit 451,* everybody swears by television, from laughing along with the Three White Cartoon Clowns as they chop each other's limbs off to reveling at X-ray shots of a lady smiling and drinking orange juice. Look at her delighted insides!

From the vantage of innocent 1953, of Uncle Miltie and *Your Hit Parade* and Dave Garroway and *Captain Video* and Bud Collier's *Beat the Clock,* and those McCarthy hearings again, Ray Bradbury looked glumly ahead to America hooked at home, under the spreading antennas.

And that's exactly where French director François Truffaut turned on his 1966 film of *Fahrenheit 451,* with a montage of TV antennas. . . .

With the extraordinary success of his first feature, *The 400 Blows,* at the 1959 Cannes Film Festival, Truffaut became an instant international directorial name. And immediately he began looking for new projects to match the success of his initial picture. Truffaut first read *Fahrenheit 451* in 1960, and began thinking about it for the screen. (He also considered Bradbury's *The Martian Chronicles.*) In 1962, Truffaut purchased the screen rights. He had just transformed David Goodis's hardboiled novel of Philadelphia hood-

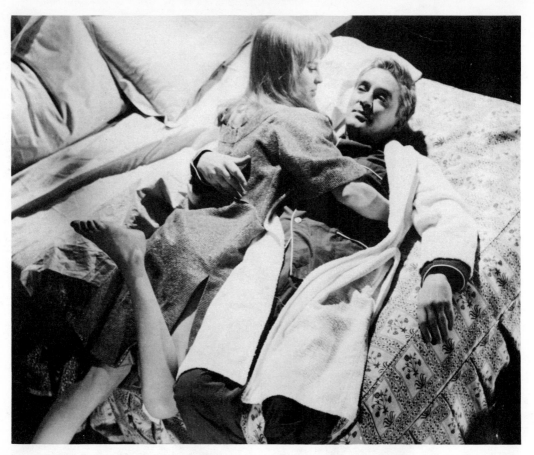

lums, *Down There,* into his brilliant French-set "noir," *Shoot the Piano Player* (1962). Why not a Gallic *Fahrenheit 451*?

Truffaut was aware of the challenge: No Frenchman had made a truly successful science fiction film since the pioneering silent days of Georges Méliès's *A Trip to the Moon* (1902). If even British directors could fashion science fiction movies for thinking people, such as *Village of the Damned* (1960) and *The Day the Earth Caught Fire* (1962), why not a cinéaste from the land of Jules Verne?

And why not an *arthouse* science fiction film? It had been decades since the silent classics of Fritz Lang—and Stanley Kubrick's *2001: A Space Odyssey* (1968) hadn't been made yet!

Additionally, the bookburning theme of *Fahrenheit 451* held personal meaning for Truffaut, who included Nazi documentary footage of bookburning in his 1961 film, *Jules and Jim.* While developing his script for *Fahrenheit 451,* Truffaut took note of a May 1964 bonfire in Indonesia of books disapproved by the Sukarno government. Back home in France, Truffaut was appalled by the DeGaulle government's banning of Jacques Rivette's anticlerical film, *La Religeuse,* based on Diderot's sensationalist eighteenth century tract about the oppression by the Catholic Church of a French nun. In his film of *Fahrenheit 451,* Truffaut's only topical reference was in regard to this infamous cinema incident: a burning by his firemen of a photo of *La Religeuse*'s star, Anna Karina, in her nun's habit.

When Truffaut purchased *Fahrenheit 451,* he envisioned making a high-tech extravaganza. He talked of "an sf film set in the future and backed by inventions and gadgetry and so on." But in the interim, *Dr. No* (1963) came to the screen, co-opting Truffaut's technological schemes, and in terms that Truffaut absolutely loathed. In 1979, Truffaut explained his repugnance for the first James Bond: "For me, the film that marks the beginning of the period of decadence in the cinema is...*Dr. No.* Until then the role of the cinema had been by and large to tell a story in the hope that the audience would believe."

So Truffaut changed his concept completely: *Fahrenheit 451* would be an adamantly *anti*-James Bond movie. As Truffaut approached shooting, he wrote in his diary kept for the magazine *Cahiers du Cinema:* "Obviously it would be too far to make *Fahrenheit 451* a period film, yet I'm heading in that general direction. I'm bringing back Griffith-style telephones, Carole Lombard-Debbie Reynolds style dresses, a Mr. Deeds-type fire engine. I am trying for anti-gadgetry....I am working contrawise, a little as if I were doing a James Bond in the Middle Ages."

James Bond by Robert Bresson. Truffaut's future is indeed a minimalist one, without even the

Although viewers probably are more attracted to rebellious book-reader Clarise than Linda (left, trying to seduce her husband), director Truffaut believed Linda's desire for sex was a quality that shouldn't too easily be overlooked. Right: The pathetic side of Linda: In her hedonistic pursuits, she overdoses on pills.

bare-bones technology in Bradbury. There are no speeding automobiles in the 1966 British production, no airplanes and helicopters in the air, and certainly no "spidery metal hand" to butter the toast. Even the ominous three-wall television from Bradbury's book has shrunk down (disappointingly) to an anemic screen, smaller than the video blowup for NFL Monday Night Football in any 1980s neighborhood tavern.

Also, Bradbury's ticky-tacky Mechanical Hound has been eliminated in the *Fahrenheit 451* movie. And there's no war, and there's no atomic explosion to contend with. In 1966, nobody cared about the day after, so Bradbury's post-Hiroshima apprehensions are trimmed away.

So what's left in the movie?

Best, there's the little red firehouse, and the little red fire engine racing through the street. They look like children's toys, the equivalent of an electric train set. It's a decidedly spooky sci-fi sigh to watch the firehouse door open and the diminutive vehicle come charging out, on the way to *start* a fire.

Truffaut's other set-design coup is the elevated monorail, what the director called "the only vaguely futuristic element in the film." The monorail was a real one, though no longer utilized. Truffaut had scouted it at Chateauneuf-sur-Loire, France, near Orleans. The interior of the monorail was likewise effective, a set designed by Truffaut to replicate the Paris Metro.

A colossal failure of *Fahrenheit 451* on film is Montag's home. The exterior is okay, a bland brick veneer, but the interior is characterless, saying nothing about either the Montags (Oskar Werner is Guy, Julie Christie is Linda) or the future. While shooting, Truffaut admitted the problem in his *Fahrenheit* diary: "Montag's apartment isn't a success.... Instead of the ancient-modern contrasts I had hoped for, what we have is just a rather good-looking middle-class interior, except for the wall television screens plus the few things I expressly asked for—the three old-fashioned telephones, the automatic doors, the electronic peep-hole in the front door."

In fact, the curve of the silent sidewalk that Montag takes from the monorail to his house every day says more, in a minimalist shot, about melancholy suburban life than all the contents of the Montag household, including what's on TV. And that's it for the look of the future, except for a certain Hitchcockian *Birds*-and-*Marnie* color that makes the world look strange. "This is really not a science fiction film," Truffaut told an interviewer about his *Fahrenheit 451*. "If I wanted that I would make it about two robots."

The movie is also wafer-thin thematically. Drained of its anti-McCarthyist and antibomb themes, *Fahrenheit* on screen has little to say, except that people in the future will be unblinking dead like actor Oskar Werner's comatose Montag, and that sex in the future will be further

In preparation for a scene set in the woods where the book people hide out, Truffaut explains to Werner what he wants. Throughout filming, the two had strong disagreements.

fetishized—witness the narcissists in the train stroking themselves and kissing their images, a scene invented by Truffaut. (Julie Christie's miniskirted bare legs are the only humanly alive image in the whole movie. Even Truffaut couldn't neuter Christie.*)

Truffaut has claimed that his film was inspired a bit by the French Resistance, and that Montag "is in the uncomfortable position of the character in the Gestapo who would like to get interested in the Resistance without it really upsetting his life." But anti-Vichy sentiments don't get to the screen, not until Truffaut's *The Last Metro* more than a decade later.

As for the bookburning motif, Truffaut ruins it by making the books-on-fire scenes so impersonal and arbitrary. The pages ignited have no special meaning for Truffaut, nor for a viewer. In his astute essay on *Fahrenheit 451,* "The Fire and the Future," critic George Bluestone observed: "For me, Truffaut's mistake was making a film about books instead of a film about movies. Not only does no one read in Montag's world, no one goes to the movies.... Especially since Truffaut, I sub-

*Truffaut made Montag's wife more sympathetic than she is in the book. In fact, because Linda (Helen in the novel) still desired physical pleasures Truffaut found her more interesting than Clarisse (also played by Julie Christie), the young renegade who has a purely intellectual, asexual relationship with Montag.—G.P.

mit, clearly loves movies *more* than he loves books." Bluestone's hindsight idea: that Truffaut's firemen go after secret movie theatres, where film buffs of the future hide out.

Ray Bradbury has always been diplomatic about the movie version of his novel, even praising Truffaut at length for how the film director handled Bradbury's difficult ending, at the encampment of book people. Yet reading between the lines of Bradbury interviews, one feels his disappointment, especially at Truffaut's failure to create a walking, talking future world. "The film is soft at the center," Bradbury told an interviewer. "Montag gets out of the city too easily. You can't get out of a major city running on foot that easily, especially in a time of helicopters and all sorts of devices, that can keep track of you."

François Truffaut was more blunt about *Fahrenheit 451*'s calamities on screen. Even before the film was released, he felt uneasy and unhappy about it. "Suddenly the construction of the story seems weaker than I thought it would," he said in his 1966 diary. "I like the film quite well when I see it in pieces or three reels at a time, but it seems boring to me when I see it from end to end."

That's been the verdict ever since: Truffaut's 1966 *Fahrenheit 451* is not bad enough to consider burning, but read Ray Bradbury's 1953 novel instead.

No Blade of Grass:
A Warning for Our Time

Cornel Wilde

In 1954 I was in London, working with my editor on the postproduction of my film *The Naked Prey* (1966). Frequently, when I had some spare time, I would drive over to Foyle's Book Store and browse through the shelves, looking for something exciting to read—hopefully the basis for another movie. One afternoon, I pulled out a paperback, *No Blade of Grass,* by John Christopher, who I knew was an excellent writer of imaginative thrillers.

I read the book straight through that night. It dealt with what could happen to the world if a new virus attacked and destroyed all grasses: famine, followed by anarchy, and a return to primitive, basic survival.

Christopher's story follows the flight from London of an average, well-off family (a father, mother, fifteen-year-old daughter, and ten-year-old son) after word leaks out that England has only a week's supply of food left. In the middle of the night, they leave in their fully packed station wagon, hoping to go to the farm of the father's brother in northern England. The brother had been forewarned and had stocked considerable food supplies—enough for a few years.

But the family is not alone. Before long, and throughout their harrowing trek, they must fight for their lives against looters, other escapees, and hungry, hard-eyed villagers, who take their car, weapons, and food, and order them to move on.

Early in their odyssey, they add an elderly sharpshooter from a gun shop to the family group. They find him to be the perfect example of a man who will survive at all costs. The sharpshooter is cold and ruthless, the man of the hour.

Along the way, they also join forces with a large number of other desperate, honest folk who have armed themselves and will kill rather than be killed. Together they make their way north, enduring perils and hardships at every turn, hoping to find salvation at journey's end. Until the very end, the novel is a breathlessly exciting and logical thriller about a topic that greatly interested me.

A nature lover all my life, I had a keen interest in ecology and was by this time seriously concerned about our environment. I had read Rachel Carson's *The Silent Spring,* and had been appalled by what I had learned. I had noticed the absence of the robins that had always arrived punctually every spring in my garden. I kept finding birds' eggs in the trees and shrubbery, one after another cracked and spoiled before they could be hatched. This was the result of pesticides, especially DDT, which the birds had ingested along with their daily diet of worms. The poisons had accumulated in their bodies and caused the egg shells to be too thin and weak to withstand the hatching process. At our beaches, the impressive flocks of pelicans were gone, also because of DDT. Tide waters, lakes, rivers, and even the great oceans were becoming polluted; and so was our air.

When I read *No Blade of Grass,* I saw the

Cornel Wilde directed *No Blade of Grass,* and both directed and starred in *Maracaibo, Storm Fear, Sword of Lancelot, The Naked Prey, Beach Red,* and *Shark's Treasure.* His many starring films include *A Song to Remember, Forever Amber, At Sword's Point,* and *The Big Combo.*

opportunity to use it as the basis for a powerful adventure film with an ecological warning to the world. As soon as I could, I made inquiries about the rights to the book. I was extremely disappointed to find that MGM had bought the film rights, as well as sequel rights, television rights, etc. I had to wait. In 1969, I read that MGM had a new head of production, Herb Solo. During the few years that had passed, I had read nothing at all in the trades about *No Blade of Grass,* so I suspected that MGM had been unable to get a satisfactory screenplay written. I telephoned Solo, an intelligent, charming man, and told him of my interest in *No Blade of Grass,* and that I had a new, topical approach to the property. We made an appointment for the following week.

I was well prepared for the meeting. I had, for years, done prodigious reading in ecology and had many ecological facts at my fingertips. Also I had a fifteen-page treatment I'd written with me in my briefcase. But I didn't take it out. Instead I talked to Solo and his creative assistant, Russ Thatcher, for an hour straight, telling the story, but with my changes and additions. They were impressed and asked me to turn in a script.

I chose a young English writer to do the screenplay, but the studio did not like the result. I told them I'd be happy to write my own version, if they would give me a month or two. It was agreed and I went to work. Fortunately, they liked the new version and, with a happy heart, I went into production in England in the spring of 1970 and shot into early summer.

My approach to the property was to make it contemporary in fact and feeling, with *pollution* the piece's villain. The film would begin with footage of pollution from all over the world—on land, in seas, and in the air. Over this, the credits would play. Thus, the audience would be well prepared for the premise. In my version, the lethal virus would *not* be a happenstance, but a result of man's heedless assault on the environment; pollution was its source. Whereas in the book, the virus was deadly only to grasses, in my film it would also destroy *grains.* One season of such a crop failure could produce practically instant, worldwide famine.

I changed the elderly sharpshooter of the book to Tirrie (Anthony May), a young "mod" who'd apprenticed at the gun shop. He is a crack shot and enjoys the power a gun gives him. He joins the family—Nigel Davenport and Jean Wallace played the parents, John and Ann Custance— and soon asserts his right to the fifteen-year-old-daughter, Mary (Lynne Frederick), as the "best man to protect her" in this new world of anarchy, rape, and pillage. Another new element I added, in keeping with changing times, was a marauding, well-armed, vicious motorcycle gang.

There was also a childbirth. Actually, there were two. One involved a young couple who had joined the fleeing families. The wife is only about seven months pregnant, but the arduous journey brings on premature labor. With the assistance of Ann and John, she gives birth, after excruciating labor pains, in the barn of an abandoned, fire-

Left: Ann and John Custance (Jean Wallace, director Wilde's wife, and Nigel Davenport) lead their daughter Mary (Lynne Frederick) and many desperate people northward, hoping to find safety and food.

Right: The journey is filled with encounters with people only concerned with their own survival.

gutted mansion. But the baby is dead—pollution was the indirect cause. This childbirth scene is intercut with Ann's recollection of the birth of her own daughter, Mary, in a hospital delivery room, white and gleaming, with an obstetrician, a nurse, and all the other civilized advantages. I wanted to show that a pollution-bred famine would, in a matter of days, destroy not only food but also the most important, taken-for-granted gifts of civilization.*

I was surprised by audience reactions to the childbirth scene. At sneak previews, some older people, especially men, were upset by the graphic reality of the sequence; but young people, although moved by the tragedy, felt no revulsion. Ironically, the younger viewers had seen childbirth films in school, while older viewers had never seen an actual childbirth.

As in the novel, the journey is filled with danger, death, and many brutal examples of man's inhumanity toward his fellow man in a lawless world. In the final sequence, the family arrives at the brother's farm. About fifty people are with them. But John's brother David (Patrick Holt) informs them that he has taken in so many of his neighbors that he can accommodate only John's fam-

*We photographed an *actual* birth (with a baby emerging from the womb) for the hospital scene, through arrangements with a pregnant woman and her husband. It was done in a nearby hospital and our props and wardrobe were properly sterilized. The actual birth was intercut with the acted birth in the barn. (The production paid all the expenses of the mother. I also delighted the couple by giving them a 16 mm copy of the sequence.)—C.W.

ily. So John has to choose between the safety of his family and loyalty to his fellow travelers, who had fought and struggled side by side with him. He chooses the latter, on principle.

John and the others fight their way onto the barricaded farm, with the help of the mod sharpshooter. Inadvertently, Tirrie kills the brother. So the victory is a tragic one, the final price of man's greedy folly in destroying his environment. The picture ends with the two warring factions joining together to live on the farm, not knowing what the future will bring or, indeed, if there will be a future at all.*

At one of the earliest openings of the picture, at the five-thousand-seat Science Theatre in Toronto, there was a question-and-answer session following the screening. The panel consisted of ecologists, conservationists, officers from government health and welfare agencies, and myself. One of the first questions the audience asked an eminent ecologist and editorialist: "Do you think this film is overdramatized to shock people?" His answer was: "Quite the contrary. I look on this film as a prophecy. In my opinion this is exactly what could happen, and people had better believe it."

In producing and directing *No Blade of Grass,* I made every attempt to show only what seemed absolutely real and logical. Some of the elements in the film were based on historical precedents,

*I had wanted to film an additional scene, taking place one year later. A girl discovers a new blade of grass growing in a barren field, signifying there was hope for recovery. Unfortunately, I hadn't the budget to do it.— C.W.

and others on logical deduction and extension of fact. Historically, famines have bred anarchy, and anarchy has always resulted in mass killings, rape, pillage, and the loss of human rights and basic dignity.

During production, some eerily coincidental events occurred. In the film, as previously mentioned, the cause of the famine is a virus mutation that attacks all grains and grasses and for which there is no control. In the summer, during the final days of shooting, there were headlines in the British press about the fungus blight that was devastating to the United States' corn crop, the biggest of all grains. There were full-page articles about it in *Time, Newsweek,* etc. The London *News* stated "BLIGHT MOWS DOWN $5 BIL-LION U.S. CORN CROP....PRICES OF ALL GRAINS SOAR BECAUSE OF FEARS THAT THE BLIGHT MIGHT ATTACK OTHER GRAIN CROPS."

The fungus was of a new type—which none of

the usual measures could control. Top scientists had been called to Washington by President Nixon to discuss the emergency situation. Many farmers lost their entire crops. Some states, like Wisconsin, estimated they would lose more than 25 percent of their corn crop. Well over $1 billion worth of damage was done.

One newspaper item I came across advised that the fungus be controlled by burning the affected areas—*exactly what we had already shot in the film!* On November 2, I saw a small article with a Mississippi dateline that stated that the corn blight had spread to wheat and oats and that the spores of the fungus were borne by the wind—just as it is in *No Blade of Grass!* If the blight had hit rice and wheat as well as corn, especially in Southeast Asia, much of the world would have had the same conditions depicted in the motion picture.

In the film, as anarchy erupts, there is an attack on the band of fleeing families by a motorcycle

world today, there will undoubtedly be more such outbreaks.)

When a typhoon struck Pakistan not long before the start of filming, the horrifying tragedy showed what can happen to people when they are thrown back to basic survival. Starving mobs attacked helicopters that brought food. The stronger took several bags of rice, the weaker got none: they were left trampled and crawling on the ground to starve to death. Underneath our veneer of civilization, the basic survival instincts have not changed much.

All it takes is one major destructive element to overturn the ecological balance. The corn fungus, for example, could have been such an element. Today, it could be the hothouse effect, caused by excessive carbon dioxide in the air and resulting in the melting of polar ice; or untimely rainfall (which we've been having) in the "bread basket" Midwest for three or four years in succession; or frigid temperatures in the great agricultural areas; or an increase in acid rain and ocean pollution, killing fish by the millions, which has already happened from San Francisco Bay to Pensacola, Florida; or drought, which occurred recently in this country and has been devastating Africa in recent years; or the proliferation of nuclear plants, which use cold water for cooling their apparatus, and send it back to rivers and oceans *hot,* which increases the toxicity of pollutants and encourages blue algae, which, in turn, uses up the oxygen the fish need; etc., etc.

Before *No Blade of Grass* was filmed, a great deal had been written and said on the subject of ecology and pollution. There had been marvelous documentaries on television, books, and articles. These caused concern and discussion but they did not, I felt, involve people emotionally, subjectively, and personally enough so that they would identify with the situation. *No Blade of Grass* was a hard-hitting film, factual and semidocumentary in approach, with one objective: to show audiences what could happen to all of us, not to someone else, but to *us,* and not in the year 2000, but any time now.

No Blade of Grass was made in the hope that it would remain fiction instead of become a reality. But right now, the odds are not good. World population has been rising at an alarming rate, especially in the underdeveloped countries that cannot afford expensive, modern agricultural techniques. United Nations studies have shown that a third of the world exists under conditions of hunger and starvation. A recent article in the Los Angeles *Times* stated: "If present trends continue in world hunger for another twenty years...the number of severely undernourished people will grow from *450 million to 685 million.*"

I would like to see *No Blade of Grass* released again, in theaters, on television, and on cassettes. It might drive home a vital point about survival better than a thousand words.

gang. By another strange coincidence, while we were shooting this big and difficult sequence during Easter week, the British newspapers carried headlines: "MOTORCYCLE GANG WRECKS TRAIN," "BATTLES IN THE TOWN OF SOUTHEND," "POLICE ROUTE SKINHEADS AT RESORTS," "BRIGHTON INVADED." The gangs attacked men, women, and children on holiday, bombarding them with rocks and bottles in restaurants, and they terrorized townspeople, as well. In Brighton alone, over five hundred cars were vandalized in one night. And all of this happened during general conditions of law and order!

In the film, a newscast mentions cholera breaking out in the city of Leeds. Before the film was in release, cholera was in the news for the first time in years when there were severe outbreaks in Africa, Egypt, and other countries in the Mideast. At one point, Turkey closed its borders as a safeguard. (With the polluted conditions of the

A New Beginning on *Terminal Island*

Stephanie Rothman

The future may be a great place to visit, but I wouldn't want to live there. Outer space swarms with hostile aliens and the planets are perpetually at war, although why they are warring is unclear, since despotism seems to be nearly everyone's favorite form of government. Even on that rare occasion when there is no war, no one is left in peace. Scientists are destroyed by the ungrateful monsters they create; machines bearing grudges rise up and enslave their masters; and nauseating organisms invade, mate with, and/or devour anyone who is left. No one ever collects stamps, rakes leaves, or waits in an unemployment line. Who can blame them? Something is always out there waiting to attack.

Yes, the future is a dangerous place.

Of course this is an exaggeration, yet there are a substantial number of films whose narratives include these ideas. Why? No doubt for such mundane reasons as feeding the audience hunger for chills and thrills, or imitating whatever is the hot commercial formula of the hour. There is also another possibility: Perhaps nightmare utopias are easier to imagine than benign ones. Filmmakers are prisoners of their age like everyone else, and the twentieth century, the age of genocide and nuclear holocaust, provides ample reason for pessimism about the future.

But these grim visions, these projections of our fears about our own human nature, raise an interesting question. Are we so unadaptable that we are doomed to repeat the errors of the past,

Stephanie Rothman directed *Terminal Island, The Student Nurses, The Velvet Vampire, It's a Bikini World, Group Marriage,* and *Working Women.*

continuing to wage war in space as we did on earth and to recklessly unleash destructive forces that we cannot control?

Terminal Island is a film that rejects this deterministic view of human nature. The future there is dangerous too, but the possibility of change, including change for the better, survives. Because this idea appears in a context of violent acts and words, occasionally interrupted by low comedy, this film has been called everything from an exploitation cheapie to *Lord of the Flies Visits Devil's Island.*

The story itself was suggested by the long-existing public resentment over the cost of caring for criminals with life sentences. Maybe you have even heard someone say that these murderers should all be dumped on an uninhabited island, left to fend for themselves, and forgotten. Well, in *Terminal Island* it happens.

Made in 1973 on a very low budget, the film lacks dazzling special effects or elaborate production design. Many scenes occur in outdoor settings designed solely by the last ice age. No doubt more time and money would have yielded a fancier film, but not, I think, an essentially different one.

The story takes place in the near future, opening with an eyewitness news report in which an off-screen reporter asks people on the street what they think of Terminal Island. Mostly, they think it is a good idea.

Some newswriters see this report at a television station as they prepare a program on the island's

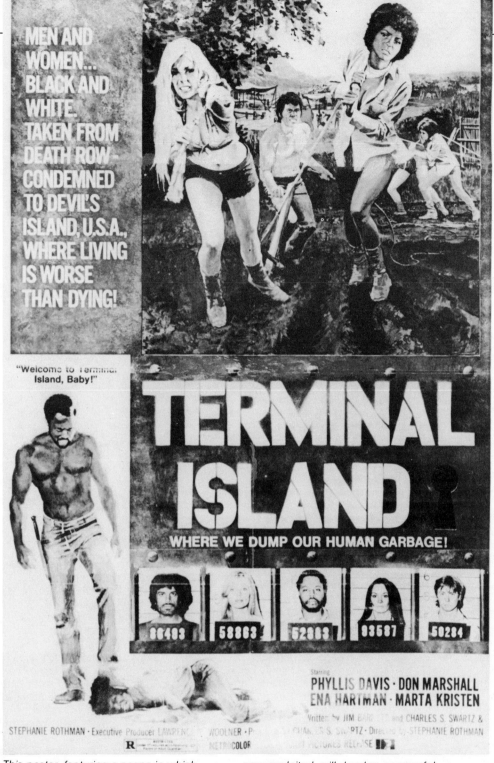

MEN AND WOMEN... BLACK AND WHITE. TAKEN FROM DEATH ROW CONDEMNED TO DEVIL'S ISLAND, U.S.A., WHERE LIVING IS WORSE THAN DYING!

"Welcome to Terminal Island, Baby!"

TERMINAL ISLAND

WHERE WE DUMP OUR HUMAN GARBAGE!

86403   58863   52803   88587   50284

Starring
PHYLLIS DAVIS · DON MARSHALL
ENA HARTMAN · MARTA KRISTEN
Written by JIM BARNETT and CHARLES S. SWARTZ &
CHARLES S. SWARTZ · Directed by STEPHANIE ROTHMAN

STEPHANIE ROTHMAN · Executive Producer LAWRENCE WOOLNER · P
R   METROCOLOR

This poster, featuring a scene in which women prisoners Lee (Marta Kristen, L) and Carmen (Ena Hartman) are treated like cattle by male inmates, reveals some of the harsher realities of Terminal Island. But from this hell on Earth, populated by the discarded and now exploited, will develop a peaceful society, distinguished by sexual and political equality. To the left on the poster, Carmen endures rough treatment from Monk, played by Roger E. Mosley. At the end, even he is forgiven.

Sadistic, crazy, self-appointed dictator Bobby (Sean Kenney) dishes out punishment to his uncooperative mistress, as part of a plan to draw the rebels out of hiding. Terminal Island is, in part, about women who refuse to stay in the "place" men such as Bobby have set aside for them.

first anniversary as a prison. They also review some file tape on its history. When the United States Supreme Court ruled the death penalty unconstitutional, Californians overwhelmingly voted to send the state's first-degree murderers into lifelong exile on an empty Pacific island. There is no possibility of escape, since its surrounding waters are mined and monitored by radar. Periodically, some basic supplies are delivered. These deliveries and the arrival of a new prisoner are the only contact with the outside world. Because it is the end of the line for anyone who goes there, this lonely knob of land is popularly known as Terminal Island.

The latest prisoner to be sent is Carmen Sims (Ena Hartman). The last piece of footage the

newswriters see shows her leaving the courthouse after her final appeal has been denied. Carmen does not go gently. She smashes an aggressive photographer's camera before being dragged away. But the photographer's loss is the newswriters' gain. Her flare-up is a welcome little nugget of sensationalism that they can mine to hold audience interest until the next commercial.

Carmen's arrival on Terminal Island is not too promising. The first prisoners she sees are corpses floating in the surf, and the first live one she meets, a distraught doctor (Tom Selleck), invites her to kill him. Even this doesn't quite prepare her for her introduction into island society when she arrives at the prisoners' inland camp. Before a listless assembly of her future colleagues and neighbors, she is robbed and beaten by a thug named Monk (Roger E. Mosley).

Life is mean and short on Terminal Island if you don't learn your place. The only social division that counts is between the strong and the weak. Predictably, the strong have most of the property and the weak do most of the labor. Race has no bearing on this division. Blacks, whites, and Asians belong to both groups, and I suspect this racial mingling was the reason that the film was banned in the Republic of South Africa.

Carmen's place is at the bottom of this pecking order along with the island's few other women, who are all doubly enslaved, forced to work like beasts of burden by day and sexually service the men at night, which sounds to me a lot like a job description for the position of traditional wife in any patriarchal society.

Bobby (Sean Kenney) and Monk, the bullies who orchestrate all this misery, share a cozy symbiosis based on Monk's brute strength and Bobby's vicious cunning. But they haven't the knack to run a thriving tyranny. Murder, suicide, and disease have all taken their toll. Nearly half of those originally sent to the island have died or disappeared. History demonstrates, I think, that there is a limit to how violent a society can become before it destroys itself. Bobby and Monk, who probably failed History, have also failed to grasp that enduring power is based on more than violence.

Yet even in a land of killers there are variations in character and temperament. While they have all killed, each one has done it for a different reason, and some never want to do it again. In the hope of leading a saner life, a few tried to revolt against Bobby and Monk. When they failed, they fled into the island's wilder parts where, led by a man named A.J. (Don Marshall), they have become nomads, living off the land and whatever they can grab in lightning raids on the camp. While their revolt marked their political awakening, their political education is still incomplete. They have not yet learned that their freedom sets a dangerous precedent that threatens Bobby and Monk's tyranny over the other prisoners.

But Bobby knows it. For protection he decides to build a stone bunker in which he and Monk can hold out against any future attack or revolt. When construction begins, Carmen is yanked off her regular job, pulling a plow like an ox, to lug heavy rocks for the walls. She literally works her fingers to the bone as the rocks abrade her bleeding hands because Monk won't let her stop to bandage them. All suffering in the camp is treated with equal apathy. So is death. In a Terminal Island burial the hapless corpse is flung into the sea, while someone mutters "good riddance" as a final benediction.

Then, just when Carmen accepts that nothing will change, everything changes. A.J. and the other nomads kidnap the women. It is an act born of defiance and sexual hunger. The women enjoy their liberation only briefly before one of the nomads argues they should control them the way Bobby and Monk did. Carmen, who has resourcefully lifted A.J.'s knife, holds its blade to the throat of the nearest man and vows to cut it open if anyone tries to enslave her again. Her argument wins. What the rest of them want, says A.J., is for the women to pull their own weight.

That is how democracy comes to Terminal Island; not out of justice but necessity.

The resultant division of hunting, gathering, and other labor is based on interest and ability, not gender. Since they are so few, the nomads can't afford the wastefulness of strict sex role divisions. With more hands to share the work, and share it more equitably, life becomes easier for everyone. Bonds of friendship and affection develop; sometimes they are sexual, sometimes not. There are personality conflicts too, but group pressure and mediation keep them within bounds. Gradually, without consciously intending to, this odd assortment of people begins to act like a family.

Once the bunker is finished, Bobby and Monk move to retrieve the women and crush the nomads. In a surprise attack, Monk and his men kill several of them. Those who escape draw even closer together and, unlike the numb mass in the camp, they mourn their dead and bury them with dignity.

The nomads' political education is now complete. They realize they cannot coexist with tyranny and that this attack is merely the opening skirmish in a war they can only hope to win if they win it quickly. Outnumbered and underequipped, they have no use for that peculiar tradition of war in which men are trained and armed to defend themselves, while women must remain untrained, unarmed, and defenseless. In this family, everyone prepares for combat.

An arms race begins and the nomads use every resource at hand. Carmen brews some poison, which her voodoo-practicing mother had taught her to extract from plants, for use on darts and spears. A woman named Lee (Marta Kristen), an ex-chemist and terrorist, discovers an abundance of natural ingredients for making gunpowder, which the nomads laboriously produce in enough quantity to make homemade grenades.

Bobby goes after more sophisticated weapons. He and his men entrap and kill the prison guards who deliver supplies, to get their guns and ammunition. With these and the bunker, Bobby is convinced he and Monk will be invulnerable to any threat. Luckily, the nomads witness this theft and get a gun of their own by picking off one of Bobby's men with a poisoned dart. With this and some gasoline Bobby overlooked, they manage to partially redress the balance of firepower and are now ready for war.

Nomads of both sexes attack at dawn, momentarily catching the camp unguarded. But it soon rallies and both sides fight and die until the only operational weapon left is the gun Bobby fires from the bunker. The nomads' last hope is the gasoline they pour down a water trough leading

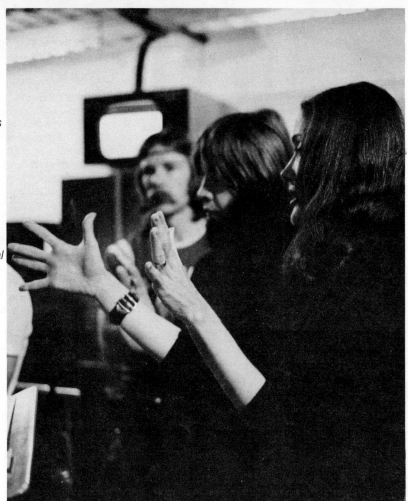

Stephanie Rothman directs an early scene that is set in a television control-room. *Terminal Island* is consistent with her other films in that it is about several men and women who unite, then live together as friends and lovers without sexual distinctions being made, or infighting and petty jealousies developing. Her ideal world is one of equality and harmony.

into the bunker. Their tactic works. The gas burns its way into that ammunition-packed stronghold, causing a fiery explosion that barbecues Bobby and blinds Monk.

But even killers tire of killing and so the survivors build a pacific new society, located somewhere between tyranny and chaos. Victors and vanquished alike are kinder to each other; Monk, now blind and relatively helpless, is well cared for. One of the women becomes pregnant (Phyllis Davis), bringing the promise of new life. And when the doctor—the very one who invited Carmen to put him out of his misery when she first arrived—is unexpectedly pardoned and given a chance to go home, he refuses. Concealing his identity, he sends back word of his own death. Because he rallied to the side of the nomads and fought along with them in the final showdown, Terminal Island is now precious to him and has become his home.

What does all this bondage and bloodletting have to do with the future of us all? Only this: Human nature is contradictory and in its contradictions lies our hope. *Terminal Island* is not the story of a utopian community built on a bedrock of ideology, but of how a group of antisocial people rediscover their own social needs, needs for companionship and cooperation that exist within us all.

George Bernard Shaw believed that no specific virtue or vice in a human being implies the presence of any other specific virtue or vice. He didn't believe in writing anyone off and neither do I. Just as the dark side of human nature did not prevail on Terminal Island, it need not dictate the character of future societies if we struggle to prevent it.

What, if anything, can filmmakers do about this, so that as we advance into space in greater numbers, we don't repeat the mistakes we have made on earth? Instead of making films glorifying wars in distant galaxies, it would be far more valuable if at least a few made films exploring the real threat of war in near space.

But can we afford to wait for this to happen when this threat is now almost a reality? Time is running out. Therefore, dear reader, my modest proposal is that we all act now to throw out of office any head of state who even *dares to think* of putting weapons in space.

And may the future have mercy on us all.

A Cannibalized Novel Becomes *Soylent Green*

Harry Harrison

As is standard Hollywood practice, the author of the book upon which this film is based was treated shabbily. All the usual tricks were used: a dummy company was set up to disguise the fact that it was really MGM buying the film rights; a contract was drawn up to prevent the author from having any control over the screenplay—and, of course, creative bookkeeping made certain none of the film's profits reached the author. But these sordid facts are of importance only to the well-screwed author; let us put them aside and look instead at the transition from book to film, since this is where the heavy hand of corporate filmmaking is so revealing.

The originators of the film, its star Charlton Heston, and its producer Walter Seltzer had been pressing MGM for years to make a film on the theme of overpopulation based on my novel *Make Room! Make Room!*. (That they neglected to inform me of this fact is part of the author-screwing syndrome: see paragraph 1.) MGM, in its infinite wisdom, thought this theme of little importance. So in an attempt to breathe life into the "inconsequential" topic, the film's originators introduced the theme of cannibalism: "soylent green," the food that the authorities give the masses, is made of human remains. Heads nodded in high places at the studio, agreements were signed—and the film went into production.

This is when I came onto the scene, to be instantly impressed by two inescapable facts: the truly professional ability of everyone connected with the making of the film and the truly appalling quality of the script, which transmogrified, denigrated, and degutted the novel from which it had been taken. That a successful film was made despite what might be considered a major obstacle can be credited to the art and set designers, the director Richard Fleischer, and to the fine actors (as well as to, I submit with suitable humility, the strength of the novel).

Although forbidden by contract to make any changes in the script, I nevertheless pointed out a number of inaccuracies and mistakes I discovered. Credit goes to the filmmakers for taking instant action on them. The film's opening is a prime example. In the original script the action began in Manhattan, no date given. I pointed out to Walter Seltzer that my novel was special specifically because it took place in the very near future, at the turn of the century. By ignoring this element, the film would lose the sense of immediacy and relevance for which the rights to my book had, presumably, been purchased in the first place.

Soon after acting upon my remarks, Walter chided me because I had made him spend a lot of money. It proved to be money well spent—on Chuck Braverman. His impressive opening montage, comprised of still shots tracing the settling and growth of the USA, ending with the overpop-

Harry Harrison wrote the novel *Make Room! Make Room!*, which was made into the movie *Soylent Green*. Formerly the editor of *Science Fiction Adventures, Nova, Amazing Stories, Year's Best SF,* and *The Year 2000,* he has written many short stories, including "Rock Diver," his first, and more than twenty novels, including *Deathworld, The Stainless Steel Rat, Captain Universe, Skyfall* and *Bill, the Galactic Hero*.

ulated and polluted New York City, firmly places the film in time.

There are other examples of the filmmakers' dedication. When I was shown the set for the "meatlegger" sequence I was suitably impressed. However, I thought that the pile of plastic bags was out of place since plastic is a petroleum product and all of the world's petroleum had been used up by this time. The bags were instantly whisked away.

I propagandized everyone in sight, from grips to actors, by giving them copies of the original book. When Chuck Connors got his, he called across the set to the director, "Hey, Dick, why aren't you using this title instead of the crappy *Soylent Green*?" The answer, which Fleischer perhaps did not know, was the decision made in high places that my title might be associated with a long-dead TV series named "Make Room for Daddy." Moral: when you throw away a good title you always get a bad one.

Real evidence of the dubiety of the screenplay was driven home to me when I overheard a remark made by Edward G. Robinson to the director. His worry was a simple one: There was nothing in the script that gave him any idea of what his role was to be. Summoning up my courage I introduced myself and offered to provide answers about his character. He ignored my rudeness, invited me to lunch with him, then listened closely when I explained the character he played as I had visualized him in the book: Sol is the sole survivor of the good days, the only

person who had lived in the world of plenty. He can survive in this new world of pollution, overpopulation, and chronic food shortages. That doesn't mean he has to like it.

This conversation led, a few days later, to an act of cinematic creation that it was my privilege to witness. They were shooting a key scene where Sol and Thorn (Heston) are eating some pilfered blackmarket food. The script was devoid of directions or content, the dialogue banal. Yet before our eyes the director and the actors built a new scene that embodied the essence of the book—and the film. Heston pantomimed simple pleasure at the loathsome artificial food—all he had ever known. Robinson virtually *embodied* repulsion and despair. When Fleischer called out "Cut!" the professional audience, only carpenters, grips, and technicians—no visitors—burst into spontaneous applause. This was artistic appreciation at its very best. The impressive results grace the film.

A great strength of this film is its strong visual content, the correct utilization of the large screen, the escape from TV's talking heads. Much credit to the art director, director, and cameraman. The green pall that hangs in the air makes the viewer aware at all times of this polluted and overcrowded world. It also adds emphasis to the beautiful Braverman graphics—with Beethoven's "Pastoral" playing in the background—during the suicide parlor scene. A perfect example of visual strength overriding content. In the book, Sol is a loner, a survivor, and dies after taking a public stance for the very first time in his life. The one thing that he would *never* do would be to commit suicide. Completely ignoring this fact, the inept screenwriter brings in that old sf cliché, the suicide parlor. Something *I* would never do. Ironically, it works in the film since it is new to cinema audiences. The scene, which includes images of the clean and beautiful world as it once had been, also adds to the film's impact.

This continual visual onslaught conveys the message of the book—modified for film. The idiotic cannibal-crackers (not in the book) and the "big" revelation that they are made from corpses will have been twigged by the audience early on. This, and the murder and chase sequences, the

Left: In 2022, New York's fume-infested streets are crowded with unhealthy, hungry people.

Right: Roommates Sol (Edward G. Robinson, in his last film) and Detective Thorn (Charlton Heston).

Below: After a man is murdered, Thorn meets two people in his employ: villainous Tab Fielding (Chuck Connors) and "furniture-girl" Shirl (Leigh Taylor-Young), the dead man's live-in mistress.

Thorn's investigations take him to the plant that manufactures soylent green. There he finds men who don't want him to learn the terrible secret. In Harry Harrison's novel, the word "soylent" was a combination of "soy beans" and "lentils"—in the film, the food given the masses is made from human remains.

"furniture" girls (not in the book) are not what the film is about—and are completely irrelevant. The film, like the book, shows what the world will be like if we continue in our insane manner to pollute and overpopulate Spaceship Earth. This is the "message" of film and book. Both of them deliver this message in a manner unique to science fiction: The technique of background-as-foreground. This means simply that the story played out by the characters is not the major story. It is the means to capture the reader/viewer's attention, to reveal a greater truth in the setting where the foreground takes place. Other examples of background-as-foreground films-from-books are *1984* (1956) and *On the Beach* (1959).

All right then—what kind of a film is *Soylent Green*? Put all thoughts of the book aside and judge the film on its own merits. Its greatest strengths are the design and the acting. The cornball chase sequences, the overdramatic ending, the numerous infelicities of writing and plotting can be ignored. The film is a visual success. The background of this terrible world is punched home like an inescapable drumbeat. The aftershock is very strong. Almost every person that I have talked to had the same delayed reaction: A week or more after viewing the film, memory of

the action had dimmed—but the feeling of horror of this world had grown and intensified. The background had become the foreground.

Am I pleased with this film? I would say fifty percent. The message of the book has been delivered. It was an exciting experience to see a major film produced by a major studio. It was a humbling experience to meet Edward G. Robinson. A great actor and a great human being. He alone knew that he had terminal cancer when he made the film. He must have chosen to make one more film rather than sit quietly at home and await death. He died before the film was released and it is a tribute to the hard-nosed film executives that they did try to cut out the suicide-parlor scene before the film was released. But it is such an integral part of the film that it could not be done. (Credit also to critics and film-goers, none of whom complained about bad taste.)

Ultimately, *Soylent Green* works as a film. It moves, it keeps the interest, it is visually exciting. The message it delivers raises it above simple entertainment.

But it was a hard battle. With my hand raised, I promise never to let anyone screw me or one of my books again. I look forward to the day when, sink or swim, I can translate one of my other novels into an interesting and successful film.

The Remaking of *Dark Star*

Dan O'Bannon

When Danny Peary asked me to contribute an article to this Omni anthology, I didn't know what the hell to write about. The future? I don't know what's going to happen in the future. I make things up. I can make up lots of different "futures," each depicting what's going to happen to the world in the next fifty, hundred, or million years, but I haven't the slightest idea what's really going to happen. I don't want to know what's going to happen.

I didn't know what was going to happen with this article, either, until Danny started corresponding with me about his previous book, Cult Movies 2, in which he discussed Dark Star, the 1975 * film I did with John Carpenter. Danny wrote to me, "Truthfully, it was hard to find out exactly what you did and what Carpenter did...." I wrote Danny a lengthy reply to that comment. To my surprise, he said he wanted to use it as my Omni book contribution. It pleased me because it saved me having to think up a topic.

I don't know if my little memoir really fits in with the theme of this book; it is not a vision of the future, but of the past. But it does give a glimpse of what people will endure in order to create a vision of the future.

The *Dark Star* story is this.

In August of 1970, John Carpenter and I had dinner at the International House of Pancakes on Jefferson Boulevard in Los Angeles, across from the University of Southern California's cinema complex. John told me that he wanted me to act

in his graduate 580 project. It was to be a science fiction film called "The Electric Dutchman," about four seedy astronauts in a small spaceship who are bombing a sun that is about to go supernova. The bomb gets stuck in the bomb bay, so one of them dons a spacesuit and goes outside with a crowbar to pry it loose. While he's doing so, another of the men goes crazy and goes out with a gun to shoot it loose. When he does, the bomb explodes, hurling the two of them away into deep space, and they talk to each other over their helmet radios as they fall away to their destinies. It was to be twenty minutes long, in black-and-white.

I said, not only did I want to act in it, I wanted to help him with a lot of other things, like the script and the special effects. He accepted, and we embarked.

Just then, my parents stopped sending me money and told me to come back to Missouri. To forestall my departure from L.A., John offered to let me stay in his apartment and eat his food. So I moved in and we started to work.

John and I did two or three drafts of a script that was forty-odd pages long. The plot was as John had described, but fleshed out a bit. I contributed some new ideas, such as: (1) the bomb talks, and

---

Dan O'Bannon was cowriter of *Dark Star* (with John Carpenter), *Alien* (with Ron Shusett), and *Blue Thunder* and *The Space Vampires* (both with Don Jakoby). He was also production designer and star of *Dark Star* and a visual effects consultant for *Alien*. He provided source material for *Heavy Metal*.

Dark Star is often listed as a 1974 film. However, while it was presented at Filmex in L.A. in 1974, it wasn't released officially until 1975—ed.

*Left: The scoutship
Dark Star, which for
twenty years has been
bombing unstable
planets—while its
four-man crew has
become increasingly
unstable and
depressed.*

*Right: In the confined
control-room (front to
back) Pinback (Dan
O'Bannon), Doolittle
(Brian Narelle), and
Boiler (Carl Kuniholm)
groove to music and
get on each other's
nerves.*

they have to argue it out of exploding; (2) they once had a captain (Joe Sanders) and now he's dead and kept in cold storage where they can talk to him; (3) star-struck Talby (Andreijah Pahich) is obsessed with the mythical Phoenix Asteroids, and in the end he fulfills his destiny by drifting away with them. John came up with the idea that former Malibu surfer Doolittle (Brian Narelle) meets his destiny by surfing down to the planet on a piece of ship debris. We each wrote the scenes we had thought up. John wrote the haunting observation-dome scene, in which Talby and Doolittle talk about their loneliness while looking out at the stars of deep space; and I added Talby's words about the Phoenix Asteroids. The way we wrote together was: We would each go off separately and write the scenes we liked best, and then John would assemble all the material into its final form. We worked on the script through the entire fall semester. It went through a couple of title changes; for a while it was called "Planetfall." The name *Dark Star* didn't arise until the following summer, after principle photography was completed; up until then the ship was called the Centaur. We had a hard time naming the thing.

The film was taking shape as a strange mixture of poesy and low comedy. On the one hand we were in love with the look and feel of space, and we wanted the audience to feel the dilemma of these men, cast off into their eerie isolation. On the other hand we were contemptuous of pomposity, and the piece was equally a sly, deadpan mockery of sci-fi traditions, a put-down of corny or heroic values. The characters and their spacebound living conditions became a reflection of the way we ourselves were living our lives: young, alienated males, forced together in communal poverty. That astronauts' days aboard the Dark Star resembled the days and nights of our lives ...inspiring, sad, ridiculous. Sometimes we went too far in expressing this; such, at least, was the opinion of John's faculty advisor, Mort Zarkoff, who had us remove such scenes as the "Toilet Emergency," in which the space toilet malfunctions and Boiler (Carl Kuniholm), who is floating outside on EVA, gets a faceplate full of bodily waste. "Do you mean to tell me," Zarkoff said to John, "that you're going to have one of your characters get hit in the face with *shit*?"

While we were writing the script, John was assembling a cast of his friends and finding a cameraman and such. John was the director, of course; it was his student project and his idea; my credit, aside from acting, was undecided. I was doing set sketches and putting together props and bits of sets, picking them out of dumpsters and wherever I could get things free. By Christmas we were ready to shoot our first scene, the "Kitchen Scene," in which Pinback babbles about how he became an astronaut (John said he wrote the part of Pinback specially for me; he said he wanted me to play somebody "idiotic and stupid"). The scene was shot over Christmas

Danforth did some astronomical paintings for us. And I did a little bit of everything myself. And it was all for free. Nobody got paid a dime to work on *Dark Star.* It was a student film, a labor of love.

Christmas came again, and the special fx work continued. Carpenter took it easy during this period, kicked his heels back, dated a string of girls. By the spring of that year, 1972, we were basically done. We faced a few pickups, a lot of sound fx and music scoring, and opticals and prints. But aside from that we were done. The film was fifty minutes long.

There is no more useless object in the film world than a fifty-minute film. A film twenty-minutes long or shorter can be distributed as a short. It can be sent to film festivals. A film eighty-minutes long or longer could be released in the-aters as a feature. But for a film between twenty and eighty minutes in length, there is no distribu-tion market. We had the most impressive student film ever made, and the likelihood was that no-body outside of USC would ever see it. John had pumped several thousand dollars into it, and I several hundred, and we wanted the film seen. But the faculty was not especially supportive, beyond simply not interfering with us. They had no plans that we knew of to do anything with it.

That was why John and I were receptive when Jonathan Kaplan approached us with a business proposition. Jonathan was a fellow student who had taken an increasing interest in the film throughout the previous year, and had helped us with the shooting. He now proposed that he and a Canadian business partner would invest $10,000 in *Dark Star* if we would expand it to eighty minutes for theatrical release.

This was a serious matter. It would mean changing our plans entirely. It meant changing *Dark Star.*

The problem with adding another half hour to the film was twofold: (1) The script was perfectly structured for fifty minutes, and to add much to that would damage the story structure; (2) we had torn down all of our sets, most notably the "Con-trol Room," and couldn't possibly rebuild them to look anything like they had (a lot of the props were "found" items); so any new scenes would have to take place in brand-new rooms in the spaceship that hadn't existed before. This totally crippled our ability to expand the story smoothly, and would transform *Dark Star* from a tightly plotted film into an "episodic" film, a weaker format.

For that matter, the very content and style of *Dark Star* was meant for a pocket-sized film. It didn't have the conceptual size to support a full-length treatment. It was a delicate little piece aimed at college audiences, not the general mar-ket. And although the film looked staggering for a student film, up there on the big screen, com-pared with real movies, it would look pretty pa-thetic.

vacation in a closet in the USC student union. By this time I had talked John into shooting in color, and when the footage came back from the lab, we were thrilled. An actual scene from our actual science fiction movie. I quickly edited it together in the cinema department editing room, and we gloated over it, running it again and again.

We launched into full-fledged principle photog-raphy right after Christmas, throughout the spring 1971 semester. We shot the "Computer Room" scene with Talby, and the "Observation Dome," and the "Emergency Air Lock." All this time I was constructing our main set, the "Control Room," in USC's tiny soundstage, monopolizing every square inch, to the chagrin of all the other cinema students. We·spent the summer shooting the "Control Room,"·and the last thing we squeezed in before our actors fled was the "Freezer Room" with Commander Powell.

The footage was looking incredible, and we were euphoric. But we were getting tired; it was the end of summer, and we faced another school year in which we'd just be doing the special effects. By this time neither John nor I was en-rolled in school any longer; but the cinema de-partment was accustomed to such situations, and tolerated it.

I undertook to supervise the special fx, and I got a lot of brilliant people to help—most notably Bill Taylor, my chief advisor, who led me to most of the people who worked for us, and later did all our opticals. John Wash from USC did our anima-tion (computer readout fx). Greg Jein and Harry Walton built our miniatures. Bob Greenberg did our "realistic" animation on the Oxberry at Cal Arts. Ron Cobb designed the outside of the spaceship. I'm damned if I can remember all the people who worked on *Dark Star*—oh, yes, Jim

Left: The fourth crew member, Talby (Andreijah Pahich), has withdrawn from the others, and just sits in the bubble at the top of the ship and contemplates the universe.

Right: The ship has been blown apart, and former California beach boy Doolittle "surfs" through space on a part of the debris.

And so John and I faced a heavy decision: We could have the best student film ever made, or one of the worst features.

Our beautiful fifty-minute student movie stood little chance of being seen. A feature—however bad—was a feature. It was a *credit,* and thus an entree into The Business (we naively thought). That was the way we reasoned when we decided to accept Jonathan's offer.

Jonathan and his partner invested $10,000 that spring, and John and I buckled down to hard work in the hot summer of '72. We invented new scenes, primarily involving an alien made out of a beach ball, and proceeded to shoot them outside of USC. We rented stage space at Producers Studio, the dump of all time, and I started building sets. We then discovered something horrible: while $5,000 would get us an infinity of resources at USC, $10,000 would get us crap in the real world. We shot that August in a record heat wave, and it was the worst-looking stuff yet.

That fall we rented editing space in Hollywood and cut in the new footage. John and I were starting to get on each other's nerves. This was going on too long, and was getting debilitating. We had no means of livelihood and were living like bums, borrowing money to eat. A lot of people helped us, worked hard, a lot of friends, a lot of talent. But by the fall we were faced with a glum reality: We had a ninety-minute film in the can, but now we needed opticals, sound cutting, music, re-recording and prints. But we were out of money. The $10,000 was all spent. With our knowledge of movie costs, we calculated it would cost us $35,000 to do the postproduction and complete the film. Kaplan didn't have it. And his partner didn't have it.

To get the money to finish the film, we were

going to have to sell the film. In workprint form, the worst it would ever look. And we were running against an absolute deadline: The only place in town capable of running our film, due to its unusual (USC-type) sound format, was the F&B Ceco screening room on Highland. And our deferment with Ceco ran out on Christmas. After that we wouldn't be able to show the film to anybody, anywhere. So we had to make our deal, find our buyer, before Christmas, or we were faced with disaster.

We ran every distributor in town through that screening room. They all hated it. "You can't mix comedy and science fiction." "The public won't buy mixed genre." "No sex." "No names." "No violence." By the middle of December we still had no buyer, and there weren't too many left. Then Bob Greenberg introduced me to Jack Harris.

Jack Harris was an independent producer-distributor who had released an animated short of Bob's, and Bob thought he might want *Dark Star*—he distributed low-budget sci-fi. And so I met Jack Harris. And then John met Jack Harris. He saw the film just before our contract ran out at the screening room. And we struck a deal with him.

It was a bad deal. We sold the film outright, for beans, no points, payment deferred against the film's profits. John and I had a tired little get-together that dark winter night. We were both depressed, especially John. We had been best friends since *Dark Star* began, but tonight John was different. There was a distance.

With the dawning of 1973 we embarked upon the horror. We had already made this film twice, and now we had to do it again for a third time. Harris demanded reshoots to bring the film up to his standards. We wrote more script, with little

relish this time, built more sets, and dragged the resistant and aging actors back for yet one more shooting, in a tiny little studio on Western Ave. The actors no longer looked the same; some of us had gained weight; all of us had changed our hair and beards. I had to get wigs and false beards to approximate our former appearances. John and I were both worn out, it wasn't fun any more. It wasn't for *us* any longer. It was for Harris. He owned the film, and he owned us, and he let us know it. He was a tyrant who terrorized and demoralized us. I started losing my temper; I shouted at people who didn't deserve it.

The summer of '73 was spent on animation; in rented animation studios now, like Wally Bulloch's and Dickson-Vasu, John and I slaving at adjacent tables over endless rotoscoping. The fall was devoted to opticals and blow-up, and now Bill Taylor came to the fore. He blew up all our 16-mm ECO to 35-mm camera negative, and did all our optical effects at the same time. We saw poetry, watching Bill work through the night over a glowing optical printer. He gave the film a touch of gloss without which it would not have survived.

John composed and conducted the musical score. He played it dramatic, deliberately against the comedy, except in the main title music. It had been John's idea since our first discussion to use country music over the titles, in spoof of *2001*'s pompous use of classical music. He had written a song called "Them Interstellar Cosmic Blues," which I quite liked ("I got them interstellar cosmic blues; I got to wait ten years before I hear the news"). But Bill Taylor wrote a song called "Benson, Arizona," and since Bill hadn't been paid a dime for all his work, John recorded that instead.

Our sound mix was less brilliant. We had to cut corners here, and the result was barely passable—no, let's be honest, it stank. But it was done.

DARK STAR was done. After three and a half years of incredible work and heartache, it was finished, in February of 1974, during the big gas crisis, in the Metrocolor screening room, when they told us this was the last answer print they were doing till they saw some money.

But Carpenter and I were finished the year before. It had ended, appropriately, as it began—in a restaurant. Late in the summer of '73, in the now-defunct Copper Pan at Gower and Sunset, John told me it was time our careers went in separate directions. He told me he didn't want to work with me any more. I asked him why. "You're too hard to get along with," he told me. "Too demanding. You take but you don't give. You always talk about yourself but you're never interested in me."

What about all the films we were planning to do together, I asked him. I had predicated my future on doing films with John—being his right-hand man—until both of us made it big, and then he would produce a film for me to direct. Without him I'd be back to scratch.

"Forget it," he said. "I may make mistakes without you, but at least they'll be *my* mistakes."

In that case, I asked him if he would at least give me a credit that read "A FILM BY JOHN CARPENTER AND DAN O'BANNON," or "PRODUCED BY JOHN CARPENTER AND DAN O'BANNON," so that I'd be able to go on without him.

"No," he said. "There's only room for one person to get anything out of this film, and it's going to be me."

Thus began the great *Dark Star* credit debate, which lasts, tiresomely, until this day.

Death Race 2000: New World's Violent Future

Paul Bartel

Films about the future usually have been metaphorical statements about contemporary societies, suggesting more about the styles, tastes, and politics of the periods in which they're made than of the times they are supposedly projecting. For instance, Fritz Lang's *Metropolis* (1926), one of the most influential futuristic films, was really a Deco fantasy, concerned less with the distant future than the dehumanizing industrialization of Germany in the mid-Twenties. Even the *Buck Rogers* and *Flash Gordon* serials were, in all their attitudes, melodrama, and design, essentially about America in the Thirties rather than any future reality. *Death Race 2000,* which I directed for Roger Corman's New World Pictures, was released in 1975 but made in 1974, when there was still much dissension in this country. It was the ideal time to make a film that depicted a dark future, with a repressive one-party system in America, and a cruel, super-bloody national sport.

In fact, United Artists was about to release a similar film, Norman Jewison's *Rollerball* (1975), in which an oppressive government keeps the masses at bay, happy with bread and violent circuses. The history of New World under Roger Corman was the making of inexpensive variations on high-budget major studio releases, like *Jaws* (1975) and *Star Wars* (1977), and certainly *Rollerball* was the model for *Death Race 2000.* Roger realized that a futuristic film would be commercial,

---

Paul Bartel directed and made a cameo appearance in *Death Race 2000.* He was star and director of *Eating Raoul* and also directed *Cannonball, Private Parts,* and *Not for Publication.* He has appeared in numerous films, including *Hollywood Boulevard, Heartbeeps,* and *Rock 'n' Roll High School.*

---

and he added the year *2000* to the title to tie it in to *2001: A Space Odyssey* (1968), but really the only reason our picture was set in the future was because *Rollerball* was set in the future. Neither Roger nor I took the futuristic aspects of our film seriously. Indeed, whereas *Rollerball* was so humorless and self-important in its futuristic vision that it eventually crumbled under its own weight, *Death Race* had no pretensions to being a serious cautionary tale about where our preoccupation with violent sports and corresponding apathy toward political issues was taking us. It was, at least for me, a black comedy, a black joke, a funny satire. The basic intention was, simply, to make people laugh through humor that related to violent subject matter.

The central idea of *Death Race* is that the national sport in the year 2000 is a coast-to-coast New York-to-New Los Angeles auto race, in which five champion drivers (each with a navigator of the opposite sex) score points by running people over. Meanwhile political subversives try to sabotage the event. That's because the annual race is held and televised as a ploy by the repressive government to keep the people happy and out of politics. The most famous racer is the legendary masked Frankenstein (David Carradine), the government's representative. Annie (Simone Griffeth), his navigator, is one of the rebels and she's part of a plot to kidnap Frankenstein to force the President (Sandy McCallum) to abolish the race. Luckily, her plan fails because it turns out Frankenstein is actually a masked crusader,

The race is on.
Above: A team of political
dissidents attempts to disrupt the contest by
killing Calamity Jane (Mary Woronov). Below:
Machine Gun Joe Viterbo (Sylvester Stallone),
with his navigator Myra (Louisa Moritz)
at his side, picks up some points by
running over a bystander.

Left: During a break in the race, government driver Frankenstein (David Carradine) is tempted by Annie (Simone Griffeth), whose job is to be his navigator and sexmate. They will fall in love and marry.

Right: The film's one use of a matte (a shot of a New York skyline is placed behind a shot of an L.A. track's grandstand) is responsible for the lone visual with a truly "futuristic" look.

on her side. In fact, at the end, when Frankenstein is the only driver who survives the race, he drives into the presidential platform and kills the evil leader. With the adoring public's blessing, our hero becomes President himself, marries Annie, and abolishes the Death Race.

When I was assigned to direct *Death Race,* it was already a fait accompli in many ways. The cars were under construction and there was a finished script by Robert Thom. That script was extremely black and, for my money, not very funny. Many of the characters were transvestites and Frankenstein was monstrous rather than sympathetic. Roger felt the script needed a little touch-up. I thought it needed a total overhaul, which it finally got. My principal contribution was to lighten it and give it a satirical mix so it wouldn't be just a poor man's *Rollerball.*

The original story on which the film was based was a little three-page shocker called "The Racer," by Ib Melchior. It dealt with only one anonymous racer and it ended at the moment the reader is made to realize he's deliberately trying to run over people to win the event. There was no Frankenstein character and no mention of a "Death Race" being our national sport; it was just the one idea, and it was serious. The conceptual problem I had when making an eighty-minute film was how to keep this guy who keeps running people over sympathetic to the audience.

For a long time, I wanted to build the plot around a central character who didn't want to run people over and managed to amass a winning number of points without killing anybody. Roger

wouldn't hear of it. The only solution then was to make the people he runs over so unsympathetic that viewers wouldn't mind his running them down. So we had to continuously set up, in quick broad strokes, various kinds of awful people and knock them off. As an exercise, it was fun because it gave me a chance to make up different kinds of jokes. In a sense, this was similar to how we set up obnoxious victims in *Eating Raoul* (1982), but in that film, victims were hit on the heads with frying pans and you hardly saw anything—there was no blood at all. Roger wanted *Death Race* to be violent and bloody. Consequently, in a way an equation was set up between the movie viewers who were enjoying our blood-filled movie and the fans of the blood-filled race in the movie. I hoped that since the movie was intended as satire, its audience was less culpable of simply enjoying mayhem and destruction; in fact, I made the violence look unreal so people could laugh at it and not be appalled. Still, one reason I'd never make a *Death Race 2000* today is that I'm not interested in movies where it is assumed the audience will get pleasure out of the spectacle of people being run over.

But in 1974, I did make *Death Race 2000* into a violent action film—full of fights, crashes and explosions—and even threw in a little extra blood to have something to take out later to pacify the MPAA ratings board, which we knew would insist on some deletions. Ironically, Roger rejected one violent bit I proposed. I'd had come up with a gag based on the already existing national black joke

about drivers on American roads scoring high point totals by striking children, old people, cripples, pregnant women, or nuns. Two characters come to a fork in the road and see on the left a blind, pregnant nun on a bicycle. Figuring this ideal score is too good to be true and is just part of a trick to get them blown up, they wisely go down the right lane—and they are immediately blown up. I don't know if it was Roger's latent Catholicism, but he was offended by the scene and wouldn't allow it.

The women characters in *Death Race* were all supposed to be great athletes and star drivers, so I imagined them all being very tough, efficient and hip. I filmed an early scene in which Roberta Collins's character talked to her sidekick about changing her image. She'd been racing as Matilda the Hun, and there were Nazi insignia on her car, the "Buzz-Bomb," but now she was considering becoming "Matilda the Nurse," and wearing a cute little white outfit and driving a beautiful white ambulance. This was meant to be an in-joke about New World Pictures, which at the time was doing a series of nurse films that employed the same actresses who played jungle rebels in their action pictures. But Roger cut the scene from the picture.

One of the few scenes that I invented and wrote entirely myself that made it to the screen was one that satirized the way young fans idolize violent, superdestructive sports stars (and rock music stars). There is a fan club for Frankenstein, which turns up to watch him race. They elect a representative, played by my sister Wendy Bartel, to sacrifice herself to him during the race, to give him extra points. And she wants to meet him beforehand so her death will have special meaning. I found resonance in this sort of teenage notion of imbuing the final act with significance by having personal contact with one's idol and, in fact, having him participate in the act. Sure enough, the next day, the girl, who holds flowers for Frankenstein, stands in front of his speeding car and is struck dead—at that moment, I cut to the other fan club members, one of whom is snapping pictures of the incident with her Instamatic.

I also sneaked a dance number into the picture, wherein Frankenstein and Annie do an impromptu stylized "foxtrot." This infuriated Roger. He came on the set the day we were shooting it and said something like "I don't recall this being in the script." Luckily David Carradine, who was the star and had much more clout than I did, really liked the dance idea—so it was left in.

With our miniscule budget, we made no attempt to create an elaborate futuristic setting. This was no *Blade Runner* (1982). I was obliged to make the most of the "futuristic" locations that abound in the Los Angeles area. I also used one, count 'em, *one* matte shot. We went to an auto race track just outside of L.A., and shot the live-action part. We actually filled one area of the grandstand with people and reproduced that image several times and put the shots side by side to make it look as if many, many people were present (close observation would reveal that the same individuals are seated in at least three

places within the frame). Then a shot of a New York skyline was matted in directly behind the stadium to make the setting seem futuristic. This was used in the opening sequence.

To give an idea about the nature of our low-budget production, let me explain our car situation. Prior to production we had five different cheesy-looking cars in production. And every week or so we'd check on how they were coming along. If one car looked as if it were developing better than the others, then it immediately became our principal car, and we'd start re-imagining and re-designing the Frankenstein character so that the car would fit his image. The car that Frankenstein ended up driving was originally planned to be an alligator car for a minor character named Cleopatra (Leslie McRay).

Because Death Race was so cheap and looked so cheap in many ways, it was easiest to do it satirically and not have to worry if it seemed futuristic. That was fine with me because, being an optimistic person, there was no way I could treat the material seriously. But since Roger made a string of trailers for the picture's American release that didn't suggest that it contained any humor whatsoever, some people were disappointed about the presence of satirical elements.* They wanted a straight action film. How-

---

*The audience reaction in England was different than in America. That was because the English trailers left no doubt that the picture was intended to be comical.—P.B.

ever, my guess is that if the film had been done seriously they would have been equally dissatisfied because the hardware couldn't match a serious concept.

There were a number of people who felt that if Death Race had been more serious and less fantastical that it would have attracted a larger audience. I think it would have been a meaningless film. When Frankenstein runs over the President and becomes President there's a hint that usurpers by nature are as ruthless as those they replace, and when Frankenstein then runs over the obnoxious TV announcer Junior Bruce (Don Steele), who criticized him for abolishing the Death Race, there's an inference that it takes violence to eliminate violence, but Death Race's themes were basically weak throwaways. Moreover, the film had little to say about politics. None of the racers other than Frankenstein and Annie represent any actual political faction; there's a revolutionary movement but it has no real significance. Even our President—who I believe is the only fictional American President ever actually killed in a film—is just a watered-down version of Big Brother. Ruling from a palace in China, he was like a public-relations invention, an artificial character who's always on television speaking in platitudes.

However, since the premise of the film was this violent futuristic sport (a combination of football, demolition derby, car racing, and bowling), we were forced to conceive a world to support its

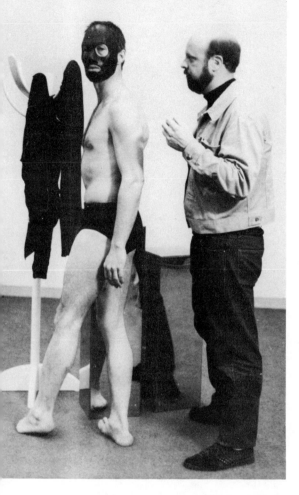

rebels attack the various drivers and the President not only blames the French for this, but also for "crippl[ing] our once great economy and wreck[ing] our telephone system." That's my favorite joke in the movie.

Otherwise, the film said very little about the time in which it was set. There had been a market crash in '79, our economy was in shambles, pills could put people to sleep for an exact time. That's about it. The whole notion of a repressive government of the future, a Big Brother-type President, and the extreme violence that characterized the society was, it seems to me now, just a second-hand cliché utilizing proven plot devices. It was all part of a formula. It was good for setting up satirical jokes but certainly could not have been taken as social commentary.

Even so, there is much I like about *Death Race 2000*. It's one New World Picture that I think was aesthetically superior to the film that inspired it. It has speed, and it has humor that, my friends tell me, still holds up. I'm proud that for the Calamity Jane character I cast Mary Woronov, my *Eating Raoul* costar, because this was her first Hollywood role. In fact, the picture had a very good cast, including Sylvester Stallone as Machine Gun Joe Viterbo (who dressed like a Thirties gangster), Louisa Moritz as his daffy partner Myra, Roberta Collins, Simone Griffeth, and, of course, David Carradine.

I also think we did a very interesting thing with Carradine's character. Because it was said that Frankenstein had experienced a terrible series of accidents and had been put back together with the pieces of different dead people, he was thought to be like the Frankenstein monster. But, we made this story into a myth rather than have it be fact. It turns out that a number of Frankensteins have been killed and replaced: David Carradine's character is actually only the latest of the Frankensteins. We kept the audience from discovering this fact by keeping David covered with a black mask and costume for much of the picture. Only later, when his unscarred body is revealed, do we learn the secret.

I think that if *Death Race 2000* were made today, it would be successful, but I think it was more suited to the time when it was made. It wasn't ahead of its time. Anyway, filmmakers change emotionally and, as I stated earlier, I wouldn't want to do this movie today. I'm much more interested now in the themes of reconciliation and positiveness than in presenting a dire vision of a future world. My own vision of the future is much different than the one expressed in *Death Race*. I see people making realistic appraisals of their needs and those of others and coming to an accommodation—there will be compromising. I'm optimistic in terms of personal relationships and I project that on the world. I don't think we're going to have a war with Russia. I think we're going to find a modus vivendi.

existence. So in story conferences, we halfheartedly hypothesized a cruel future that was divided into several armed camps. This idea, like much of the film, was probably borrowed from *Nineteen Eighty-Four*, which was original in its time, but has been much imitated since. Looking back, I think our vision of the world was terribly dated, unrealistic, and childish. We weren't even specific about the exact divisions of camps, just that America had become part of a united North American continent, which was constantly in a state of war with some enemy camp. We didn't want the conflict to be between the U.S. and Russia, but the only opponent we bothered to mention was France. What happens is that the American

Playing Ripley in *Alien*

An Interview with Sigourney Weaver by Danny Peary

Danny Peary: Did you go to movie casting calls before *Alien* [1979]?

Sigourney Weaver: Not many. I'm sure I'd turned down a couple of films. One of the reasons I wasn't crazy about getting *Alien* was that I felt responses had been so encouraging at past auditions that I'd soon get another role if I didn't get picked for *Alien*. That's not to say I didn't want the job. I did. I had no money for one thing. I was delighted to be considered. But I had high hopes. The fact that I didn't slobber at the mouth when I was told I'd get a screen test helped me get the part.

DP: How were you even selected to audition for the lead part in a *major* film when you had never been in a film before?

SW: I had been out on the West Coast the year before, visiting my parents, and had met a few people out there. And I'd done enough work in

Sigourney Weaver has starred in such films as *Alien, Eyewitness, The Year of Living Dangerously,* and *Deal of the Century.* In addition, she has appeared in many New York stage productions; with costar Christopher Durang, she wrote the Brecht parody "Das Lusitania Songspiel."

New York already so that I wasn't completely unknown. I was highly recommended to everyone involved with *Alien*. They had been trying to sell Fox on having a newcomer play Ripley. Fox had mixed feelings at first and casting took a long time. They saw a lot of actresses. I was asked to meet everyone here in New York, soon after I'd opened in the play *The Conquering Event*. I remember going to the wrong place for my appointment and having to rush around in confusion. I met Ridley Scott right away, and the producers Gordon Carroll and David Giler. And then I met Walter Hill, who coproduced *Alien*. And they all liked me. Walter Hill and David Giler wrote the script I read, although Dan O'Bannon had written the original script and got the screen credit. You can tell Walter's influence. He writes so sparely because he expects you to improvise. When I read it, I found that his characters, especially the males, seemed identical. That's why when they cast *Alien* they chose distinct types who could make the characters interesting in ways other than just by saying the dialogue. It was a very skeletal script and that's one of the reasons I liked it.

DP: At that stage of your acting career, were you secure enough to argue over problems you found in the script?

SW: Sure. That's what it's all about. On *Alien,* I immediately commented, "It's a very bleak picture where people don't relate to each other at all," and the casting director was there signaling me to not blow it by making such strong objections. But I figure if you put all your cards on the table, they can use that. After all, they're hiring *you.* They can disagree with you but you must air your feelings so you can arrive at a resolution. You have to be careful and specific about what you disagree with. And you also have to express what you find positive about the project. I happen to have worked on many new plays

The crew of the commercial starship Nostromo: (L–R) Brett (Harry Dean Stanton), Ash (Ian Holm), Kane (John Hurt), Lambert (Veronica Cartwright), Dallas (Tom Skerritt), Ripley (Sigourney Weaver), and Parker (Yaphet Kotto).

with new playwrights so I have been encouraged to speak up—I didn't know if people in movies were used to that. I thought they should be. You shouldn't work with a bad director, one you can't have a dialogue with. I just think it takes too much out of you if you don't absolutely love the project. If you love it you can put up with a lot, even a jerk director—which Ridley Scott definitely was not. I think when you're not fully committed to something, you shouldn't do it. I have only done things I've felt strongly about. Even *Alien.* I sat down and thought about Ripley a long time before deciding I really wanted to play her.

DP: When were you told you had the part?

SW: I flew out to Hollywood to meet Alan Ladd, Jr., and Gareth Wiggin at Twentieth. I lost my bags on the plane and went in my rotten clothes. We had a typical chatty Hollywood meeting where you're all supposed to pretend you're there for social reasons and no one mentions the film. Ladd agreed to screen-test me, so the next week I flew to London where Ridley had built a whole set for me. I hadn't yet been hired but I was the only actress they were screen-testing. They hoped I would do well. And we did a run-through of the entire script. I wore old army surplus stuff for the screen test. We didn't want it to look like *Jackie Onassis in Space;* we wanted to look more like pirates. On the day I left for home, Ladd came to look at the tests. He asked all the *women* in the studio who worked as secretaries to watch my tests, too, and tell him their opinions. And the women just

said, "Well, we like her." So *they* got me the part. On the day I got back to New York, they called and said I got it. I had sort of written it off every step of the way.

DP: Is there anything you tried to bring to Ripley when you were trying out for the part?

SW: A no-nonsenseness to her. She's a very matter-of-fact person. I think she grew up believing there is a certain order to things that could not be broken or changed. She had very rational training. And her beliefs are exploded in the film when she suddenly has to work on instinct and emotion rather than intellect. Looking back, in some ways she was the most unimaginative character I've ever played—which isn't to say I don't like her. Actually the part I wanted to play was Lambert, Veronica Cartwright's part. In the first script I read, she just cracked jokes the whole time. What was wonderful about it was that here was a woman who was wise-assing, telling stupid jokes just when everyone else was getting hysterical. And she didn't crack up until the end. That's a character I could identify with because that's how I assume I would act. If the elevator gets stuck that's what I do. The character changed however when Ridley and Veronica decided to give viewers a sympathetic character.

Sexual imagery. Left: Dallas, Lambert, and Kane approach the peculiarly designed entrances to the derelict alien ship they discover. Below: Kane explores the ship's vast chamber and discovers a liquid-filled hatchery for alien pods.

Right: Ripley, Parker, and Brett attempt to ferret out the tiny, eel-like alien that burst through Kane's chest and has hidden in the ship. They don't realize that it has grown considerably.

©1979 TWENTIETH CENTURY-FOX FILM CORP.

©1979 TWENTIETH CENTURY-FOX FILM CORP.

DP: It's obviously great getting a starring role in your first film.

SW: It's also dangerous in the sense there are so many good supporting roles that I'll never be considered for. I really developed in the theater by taking character parts and in a way that's what I'd like to do in the movies. I think I'm considered for parts that are nothing like those I'm drawn to. That's the "actor's dilemma." It's not unique to me. When you are the lead in a film that costs a few million dollars, you do get the best hair and make-up people, and you don't

have to worry about things in rehearsal you might not get if you were making an independent film or if you had a supporting role. On *Alien* there was some resentment toward me because I came from New York and got such a good part, the one character alive at the end. That was very difficult for me to deal with. There is a segregation between leading and supporting people in films that I find stupid and distasteful.

DP: So could you enjoy working on *Alien?*

SW: *Alien* was fun. I was excited about being in a movie and since it was my first time out, I was

very easy-going. I didn't realize until the four
months were over that I'd been experiencing
such tension. Every day Ridley would let me get
behind the camera to look at each scene and I
could tell *Alien* was an incredible film to be a
part of. It was always fascinating seeing Ridley
work and how he put it all together. And I loved
working with Tom Skerritt, who played Dallas,
the captain of the Nostromo. He's great, a
truly interesting person. Also I learned a lot
working with actors who had so many varied
acting backgrounds. For instance, the scenes I
did with Ian Holm, who played Ash, the science
officer who turns out to be a robot, were done
word-for-word perfect, like I was used to doing
on stage. However, the scenes I did with Yaphet
Kotto, who played Parker, were probably nothing like the scenes that were written. However
an actor worked, I was willing to work with him
that way. I would have liked to have done more
inprovisation because we might have made ourselves into the *ensemble* we should have been.
DP: What did you think of the sets?
SW: They were great. In fact, I think the *main*
reason I wanted to do *Alien* was because they
had showed me H. R. Giger's incredible designs
for the alien and the planet. I had never seen
anything like it. I wish you could have seen the
filming on the planet set because it was so fascinating to watch. They had Ridley's two boys and
Tom Skerritt's son walking around in space suits
being doubles so everything around them would
look bigger. The amount of incense used was
not to be believed—it was also used to diffuse

light on the bridge and mess-room sets, where
the ceilings were very low. It was like the incense burned at a Catholic funeral I once
attended—people wore masks. I remember taking my parents around this set. It was like wandering through some Playboy orgy room. There
was this huge spaceship with vaginal doors and
there were beautiful female bones. They were
gulping, "Very interesting, very interesting." It
was funny having never done another film, except for a week on something that was never released. I thought every actor got up, had break-
fast, and went to another planet. It seemed so
natural to me.
DP: Did you like working with Ridley Scott?
SW: We got along very well. He's an amazing
man, a genius, and I think *Alien* is beautifully directed. He is one of those directors who will
come up to you after you've done a scene and
say, "Well, I don't *fucking* believe that." At first
I'd be taken aback and wonder, "Where's the
stroking, where's the diplomacy?" And there just
wasn't any. And that's why I liked him so much.
In an industry where there's so much bullshit, I
really appreciated his just getting to the point.
We didn't have to waste time. We rarely re-
hearsed and if we did it was only a day in advance of shooting. It was a high-pressured set.
Ridley operated the camera. He hadn't worked
that much with actors and I think one of his pri-
orities today is to become not an "actor's director," but to be better with them. I remember one
time when I asked for his help on a problem I
was having with Ripley. And he thought about it

for a long time and then he came over to me and said, "What if you are the lens on ... (and he named a sophisticated camera) ... and you're opening and shutting." And there was a long pause. Finally I said, "Ridley, I'll have to think about it." And he looked crestfallen because he hadn't helped me and he added, "Well, let me think, too." He really wanted to be part of the process. But having me be the iris of a lens? I said, "That's okay, Ridley, I'll figure it out myself." And I did. But I loved him.

DP: Had you seen many science fiction films before being in *Alien*?

SW: Only a handful, if that many. Being in *Alien* made me want to see *Dark Star* [1975] because Dan O'Bannon wrote that, too. I didn't really remember *2001* [1968], but Ridley kept saying it was a masterpiece.

DP: That's another film with a sterile environment.

SW: I was reading Isaac Asimov's *Foundation*. There are no women in that at all. Where did we all go? Are we in a hen house hatching babies?

DP: Many space travel stories have no women. The male writers don't know what to do with women in such a situation. They need an excuse to put them on board.

SW: They're always scientists. If women were drafted in America, all images might change.

DP: In *Alien* there are two women who are integral members of the crew.

SW: At one point, Ripley was supposed to be a man.* They changed the character to a woman just before casting was started. There is just slight sexual differentiation in the film. There's also slight sexual innuendo. There was supposed to be a love scene right in the middle of the picture. It was one of Ridley's favorite scenes but it was never filmed. Ripley sees Dallas and starts to take off her clothes, saying, "I need some relief." And they built a special chair for us to make love in. It was a ludicrous idea—with that alien running around loose in the ship, who would have wanted to take one's clothes off to make love?

DP: Was there discussion over your famous strip toward the end of the film?

SW: Originally there was going to be a lot of nudity in the film. Of the matter-of-fact variety. There were going to be lots of shots of naked people walking around, which I thought was a good idea because it was such a harsh environment. It would have been a nice contrast. As for my strip ... people have said, "Aw, how could you demean yourself by doing a striptease?" And I say, "Are you kidding? After five days of blood and guts, and fear, and sweat and urine, do you think Ripley wouldn't take off her clothes?" It never occurred to me for a second

that people would think my strip exploitive. I think it's kind of provocative—you're almost seeing me through the alien's eyes. Suddenly I go from dark green animal to a pink and white animal. Ridley and I had so much fun working out the ending. There were so many different endings. One of them was that the alien would surprise me and I would run into the closet where I'd take off my suit and put on another. So there would have been a moment when the alien would see me between suits and be fascinated. Because the alien isn't evil. It's just following its natural instincts to reproduce through whatever living things are around it. Every now and then a reporter would ask, "How could you have been part of a film about such *evil*?" And I'd go, "Good Lord! You take this very seriously, don't you?" So I liked all this stuff. You see the alien in its birthday suit the entire film; so I thought it was a cop out having me wear the underwear, and not stripping entirely. Fox is always concerned about losing Spain, losing Italy, etc. But I must say, having received the mail I have, I would now think twice about taking off all my clothes in a movie and scampering around for an hour.

DP: Were you surprised by the amount of fan mail you received, and the obsessive nature of some of it?

SW: I never expected much fan response from *Alien*, certainly nothing as tremendous as I got. My agent had been in the business a long, long time, and he said he had never had so much trouble dealing with fans as those who tried to get in touch with me. For a long time someone sent roses, and I'd get lavish gifts from around the world, which were returned. Most of the letters I got were sincere and sweet and I appreciated the compliments and sentiments. But I had trouble with the ones that said, "You must write me today. I can't live unless you write me now! You are the *only* person who can understand what I'm feeling." What can you write back to these people?

DP: Was there talk of *Alien II*?

SW: It was a great joke among us after the movie came out. Everyone at Twentieth wanted one because *Alien* made so much money, but none of us ever talked seriously about a sequel.

DP: You took a long time before doing another film. ...

SW: I was astonished to discover after finishing *Alien* how traditional scripts are in regard to women. For one thing, there's rarely a script in which the woman can keep on her clothes.

DP: Would you like to do more science fiction films?

SW: Having made *Alien* with Ridley Scott—yes, I'd like to.

---

*In Dan O'Bannon's original script, all characters could be played by either actors or actresses.—D. P.

The preceding is an excerpt from an interview published in the British movie magazine *Films & Filming*.

The mysterious poster for Alien, *the surprise commercial blockbuster of the summer of 1979.*

The terrified Ripley (Sigourney Weaver, above) realizes that she has unwanted company (R) in the shuttle. Viewers were titillated by Ripley's strip before she spots the alien—it's possible that the alien (which, after all,

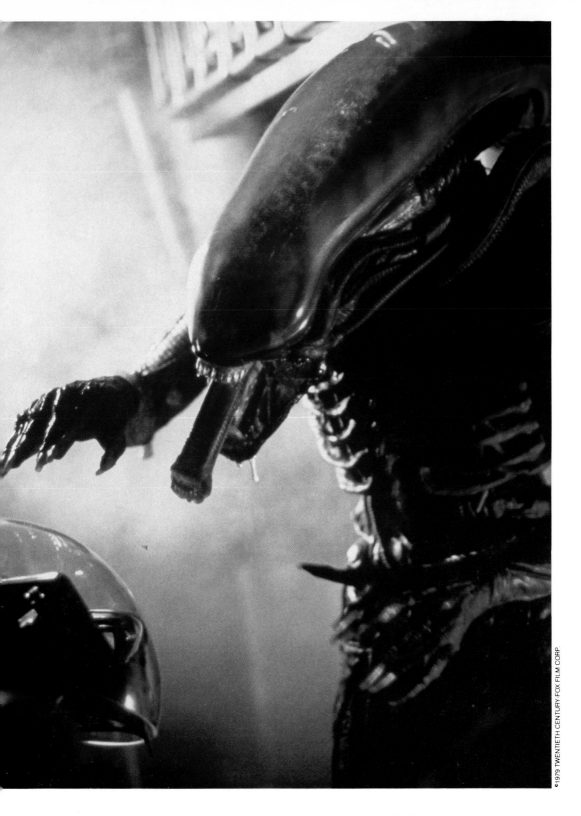

has a phallic design) was excited also. The alien was designed by H. R. Giger. Carlo Rimbaldi, of E.T. fame, designed and constructed the alien's heads. Actor Bolaji Badejo wore the articulated heads.

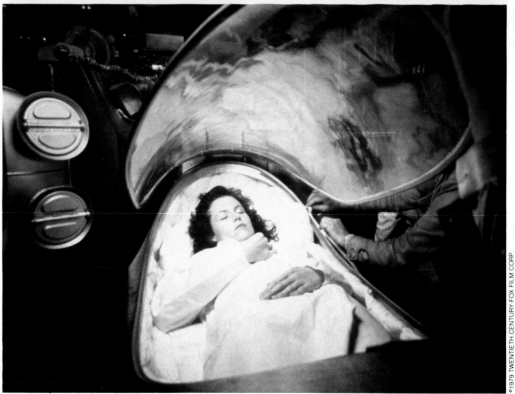

Top: Ripley is on the job, talking to Earth base. She is second in command on the Nostromo—when Dallas is killed, she takes over. Above: There is preparation of the final "Sleeping Beauty" sequence, in which Ripley—the lone survivor—puts herself into suspended animation for her long journey back toward Earth.

Battle Beyond the Stars: Notes from a Tacky Galaxy

John Sayles

I think my greatest advantage in writing my first science fiction screenplay was that I had read almost nothing of the genre. One or two obscure titles almost by accident, a few of Kurt Vonnegut's crossover books, and that was it. This gave me a freedom to invent without fear of precedent, to feel like I was going into unknown territory. I'm sure anybody deeply into sci-fi literature can look at every concept in the screenplay and say, "Oh, yeah, that was done first in *The Gerbil-Women of Zuma*" or whatever, but to me it was virgin turf. I'd seen many science fiction movies, but knew they were pretty tame stuff conceptually compared to what existed in the novels. So when New World Pictures called up and said "The Seven Samurai in Space" the possibilities seemed endless.

Well, almost endless. In all screenwriting one has to keep in mind the probable budget of the project one is writing. At New World when Roger Corman was running it, things usually looked better than they should have considering the cost, and cost less than they should have if you wanted to make a good movie. High on inventiveness from all involved and low on production value, unless you wanted to blow up motorcycles. With this in mind I realized that whatever galaxy I set my story in was going to be a somewhat tacky one, and decided to build elements of low-tech into the script.

The model I was working with, Akira Kurosawa's *The Seven Samurai* (1954) (and its successful 1960 American remake, *The Magnificent Seven*) seemed to adapt perfectly to science fiction—mercenaries with various personality traits became beings from different planets, the beleaguered village became the inhabited green spot on the desert planet Akir, the maurauding bandits became Sador (played by John Saxon in the film) and his Malmori mutants, etcetera. But what interested me more than finding equivalents was playing with beings whose perception was different than ours, who played by different rules. Before I knew it I was writing a sci-fi comedy about different concepts of death.

This is not the kind of thing you want to let slip when you're sitting at Orion with Corman trying to help him get half the financing for the picture. It's not the kind of thing you want to have any of your characters start rapping about while they're blasting Malmori mutants out of the sky. But it does help hang your story together to give it a subtext.

There has always been something cold about death in outer space movies. A little video-game blip and the screen is clear. No bodies and blood, just straight to atomized particles and oneness with the cosmos. (George Lucas's laser-swords were a great invention, bringing in some physicality to the fighting you can't get with those silly ray-guns.) The vastness of space does not give a damn whether Planet X is vaporized or not and it's tough for the viewer to get that worked up Out There either. So I started playing with various earth cultures' concepts of death and tried to add a few I'd never heard of.

John Sayles wrote the screenplays for *Battle Beyond the Stars, Piranha, The Howling, Alligator, The Challenge,* and *The Lady in Red.* He wrote and directed *Return of the Secaucus Seven, Lianna, The Brother from Another Planet,* and *Baby, It's You.*

I based the beseiged Akira on Kurosawa's Japanese villagers, with life and death being a part of a never-ending cycle, and the society's richness being its culture—fairly traditional earthling stuff. For the character of St. Exmin (Sybil Danning in the film), I used the model of the ideal Plains Indian warrior in lean times—her motto of "live fast, fight well, and have a beautiful ending" belongs to an overpopulated culture that needs to kill off a high proportion of its young before they can get the chance to breed. For Cayman of the Lazuli I had the idea of a being who was the only survivor of his kind, someone to whom personal death no longer has a context, sort of an intergalactic *Last of the Mohicans*. The hit-man Gelt (Robert Vaughn) was a character "born in space," as alone as Caymar but without even a memory of connection, an organism aware of its existence but with no illusions that it has a meaning. And I included an earthling, Space Cowboy (George Peppard), to provide a familiar set of values the others could be measured against. But the most interesting characters to me are Sador, Dr. Hephaestes (Sam Jaffe), and Nestor.

Sador is a character obsessed with immortality, a classic attribute of horror movie heavies. His personal physician is able to keep him alive indefinitely by grafting limbs and organs from other beings on to him as his increasing age and atrophy threaten him. His only interest in the Akira is as a potential supply of spare parts. His final words in the script are "I want to live forever." It's always good to have a bad guy you can sympathize with on some level. One also feels for Sador

because of the company he is forced to keep. Saddled with a death ship full of "genetic mistakes," he laments, "Why can't our mutants be superintelligent like the Eli?" There are no women on the ship—the Malmori are not only misshapen and slow-witted, they are, like most mutants, sterile. If one can't reproduce one's own kind, death seems much more final.

Dr. Hephaestes also wants to live forever, but rather than replacing his failing body with organic flesh he replaces himself bit by bit with technology till he is a brain in a jar connected to the cameras, microphones, androids, and robots that provide his senses and carry out his will. His space-station, relentlessly monitored, is not just an extention of his body, it *is* his body, in which he keeps his daughter Nanelia (Darlanne Fluegel) locked, as in a womb. His strategy against death is to retreat from life, to replace what is organic and mortal with the inorganic. When Nanelia deserts him, and follows hero Shad (Richard Thomas) to help the Akira, he is left with the capacity to live indefinitely but nothing to live *for*.

Nestor is a being who is represented by five "facets," identical bodies with a single conciousness. Whatever one facet experiences, all the others, no matter where they are in the galaxy, experience as well. On the home planet are more facets but only one consciousness, one being: Nestor. As soon as one facet is "ended" (killed or ceases to function) another is created on the home planet, like skin cells dying and being immediately replaced. The problem, of course, is who do you talk to if you're all alone on the

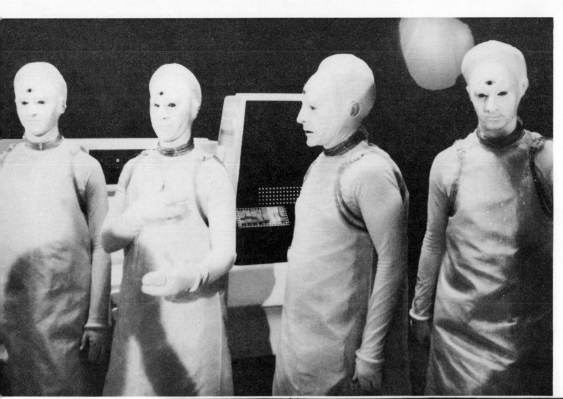

Left: As the lizard-faced Cayman and two facets of Nestor look on, Shad (Richard Thomas) and Nanelia (Darlanne Fluegel) discuss strategy for battling the evil Sador.

Above: Four facets of Nestor.

Right: Other recruits include Space Cowboy (George Peppard) and St. Exmin (Sybil Danning), who seems to be bursting out of her seams.

Sador (John Saxon, right) is kept in working order by his doctor, who constantly gives him tune-ups and replaces his imperfect parts.

planet? Nestor is in danger of being *bored* to death and has to send facets out to have adventures to keep his mind stimulated. In that each facet anywhere in the galaxy is conscious of what adventure each other facet anywhere else in the galaxy is having at any given moment, Nestor gets a lot of stimulation. He is the character who comes closest to immortality—as long as one facet exists no bit of memory or consciousness he had ever had will be forgotten. The facets have no more fear of "ending" than you do in brushing off a flake of dandruff. With this trait, of course, comes a certain detachment. Nestor is the only one of the Protectors of Akir who has no *courage*—there is no death for him and at even the hint of pain a facet will end itself (only considerate—why let the whole consciousness suffer for the pain of a single cell?).

All this time, of course, I've been talking about the screenplay—not the movie. Movies are generally mutants of the screenplays they are based on and only rarely are mutations improvements over their basic models. There were phone calls during the shooting asking me to replace all scenes where spaceships either took off or landed, to have all the fights in space be between ships in multiples of three, and to considerably reduce the number of Malmori invaders. (A lot of

this happened in phone booths, and I remember one guy waiting to make a call turning pale when he heard me say, "Okay, so we cut the mutants in half.") Somehow Cayman, described in the script as a huge black man with a Yakuza-type tattoo on his back, turned into a guy with a lizard suit doing his version of Cyril Richard's Captain Hook. And Dr. Hephaestes's brain in a jar became Sam Jaffe's head sticking out of a steam cabinet, and St. Exmin, meant to be a tough, battle-wise Valkiri warrior, became a walking double-entendre wearing breast plates three sizes too small. It is a tacky galaxy, but I had a good time when I went to the movie anyway.

The death stuff worked as it was supposed to—as a subtext that helped a woefully underbudgeted movie hang together. Some excellent character work by George Peppard and Robert Vaughn also helped, as did some inventive production design (though the planet surface itself suffered from its resemblance to the Venice landscape that it had been some few weeks earlier). The movie did very well financially and shows up on TV now and then, with vast areas of Sybil Danning cropped off. Some people can't get past the gaps in the production values, but as Cayman says in the script, "Different norms for different forms." My biggest regret is that they dropped the idea of having Akir be a planet with two suns. I wanted to see the cinematographer deal with the concept of everybody having two shadows. There is a bit of Sador in all of us.

Outland:
Out of Its Mind
But, Sadly, Not Out of Sight

Harlan Ellison

One of the basic tenets of *good* science fiction has always been that it has an intellectual content that sets it apart from and above the usual sprint of merely-entertainment diversions. While we'll suspend our disbelief to allow James Bond or Burt Reynolds to jump a car in a way that we know defies gravity and the laws of impact or whiplash, we balk at permitting that kind of mickeymouse stunt in an sf film. Because we know that science fiction deals with the laws of the known universe and its accepted physics.

So when the error, the lapse in logic, is a simple one that could have been avoided without slowing or crippling the plot, that need not have set the snail on the blossom of our enjoyment, need not have darkened our feeling that we are safe in the hands of a creator who will reward us for our attention and the price of a ticket, we react more sternly than were it just another *Blues Brothers* or *The Hand,* which are brainless loutish films but from which we expect nothing better.

Reiteration: If you cast back over the reasons why certain sf films disappointed you, chances are good many of them will be of this sort—silly, sophomoric, kindergarten-level scientific illiteracies that defy what even the densest people know about science and pragmatic reality.

I speak of the kinds of errors—and I'll offer a flagrant one in a moment—that are made by directors (and in this case a director who deludes himself that he can write) who are too arrogant to hire and listen to a knowledgeable consultant. They wouldn't have the gall, the nerve, the temerity, the *chutzpah* to make a film about the Civil War without engaging the services of a savant like Bruce Catton to authenticate detail and his-tory; or a film about quenching an offshore oil rig fire without getting Red Adair to validate the technique; or a film about Cortez's depredations in Mexico without constant reference to Bernal Díaz del Castillo. But they are such self-important spoilers that they blunder into the arena of science fiction with some half-baked derivative idea and they sell it to an even *less* literate studio executive and proceed to make the film without even a passing nod to the possibility that they are cramming their cinematic feet in their cinematic mouths.

The writer and director of *Outland,* one Peter Hyams, is the man responsible for an earlier exercise in stupidity, *Capricorn One* [1978]. When I consider Hyams's abilities as a plotter of sf-oriented ideas, I am put in mind of the rhetorical question, "If you nail a duck's foot down, does he walk in circles?"

Lemme give you a f'rinstance that brooks no argument, not even from the most slavishly adoring fan of this film.

There is a scene in *Outland* where Space Marshal O'Niel, played as well as can be expected in a drone scenario like this by Sean Connery (who looks as if he wished he were back making a worthwhile flick like *The Hill*), draws blood from a corpse to ascertain if narcotics are present in the

Harlan Ellison wrote scripts for *Star Trek* and *Outer Limits* and created the television series *The Starlost.* In 1975, his novella *A Boy and His Dog* was made into a prize-winning movie.

Left: Federal District Marshal William I. O'Niel (Sean Connery, center), assigned to a mining complex on Io, a moon of Jupiter, has deputies (including the crooked Montone played by James B. Sikking, left). But when the chips are down, he's on his own.

Right: O'Niel looks for trouble in the beehivelike workers' quarters.

dead man's system. For the moment we'll ignore the implausibility that they have maintained the corpse in a plastic bag rather than simply cremating it in one of the mining colony's furnaces, which would be de rigueur in an enclosed life-system such as that portrayed on Io. Since space on shuttles would be at a premium, logic dictates that a clause would have been inserted in every laborer's contract with the mining corporation, Con-Am, that should death occur while on the job, the body could not be shipped back to Earth for burial. So they'd simply blow it out into space or burn it. But I'll even go along with the unexplained (to my satisfaction) plot-device that the body is conveniently left in transit storage for Connery to examine. (Which wouldn't happen, also, because the baddies wouldn't want an autopsy done that would show their dope had been instrumental in killing the guy. See what I mean? The more you examine the story, the more easily it falls apart.)

To get to the point. Connery sticks a needle into the tracheal cavity, ostensibly into the carotid artery, and up bubbles about a quarter of a pint of bright red sloshy blood into the barrel of the hypodermic.

The only trouble with *that,* as any dolt who has ever watched Quincy on TV can tell you, is that it ignores the reality of forensic medicine and the reality of lividity. For those of you unfamiliar with the concept, lividity is what draws the blood to the lowest part of the body in a corpse. (Don't try to fudge it by saying, "Yes, well, that's how it is if

there's *gravity,*" because even on Io, innermost moon of Jupiter, gravity is on the order of one-twelfth to one-fifteenth Earth g, which would make lividity work the same way, especially after the unstated number of days the body had lain in that plastic bag. And even trying to rationalize the gravity question doesn't work, because we can see that the mining colony has *artificial* gravity. Take *that,* Saracen dog!)

So if Connery stuck that needle into the neck hollow, all he'd bring up would be *air,* because all the blood left in the corpse would have long since drained into the ass! And any first year high school biology student knows that. But not Pete Hyams, who fancies himself a writer of sci-fi movies.

And as if *that* ain't moronic enough, there is also the reality of coagulation. Days after death, you stick a needle into the body *anywhere* and nothing bubbles up like Old Faithful. What you get is clotted brown glop.

One cannot help but resent and distrust a film that makes so many gratuitous errors; that fails to demonstrate even a first year high school student's basic understanding of science or medicine or logic; that manipulates plot and characters in such a patently cheapjack manner to the service of a ripoff comic book plot; that denies everything we know about human nature; that is, simply put, so clearly a derivative shuck.

The core of contempt this film congeals in me lies with the basic concept. By admission of the writer/director Peter Hyams in many interviews,

he approached the producing entities Warner Bros. and the Ladd Company with this single sentence *précis:* "It's *High Noon* in outer space." And they cut a deal on the spot.

Hyams performed that cliché act best typified by the back cover ad *Galaxy Magazine* ran in its earliest days: he had converted a non-sf story into a kind of witless space opera by changing the equivalent of *cayuses* to *spaceships.*

Peter Hyams stood in front of the deal-makers at the Ladd Company and said, "*Outland* is *High Noon* in outer space," and the wee, limited, horizonless mentalities of those whose purses he wished to wallow in, twitched their noses and once again conceived of the audience as *average* and cut him a contract. They subsidized mediocrity.

But *Outland* is not *High Noon.*

The latter is a film of passion and courage, with a clear subtext that speaks to the fog of fear and cowardice that covered Hollywood during the Fifties due to the House Un-American Activities Committee witch-hunts that blacklisted, among others, the scenarist of *High Noon,* Carl Foreman. It is the story of a dedicated man doing his job and not being swayed by the self-serving timidity of his community.

The former is a crippled and dishonest mockery of that noble 1952 effort. And the core of corruption that is *Outland*'s most notable feature is redolent of that slavish mockery. More, it is a screenplay that demonstrates Peter Hyams has the plotting sensitivity of a kamikaze pilot with eighteen missions to his credit.

Wedded to the bone-stupid *idée fixe* of transposing *High Noon* one for one, without expanding or restructuring the plot to account for alien conditions and a different societal mesh, Hyams made this film an exercise in repeated inconsistencies, illogicalities, and contrivances sufficient to give a coprolite a tic.

Let me enumerate.

In *High Noon* we have a prairie community setting with a population of maybe two hundred people, most of whom are farmers and small businessmen and ranchers. They are not gunslingers, they are middle-class burghers and common laborers. It is not surprising, therefore, that Gary Cooper's Marshal would find almost no one to help him. They were people who had relied entirely on the Marshal for peacekeeping, of which there had been no serious necessity in some time as the film begins. It was a slow, slumbering town without danger.

Contrast that with the mining colony of Io, where the toughest, burliest laborers in the Solar System have come to brave incredible adversity to burn titanium out of a hundred-meter deep

Left: The corrupt Sheppard (Peter Boyle).

Right: O'Niel's only loyal friend is a tough female doctor (Frances Sternhagen).

crater in airless, high-pressure circumstances. Over twenty-one hundred men, the equivalent of oil riggers and high steel workers and gandy dancers. Not cowards, but grizzled roughnecks who work hard, drink hard, and whose lives of confinement would produce not—as Hyams contends—passivity, but a tendency to brawl, to seek hardy entertainments, to get involved in the politics and work-problems of their enclosed society.

In *High Noon* the character of the town is so clearly laid out that we have no difficulty believing the timid mouselike citizens would hide behind their shuttered windows. But in the Con-Amalgamated refinery 27 it is impossible to believe that Marshal O'Niel could not find enough mean, sympathetic, tough hands to make up a cadre of deputies. For God's sake, look at yourself! Are *you* a coward? I'm not, I'd join the cause. And so would you. And so would all those lineal descendants of long-haul truckers, anthracite miners and merchant marine deckhands. It is simply impossible to accept that men recruited and signed to time contracts for their burliness and ability to suffer life under such extreme conditions would *all* be sniveling, head-in-the-sand cowards.

But to maintain with blind illogic that trope of *High Noon,* Hyams defies what we all understand of simple human nature.

Further. Con-Am is government regulated. All

through the film O'Niel says they're afraid of losing their franchise, that's why the Earth government has placed Marshals on hand. If the police of any city found they had a serious situation for which they needed more men, they would simply go out and deputize. Conscription. And there are *always* men who sign up for such *posse comitatus.* But not at Con-Am 27 where the moron plot demands that to maintain the *High Noon* parallel, Sean Connery has to go it alone. That is manipulation of reality in deference to the belief that an audience is too stupid to perceive the corruption of real life.

Further. O'Niel acts stupid throughout. If he intercepts the phone conversation between refinery foreman Sheppard—the Peter Boyle villain—and the shadowy criminal cartel from whom he's been buying his narcotics, all he has to do is tape the call and then go arrest Sheppard, lock him up till the next shuttle, and send him back for prosecution. But he doesn't tape the conversation, which is solid evidence.

Further. He *finds* the drugs stashed in the meat locker. What does he do with this valuable evidence that will be needed for a trial? He flushes it down a toilet. Very smart. Show me even the stupidest country hick deputy who would find dope he needed for a bust, who would then flush the evidence.

Further. O'Niel knows two gunmen are coming

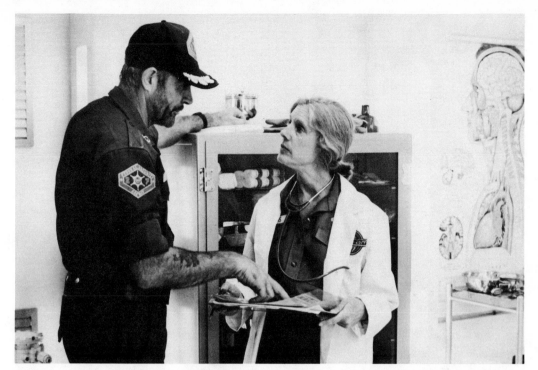

in on the shuttle. Instead of calling the space station and having authorities there check the luggage of all passengers for weapons, thus stopping them at the start, he allows them to board. Or maybe I'm being too picayune. So then, if he isn't a complete asshole, let him stand with his deputies (even the traitor deputy) at the egress port of the shuttle when it arrives. Let him speak to the onboard personnel and have them send out passengers one at a time, have them drop their pants while their baggage is searched, and catch the two "best professional killers in the Solar System" (as the voice on the space-phone called them) before they gain access to a huge refinery complex where they can set up an ambush. And if your deputies say, "We don't want to get involved," then if you are the topkick of the peacekeeping force you simply say, "Your ass is fired, collect your gear." Try and convince me that all these space cops, career men, obviously, will risk loss of pay and being drummed out of the service, because they're afraid to help O'Niel... *which is their job!*

Further. If O'Niel has such certain knowledge that Sheppard is the power behind this scam, and if you don't want to acknowledge that all O'Niel has to do is take the fucker into custody till help arrives, then have him simply go to Sheppard's office—as he does on several occasions—tie the clown up and sit there with his laser rifle trained on the port. Have him wait for these two skillful assassins and when they come to check in with their boss, to find out why they can't find O'Niel, let the Marshal blow them out of their socks.

But that's too logical. Too simple. Too direct. It would deny us the joys of that imbecilic chase

through the refinery. A chase that defies its *own* internal consistency, not to mention the simple precepts of logic. Let me point out a few to you.

"These guys are the best," said the mysterious criminal voice on the space-phone, when Sheppard called for help. (And do you perceive another lamebrain manipulation of reality in that Sheppard can call for help whenever he needs it, but O'Niel can't? Or won't. Simply put: *he doesn't,* thereby making him seem even more a dolt, rather than the superior cop we're asked to believe he is.) These heavy-duty killers come fully equipped with laser rifles that sport heat-seeking telescopic sights. We are treated to shot after shot of these infrared heat-seeking devices tracking back and forth. But each time they get O'Niel in their sights, with him unaware of the danger, *they miss the first shot!* Every single time. Thereby giving O'Niel a chance to escape, to fire back, to pull a diversionary maneuver. What science, what technology, what skilled trackers! What horse cookies!

If these are the two best assassins the crime syndicate and Sheppard can come up with, I'll throw any two of the punchiest button-men in Brooklyn against them and relax.

And for a big finale, for the towering moment of absolute idiocy, Hyams asks us to believe that these killers who are "the best," who apparently have been out in space a long time, who understand the laws of physics (which is more than can be said for Hyams), are simpleminded and/or distracted enough to fire a laserblast at a greenhouse window, thus exploding them out into the vacuum.

The night I saw the film, the audience booed

and hissed at this ridiculous climax. I was pleased to see that not even an audience slavering to enjoy one of these "sci-fi flicks" for special effects was prepared to let themselves be so intellectually insulted. I wish Mr. Hyams had been there. And I wish I had the spoiled fruit concession.

I've spent almost three thousand words stripping this gawdawfulness to the rotten core, and I could go on for another five thousand. The phony scare technique of having a cat jump out at Frances Sternhagen. The avoidance of common sense in O'Niel's being able to tap Sheppard's line but in not putting a recorder on the wire so he could find out who the traitor in his midst might be. And the big moral shuck of not having O'Niel simply walk into that dining bay and say, "Okay, you hundred working stiffs, you're all deputized, let's go get the Bad Guys!"

Further. Where is the labor union for these workers? Don't tell me that the United Mine Workers or the Teamsters or the futuristic equivalent of an AFL-CIO wouldn't have shop stewards there protecting the rights of the men. Don't tell me that in that vast body of over two thousand men there wasn't *one* like Victor Riesel, the columnist who had acid thrown in his face for trying to expose union corruption. Don't tell me that there wasn't *one* union man who would see his fellows were being killed by contraband junk proffered by a company man, who wouldn't spread the word and organize other workers. And what kind of schmucks are these 2000+ workers supposed to be, that they can see others of their number

Above: Two assassins arrive to kill O'Niel. In High Noon, *a whole gang threatened the marshal—why only two men in* Outland? *(Even if he weren't a trained lawman, O'Niel would need only one assistant to even up the odds.) Worse, why is the more frightening of the two men killed first, leaving the weaker opponent for the finale?*

Right: An assassin plummets to his death.

running amuck and dying from some nasty substance, who don't blow the whistle? Even in wholly owned company towns the miners and factory workers stand up for their rights. To ignore that entire aspect of the situation denies the realities of the Labor Movement for the past hundred years. Only in the incomplete, manipulate-as-you-will duplicity of a bad writer can such factors be eschewed.

High Noon was about something important. Like Arthur Miller's *The Crucible* it was about being a "good German," about letting the powers of repression and censorship and evil do their dirtywork unhampered. It might be shown today as a warning against the New Puritanism of the Moral Majority.

Outland is about nothing. It is simply a cheap filmic device to give the makers of little plastic models a chance to convince you your sense of wonder has atrophied. It is an untalented man's career getting another boost from your innocent desire to see a good science fiction film. It is the

bastardization of someone else's original idea, ineptly translated into a genre where it does not work.

In an interview published just about the time the film was released, Frances Sternhagen said, "This isn't really science fiction. It is set in a science fiction ambiance, but it is more like an old Western. It just happens to be an old Western on a satellite of Jupiter."

And *that* is the most corrupt thing about *Outland*.

Thirty years after *Galaxy Magazine* conceived the perfect example of what sf would look like if it were put in the hands of dabblers, fools, and perverters . . . the template becomes a nasty reality. It is called *Outland*.

Ms. Sternhagen, an intelligent actress who, in this case, has made an incredibly dumb statement, does not seem to perceive the invidious-

ness of her comparison. I won't comment on how Ms. Sternhagen—recently on Broadway in Strindberg's "The Father"—would look on such a transposition of the classics. "Oh, it's just 'Miss Julie' rewritten as a superhero comic." "Oh, it's just 'Richard III' as a roller disco comedy." "Oh, it's just 'An Enemy of the People' as an underwater ballet for Esther Williams."

But the inept and inappropriate warping of *High Noon* into a genre where it doesn't work bothers her not in the least.

Such tenebrous thinking from a respected artist only serves to validate for the jimooks who made *Outland* their arrogant stupidity in cobbling up such a piece of duplicity.

And the most chilling news of all is that a director has been signed for the filming of the sequel to *2001,* and that creative consciousness is none other than Peter Hyams.

Cafe Flesh: Midnight Hit for a Pornographic Age

Jerry Stahl

Travesties abound. By any estimate, a catalogue of torments in the twentieth century would ravage twice as much virgin forest as the Manhattan Yellow Pages. But who'd read it? At best, all but the most saintly or sadistic would be nodding off by the second yellow page. For it's the peculiar charm of the Present Era that, faced with a glut of agonies—Lonesome Gunmen, Industrial Strength Tumors, Tylenol Monsters, and the Slaughter of Innocents Abroad—its inhabitants succumb to a sort of hormonal apathy, some bone-deep "Ho hum!" immunity to horror that seems to breed in direct proportion to life's horrific potential.

Indeed. Whether such resistance portends salvation or certain doom depends on your P.O.V. What *is* certain is that all that really shocks us any more are details. Statistics pale beside that juicy close-up. (It's not that John Wayne Gacey disposed of 27—or was it 37?—wayward lads beneath his rec room that really grabs you. It's that he did them in dressed in a clown suit. What an image!)

Abstractions simply fade without that visceral peek. Half a century after the fact, folks chat about The Six Million with less emotion than they once mustered for The Fab Four. Which means something. When time, or applied narcotics, manages to neutralize even our Holocausts, then what may be required is a more vivid fix—a little movie, say, of Ilse Koch whistling "Deutschland

Uber Alles" as she waggles the blade that will castrate her *amoroso* in far-off Buchenwald—something brutal enough to rip through the gauze in which we've cast the past, to let its true impact, its flames and horrors, illumine us anew.

What we need, in short, are images more shocking than the truths that shocked us into numbness to begin with. Which takes us to *Cafe Flesh*.

It would be the height of pretension to claim that Rinse Dream, the director, or I knew what sort of twist-o shocker we had on our hands when we wrote *Cafe Flesh*. The film that you know, and (if the gods of strangeness are good) the one you will continue to see midnights at your fave Revival House, is a far more brazen, flawed, and schizophrenic stretch of celluloid than we'd originally planned. But then how *do* you plan on schizophrenia? What do you pack?

To make a long, squirmy saga short and printable, Dream and I came up with the idea for a film about the burned-out future back in 1981. Our object, in that shining epoch, was to put on the map a postnuke musical, a kind of irradiated *Guys and Dolls,* where slap-happy mutants and atomic mobsters held sway over a society deprived of all wholesome pleasures. Bleak-but-bouncy was the universe we envisaged—all rendered in the nascent New Wave fashion that films from *Flashdance* (1983) to *Liquid Sky* (1983) have long since altered into the aesthetic leisure suit of the Eighties. But never mind.

Not only was New Wave the Next Big Thing,

Jerry Stahl was cowriter (as "Herbert W. Day"), with director "Rinse Dream," of *Cafe Flesh*. He has written for *Rolling Stone, California, The Village Voice,* and *The Movies*.

Above: No longer able to control her sexual desires, Lana (Pia Snow)—"coming out of the closet" to reveal that she is a Sex Positive—makes her way through the impotent postnuclear punks and toward the Cafe Flesh stage. Below: Lana (on her back) puts on a sexual exhibition with Angel (Marie Sharp), another recent addition to the government-run sex circuit. The sex in Cafe Flesh is graphic, but is stylized rather than raunchy and has thematic relevance. Indeed the film itself is one of the few XXX-rated pictures that is not only well made but also has a thought-provoking storyline.

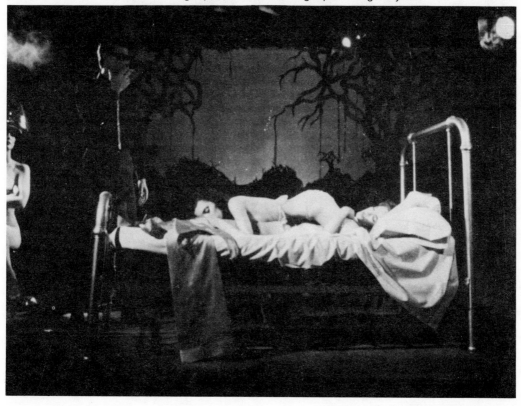

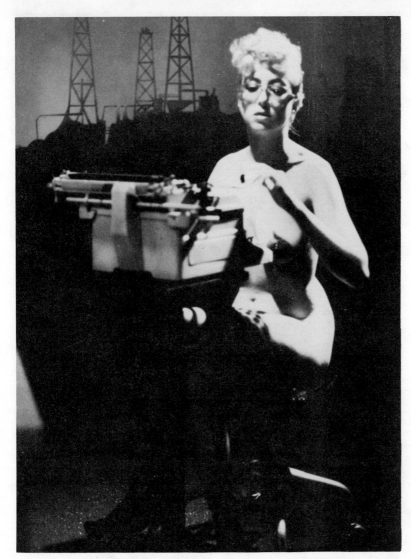

Two stills showing one of the oddly choreographed, stylistically filmed sex acts put on by performers at the Cafe Flesh.

but so was the New Apocalypse. This was, old-sters will recall, pre-*The Road Warrior* (1982), pre-*The Atomic Cafe* (1982), before sobbers like *Testament* (1983) and *The Day After* (TVM-1983) captured the public's fancy. Legions, we knew, would soon be lining up to rouse a moribund public with all manner of nuclear entertainment. And for a few million we were prepared to do it our way.

Only—grim surprise—no one seemed to share our ardor. For months on end we made like Brylcreemed Isaiahs, pitching our prophecies of Atomic Dollars, of the Box Office Magic to be had by showing-the-folks-out-there-what-life-will-be-like-after-they-bounce-the-Big-One. But playing prophet barely pays for lunch.

No need to chronicle our visits to sloe-eyed studio execs, those lupine producers and twitchy V.P.s, the low-budget magyars and would-be mo-guls just in from Dallas where "Dad's in plastics." Suffice it to say they all bowed out, but not before we got to watch the panic glaze their pupils. For

these stalwarts did not just say "No," they said "Never," a parlous signal that spooked us into collusion with the unlikely swells who finally said "Okay."

As it happened, a group of "Adult" financiers—the sort of fellows whose idea of heaven is a button-down banlon and a black El Dorado with tinted windows and "XXX" plates—had a hun-dred thousand they wanted to sink into "a more highgrade product." They were, in their way, ready to make the leap from *Teenage Sushi Girls* to something like a Real Movie. And *Cafe Flesh* struck them as just the right hot little property. With minor changes, of course.

To qualify as Triple X (and avoid costly artificial kneecaps) we swore solemnly to insert half a dozen shots of "poundcake," or "money scenes," as hard-core pros are wont to call the *Cinema Gyno* that feeds their families. But to qualify as art (sop to our pretensions), we were permitted to cram whatever livid riffs or visuals we chose into the rest of the film. All in ten days, on a

single set, in a studio roughly the size of a large Laundromat.

Drab but true. To get what we wanted made, we had to agree to make something else. Which is, of course, the Hollywood Way. The constraints clamped on our vision, dictates of the Porn Politburo whose system we'd bought into, meant that we had to work around the flesh-on-flesh; to squeeze our message, if you will, in between the cracks.

Like many apple-cheeked young artistes, we just assumed it would all turn out okay, that we could change everything back later. Surely the Big Boys would go along! We told ourselves we'd simply excise the rut-and-snuggle, then laugh about the whole fiasco over Rob Roys at Jack Valenti's when we popped in to pick up our R rating. Self-delusion, as Voltaire tells us, is the key to contentment.

Our original vision of the future, hardly Disney turf to begin with, thus took its first, fatal lurch down the road to Big League Strange. Without meaning to, we created our own mutant genre, Eschatological Erotica, as we reshaped Doomsday to accommodate libidinous incidentals. The result was as fortuitous as penicillin, if less socially redeeming.

The revised foundation of the script was simple: After the Blast, survivors would break down into two unequal camps: Sex Positives and Sex Negatives. The latter, 99 percent of the populace, would be unable to have sex. The former, the lucky one percent, would be not only able but obliged to perform for the deprived majority, who suffered seizures when they tried it themselves. A special team of men in raincoats, the Enforcers, were dispatched by authorities to flush out Positives who failed to fulfill their civic duties. Etc., etc. . . .

All performances would take place in the atomic hotspot called Cafe Flesh. And the act itself was reduced (or elevated) to ritual: symbolic pageants where lugs in cartoony masks serviced the fair sex against a backdrop of barbed wire, The Berlin Wall, heads in cages, or bearded infants impaled in their high chairs, pinned in the swaddling and forced to watch. . . .

Max (Andrew Nichols), a malevolent emcee, was written in to comment on the action. And a love story, radiating angst, played itself out against the background of those prurient floorshows. Nick (Paul McGibboney) and Lana (Pia Snow), a pair of pre-Holocaust lovebirds, suffered the spasms of romance that had outlived its function—Tristan and Isolde in Post-Nuke Purgatory.

Lana had a secret, discovered by the heinous Max: she wasn't really a Negative. Here was a woman who, for love, faked that she *didn't* feel anything. To let her one-and-only know that she could, in fact, get physical and join the Positives onstage would certainly destroy him. And so she pretends otherwise, until the lure of erotic fulfillment becomes too strong and she sacrifices their platonic companionship—a relationship based on mutual nausea—for the ecstatic oppression of the Positives, who must exercise their passion in public or perish for it. Her climactic exposure and onstage betrayal with Johnny Rico (Kevin Jay), star beefcake on the Terminal Thrill Circuit, drives the sullen hero to zombiedom. At film's end, Nick gazes up at his lover's performance, then staggers insensate out into the Nuclear Night. . . .

It might be argued that all climax will be anticlimax after the Nuclear Kiss, that whatever decadence may have driven us to the bitter end will be canceled out in the flesh of those who live beyond it. This is, at last, redemption through radiation, final proof that the Falwells were right, the fruits of passion do ripen into running sores. In *Cafe Flesh,* each soul arrives wrapped in their own poisoned mortality, denatured as the scorched earth he, she, or it inhabits, yet driven to come and slaver over sin they can no longer commit.

An audience of lickerish casualties—Max calls them "Mutants and Mutettes"—drift in nightly to sample the club's spectacles. They groan; they drool. They weep and panic and scratch their eyes . . . but they never turn away. That audience, in a sense, stands out as the most telling element of the film, most evocative of a future well on its way from nightmare to real-life *Walpurgisnacht.*

Halfway through the picture, pretty Lana asks her beau why he continues to frequent the Cafe, when everything he sees there only tortures him. "Because," Nick answers, in the deadpan of the fully damned, "torture is the one thing left I can feel."

Precisely. To a generation that kicked off adolescence jamming Mom's old safety pins through its cheeks, this can pass for Gospel. *Cafe Flesh* is very big with Punks. Perhaps because, as with youth movies of old, your eager teens look to the Big Screen for archetypes of cool. You have to be eighteen or older to see this one, but the lure remains. Wasted youth of every age peg the Flesh-ites as themselves in a few years: high-style mutants hanging out in an underground bar, fed up to their mohawks with the Nowhere they've grown up to inherit. Nuclear war, when it finally hits, will prove that all those postadolescent nihilists were right all along.

Sex, clearly, is not the issue here. Apocalypse itself is what titillates. For the jaded throng who view their own future as a function of a World Gone Rotten, *Cafe Flesh* is a logical destination. The movie exists as graphic proof that, if you're not obliterated one way, you're obliterated another. There are a million dirtier movies in the cosmos. But for an alarmingly large segment of our little world, obliteration seems the sexiest ticket around. A fact your humble author is still not sure he needed verified.

But what the heck? Sometimes a guy just has to scrape the Weltschmerz off his loafers and keep going. What no one knew is how virulent a combo carnality and apocalypse would prove to be. Like testy Mendels, we cross-bred obsessions, tossed sex and self-destruction in the gene pool to see what rose to the top. In this way some viler strain was engendered, and the public exposed.

Considered, then, as the sum of its parts, *Cafe* qualifies as yet another romp through millennium, latest in a grand tradition from *Metropolis* on. Lang propped his parable of capital and labor on geometric sets. *Flesh* foisted its high-rad Haves versus Have-nots against a stylish *nuevo* stage. In our version, we set up Negatives versus Positives, a clash only as metaphoric as your morals require. Perhaps Ilse Koch would have understood.

Cafe's concerns are terminal: the mechanics of lust *après* mega-death; the impotent salacity of the living doomed; the fetish for fiery climax that gives some folks a secret frisson at the prospect of the Holocaust to come, so that survival itself hinges on continued repression. How long *can* we fight off that mushrooming desire?

Just considering such repulso topics, giving them air-time in the brain, amounts to a kind of admission. I remember, by way of pertinent digression, the peculiar self-consciousness of the audience at an L.A. screening of *Salò* (1979), in which Pasolini shifted De Sade's *120 Days of Sodom* to fascist Italy. The eight souls (the rest had walked) still left in the theater to see the climactic series of tortures and atrocities (a screaming young woman is scalped, another is hanged, a young man's tongue is sliced off) had sunken almost out of sight in their seats. And after the lights went up no one could meet anyone else's eyes. For they—we—knew we were all doubly indicted. First, for just being there, for bearing witness and somehow sanctioning the gesture. And second, for simply belonging to a race of creatures that could conceive of such a thing, let alone sit passively in the dark and savor the image.

These films merit comparison on no other level. Only that edgy after-effect connects them; that shock, ultimately, of grim recognition. The audience within *Cafe Flesh* exists as more than a symbol for the one outside. The onscreen voyeurs emerge as our shadow selves: postbomb doppelgangers, just plain folks adapting to an option that's never more than a shudder away.

This is the rank secret at the heart of *Cafe Flesh.* The survivor's quotidian, that scabrous carnival, does not mark some vast departure from Life as We Know It. Au contraire! Their itch for a vicarious fix is the same as the one that brought the paying public in off the streets.

In *Cafe Flesh,* the impotent are driven to have their fate paraded before their eyes. In the here and now, they also watch. Unmanned by a looming horror that leaves them powerless, the audience can't help itself. They're aroused by the image of their own ultimate debasement. They seem to need it.

Torture, our hero says, is the one thing left he can feel.

If the future portrayed in *Cafe Flesh* is an obscene one, it may be because the present long ago became unspeakable.

There has been a nuclear holocaust, but the sexual show must go on at the Cafe Flesh.

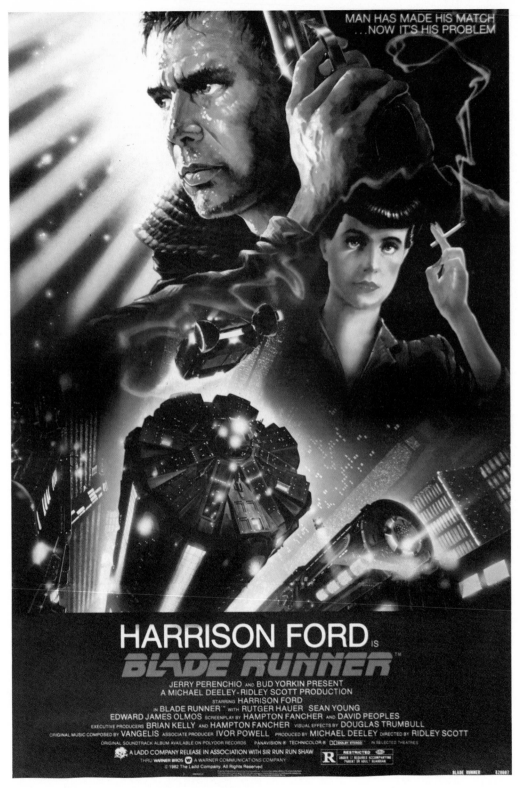

MAN HAS MADE HIS MATCH
...NOW IT'S HIS PROBLEM

HARRISON FORD IS
BLADE RUNNER

JERRY PERENCHIO AND BUD YORKIN PRESENT
A MICHAEL DEELEY-RIDLEY SCOTT PRODUCTION
STARRING HARRISON FORD
IN BLADE RUNNER WITH RUTGER HAUER   SEAN YOUNG
EDWARD JAMES OLMOS SCREENPLAY BY HAMPTON FANCHER AND DAVID PEOPLES
EXECUTIVE PRODUCERS BRIAN KELLY AND HAMPTON FANCHER VISUAL EFFECTS BY DOUGLAS TRUMBULL
ORIGINAL MUSIC COMPOSED BY VANGELIS ASSOCIATE PRODUCER IVOR POWELL PRODUCED BY MICHAEL DEELEY DIRECTED BY RIDLEY SCOTT
ORIGINAL SOUNDTRACK ALBUM AVAILABLE ON POLYDOR RECORDS   PANAVISION ® TECHNICOLOR ®   DOLBY STEREO   IN SELECTED THEATRES
A LADD COMPANY RELEASE IN ASSOCIATION WITH SIR RUN RUN SHAW
THRU WARNER BROS   A WARNER COMMUNICATIONS COMPANY
© 1982 The Ladd Company. All Rights Reserved.

R RESTRICTED
UNDER 17 REQUIRES ACCOMPANYING
PARENT OR ADULT GUARDIAN

When adapting Philip K. Dick's novel Do Androids Dream of Electric
Sheep? *director Ridley Scott "asked my writer Hampton Fancher to think
up a term for detective that would be suitable for the exotic, futuristic time
period we were presenting. He came up with 'blade runner.' I thought it*

was marvelous and it became the film's title." Although the film didn't do well in America when first released, it has since emerged as a cult favorite, a midnight movie staple, and perhaps the first "thinking person's sf film" since 2001: A Space Odyssey (1968). Left: The images on this poster are of blade runner Rick Deckard (Harrison Ford) and his replicant lover Rachael (Sean Young). However, their story may not be as important as the backgrounds; specifically, the streets, buildings, and atmosphere that characterize the year 2019. Above: Deckard searches the hazy streets for a replicant he must kill.

Top: A photo of the megastructure in which the Tyrell Corporation is situated. Buildings such as this dominate the film—in this case, the building is a model created by Doug Trumbull's Entertainment Effects Group. Above: The inhospitable, unhealthy streets of L.A. in thirty-five years. Filming was done on the main street of Warner's Burbank lot.

The Way the Future Looks: *THX 1138* and *Blade Runner*

Robert Silverberg

We are in Los Angeles, but it is not the familiar city of palm trees and perpetual bright sunshine. Above us loom colossal, sloping high-rise buildings of intricate and alien design, patterned, perhaps, after Aztec temples or Babylonian ziggurats, that turn the narrow, congested streets into claustrophobic canyons and hide the dark, pollution-fouled sky. A cold, bleak, maddening rainstorm goes on interminably. Great searchlights intended, possibly, to substitute for the absent sun, send intrusive beams slicing across vast distances from sources mounted somewhere far overhead.

Down here on surface level we move warily through a densely packed district, largely Oriental in population and in architecture, a crazy, hyped-up version of Hong Kong or Tokyo, where a dizzying multitude of flashing electronic signs seeks insistently to draw our attention to games parlors, massage houses, noodle counters, drug-vending shops, and a thousand thousand other commercial establishments. Dull-eyed coolies, bending under immense burdens, jostle us aside without apology. Myriads of spaced-out fanatics in fantastic costumes dance along beside us down the street, each lost in some private bubble of self-absorption. High above us, helicopters moving with reckless velocity buzz like crazed dragonflies between the skyscrapers: police, most likely, searching for the deadly fugitive androids that are said to be loose in the city. At any moment, we think, one of those helicopters may descend from the sky in lunatic spirals and land in the middle of the next block, disgorging policemen who set about making arrests with Kafkaesque implacability.

The mood is oppressive and scary. We are trapped in one of the ultimate urban nightmares: a city of a hundred million people, every one of them hostile to everyone else. The look of the place—dark, menacing, congested, dominated by those immense ponderous towers that crouch like monsters upon the land—is unique and uniquely horrifying. Everything manages to glisten with futuristic pizzazz and nevertheless reveals itself simultaneously to be tinged with rot and decay: new and old, light and dark, airy and ineluctably heavy, both at the same time. The year is 2019, and this is the world of Ridley Scott's 1982 motion picture, *Blade Runner*.

Try another world? Well—

We are indoors. Perhaps within some giant building, perhaps deep underground in a labyrinth of tunnels—it makes little difference. The essential point is that there are no windows and no doors to the outside, that the sun and the sky and the stars are no part of this place, and we inhabit a realm of sterile corridors, bright lights, white walls, a megalopolis with a hospital's grim aseptic dazzle. Here there is neither clutter nor squalor: The prevailing esthetic here is that of the surgical operating chamber, not of the crowded

Robert Silverberg is the award-winning author of *Nightwings, Tower of Glass, Dying Inside, Recalled to Life, A Time of Changes, The Book of Skulls, Born With the Dead, Lord Valentine's Castle, Majipur Chronicles, Master of Life and Death, The Seed of Earth, Up the Line, Son of Man, Sundance,* and *Downward to the Earth*. Probably the most prolific science fiction writer, he also has edited numerous anthologies.

Oriental marketplace. Though the population density is high, perhaps as high as in the world of Blade Runner, there is no sense of overcrowding because there is no random motion. A bland, lobotomized-looking populace, clad in standardized costumes rather like prison garb, makes its journeys from place to place in obedient tidy files, while guards with impassive inhuman faces step in quickly to see to it that no one gets out of line or deviates in any other significant way from the flow of traffic. From gleaming grilles in the walls comes a constant low incomprehensible electronic static, an aural wallpaper of blurps and bleeps and soft crackles, interrupted at frequent intervals by cryptic instructions that are instantly accepted and followed by those to whom they apply. Flickering television screens provide two-way monitoring; computer eyes scan and count and record; Big Brother's minions, unseen but omnipresent, oversee the flow of data. The color scheme is a blinding white-on-white: There is no room for untidiness here, no space whatever for irregularity. The mood, once again, is oppressive and scary. We are trapped, once again, in an ultimate urban nightmare, though of a kind quite different from the last one. The year is something like 2200 A.D., and this is the world of George Lucas's first film, THX 1138, released in 1971.

These movies, Blade Runner and THX 1138, strike me as two of the most valuable science fiction movies ever made. To me they embody the highest virtue the science fiction film can offer: They show the way the future looks, and they show it with such conviction, such richness of detail, such density of texture that the visions of tomorrow they offer will remain embedded forever in my imagination. They have provided a kind of time-travel experience, in a sense, and they have done it so well that I am willing to ignore

entirely the manifest failure of both these movies in most other aspects of the art of science fiction.

If Blade Runner and THX 1138 were novels, they would be undistinguished ones. Blade Runner is indeed based on a science fiction novel, and an outstanding one: Do Androids Dream of Electric Sheep? by the late Philip K. Kick. But—although Dick reported himself pleased with the screenplay that Hampton Fancher and David Peoples drew from his novel, and would, I think, have been pleased by the finished film itself had he lived to see it—Blade Runner bears only the most skeletal resemblance to the book on which it was based, taking from it nothing but the essential plot idea of hunting down a group of escaped androids. As for THX 1138, it began life not as a novel but as a film treatment, produced by the very young George Lucas while he was still a student at U.C.L.A. After Lucas and Walter Murch had expanded it into the full-length script for the final version of the movie, that script was indeed "novelized" for paperback release by the experienced science fiction writer Ben Bova, but not even Bova's professionalism could lift the story beyond the level of the perfunctory. Science fiction is, among other things, a literature of ideas; and the problem that each of these movies has as science fiction literature is its mediocrity on the level of idea.

Blade Runner is simply silly. We are asked to believe that humanity, just a few decades from now, has colonized not merely the Solar System but the stars; that we have populated those stars with "replicants," synthetic human beings that are superior in most ways to ourselves, although they are designed to live only four years; and that a handful of these replicants, having rebelled at being assigned to slavery in the star-colonies, have found their way back to Earth and are

running amok in Los Angeles. Out of this cluster of manifest implausibilities is generated a perfunctory plot in which the androids, hoping to find a way to have their lifespans extended, seek to enlist the aid of their designer, while a police officer follows their trail, taking desperate measures to destroy them—at the risk of his own life, even though the androids have only a few weeks left to live anyway. Since none of these concepts makes much sense, either taken by itself or in conjunction with any of the others, it is hard to find much useful speculative thought of a science-fictional nature in *Blade Runner:* It tells us nothing much that is useful about the human-android relationship, the colonization of the stars, the use of genetic engineering to produce superbeings, or anything else that might seem to be contained in the main premises of the story. If we filter out the self-cancelling absurdities of the plot, we are left with only two concepts that a demanding reader of science fiction might find nourishing. One is the depiction of the female android Pris (Daryl Hannah), a mysterious acrobatic creature in whom the life-force rages so powerfully that when she dies it is with an astonishing display of superhuman fury, the outraged death of an extraordinary though limited being; the other is the question of how to distinguish readily between humans and androids, which was at the core of Dick's novel and which here is crowded into convenient corners of the script, only occasionally to be confronted directly. The rest is straight private-eye stuff, dogged pursuit culminating in a terrifying but conceptually empty rooftop chase.

The ideas around which the story of *THX 1138* are built are not at all foolish—merely hopelessly stale. They go back at least as far as H. G. Wells's

When The Sleeper Wakes of 1899 and E. M. Forster's "The Machine Stops" of 1909, with touches borrowed from such later but hardly recent works as Zamyatin's *We,* Huxley's *Brave New World,* and Orwell's *Nineteen Eighty-Four.* That is, we are ushered once more into the complete totalitarian state, where computers make all decisions and the populace is drugged into complaisance. Uniformity of thought, costume, and behavior is imposed by law and enforced by automatonlike humanoid police; unseen monitors keep watch on everything and everyone; any sign of individuality is relentlessly suppressed. The protagonists are those familiar characters, the rebels against the conformity of it all: THX 1138 (Robert Duvall) and his female roommate, LUH 3417 (Maggie McOmie), who surreptitiously cut down on the dosage of the drug they are compelled to take to reduce their sexual impulses, and, after restoring their libido, set about conceiving a child, which is forbidden by the regulatory powers. They are apprehended; LUH 3147 is destroyed, but THX 1138 manages to escape the hivelike city into an outer realm where other rebels and nonconformists have taken lodging. A pair of implacable robots pursue him; and the film, which until this point has been pure if overfamiliar science fiction, devolves in its final third into a mere chase story, an endless sequence of frantic zoomings through subterranean tunnels, until THX 1138 at last eludes the police and escapes into the open-air world beyond.

But—even though one of these films is cobbled together from nonsensical premises and the other is manufactured from clichés—it is, I think, beside the point to pay much attention to those failings. These are *not* novels, with a novel's scope for

Left: Deckard suspects that this mannequin is one of the replicants he must kill. He's correct: Pris (Daryl Hannah) is about to spring on him.

Right: A minimal set that seems suitable for an absurdist play. In THX 1138 such empty rooms with white floors and walls become prisons for dissidents. Here robot security guards harass THX 1138 (Robert Duvall), who almost blends into the environment.

explication and analysis. They are movies, that is, visual events, pictorial compositions extended along a narrative axis by complex technological means. It is possible to wish that *Blade Runner* had relied more on the intricacies of Philip K. Dick's novel and less on the formulas of detective fiction, or that *THX 1138* had given us more of a look at the assumptions on which its totalitarian society was founded and less of a mad chase in those tunnels, but to express such wishes is to ignore an ugly reality, the Catch-22 of science fiction moviemaking: Science fiction films require special effects, special effects are costly, costly films need to pull in big audiences in order to break even, and big audiences are snared only by reliance on familiar plot mechanisms. (As it is, *Blade Runner,* which cost something like $30,000,000 to produce, was a commercial failure. *THX 1138* was the relatively inexpensive work of a novice filmmaker, and in its way was an uncompromising and difficult movie, revealing its plot in an oblique and demanding way, but without its harrowing if meaningless chase finale it might have drawn no audience at all, with consequent difficulties for George Lucas's further career.) It is precisely in those special effects that the merits of the two movies lie; indeed, *Blade Runner* and *THX 1138* provide startling evidence that an important science fiction movie can be assembled out of unimportant science fiction material. If their failings as fiction had not been as great, they would have been finer movies yet; but perhaps that is asking too much.

They are visionary movies in the most literal sense of that word. They show us futures, and they do it, not as a novelist might, with a few deftly chosen adjectives cunningly disposed on the page, but with nuts-and-bolts reality. In *Do An-*

droids Dream of Electric Sheep? Philip K. Dick creates his atmosphere of gritty, dismaying urban decay with quick little touches ("the tattered gray wall-to-wall carpeting. . . . The broken and semi-broken appliances in the kitchen, the dead machines. . . . Tufts of dried-out bonelike weeds poking slantedly into a dim and sunless sky"). Ridley Scott, at an expenditure of millions of real dollars, builds an entire gigantic city of enormous pseudo-Aztec temples and flashing pseudo-neon signs, fills it with weird little shops where commodities as yet uninvented are sold, and whisks his camera swiftly through it, giving us tantalizingly elliptical glances at a future world that he has in fact realized in immense detail. I have seen it argued that it is somehow a higher achievement for a novelist to create the texture of a world by quick descriptive touches than it is for a movie producer to turn loose a battalion of carpenters and electricians, but—despite my own novelist's bias—I'm not so sure of that; the effects that Scott creates by building sets and letting us have mere glimpses of them are at least as elegant and cunning as any instance of the science fiction writer's descriptive art. The Los Angeles of *Blade Runner* is a unique invention, actually owing relatively little to the Dick novel; however preposterous the adventures of Rick Deckard (Harrison Ford) may be as he stalks his way through that somber, ominous city in search of the crazed replicant Roy Batty (Rutger Hauer), the city itself remains the essential imaginative achievement, and it does the essential science-fictional thing of displaying and illuminating a landscape not otherwise accessible to the eye. It mattered very little to me whether Deckard pushed Batty over the edge of the roof or Batty pushed Deckard over; what did matter, and a great deal, was the hypnotic

power of Scott's camera as it panned down the face of one of those overwhelming buildings, and showed me the architecture of an era yet to come.

So too with *THX 1138*. "Imagine, if you can, a small room, hexagonal in shape, like the cell of a bee," wrote E. M. Forster in 1909. "It is lighted neither by window nor by lamp, yet it is filled with a soft radiance. There are no apertures for ventilation, yet the air is fresh." And we are launched into the stiflingly circumscribed world of "The Machine Stops." Or we turn to Zamyatin's *We,* on which, I suspect, *THX 1138* was founded, and we read, "As always, the Music Plant played the 'March of the One State' with all its trumpets. The numbers walked in even ranks, four abreast, ecstatically stepping in time to the music— hundreds, thousands of numbers, in pale blue unifs, with golden badges on their breasts, bearing the State Number of each man and woman." But Lucas makes us *see* it. He makes us *hear* it. The faces, the eyes, the shaven scalps, the white-on-white corridors, the electronic buzzes and murmurs, the flow of computerized commands so baffling to the twentieth-century eavesdropper— the movie is an astonishing experience, an all-out immersion in a world of the future, without explanation, without apology. If Lucas is using other writers' material, he is making it altogether his own by the vivid way he realizes it and by the sheer uncompromising strangeness of the place into which he thrusts the viewer. (Scott does that too. Though he uses a crude voice-over technique to explain details of the plot, he offers the startling urban landscape largely as a given, without footnotes or commentary, thereby greatly enhancing the power of its strangeness.)

The task of the science fiction novelist, ideally stated, is to discover a unique speculative concept, develop its implications through a rigorous intellectual process, and make it accessible as fiction through an appropriate choice of characters, plot, and narrative style. Since science fiction usually involves the depiction of an unfamiliar landscape, the novelist's craft requires the mastery of descriptive techniques that will convey that landscape to the reader with maximum visual impact (a craft that entails more than a little collaboration on the part of the reader, but is a collaboration that the skilled novelist knows how to elicit). The task of the science fiction moviemaker, ideally stated, should be the same, and perhaps some day it will be, although, as I have suggested, commercial considerations at present seem to demand certain oversimplifications of concept and plot and character, and, in any case, even the most uncompromising of films are necessarily unable to achieve some of the things a novel can manage.

So far, I suppose most and perhaps all of the science fiction movies that have been made have failed the highest tests of science fiction excellence; but in the domain of depiction of an unfamiliar landscape, that is, in the domain of special effects, there have been notable successes: *Alien* (1979), *2001* (1968), *Star Wars* (1977), *Forbidden Planet* (1956), and many more. I think it is no trivial achievement to make futuristic visions concrete in that way; as I have said, I am not among those who would claim that building a movie set is somehow a less worthy artistic accomplishment than composing a paragraph of vivid descriptive prose. What those films managed in the way of putting the look of the future on the screen was far from trivial. But I can think of no others in which the special effects are dedicated so powerfully to

Right: Following a long, suspenseful chase, THX 1138 escapes the oppressive underground world. In director George Lucas's student short THX 2238 4EB, on which he based his feature version, the chase took up the entire twenty minutes. (Moreover, the lead character had hair.)

Below: On the ledge of one of the city's many dilapidated, abandoned buildings, Deckard battles powerful replicant Roy Batty (Rutger Hauer).

the creation of a coherent imagined environment that wholly enfolds and houses the story that is set within it. That the story is foolish in one case and stereotyped in the other is regrettable but fundamentally unimportant. What Ridley Scott ac-complished in *Blade Runner* and George Lucas did in *THX 1138* is notable despite all peripheral failings: to create a landscape of the mind, vivid and compelling and complete, that for one breathless moment of suspension of disbelief seems to be the real thing, the authentic future, which we can in no other way experience than through the medium of lens and light and screen.

WarGames and the Real World

John Badham

When *WarGames* was released in June of 1983, the most frequently asked question from the media was: "Can this really happen?" For those who have not seen the picture, *WarGames* is the story of a seventeen-year-old boy who mistakenly interfaces his home computer with the government's war games computer. Thinking he is hooked up to some fantastic video game, he almost causes World War III. "Can a smart kid like Matthew Broderick played in the film use his home computer to break into military installations and create near disaster?" This question was the subject of constant discussion for a while and the initial response from government and military experts was a loud and unequivocal "No!" Somehow the filmmakers had made all this up.

As I read the articles I began to be dismayed. I did come rather late to this film and had to accept many facts from the authors as givens. Maybe I'd been lied to. These two young authors, Walter Parkes and Larry Lasker, with shining innocent faces, were really con men in Ivy League khakis and button-downs.

Shortly after, however, small voices of reassurance were heard. Little articles appeared that said there were serious defects in the system. Item: The U.S. Navy began to worry about the security of their computers. Could they be breached by nonsecure personnel? Translated, that means could spies break into their computers? The Navy formed Tiger Teams of experts whose job was to try to break into any or all of the Navy equipment. A few weeks later, the reports came back. And the news was not good. It was very poor. In fact, it was terrible. Not only did the Tiger Teams gain access to every computer they confronted, they themselves were shocked how easy it was.

Now a few articles began to appear that detailed kids accessing school computers and changing their grades, as Broderick does early in *WarGames*. One boy almost went to jail. A whole group of kids were then arrested by the FBI and had their computers confiscated for stealing computer time from the Datanet telephone computer link-up. In another case, one boy almost crashed the Sloan-Kettering medical computer. But best of all occurred last August when the press broke the story of a group of kids who came to be known as the "Milwaukee 414." In one fell swoop, they gave the lie to all the articles written by the "experts." Not only had they broken into computers all over the country, they had accessed the Los Alamos nuclear computer. Forget that it was a noncritical area, because the fact is, they broke in.

I began to believe that the nay-saying experts of the early articles didn't really know what they were talking about. You all remember Mark Twain's definition: "An expert is just some damn fool from out of town."

One thing that really intrigued me in all the controversy surrounding the film is that most everyone focused solely on the superficial issue of

John Badham directed *WarGames, Blue Thunder, Dracula, Whose Life Is It Anyway?, The Bingo Long Traveling All-Stars and Motor Kings,* and *Saturday Night Fever.*

Left: Teenagers David (Matthew Broderick) and Jennifer (Ally Sheedy) use David's home computer to interface with their school's computer to alter their grades. Soon David will try another prank: He'll tap into the Defense Department's WOPR computer and initiate a friendly game of "Global Thermonuclear War"—not realizing that WOPR is playing for real.

Right: Dabney Coleman (L), who plays a Defense Department executive, talks with director John Badham.

computer security. No one addressed the more substantive issues. Nobody touched on the kinds of things Dr. Helen Caldicott deals with, which is clearly what the end of *WarGames* deals with: The idea of winning or even fighting a nuclear war is insane. The piling up of nuclear warheads is ridiculous because we can never use them: "if you love this planet."

Tied in with this idea is one that is secondary in *WarGames* but key to understanding the whole idea. I'm referring to runaway technology. Now, we have always had a kind of love-hate relationship with technology. We love all the things technology will do for us. It does have its good points: It can give us control over the environment, it can give us pleasure and can certainly do a lot of work for us. I personally have no fear of technology. If you judge by my house, I seem to be in love with it. I have video equipment and various cooking gadgets, solar-operated microwave ovens, electric sundials, computerized banana peelers, and so on. They're all great fun, when they work. But have you ever noticed that they very often do not work? What they do is control your life. The servant becomes the master; the tail wags the dog. The labor-saving device very often turns out to be the labor-intensive device.

As technology gets more and more complicated you can expect more and more major complications. You remember how many back-up systems and safety devices were built into nuclear power plants and yet under the right combination of circumstances, those one in a million shots, we have Three Mile Island. That's pretty big stuff, right? All the nuclear power plants have had their share of troubles but that was your basic biggy. Did you notice in the articles and

interviews with the guys that run these plants that they think of them as just over-sized generators? Just another diesel engine, only bigger. Utility companies don't seem to grasp the nature of the beast they have by the tail. What actually went on at Three Mile Island in the context of a normal power plant would never have been a problem. Even the shift supervisor might not have been notified. But with this technology and its possibilities for disaster, it was a four-hundred-million-dollar disaster. From what? A man sitting at a desk with an open valve and a tag hanging from the valve saying don't worry about this because we're working on it. Something went wrong and in a matter of seconds, disaster. Importantly, the technology was not so much at fault as were the people operating it.

Certainly the terrifying incident with Russia and the KAL plane exemplifies runaway technology in so many ways. No one has yet answered the question of why the plane was off course. Was it the navigational system, the pilot error, a spying mission, or what? But there they were, off course over a country that historically is paranoid in the extreme about their borders. The KAL pilots knew that better than anyone. Wasn't a KAL airliner shot down five years before by the Soviets, when it was off course? You also know the Soviets would be aware that the flight regularly passed through that area at one o'clock in the morning. But Soviet paranoia was in full swing, so missiles with sophisticated heat-seeking technology were launched successfully, murdering two hundred and sixty-nine people. Here the technology may or may not have been at fault, but one thing is for damn sure. The people who were in charge had no business operating it. We know not to give an

angry ten-year-old boy a fast car to drive or a rifle to shoot, but we haven't learned that lesson with our adults.

Thank God that Reagan chose not to rattle his saber in the KAL situation. His first reported reaction was "we don't want to overreact." In the future, may the President always be that controlled and that sensible. But whether he is able to is another interesting question.

Robert McNamara had an article in *Foreign Affairs* (Fall 1983) that quickly controverted the Administration. In an interesting turnaround for the hawkish McNamara, he urged NATO to renounce its reliance on "the threat" to use nuclear weapons. He said, "using nuclear weapons against the Soviets would be an act of suicide because it would touch off a chain reaction of escalating nuclear exchanges. The threat of first strike has lost all credibility as a deterrent to Soviet aggression. You cannot build a credible deterrent on an incredible action." According to the article, this view seems to be shared by a lot of people who were very involved in the government defense establishment: McGeorge Bundy, the NSA advisor to Kennedy and Johnson; George Kennan, the former Soviet ambassador; and George Smith, the chief negotiator on Salt I. This group advocated what any reasonable person would advocate. They all favor a "flexible response." A response tempered by the knowledge of what an opponent might or might not do, and whether or not there is some chance that the conflict might be contained without going into nuclear retaliation. Seems reasonable, right?

But it will come as no surprise that not everyone shares this view, unfortunately. A book published in October 1983 called *SIOP: The Secret U.S.*

Plan for Nuclear War by Peter Pringle and William Arkin gives us another instance of runaway technology becoming the master of the situation. The SIOP appears in *WarGames* under another name: the "WOPR." Many people thought we made that up. However, the only part that was invented for the film was the name WOPR. Anything for a cheap laugh. SIOP stands for Single Integrated Operations Plan. It is a computer whose function is to evaluate war plans twenty-four hours a day, three hundred and sixty-five days a year. It is constantly fed updated military information, political information, weather patterns, etc., from all the countries in the world. Based on this shifting information, the SIOP constantly plays war games and creates war scenarios. For example, a war scenario might begin like this: U.S.S.R. launches a missile at China. Then China retaliates. Then the U.S. sends up a missile. Now the Soviets send up several, etc. Theoretically, in the event of a nuclear attack, the most up-to-date war plans made by the SIOP could be handed to the President to aid in his decision making. That decision could have to be made in twenty-three minutes or as little as six minutes if the attacking missiles were submarine launched.

It is hard to understand what kind of rational, well-considered decision could be made in six minutes. According to *SIOP: The Secret U.S. Plan for Nuclear War,* the SIOP was tested in 1982 by the Reagan administration and found severely wanting. It certainly did not live up to expectations. However, according to the authors of the book, the government has gotten itself into the alarming position of no longer being able to employ Mr. McNamara's flexible response. The

Above: With world destruction only seconds away, David and all the people in the war-room desperately try to stop WOPR from playing the war game until the end. Left: WOPR's computer display screens tell the viewer the point of the movie: In a nuclear war there will be no winners.

SIOP is geared for massive retaliation only, not flexible response. "The nuclear battlefield," according to the authors, "no longer allows the luxury of presidential control." How's that for unnerving? Control is referred to as "luxury." This is all a nightmarish version of when you call to question your telephone bill, only to be told that it has to be that way because the computer needs it like that. This is not a satisfactory answer.

WarGames emphatically advocates the thoughtful maintenance of hands-on human control. We have seen over and over again how easy it is for technology to get out of hand. With nuclear technology we are talking about the ultimate Out of Hand. All of us now find ourselves saddled with a responsibility that neither our grandparents or even our parents ever had to face, much less conceive of: the containment of a technology that can quite simply wipe out life on Earth, not once but *forty* times over with the present stockpile of nuclear weapons. Talk about overkill.

We clearly cannot shrug off the responsibility and pass it onto our government, our religion, or our scientists. We need to take that responsibility ourselves. How? I cannot tell you. I don't even know if it is possible. I do know that if we fail we have no one to blame but ourselves.

This article was written to be simultaneously an inclusion in this book and, in a slightly different form, an address before the Physicians for Social Responsibility.

PART III

THE CREATORS

Designing the Future

Syd Mead

I drew pictures from the time I was two or three, like all children do. The difference was that I tended to make more elaborate drawings earlier in the process and, as I got older, became more and more proficient at making the scenes I depicted look real. In a way, it was an escape: I thought that the worlds I dreamed up were more interesting than the one I lived in. Indeed, it was because I enjoyed imagining what the future could be like that, after leaving the army, I was prompted to study industrial design at the Art Center School in Los Angeles, and, later, to choose my particular career.

I supply *ideas*—I call them "additional visual vocabularies"—to clients in fields as diverse as boat design, aircraft interiors, mass transit, product design, motion pictures, and automotive exterior design. There are innumerable engineers, materials specialists, techniques, and plant facilities available to make production of objects relatively simple, but the fact that for more than fifteen years I've been hired over and over again by clients with large production staffs proves to me that *ideas* are at a premium. You must have an idea of something before you can start figuring out how you can make it.

The term "conceptualist" was invented for me to use as my screen credit on *Blade Runner* (1982). Whereas a "futurist" predicts general world trends, on anything—food, housing, the nature of government evolvement, the economy —a conceptualist, in regard to design, is someone who thinks up how things might *look* according to a very exact client-supplied scenario involving a specific setting and time frame. If the client tends to be conservative, he can be his own worst enemy because conceptualizing is essentially a freewheeling, radical procedure. I deal with the look of the future in the whole lifestyle spectrum. This means that I theorize on everything from how architecture might look to how people might dress. Politics and economics don't really fit in, but I suggest what forms higher levels of technological achievement will take and I cover what might occur in the whole social scene. All of these things together produce a picture that has that odd look one would get if one could peer through a time telescope.

My design company usually works on several projects at once. Now, for instance, I'm doing two architectural projects, gearing up for a major design job in the transportation field, and finishing up on my involvement on *2010: Odyssey Two* (1984). In the last five years, movie design has contributed between 20 to 25 percent of our gross company income. As far as I'm concerned, doing conceptual art for film companies is just the same as working for other clients. You work with a director, who in turn is working with a script, either

Syd Mead has done conceptual art for *Star Trek—The Motion Picture, Tron, Blade Runner,* and *2010: Odyssey Two.* Internationally recognized as a leading innovator in the design of the future, he has been engaged as a consultant and/or designer for many leading corporations, including Ford, Honda, Chrysler, BMW, Jeep, Phillips, and General Electric. His book *Sentinel* contains illustrations of futuristic architecture, transportation systems, and computerized environments.

one that the studio or film company purchased or one he wrote himself. It's his picture—I'm just hired to be his eyes and imagination and to conceive the visual ideas that were suggested in the script. The overview is the director's and what I hope to accomplish on each film is to design specific fixtures, props, or a look that will satisfy him. Working for someone else doesn't affect my creativity—they hire me because I have a record of being creative.

Being a film designer has not affected my other design, but my background as a corporate designer has influenced my film work. Although I'm not an engineer or necessarily a materials specialist, I do have an awareness—a *heightened* awareness—of how things have to be built; so I can think up something that doesn't exist and indicate a detailed assembly system that will make it look real. The procedure for satisfying requirements on a film assignment is exactly as it is for a corporate design: There is the classic progression from sketch to finished art. I am an illustrator really for my own convenience; it's a separate facility I use or don't use, depending on the job. However, because I am an illustrator, working on films is curiously satisfying. What I invent is later built into a piece of hardware of a prop or an interior set, and the illustration *moves.* It's wonderful to see your idea come to life in a setting that was laboriously made to look as real as possible.

The best way to work on a film is to have personal relationships with the director and art director and to have day-to-day involvement with the special effects people, who do so much to make an impossible or nonexistent reality seem real. Fortunately I've had close one-to-one relationships with directors Steven Lisberger on *Tron* (1982), Ridley Scott on *Blade Runner,* and, now,

Peter Hyams on *2010.* I always presented my ideas directly to them (just as I do with corporate clients), and we got along well as co-workers and friends. I also had close discussions with Robert Wise, the director of *Star Trek—The Motion Picture* (1979), my first film project, but in that instance I worked as consultant to the film's *second*-unit. When I came on the film, in fact, the action had already been shot and only the special effects postproduction work remained.

Getting involved in film design happened by pure accident. John Dykstra called about *Star Trek—The Motion Picture.* I then contracted as a consultant for Dykstra's company Apogee, which was producing the model for the picture's celestial entity, V'ger. I was given the specific job of designing V'ger. The movie needed an ending, and it also needed a spectacular setting for that ending. The design for V'ger was a six-sided geometric extrusion, twisted and modulated along the length of the entity. The interior was a kind of outgrowth of thinking, "What would be the most awesome, awe-inspiring sight a human being could have?" I went to our common cultural base, and took a Gothic cathedral and turned it on end; imagine walking into the cathedral at Cologne with the top of the building ahead of you. The model was forty-seven feet long, and it was photographed in a zero-visibility facility. I think it met my visual expectations: It was an awesome, lovely, frightening sight.

On *Tron,* I was expected to think up the computer-generated tank, aircraft carrier, and Lightcycle. This was done by going back to in-head audience memory—constructions of what people visualize when they think "tank" or "aircraft carrier" or "motorcycle." I took actual photo scraps of all these devices and then synthesized a rearrangement of the same relative masses and

Left: Syd Mead, conceptual artist, at work.

Right: Mead conceived the logo for the computer-generated opening title for Tron *(1982).*

sizes and came up with sleek constructions that still looked like these vehicles but were floating in free space. For the aircraft carrier design, I took two aircraft carriers, placed their flight decks at 90-degree angles to one another, and then floated the bridge tower (the big mass that sits to the edge of the flight deck), having it come out of the side to float like an enormous ring. And this produced the same mass relationship in terms of profile and section that a contemporary aircraft carrier has, only it was changed into a free-floating construction.

The Lightcycle was a much more difficult problem. According to Steven Lisberger, the drivers would hold a code wand in their hands; that code wand was what triggered the energy field to produce the Lightcycle. This meant the code bars functioned like handlebars. So I envisioned the front wheel as a power source that pulled the cycle along—that's why it ended up as a sphere. And the rest of light's cycle was formed behind, under, and between the legs of the drivers as they stood up. When they put their feet up into the foot-wells, the vehicles closed around them, and away they went.

I sort of edged into working in other areas of the movie. I did some costume constructions—for instance, the clothing pattern on Tron (Bruce Boxleitner) was generated from some costume studies I did. I designed the construction of the Master Control Program tower. That was visualized, as was V'ger, as some kind of wondersome, Gothic churchlike cathedral construction. The energy field around it was conceived as an interlocking set of wedge-shaped details, which were endlessly repeated to form the circle around the MCP tower. Energy would flow out and into the MCP through and along these cracks and imaginary surfaces. The computer graphics used throughout the film were generated by first coming up with a ten-number set {1, 2, 3...0} in a peculiar geometry style. Lisberger liked that and asked if I'd like to take a crack at the title graphics. I simply did an alpha (letter) variation on the numeric design and that became the final title graphic, TRON.

For *Blade Runner,* I was originally hired to design the futuristic vehicles. Included was the police spinner—a car-aerodyne combination. I theorized that if all the power can be generated inside the vehicle through the use of turbines (the bottom of the car would be vented), the spinner wouldn't have to have extendable wings. Because the spinner doesn't change shape when it rises and flies, it is more magical.

Creating vehicles was almost like creating characters because they had to have specific characteristics that suited the personalities of the people who used them. For example, the truck used by Sebastian (William Sanderson) was a composite of add-on parts, theoretically found in a junk heap in the year 2019. The problem was making it look strangely assembled—kind of like a tinkerer's automotive dream. I envisioned all these pieces of what might be discarded technology at that point in time.

By the time I'd been working on the vehicles, the movie was progressing, the screenplay was being revised, and so forth. And with my weekly briefings from Ridley Scott, I was getting a feel for what was wanted in terms of a *look.* I started putting fixtures and ideas behind the vehicles, to put them in a futuristic setting. I don't like to do a car on a white background; it looks too isolated and strange, and the approach is too clinical. So I place my vehicles in a complete environment. As long as the scene is consistent with itself, with its own internal detail mechanics, it will look real.

Ridley liked my drawings very much—to be fair, I must say that I was the only source for these kinds of ideas at the time—so he asked me to go ahead and come up with the concepts for the picture's street sets. I also did most of the interiors because the ideas had to have the same mechanical set that the exteriors of the society had. Doug Trumbull, who did the film's special effects, designed the Tyrell (Joe Turkel) office for a very good reason: It had to look significantly different, more elegant and cleaner than the jumble of mechanical fixtures that characterized the lower echelons of society.

The city of 2019 was getting progressively dense. Buildings were over three thousand feet high, with older buildings of ten to twenty stories being used as bases for the entire superstructures. Cables and tubes, delivering air and removing waste, would climb along the outsides of old buildings. The street level would be a service alley to these towering megastructures. Street-level fixtures such as fire hydrants, parking meters, and the noodle bar where Deckard (Harrison Ford) eats, were, again, all conceived using the social theory of *retrofitted utilization*. Ridley Scott, Ivor Powell (the associate producer), Lawrence G. Paull (the production designer), and I developed the concept: Because in 2019 there was so much energy being devoted to off-world activity, for which the replicants were made, the consumer base wasn't getting much attention. This meant that the population was very actively collecting bits and pieces of add-on layers to make their original articles work. Today, in many Third World countries you'll find older vehicles, some dating back to the Thirties and Forties, that have air conditioners on top, larger batteries and generators, mud-flaps, and hang-on fixtures. They're retrofitted machine constructions that bear superficial resemblances to the original articles, but they've been overlaid by so many add-ons that they've taken on a style of their own. We labeled that style, which influenced the look of the film, "retro-deco."

Ridley also asked me to conceive the Voight-Kampff machine, which he said was to be an exotic, intimidating kind of lie detector used for exposing replicants. Since the machine would only be the size of a briefcase, I had to make it threatening in a different way. I decided that it should breathe. The machine would draw in air samples from the immediate area, reacting to a body's chemical changes as the person or replicant becomes nervous or scared because of the questions he's being asked. As soon as the subject walks into the room, the machine's arm swings around and focuses on his eye and the breathing begins. It's alive in a way, and is very, very threatening.

I have seen many films that have depicted future worlds: I thought *A Clockwork Orange* (1971), for instance, was wonderful; for its time

2001: A Space Odyssey (1968) was an incredible, startling visual tour-de-force. But I've never studied motion pictures to see how they invented the future. I'm hired for my own particular visions. My vision of the future is much different than that depicted in many of the potboiler science fiction movies. For one thing, they have a kind of shattered-icon fascination with technology going haywire, with sparks flying, things crashing, nuclear bombs exploding, and man being helpless. Setting up a disaster scenario is probably the least creative and simplest thing to do, and is not much more sophisticated than the old Frankenstein Monster kind of plot—very uninventive and boring. But the shock value of something going radically wrong is a kind of catharsis, and people flock to see these kinds of things.

Star Trek—The Motion Picture actually had a much more inventive premise than I've just described. Men are confronted with the unknown and make the brave decision to investigate what it is all about—and when nothing goes wrong, they go a little bit further. This was really a fairly sophisticated plot structure. It wasn't new, of course. They'd patched together at least seven plots from the old television series to come up with the overall framework of the story. *Blade Runner* was, typically, the original idea-gone-haywire story. When the replicant Batty (Rutger Hauer) confronts his designer Tyrell and in frustration (because Tyrell can't prolong Batty's life) crushes his head like a watermelon, it's very much like the angry Frankenstein Monster returning to his creator and demanding a little more than it had been given. *Tron* was much more a fantasy trip into a fascinating, impossible world. Everything was expressed in ego confrontation; and we had the mad, evil computer scientist taking over his creation, rather than the other way around, as is usually the case.

I have a more optimistic outlook than most science fiction films because I believe that if we've lasted this long, there's a very good chance we're going to last a lot longer. Conceiving a future that takes place after a nuclear holocaust is a favorite, much belabored failure-of-nerve scenario. If we all insist that a nuclear holocaust will occur, it probably will. But I believe that the human race has a very strong survival mentality. The idea of having a nuclear war is really quite repugnant to most of the world's societies. I think this will get us through. We're now realizing that the greatest danger comes not from the large superpowers but from the so-called "renegade" societies that have a rising level of technical capability and a highly educated, paranoid megalomaniac who has taken over the economic base of his country. A lot of people will sell weapons to these countries for immediate profit, and this is worrisome. But the superpowers are becoming increasingly aware that we have too much to lose. The test will be if we can last through the year 2000. Then I

An impressive head-on view of V'ger in space, from Star Trek—the Motion Picture *(1979). Like all images in this color section, V'ger was conceived by Syd Mead, the most innovative conceptual artist working in films today. His futuristic designs on the three films represented here—Star Trek—The Motion Picture, Tron (1982), and Blade Runner (1982)—paved the way for his recent assignment on 2010: Odyssey Two (1984).*
All photographs on these pages were taken by Erik van der Palen.

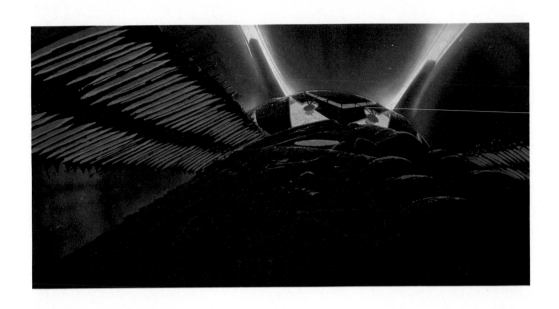

Top: View of central sphere of V'ger. Above: View down valley toward maw of V'ger.

IDEA FOR DOMAIN WALL PATTERN: LARGE NUMERALS 1 THRU 4.

Computer images from Tron. *Top: A game arena sketch for a domain wall pattern; using large numerals 1,2,3,4. Above: A freeze frame of a Lightcycle.*

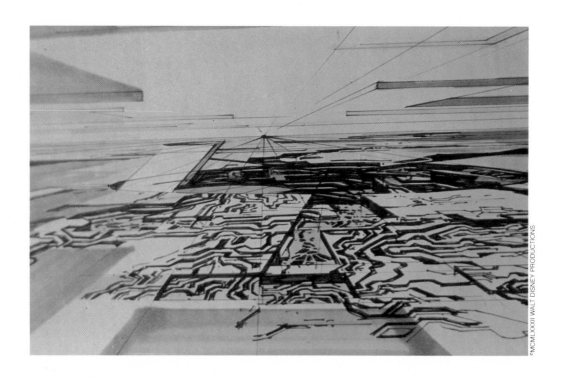

Top: Overall view of Tron *terrain. Above: Sketch of a Lightcycle—a side view.*

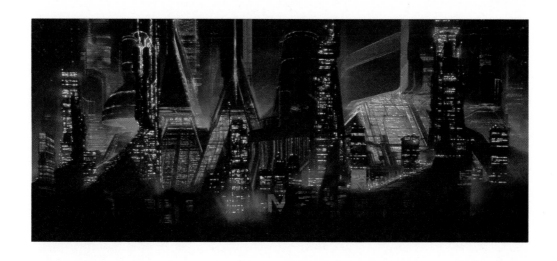

Top: Cityscape of L.A. in 2019 in Blade Runner. *Above: Mead was originally hired for* Blade Runner *to design this police spinner and other vehicles. He was later assigned the look of the whole city.*

Top: Close-up of street facades in Blade Runner. *Above: An elevation of a street block.*

Blade Runner. *Top: The Burbank studio's street set before being transformed into a futuristic L.A. street. Above: A futuristic street intersection.*

Blade Runner. *Top: interior of Intensive Care Unit. Above: interior of Sebastian's workshop.*

think we'll be home free. By then we'll have figured out some of the ways we can balance our drives and ambitions, and it'll finally start to sink in that we're all together on this cosmic speck called Earth.

My visions of the future don't have any particular limits. We're all limited by ourselves, our accumulative awareness and knowledge, etc. But there's no particular year in the future where I'd have difficulty making predictions. Of course, it's hardest making predictions about the *near* future, say five years from now, because we don't have access to corporate marketing plans and other priority information. But it's comforting to know that once you pass that magic time, you can say, "My idea is as good as anyone else's." Nobody other than geophysicists can really have an idea of what the Earth is going to be like in, say, the year 3000. What we come up with, therefore, when doing prediction exercises, are possible, visually and story-wise entertaining visions of particular futures.

A common mistake is to automatically make things in the future bigger, even limitless. If you build things today that are ten blocks across, in the future you assume you can build them hundreds of miles across. That's not necessarily true, except in space, where we'll be able to build anything we want with no particular restraints in regard to size, other than getting all the material necessary together in one place.

Architecture, I think, will continue to become more exotic and complex. It will become more natural: We'll have spectacular two-hundred-foot-high indoor waterfalls, cascading banks of greenery, flowers, and movable, adjustable landscapes. Certainly there will be very large projects, extensive interconnected indoor environments, possibly going up to the 3,000–4,000-foot-high level in high-density urban locations. Cities are already in place and they'll pretty much remain constant in terms of where they are and how much land they'll cover. Because of economic considerations, I can't see cities looking much different except for add-on structures. But the new self-contained city centers and malls that are being built will become so large they will be equivalent to whole new cities in the future.

I think we're going to clean up the environment as we find the loose ends of the various loops we've put in motion. We'll be able to control the deterioration of the air quality; and through management of the earth's resources in the biosphere and with space satellites tracking air movement, we'll be able to regulate and predict rainfall to improve crop conditions. We should get an excellent handle on preserving our natural environment.

Entertainment will become much more participatory. Even now with videodiscs and elaborate computer games, you can design your own fantasy. Once we can get into our own heads on a preprogrammed basis, we can activate, quite possibly, our dream centers. Then we can go back and visit people in history, be places we've always wanted to go, relive our most enjoyable experiences, and create new ones.

I'm not a fashion designer particularly, but I believe clothes will continue to be kind of a plaything. There will be new fabrics that can change colors, and others that can change shapes when activated by electric currents. And once we solve the XY-screen kind of technology (flat screen pixel address with on-board memory), we'll be able to weave electrified fabrics that can produce any pattern you want, in whatever combination of colors you desire.

I think we'll see floating pleasure islands that actually will be large machines. They'll be able to move into a port and either be used there or they'll sail away on a trip with a few thousand people aboard, much like an ocean liner but more leisurely and less a mode for transportation. I don't think there will be many single vehicles that can travel on land, sea, and in the air, for the simple reason people won't need such capabilities from one vehicle.

Land vehicles is a huge subject. In general, I believe we're going toward about five different types for the consumer base: Two will be most common. There will be a small, utility-rolling-cabinet vehicle, much like the Renault 5 or Ford Escort. There will also be something that will replace the normal sedan. I expect it will be a van-type, one-box profile, as car designers call them. They'll be very efficient, and be able to haul the most people and biggest loads on a minimum ground imprint.

I don't believe we'll see privately owned aircraft reach the density of automobiles on the freeway. The management required to keep a dense aerial mix of traffic in place and control the mechanical-failure percentages is simply too great. But we'll certainly have private vehicles in space. We'll have commercial traffic, bringing materials to and taking finished articles out from the Earth's orbit. We'll have traffic to and from various space worlds. . . .

Advertising is a little bit out of my field, but thinking about the way technology is going now, I believe that once we achieve high-density computer memory and a flat XY-access picture control, we can easily have moving advertising sticker spots placed on *everything*. They'd have a life of, maybe, a couple of days or a week; they might be sun-powered. There will be an avalanche of advertising access to the individual once we achieve the cell system—two-way communication areas for phone or other person-to-person link-ups—all over the country. People will have their own communications modules. Those channels in the dead spaces of conversations might be accessible for advertising that will deposit into one's local memory device. The biggest problem is going to be preserving one's privacy, because a person will have to give all kinds of personal information to a computer bank so it can facilitate his or her communication desires. All of these technologies might then be perverted to favor the needs of advertisers getting their messages to potential consumers.

As is the case today, technology will tend to invent itself back into invisibility. Solid state circuitry is getting smaller and smaller; and if we have success in building bioelectric computers (the protein computer, for instance), we can compress the entire written and recorded history of mankind into a cube one centimeter on each side.

The entertainment world's view of science in general is terribly apocryphal and naive. As techniques more and more marvelous become available to us, science will progressively be a utilitarian, problem-solving series of investigations and

a monitoring of ideas. The major wave of science will then have to do, once again, with studying nature, the workings of the universe, and the balance of forces we have to confront as we go into the future. Science might very well become a very arcane, abstract study of truly cosmic forces, rather than a means by which to solve the problems of the next one hundred years.

Artificial life will certainly be generated in many, many forms—the pure mechanical (robots), biomechanical-cyborg, cloning. It will be completely possible to have yourself cloned, and then move into yourself, into a younger, healthier duplicate—if that's what you want. Cloning will certainly have monumental social impact. For one thing, it will play havoc with inheritance rights and tax laws—are you copy #1 or copy #50? The concept of replicants that was central to *Blade Runner* is definitely the most logicial way to go, rather than trying to build an elaborate mechanical or even biochemical construction. Duplicating a human being is the least of the interesting goals for robot technology. It's more of a trick, harking back to the original fascination with anthropomorphic constructions. As a race we have long tried to figure out who we are and why we are, and

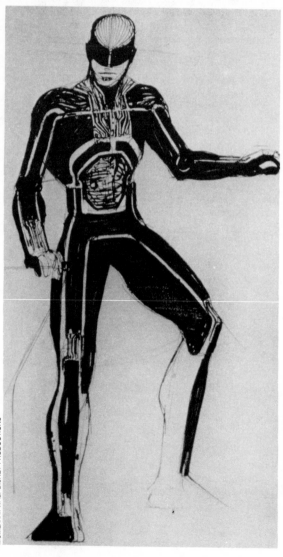

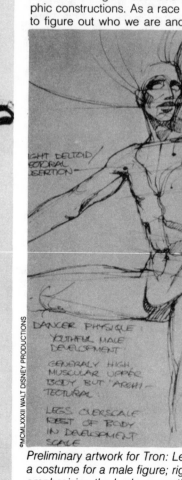

Preliminary artwork for Tron: Left, a sketch for a costume for a male figure; right, a sketch emphasizing the body proportions of a male figure.

now we're beginning to find out what we are. In the future, we'll be able to decide who we are going to be. We'll literally be able to remake ourselves in any particular shape, form, direction, or level of organization that we wish to achieve. In the future, we could ship whole colonies of people off to somewhere on a little frozen speck of protoplasm securely transported in a vacuum vial.

Earth is such a tiny bit of stuff, that logically, it will not be able to supply the human race with its needs forever. That's why space will become such an active place. There will be resources to develop and room to move and places to go in space. Here we are, coating this little speck with all our activities, all of it amounting to about the same thickness in scale as a smear of butter on a cue-ball. We have much more ambitious dreams than that, and space is where we'll make them come true.

Policeman Gaff (Edward James Olmos) and detective Deckard (Harrison Ford) take a ride in a police spinner that was designed by Mead for Blade Runner *(1982).*

In the future, the United States will become just a member of the world community and, along with everybody else, will concentrate on boosting its people off this planet. By the year 3000 there will be many, many more people living off this planet than will be left here. There will be estates and colonies in space, and eventually, in the far future, we'll generate all of our power to run our Earth society off-world. Then we'll turn the Earth back into a beautiful garden, and work to preserve our historic civilization sites. Earth will become *the* place to go back to, visit, and to trace our cultural heritage, much in the way some people born in America go to Europe, land of their ancestors.

Creating Tomorrow Today: SF's Special Effects Wizards

Frederik Pohl IV

The science fiction film and the art of special effects have grown up together. Non-sf films certainly make use of special effects, but primarily as money-saving conveniences: Obviously, destroying models is cheaper than destroying real ships in a naval battle scene. In fact, regular films have an advantage over sf films, in that viewers watching even a picture as dependent on technical wizardry as Robert Wise's *The Hindenburg* (1975) may not be aware of being tricked by special effects—after all, blimps still exist and there is at least the possibility that the filmmakers decided to burn up one for the climactic scenes. But if a viewer sees faster-than-light travel, as in Wise's *Star Trek—The Motion Picture* (1979), he has no doubt that special effects are being employed. Since science fiction films *must* show things that have never existed, they have no choice but to create images (illusions) through special effects. Because audiences rightly expect such trickery, the task of delivering convincing visuals has been accomplished only by the best special effects experts.

The emphasis that science fiction films have placed on special effects has resulted in the elevation of technicians to star status. Douglas Trumbull is as much the star of *Blade Runner* (1982) as Harrison Ford; Industrial Light and Magic is as much the star of *Star Trek II: The Wrath of Khan* (1982) as William Shatner and Leonard Nimoy. Indeed, one can trace the lin-

eage of special effects through the history of the science fiction film, covering such men as Willis O'Brien and Eugene Shuftan of sixty years ago and Trumbull and John Dykstra of today: The devices they invented to show the nonexistent are staples of all film production. But when one studies the contributions of special effects innovators through the decades, one must begin with the earliest pioneer, the great French filmmaker Georges Méliès.

In the first two decades of the twentieth century Méliès made use of "artificially arranged scenes" for his most successful releases, including *A Trip to the Moon* (1902), the first science fiction film. His effects seem primitive now; and many of them were discovered by chance, as when his camera temporarily jammed while photographing Paris traffic and the "pop in" replacement of a bus by a hearse provided a dramatic substitution. But they crudely foreshadow what is done now with great sophistication. He also pioneered in quite another way. Often he planned a film around the tricks that he had discovered his cameras could perform, the same process that can be seen when a 1980s producer demands a "state of the art" script from his writers.

For example, there is Méliès's non-sf film, *The Man with the Rubber Head* (1901). What viewers saw was a seated man whose head swelled and shrank alarmingly as they watched. That sort of illusion would later be done by combining separate strips of film in printing—the "matte shot." Méliès accomplished it in a different way. He

Frederik Pohl IV is coauthor (with his father Frederik Pohl) of *Science Fiction Studies in Film*. He is a partner in a location-finding service for film and television producers.

Georges Méliès's An Impossible Voyage (1904). Left: A train is able to fly off a mountain ledge and into space through speed alone. Below: After its journey, it has a rough landing in the sea. The special effects pioneer employed giant moving cutouts and mechanical backgrounds, multiple exposures, stop-motion, and split-screen imagery in his brief film.

draped his actor in black, but for the head which he photographed with the camera moving in and out so that it seemed to expand and contract on the film. Then he rewound the film and photographed a torso, with the head covered in black, and reshot the film. It was a crude effect—the background could be seen through the head—but it differs only in sophistication from the matte technique Kubrick used in 2001 (1968).

Méliès's An Impossible Voyage features a train traveling to the sun. To show it, Méliès photo-

graphed the train model against a rotating drum painted with clouds—the primitive, yet effective forerunner of rear projection. An Impossible Voyage was released in 1904. It took two full decades until the next significant development in special effects occurred, and that was the invention of stop-motion animation by Willis O'Brien for his 1924 prehistoric dinosaur movie, The Lost World. This technique, in which tiny puppet figures are moved a frame at a time, was later used by O'Brien himself in King Kong (1933) and Mighty

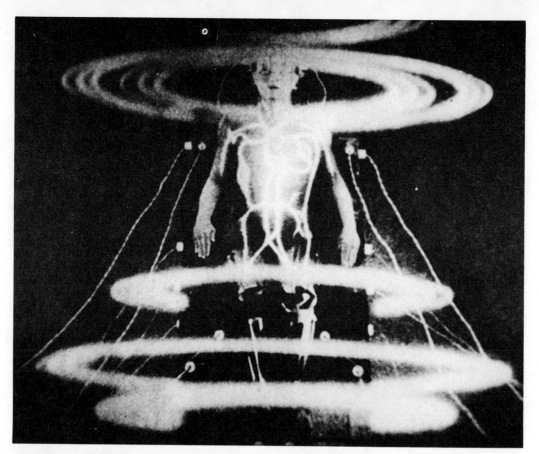

Joe Young (1949) and others in films from *Destination Moon* (1950) to Ray Harryhausen movies to *The Empire Strikes Back* (1980).

After this development, the pace began to pick up. Two years later, in 1926, came Fritz Lang's *Metropolis,* the pioneering German film that not only used true rear projection (projecting a separate film against a translucent screen from behind) to simulate then-nonexistent television, but provided the first good system for creating stationary mattes—the Shuftan process. Lang did not want to build a whole "Metropolis" for his story. He simply wanted to use models of the city, and to have live actors seemingly inhabit it. Eugene Shuftan showed him how; all of the above-ground city scenes used his process.

The Shuftan process really was "done with mirrors." First a model of the city was built, along with a smaller section done in full scale for the actors to act in. The camera was directed at the set with the actors; then a mirror was placed between camera and set, at a forty-five-degree angle. Off to one side was the model city itself, so placed that it reflected into the camera. Then came the hard part. The silvering in the mirror had to be painstakingly scraped away in a pattern that allowed the actors, and part of their full-size set, to be seen through clear glass, while the rest of the image on the film was the reflected model. This laborious process had to be done on

the set itself, usually with the actors and technicians standing around waiting for it to be completed. Heaven forbid that anyone should carelessly jar the mirror out of alignment, because then it all had to be done over again. Although there are only thirteen Shuftan shots in the film, they were at least part of the reason why *Metropolis* took a solid year for its principal photography to be completed. The process was also very limited, because the boundary between live action and model could not be changed—that's why it is called a "stationary" matte. But it worked. It was so successful that it continued to be used for many years. Alexander Korda's British production *Things to Come* (1936) utilized the Shuftan process with only minor refinements (allowing some movement in the model section of the scene); Korda's fantasy, *The Thief of Bagdad* (1940), adapted it for use with color. The process had one great advantage for the sort of demon-prince directors who tyrannized their crews and improvised as they went along: By looking through the camera they could see exactly how the scene would appear on film before shooting.

Méliès and Shuftan operated in Europe; in the Thirties it was time for Hollywood to get into the act. For the film *Just Imagine* (1930), rear projection came into its own. Two separate scenes could be combined—one a background shot, with as much live action as was wanted; the other

Left: Rotwang's robot is brought to life in Metropolis *(1926). This significant special effects sequence was accomplished through a series of double exposures.*

Right: This scene showing Everytown in 2036 in Things to Come *(1936) utilized the Shuftan process, incorporating models and mirrors, to give the impression that the people are standing in front of supposedly enormous structures.*

scene had live actors in the foreground, able to move as far as the background scene permitted, with no limitations to keep them frozen in one small area. One of its defects was that the translucent screen for the rear projection had to be large. A more serious problem was that the camera shooting from the front and the projector operating from the rear had to be synchronized so that the camera and projector shutters were open at the same time. *Just Imagine* accomplished that with a bulky and headache-causing mechanical interlock. It was a great nuisance... but it worked.

The 1950s were the first real boom period for science fiction films. Growing public interest in science and the future was matched by increasing technical expertise on the part of the film technicians; almost anything imaginable could be filmed, and audiences were ready to watch it. Of course, there were still many technical crudities in the processes—but audiences were forgiving.

A large part of this new technical competence came from the development of the "traveling matte." With this technique, the background could be shot in one place at one time and the actors could perform in another, and the two films could be combined in an optical printer (simply put, a projector linked with a camera). There are

many processes for accomplishing this—blue screen, yellow (sulfur) screen, and rotoscope are the chief ones.

For a traveling matte one needs four strips of film—two of them normally photographed, the other two technically produced. Strip 1 shows the foreground action. Strip 2 is the background action. Strip 3 is a "male" matte, which is developed from strip one by silhouetting the foreground action in solid black and leaving the rest of each frame transparent. Strip 4 is the "female" matte, the negative image of strip 3: The background action is blacked out and the space occupied by the foreground action is left clear.

The strips are then combined, two at a time, in the optical printer. The camera side is loaded with unexposed film. The projector side takes both strip 1 (the foreground action) and strip 4 (the female matte). The light of the projector is blocked by the opaqued-out areas that represent the background, and so all that prints onto the unexposed film are the actions of the foreground actors. Then the just-exposed film is rewound, and the projector side reloaded with strip 2 (the background) and strip 3 (the male matte). Again, the opaqued-out sections keep any light from getting through, so all that prints is the background itself. The result is the composite matte shot.

An artist's conception of the Id Monster in
Forbidden Planet (1956), a film known for its
sophisticated special effects.

In the Fifties this procedure still had imperfec-
tions. One was that shooting and reshooting a
strip of film increased its graininess and damaged
its contrast at each step; the composite print had
more grain and contrast than the original shots.
Black-and-white films like *The Incredible Shrinking Man* (1957) were nearly invulnerable to this
damage, but the color emulsions of the 1950s
were much more sensitive; the composite shots
were visibly different from the rest of the film. (Ten-
year-olds were able to anticipate when a monster
would appear because the film got grainy and the
colors began to look odd as the composite shot
began.)

Even more troublesome was the task of preparing the male and female mattes. In the first process used, rotoscoping, it was simply done by
hand. Each individual frame had to be gone over
by an artist with an ink brush, blotting out the
undesired sections—a job almost as tedious (and
expensive) as Méliès's original hand-painted
color films.

A better method came along with the blue
screen. The background shot was filmed in the
usual way. The foreground, however, was shot in
front of a special blue screen, with a camera that
exposed two strips of film simultaneously. One
was regular film, the other an emulsion sensitive
only to the blue light from the screen. When the

special emulsion was developed it automatically
became strip 4 (the female matte); reprinted as a
negative, strip 3, the male matte. Obviously this
was a much less painful way to produce the matte
strips—but it still was not without problems. Blue
light reflecting on the actors showed up as holes
in their bodies; fine, fuzzy detail like hair or fur
tended to break up. And the degradation of the
image with repeated photographing remained a
problem.

It is impossible to talk about futuristic science
fiction films without mentioning such landmarks
as *Things to Come, Destination Moon* (1950), and
Forbidden Planet (1956), but their contributions to
special-effects technology were relatively minor.
The quantum leap came with Stanley Kubrick's
classic *2001: A Space Odyssey*. In this film Kubrick, Con Pedersen, Wally Veevers, and Doug
Trumbull all but reinvented special effects, and
changed forever the way they are used to advance a story. We don't have space to discuss all
of their innovations, but three are particularly
important: front projection, slit-scan photography,
and in-camera compositing.

Front projection is just what it sounds like: The
background shot is not projected from the rear,
through a translucent screen (which always blurs
the image and weakens it to some extent), but
from the front onto an opaque screen, giving a
sharper picture. If you have ever been watching
home movies and seen the person in front of you
stand up, between the projector and the screen,

Below: Canadian director David Cronenberg has always utilized special effects; the more bizarre the better he likes them. In Videodrome (1983), for which Rick Baker did sfx, Max (James Woods) looks at the Flesh TV as very strange things start to occur. By film's end there will be the virtual melding of man and machine.

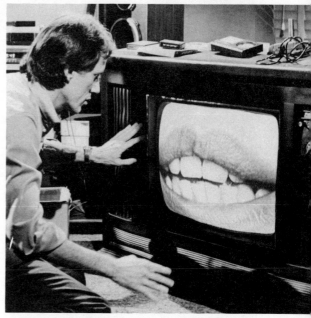

you know what the problem is with front projection: The projected image is projected onto the actors, too. However, Kubrick and his wizards found ways of dealing with that. First they used a special beaded screen that reflected a great proportion of the light striking it directly back into the camera—much like the layer of cells in a cat's eye that shine so brightly in a car's headlights. So the intensity of the image on the screen was greatly enhanced. Second, they lighted the foreground actors with high-intensity lights that washed out undesired images from the projection. It worked: The African veldt scenes in the opening sections of 2001 were done that way with great success. There is one flaw in front projection, but it is not a technical one. What's wrong is that the background images have to be ready at the time of principal photography, and for scheduling and budgetary reasons it's often easier for a producer to have them done separately and usually later, combining them in postproduction. But front projection gives a beautiful image.

Slit-scan photography was used for the "trip" (star-gate) sequence at the end of 2001. This is also a simple idea that requires precision to work well, but when successful it creates a convincing illusion of movement. As first developed by John Whitney, it consists of moving the camera, artwork, or model while the camera shutter is open, thus producing a slightly streaked image that the human eye interprets as real movment. 2001 used a computer-controlled animation stand to add the precise degree of streaking necessary, the first application of the computer to special effects. Since 2001, slit-scan has been used, for instance, for the jump to warp speed and the "wormhole" effect in the Star Trek movies (as well as in such TV network headers as that for The ABC Monday Night Movie). Why it has not been used more often in science fiction films is hard to say—one theory is that slit-scan worked so vividly in 2001 that other producers don't use it for fear of being accused of copying Kubrick.

The development of in-camera compositing demonstrates Kubrick's obsession for perfection. We've talked about the change in film quality when conventional traveling mattes are used; Kubrick wanted to avoid that. He wanted something that had never been attained before in a science fiction film: an absolute black to show outer space. Non-sf films don't need that because there are no true blacks on Earth. Attaining it through conventional matting is almost impossible because as the strips of film run through the optical printer there is enough leakage of light to slightly expose even the black areas. What Kubrick wanted was a "first generation" look—the look of the pristine film that has gone through the camera just once. To get it, he went back to the fundamental idea Méliès had used in The Man with the Rubber Head—with the refinements of sixty years later.

Take a simple example of a shot from the film 2001. You are looking at the spaceship Discovery from outside. You see it pass in front of a field of blazing stars against the total blackness of space. There is a window in the Discovery, and through it you can see the crew.

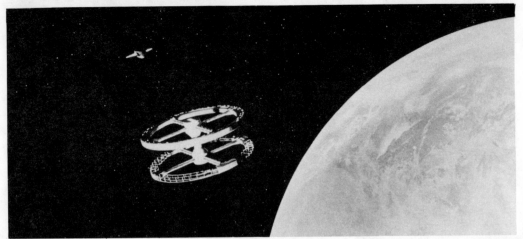

In 2001: A Space Odyssey, *the space clipper Orion approaches a space station. The three-foot Orion model and the six-foot space station model were photographed separately to obtain the proper relative size.*

The first step was to prepare the Discovery model with the window blacked out. The camera moved slowly past it (in the opposite direction of the illusion of movement they wanted to create), with the exposure time lengthened to give depth of focus and a slight motion blur. When the shot was completed, the camera and film were returned to the starting position and the entire Discovery model was draped in black. The window was now covered with a highly reflective white card, on which the action of the crew inside was projected, frame by frame, while the same transit of the ship was made by the camera.

Kubrick now had the ship and its crew; he did not yet have the star field behind it. Kubrick decided to add the star field optically. To retain his first-generation look, he broke down his full-color film of the ship into three separate black-and-white color separations, one for each of the emulsion colors. These strips were then printed (through filters to restore the color) through a rotoscope matte that blotted out the stars as the ship passed in front of them. The result: a black black and a first-generation look.

Not all of these problems were entirely solved. 2001 was released in both 70- and 35-mm versions and the star patterns that looked glorious in the 70-millimeter print tended to clot together in the smaller version, and so a certain amount of compromising was necessary. But we have taken a very simple example; many shots (like the approach to the space station) combined many more elements. All in all, 2001 was a true landmark in special effects. Trumbull, Pedersen, Veevers—and Kubrick himself (perhaps most of all)—set a new standard of proficiency and defined the state of the art at that time. They went as far as existing technology permitted—perhaps a little further.

Of course, technology did not stop with 2001. New film stocks made it possible to produce good composites without the painful, repetitive drudgery of 2001, and the computer, brought to bear in a hundred new applications, was perhaps most important of all.

Doug Trumbull's subsequent career deserves a book unto itself. He pioneered the creation of special effects in 70-mm and then reducing them to blend in with the regulation 35-mm bulk of the film. For Close Encounters of the Third Kind (1977) and Blade Runner Trumbull set himself the task of showing flight through Earth's atmosphere properly—slightly diffused by the air, instead of with the starkness of outer space (like most earlier attempts to show air passage). He did it by photographing his models in a controlled smoke environment, then printing them in with a soft-edged matte. For his directional-debut film, Silent Running (1971), Trumbull applied the lessons of 2001 to a low-budget film; and what was even more important in the long run, he passed on his expertise to his then-assistant John Dykstra and his partner Richard Yuricich, both of whom have since become leading creators of special effects.

With them the reign of the computer began to take full effect. The Dykstraflex, the camera created for Star Wars (1977); the Empireflex, for The Empire Strikes Back (1980); and all of the other flexes are computer-controlled cameras that allow whole new dimensions of freedom in creating special effects. No longer is the relationship of camera and model limited to a straight-line pass-through, as in 2001. The "flexes" let the camera-man pan and tilt at will. The movements of the camera are faithfully recorded by the computer, so that when the other elements of a shot are photographed, the camera can duplicate exactly every movement. And the creation of totally computer-generated films, barely hinted at in the Disney Studio's Tron (1982), is waiting in the wings.

Meanwhile, the state of the art in science fiction special effects resides in a small unmarked build-

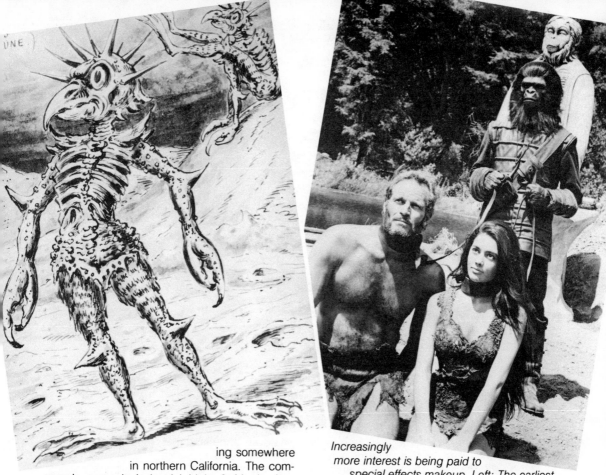

ing somewhere
in northern California. The com-
pany's name is Industrial Light & Magic, Inc.
(ILM). The brainchild of George Lucas, it so dominates the special effects category that it has won
all but one of the Academy Awards in that field in
recent years. Not long ago I was delighted to be
allowed to visit it.

One visits ILM in much the same way as one
visits the CIA—by invitation or not at all. So I was
pleased to get a quick okay from Tom Smith, vice-
president and general manager of ILM. After I
signed in I was allowed to enter the magic kingdom and was struck at once by the busyness of
the place. ILM has about 120 employees and,
although they were not heavily engaged at the
time—they had just finished *Return of the Jedi*
(1983) and were only setting up for *Star Trek III:
The Search for Spock* (1984)—they all seemed to
be busy at productive tasks. This is in considerable contrast to actual production locales for other
films, where the first impression one gets is of
people standing around and drinking coffee.

That contrast is not accidental. Lucas created
ILM for good reasons, and located it where it is
for perhaps better ones. When he made *Star
Wars* he did so in the traditional way, recruiting a
crew that stayed together for the film and scattered less than eighteen months after it was over.
Most went on to other projects; some formed their
own companies, like John Dykstra's Apogee; but,

*Increasingly
more interest is being paid to
special effects makeup. Left: The earliest
alien costumes were designed by Georges
Méliès for the Sélénites in the first sf film,* A
Trip to the Moon *(1902). Right: John
Chambers won an Oscar for his special
makeup design for the simian masters in*
Planet of the Apes *(1968). Charlton Heston
and Linda Harrison play humans who are
forced into servitude by the talking apes who
will someday rule the Earth.*

for one reason or another, very few of the *Star
Wars* people came back for *Return of the Jedi*.
Lucas thought that wasteful, and Industrial Light
& Magic was formed to keep these skilled specialists together. They don't work only on Lucas films,
of course—especially not now, during Lucas's
"vacation"—but they have taken on such projects as *Star Trek II: The Wrath of Khan* (1982),
Disney's *Dragonslayer* (1981), and Stephen
Spielberg's *E.T.* (1982), and *Indiana Jones and
the Temple of Doom* (1984).

Having decided to form ILM, Lucas moved it
out of southern California and its tightly drawn job
descriptions. ILM organizes its crews informally:
groups that work well together stay together, with
less emphasis on specialization of craft. (To emphasize the point, Lucas resigned from the Directors Guild.)

ILM is a full-service special effects company. It is in the business of providing all the techniques necessary for special effects of any kind. At the center of its effort are three motion-control camera setups, where the miniature models are shot; during major production these are in operation in three shifts, twenty-four hours a day. When I saw the cameras they were occupied with the models for *Star Trek III: The Search for Spock.* Everything else is support for these cameras, to feed them or embellish their product: model-builders, creators of background art, departments for optically compositing the results. There is a large special effects stage with a blue screen to shoot live-action shots, and a screening room to project the thirty or so seconds of finished film they will produce in a day.

Time was when the VistaVision format was headline news in exhibiting feature films. Now it is almost obsolete for most purposes, but ILM has found a new use for it. In the VistaVision format the film runs horizontally through the camera rather than vertically, and the equivalent of two frames are exposed at once. This gives ILM twice the film area of standard 35-mm film to work with, and gains them some of the advantages Trumbull finds in using 70-mm film, without the difficulties of having to deal with more than one film gauge. Even more important, it allows them to shoot effects for a wide-screen film "unsqueezed" by the anamorphic lens other systems require. (When expanding a special effects matte shot optically printed in the "squeezed" form the matte line often shows up—ILM avoids this.)

For animating the various monsters and odd creatures of its films, ILM uses both the traditional stop-motion techniques of Ray Harryhausen and Willis O'Brien in addition to its own process,

called "go-motion." Go-motion also uses puppets, but instead of hand-setting each new position and exposing the film a frame at a time the puppets themselves are made to move by computer during camera exposure by means of cables that control their eyes, arms, mouth, limbs—whatever appurtenances they may possess. There are two big advantages to go-motion. One is that, since the creatures being photographed are actually moving, the camera picks up that slight motion blur that the viewer's eye translates into real movement—rather than the sometimes jerky, stroboscopic effect of stop-motion. The other reason is simple time economy: Not even ILM could produce the volume of film needed for a major feature rapidly enough with stop-motion.

Where ILM shows its true stature is not so much in any individual process as in its ability to combine them all, through superior management and planning. It is hard to imagine how any other company could have produced the 450 special effects shots (some of which were later omitted) for *Return of the Jedi* in the time available. What's more, ILM's budgets are almost exempt from the huge cost overruns common to most special effects films—Tom Smith's original estimate for *Jedi* was off by only $200,000—picayune by such standards.

In the same complex another group of artists and scientists is working on the next generation of film technology. Here, sharing a building with Ben Burtt, Jr., and his second-effects wizards, is the Lucasfilm Graphics Project.

The first impression a visitor to the Graphics Project gets is a startling contrast of technologies, old and new. ILM and the Graphics Project add up to a capital investment of millions of Lucas's dollars. Lucas has deep pockets, but he has big

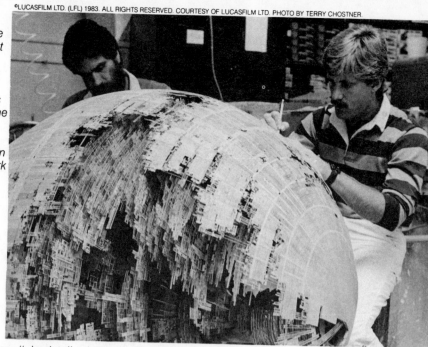

Men at work at George Lucas's Industrial Light and Magic in San Rafael, California. Left: Key sculptor Dave Sosalla gently removes the hand and arm of the miniature Rancor from its mold. Right: Modelmakers Jeff Mann (L) and Bill George work on small details on the Death Star.

plans, too. So when an "obsolete" piece of equipment—and therefore a cheaper one—will do what's needed, it is acquired. Thus you see state-of-the-art (perhaps even state of tomorrow's art) computer animation and video-to-film transfer equipment standing next to old, upright moviola editing machines and wind-up Bolex cameras.

The computer is at the heart of many of the Lucasfilm projects, among them a computerized film-editing system and a fully digital sound mixing board. Almost ready for release is a computer system to produce blue-screen mattes that will eliminate many of the faults we've already discussed in the system. It is an impressive process—somewhere between the ChromaKey used on every local weather forecast and plain magic—but it is only one part of a much greater technology. The process, like most computer-generated visuals, produces not film but videotape. Converting the electronics to film has always been a complicated and not always visually satisfying task. So to solve this problem, they have created the Pixar (which employs a laser device), a complete system for generating visuals and transferring them to film. When I saw it not long ago it was in a prototype stage and looked more like a high-school science fair project gone mad than a revolutionary new film device, but its prospects are enormous. Not only can it transfer electronics to film seamlessly, it will be able to synthesize film images much as a Moog synthesizes sound. It (or something very much like it) will fundamentally revolutionize special effects in film by directly generating computer images to show any desired scene.

We have not yet seen what this can mean to film technology. Even Disney's video-game inspired *Tron* is only a tiny first step in that direction,

like the Lumière brothers' early films of workers leaving their factories in comparison to something as advanced and sophisticated as the Méliès productions. However, contemporary computers, fast and powerful as they are, are not up to generating images rapidly or realistically enough to do the perfect job—Alvy Ray Smith, director of the Lucasfilm Graphics Project, estimates that it would take 200 years of computer time to generate a life-quality feature film now. But if there is any field of technology moving faster than film, it is the computer. Every few years a new generation comes along, working ten times faster and with ever larger data stores. If Lucas decides to end his "vacation" in a year or two and begin making some of the remaining *Star Wars* films, he may well have a fifth-generation computer to help him. . . .

And then we'll really see some special effects!

We've sketched the history of special effects technology in film, and particularly in the science fiction film. More than anything else, the history reveals itself in terms of individuals, and there is a connecting thread that links almost all of them. It started with Méliès. Then the progression moved from Willis O'Brien to Ray Harryhausen and from Eugene Shuftan and his process to Ned Mann, who used it on *Things to Come.* Mann trained Wally Veevers, who later worked on *2001* with Doug Trumbull; when Trumbull did *Silent Running* he hired John Dykstra—who then went on to do *Star Wars* with those people who now make up Industrial Light and Magic. Generation after generation, the new wizards have come along to astonish our eyes and delight our hearts in ways ever new and more believable. May they never stop!

The Special Effectiveness of George Pal

Robert Bloch

In 1953, after several years of increasing popularity, audience interest in science fiction declined. Both box office and fiction sales dropped quite noticeably.

Seeking an explanation, one critic wrote, "I'll tell you who killed the science fiction boom. George Pal and his pals."

But time plays strange tricks. Some years later that same critic went to Hollywood, met Pal socially, and ended up working with him on two projects that terminated with the producer's death.

Long before then, the self-appointed critic took a deep breath and ate his own words.

To keep you in suspense no longer, that critic was myself. And after observing George Pal's methods and motives firsthand I came to realize he was a vastly underappreciated creative force whose best efforts were all too frequently sabotaged by studio interference. The real villain was Hollywood itself.

Pal's talent was truly protean and despite the handicaps under which he labored it is reflected in his work. As an unenrolled anatomy student with a flair for drawing, he acquired the skills he'd later use as a commercial cartoon animator after leaving his native Hungary for Germany. He departed from there in 1933, when the Nazis came to power, and eventually made animated films in Paris, using a stop-motion camera of his own

design. Moving on to Holland, he began production in a garage; he ended up with a studio and staff of seventy-five. There Pal made his first venture into science fiction with a color short-subject, *The Ship of the Ether* (c. 1936), featuring a glass spaceship. Now his early experience as a licensed carpenter found expression in the carvings of his famed Puppetoons—cartoons using mobile puppets instead of drawn figures. Their popularity led to a Paramount contract. In 1939, he set up a Hollywood studio where, with a crew of twenty-five, he made more than forty shorts, plus training films for World War II armed forces. Pal's experiments with miniatures began, and he received his first Academy Award (1943) for animation techniques.

By 1947 short subjects were being phased out, and Pal turned to feature-film making.

"It wasn't easy getting started," he told me. "My reputation was as a producer of shorts, which nobody wanted anymore. And none of the major studios wanted me, either—a man with no experience working with live actors, nothing to show I could handle production problems on full-length features." In a town filled with ambitious expatriates, Pal was just another hungry Hungarian.

But he kept knocking on doors. Along the way he acquired the rights to several stories and eventually wangled a contract to film two of them for Eagle-Lion, a new independent company. His first production, *The Great Rupert* (1950), directed by Irving Pichel, was a low-budget com-

Robert Bloch's *Psycho* was adapted into a classic film by Alfred Hitchcock. He wrote teleplays for *The Alfred Hitchcock Hour, Thriller,* and *Star Trek;* his screenplays include *Straitjacket, The Night Walker, The Psychopath, Torture Garden, The House That Dripped Blood, Asylum,* and two unfilmed projects for George Pal that were aborted upon Pal's death.

A rocket ship taking off from Earth is a common sight in George Pal films. This is the ship flown in The Conquest of Space (1955).

edy fantasy featuring Jimmy Durante and a dancing squirrel—actually an animated Pal puppet.

The picture went down the tubes and Pal's reputation sank with it. In order to get the go-ahead on the second project he had to put up his own savings as part of the financing.

The second film was one he had dreamed of making for two years, ever since reading the script by science fiction writer Robert A. Heinlein and screenwriter Rip van Ronkel, based on Heinlein's juvenile novel, Rocketship Galileo. Twenty years after Fritz Lang's German production of Frau Im Mond (1928), the notion of rocket-flight to the Moon was still regarded as fantasy; Lang himself found no backers for a similar project in 1948. But Pal was convinced of the future of space-flight and, despite little encouragement, was determined to dramatize it.

In the face of obstacles and opposition, he made two daring decisions: despite a meager budget no larger than that of The Great Rupert, the picture must be filmed in Technicolor, and be given the flavor of a realistic documentary rather than a typical 1940-ish "space opera" story. Much research was done during preproduction, and Pal enlisted the services of Chesley Bonestell, an artist acclaimed for his paintings of outer space and lunar landscapes, retaining him and Heinlein as technical advisers to lend scientific authenticity to the film.

"That's where we ran into trouble," Pal recalled. "We wanted to do a straightforward, believable story of the first flight to the Moon. The studio geniuses wanted what would soon become the standard formula: boy meets girl, heroine is menaced by bug-eyed monsters from outer space. They brought in another writer (James O'Hanlon) and kept trying to change the script, even after we started shooting. With the aid of Irving Pichel, we fought to make the picture our way." Luckily the staff of artists and technicians came up with some remarkable effects, cutting corners on costs but still creating a marvelous moonscape and an impressive view of outer space. The rocket interior was built so it could be rotated and they were able to make it appear as though the crew-members were walking on the walls. They floated, suspended from wires like human puppets, their movements directed by puppeteers overhead.

"Of course we had to make compromises," Pal said. "We showed a one-stage rocket rather than a three-stage, to simplify the process for our audience, and used a cartoon insert by my friend Walter Lantz to explain technical details. By mistake the stars for our space set were all of the same magnitude of brilliance, but we couldn't afford to make changes. And we deliberately cheated by putting nonexistent cracks in the Moon's surface, in order to give our small lunar set the illusion of greater depth. But we told the story we wanted to tell."

The film that emerged as Destination Moon (1950) depicts the first lunar flight. The journey in

an atomic-powered rocket is financed by private industry after the government rejects the project. A crew of four—a young industrialist (John Archer), the designer of the rocket (Warner Anderson), an electronics technician (Dick Wesson), and a general (Tom Bowers) who believes in the military importance of the mission ("the first country that can use the Moon for the launching of missiles will control the Earth")—takes off in defiance of the authorities, who have denied permission to even test the engine. The perils and difficulties of their trip are graphically detailed, as is their touchdown in the crater of Harpalus, where they emerge to explore the lunar landscape.

But their fuel supply has been depleted in landing and they lack sufficient power for a return to Earth. Even after discarding every possible item of equipment, the ship is still almost a hundred pounds too heavy for takeoff. The electronics technician suits up and leaves the ship, radioing his companions that he'll remain behind and enable them to blast off safely. The others come up with a last-minute solution; by removing his space-suit the technician can discard it in the airlock. When the technician returns to the cabin the airlock door opens and the heavy suit is cast out into space. The ship makes a successful hurried departure behind a caption: "The End—of the Beginning."

Today the reality of space-flight has outstripped Pal's imagination. But what he conceived in 1950 was new and impressive to its audience. Much to the astonishment of the old Hollywood hands, *Destination Moon* took off like a rocket the moment it was released, and George Pal's career soared with it.

While still working on *Destination Moon,* Pal became interested in *When Worlds Collide,* a novel by Philip Wylie and Edwin Balmer that Paramount had bought in 1932 for Cecil B. De Mille. A script was abandoned in 1934 after De Mille vetoed the project. Pal found the story exciting but Paramount did not, and gladly sold him the rights. He commissioned a new script and shopped around for a buyer, but no other studio would take a chance with it. Then, when *Destination Moon* became a hit, Pal was offered a production deal and opportunity to make *When Worlds Collide* (1951)—by Paramount.

"I was delighted," Pal told me. "But I soon learned that the studio had the final word. First of all they insisted on yet another new script with a lot of changes; I still think the one I brought them

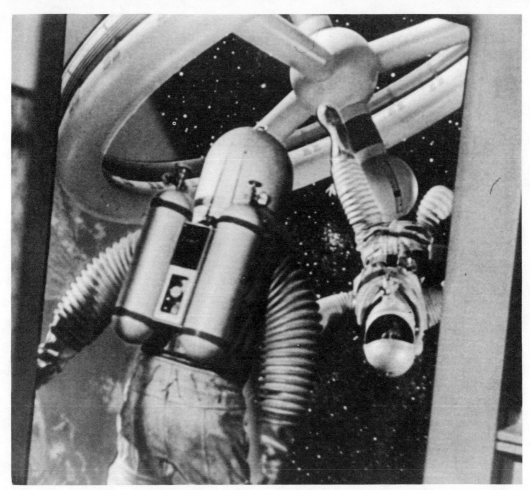

was better. In order to release the picture quickly after the success of *Destination Moon* they cut short production before I could film my intended ending and substituted an abrupt final scene of their own. Our technical staff had worked miracles with miniatures and special effects, but the biggest miracle of all was that *When Worlds Collide* succeeded in spite of the interference.''

The film, directed by Rudolph Maté, bears certain suspicious similarities to its predecessor, illustrating the Hollywood syndrome: if you've got a formula that works, use it again. In *When Worlds Collide,* the hero (Richard Derr) is a young flier who learns astronomers have secretly discovered two planets heading toward Earth. Zyra, much like our own, will barely miss us, but its passing will cause global devastation. Bellus, a giant, will actually collide with earth nineteen days later and destroy it. One of the astronomers believes a ''space-ark'' can be built in time to take off before the final catastrophe. Carrying forty people chosen by lottery from the workers who constructed it, the ship might land safely on Zyra, where the survivors can start life anew.

As in *Destination Moon,* the authorities refuse to cooperate on the project, and the rocket is built through private funding. Again the take-off of the completed spacecraft is in danger of being aborted, this time by workers who resist being left behind. And once more an heroic decision saves the day. A self-sacrificing astronomer (Larry Keating) tricks a selfish industrialist (John Hoyt) into remaining behind with him, thus conserving the launched rocket's precious fuel supply for its journey.

Despite the resemblances, *When Worlds Collide* offers more than its slow-moving forerunner— a love-triangle plot (Derr wins Barbara Rush from Peter Hanson), a race against time, and above all, a series of effects that made it the definitive *disaster* film for years to come. The construction of the gigantic rocket, counterpointed by volcanic eruptions, a tidal wave that smashes into New York City, and the final collision of Bellus with Earth (after the rocket escapes with its survivors) make an imposing spectacle. Again Bonestell and a top team of technicians transferred Pal's concept to the screen, deservedly winning an Academy Award for special effects.

H. G. Wells's *The War of the Worlds* was another property Paramount had purchased, way back in 1925. Rejected by both De Mille and Sergei Eisenstein, it collected cobwebs on the story department's shelves. Even the sensationalistic

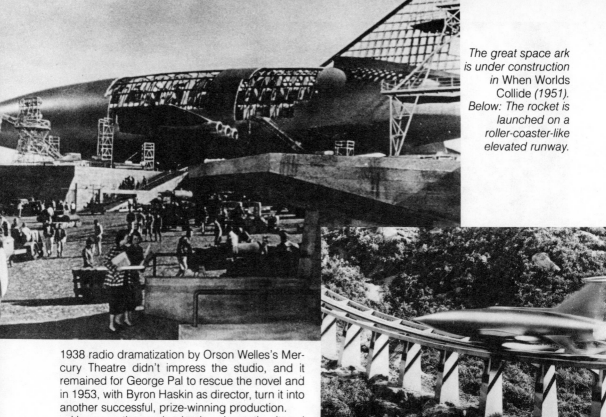

1938 radio dramatization by Orson Welles's Mercury Theatre didn't impress the studio, and it remained for George Pal to rescue the novel and in 1953, with Byron Haskin as director, turn it into another successful, prize-winning production.

However, the modernized and greatly altered story of Martian spaceships invading Earth is far less innovative in concept than the radio version's convincing news-story approach. Protected from U.S. Army defenses by a force-field, the flying war machines ravage the world with death-rays and menace the hero (Gene Barry) and heroine (Ann Robinson) in an attack on Los Angeles. Last-minute salvation comes out of left field when the Martians suddenly succumb to Earth's bacteria.

While Bonestell and the effects and art-direction staffs translated Pal's vision into exciting imagery, efforts to elevate the trite tale were blocked by the studio's vice-president in charge of production. The real warfare went on behind the scenes, and only the intervention of the studio head kept the project alive. But Pal's preference for a story about a married hero searching for his wife and child lost in the invasion got shot down, as did his idea of filming the climax in 3-D. "What I did win out on," Pal said, "was the idea that only one Martian creature would actually be shown on screen, and only for a few seconds. That kept the film from being dismissed as just another bug-eyed monster picture." This wise decision also helped keep the film from becoming dated when, in ten years, technical virtuosity created more convincing examples of extraterrestrial life-forms.

Pal's The Conquest of Space (1955), planned as a sequel to Destination Moon, was based on a nonfiction book by Bonestell and rocketry expert Willy Ley. Originally the script ("Trio of Space") dealt with voyages to Mars, Venus, and Jupiter, launched from a space station orbiting around earth. As usual, the studio got into the act, confining the story to the Mars flight alone and using four writers to turn the Haskin-directed film into another rehash of Destination Moon. Werner von Braun served as technical consultant but that didn't help the plot.

A rocket with a six-man crew, including a father (Walter Brooke) and son (Eric Fleming), and a stowaway, takes off from a huge spacewheel. Radar equipment fails en route and must be repaired from outside the ship; one crew-member is killed by a meteorite and the rocket itself is almost struck by a gigantic asteroid. The hero's father, traumatized by these perils, becomes convinced the mission defies divine will and tries to wreck the craft as it lands on Mars. His son prevents this, but during their stay on the planet the father attempts to destroy the precious water supply and is accidentally killed while struggling with his son. Now the son faces a murder charge when the ship returns to Earth. Meanwhile, when exploring the Martian environs, the water is used up; an unexpected snowfall provides a fresh supply. Then, as the ship prepares to leave, a sudden quake dislodges it from the ninety-degree take-off position. The son saves the day by firing the ship's engines, thus causing the rocket to right itself. As a reward, his companions agree to drop

In The Time Machine *(1960), George (Rod Taylor) listens to the talking rings to learn how civilization has deteriorated. Weena (Yvette Mimieux) doesn't understand why this man from the past cares so much about history and knowledge—after all, her people disappear and are killed at her age.*

the murder charge; moreover, it will be reported that his father died a hero.

These story contrivances destroyed the film's documentary flavor, and even the authenticity of the Martian locale suffered from executive tampering. Only the asteroid sequence and the funeral of the crewman killed in space retain their visual power.

Pal felt his own power ebbing at Paramount. Unable to negotiate a satisfactory deal for control of his work, he left and eventually found a new haven at MGM. It was there he made *The Time Machine* (1960)—yet another H. G. Wells story that Paramount had rejected. With the help of a new writer, David Duncan, and a new staff of artists and special-effects experts, Pal both produced and directed his best science fiction film.

George (Rod Taylor), its hero—who conceivably could be Herbert George Wells himself—perfects a time-travel machine in 1899 London and transports himself into the future. Reaching 1917, he discovers his house ruined and abandoned; proceeding to 1940, he encounters the air-raids of World War II. Continuing to 1966 he escapes (literally) in time, as London is obliterated by an atomic attack. When the nuclear holocaust triggers a volcanic eruption, George and his machine are trapped in rock. When the rock finally erodes he emerges into the world of the future, over 800,000 years later.

Here two primitive races exist amidst mysterious ruins: the gentle, overly passive Eloi, on the

surface, and the menacing Morlocks, who dwell in caverns below. Leaving his machine near a huge stone sphinx, George saves an Eloi girl named Weena (Yvette Mimieux) from drowning and is disturbed that none of the Eloi cared enough to help her; later he also rescues her from a hideous apelike Morlock. Then he discovers his time machine has been stolen by the Morlocks and placed inside the sphinx.

The girl brings him to an ancient structure where a remnant of former civilization—strange "talking rings"—reveals the history of an atomic war that wiped out the world and left only a handful of survivors. Evolution transformed the surface-dwellers into the peaceful but primitive Eloi, lazy vegetarians (their food is supplied by the Morlocks), who neither worked, developed a culture of their own, nor bothered to protect themselves from the Morlocks. Those who took refuge in bomb-shelters below became the evil Morlocks—cannibals who use the Eloi for food.

Along with other Eloi, the girl walks trancelike into the stone sphinx when summoned by a

siren's age-old warning of impending danger; it's a trick devised by the Morlocks to imprison them. George ventures alone into the gloomy caverns in hopes of finding a way to save the girl and her people. The fanged and hairy Morlocks, eyes glowing in the dark, attack him as he invades their lair. Discovering their fear of fire, he manages to lead the girl and the other newly revitalized and aggressive Eloi in overcoming the Morlocks.

Using the flame as a weapon, they escape to the surface. George enters the now open sphinx and retrieves his machine. As the remaining Morlocks close in for the kill, George takes off and returns to early 1900, in time for a dinner party he'd arranged. After telling his story, he finds his friends do not believe him. As the film ends, he seats himself in the time machine, returning to rejoin the girl and the other Eloi and assist them in restoring civilization.

This award-winning movie was Pal's most effective and successful science fiction work because its protagonist is a full-fledged character instead of a stick-figure hero, and because the visual imagery is more innovative than in earlier sf works. Pal's knowledge of the principles of time-lapse photography (so important to his Puppetoons) and his expertise in evolving special effects helped create the illusion of time-travel; his youthful education in art and architecture guided the brilliant production staff. William Tuttle designed the frightening Morlock masks from Pal's sketches.

Robinson Crusoe on Mars (1964), which Haskin directed and Ib Melchior scripted, was Pal's last venture into the genre of "pure" sf. A modern-day variation loosely based on the Defoe classic, the picture boasted a Mars set that won critical acclaim, but the somewhat pedestrian pacing of the lone-man-surviving-through-ingenuity plot failed to excite audiences that had come to expect greater scope and spectacle in science fiction fare. As a follow-up to *The Time Machine,* it seemed anticlimactic, and Pal turned his attention to other areas. Twice he would flirt with borderline sf concepts—psi phenomena in *The Power* (1968) and technological gadgetry in *Doc Savage—The Man of Bronze* (1975)—but never again was he granted the opportunity to film any of his beloved science fiction projects. One of them was a sequel to *The Time Machine,* utilizing more of Wells's novel; like the rest, it became the victim of executive turnovers and changes of studio ownership in the Sixties and Seventies. On several occasions he was given the go-ahead, only to be halted before production when new management replaced the old.

I myself saw it happen while working with Pal on two films during the last years of his life. *The Day of the Comet,* derived from a Wells story about a comet that menaces Earth and planned as a television miniseries, was to be told with an adult approach, which Pal had always been prevented from using. *Berg!* was loosely based on a novel concerning an Antarctic iceberg towed

Left: George attempts to rescue Weena and the other Eloi from the dreaded Morlocks' underground chambers. But the Morlocks won't make it easy.

Right: Pal's Robinson Crusoe on Mars *(1964) was filmed in Death Valley for authenticity. The film starred Paul Mantee (R) as the title character and, as his copilot, Adam West, destined for TV stardom as Batman.*

through thousands of miles of ocean to irrigate the Middle East. Oddly enough, although the concept might appear just as wild as the notion of actual space travel seemed in 1950, such an achievement is by no means an impossibility. Again Pal proposed to pioneer as a prophet, and again studio politics prevented him.

Of Pal's fifteen features, only those discussed here can be classified as "pure" science fiction; of these, only *Destination Moon, When Worlds Collide, The Conquest of Space, The Time Machine,* and *Robinson Crusoe on Mars* explored our future. Made in the face of obstacles and opposition, flawed by compromise and changes, they nonetheless convey his personal philosophy—his hatred of authoritarian oppression, his unswerving belief in human heroics and self-sacrifice, and his affirmation that man's intelligence will prevail in the end. Eternally optimistic, he imbued even Wells's most pessimistic predictions with his own faith in the future. Time itself caught up with George Pal. But he lived long enough to see his concepts of space stations and

moon-flight become realities, and though the actual events dated his films he rejoiced in the vindication of his vision.

None of Pal's films boasted a cast of major stars or the multi-million-dollar budgets common today. Their success was a direct result of his unique ability to transform his inner vision into screen imagery. Pal's favorite expression of farewell was "Take good care." He himself observed the injunction in his work. The good care he took when conceiving, designing, and executing special effects paved the way for today's technical triumphs.

Throughout his career, Pal never faltered in his determination to design his cinematic creations for family entertainment. His principles seem old-fashioned to today's filmmakers, but all of them owe a debt to Pal's efforts. Without his example to guide them, science fiction films might never have achieved their present stature. What we see on the screen today is a lasting legacy from the man who always signed himself, "Your Pal, George."

Two similar
publicity stills
showing nuclear
mutants carrying
helpless blond
beauties. Above: In George
Pal's The Time Machine, Yvette
Mimieux is the female in trouble.
Right: In Roger Corman's The Day the World
Ended (1955), Lori Nelson's character is
terrified of a monster who turns out to be her
former boyfriend, a victim of radiation.

Cautionary Fables

An Interview with Roger Corman by Ed Naha

Ed Naha: You first dabbled in futuristic fiction in the mid-Fifties, beginning with your fourth film as director, *The Day the World Ended* [1955]. This was a cautionary film about the aftermath of nuclear war. Were you first attracted to the science fiction genre because you felt it would allow you the opportunity to say something *meaningful* to movie audiences?

Roger Corman: I think I was trying to find an area of film that interested me and where, within the contexts of the action movie, I could possibly portray some of my ideas concerning the future. I had always been interested in science fiction— when growing up, I had been an avid reader of

---

Ed Naha wrote the screenplays for *Camp Bottomout/Oddballs* and *Wizard Wars* for Roger Corman's Millenium Pictures. His books include *The Films of Roger Corman, Brilliance on a Budget; Horrors: From Screen to Scream; The Science Fictionary;* and *The Making of Dune.*

Roger Corman formed Millenium Pictures after many years as head of New World Pictures, which he also founded. He has produced, directed, and distributed more than three hundred films, many in the science fiction genre. The futuristic films he has directed are *The Day the World Ended, Teenage Caveman, The Last Woman on Earth,* and *Gas-s-s-s.*

---

science fiction literature and had, of course, seen many science fiction films over the years. I found the science fiction genre intriguing to me as a filmmaker in several ways. First, it's an unlimited breeding ground for imagination and ideas. You can let your innermost beliefs and desires run more freely in science fiction films than you can in the somewhat limited structure offered by "realistic" pictures. Also, you can use the film medium in wilder ways. For instance, you certainly can experiment with special effects. So it's a freer type of film, visually and intellectually.

EN: Was there anything you wanted to "say" in your early science fiction films?

RC: There was not *one* specific thing that I tried to get across in my science fiction films. But ideas were important.

EN: In movies such as *The Day the World Ended* and *Teenage Caveman* [1958], you were restricted by pretty tight low-budget exploitation movie formulas. Did you find that confining in terms of editorializing?

RC: To a certain extent, but not completely. In *The Day the World Ended,* I was locked into a story that American International Pictures assigned to me about a postnuclear world filled with radiation and mutants. I did some work on it, and I think we managed to make a pretty scary movie that included a few thought-provoking situations.

Now, *Teenage Caveman* was a different story entirely. By the way, I never *made* a movie called *Teenage Caveman.* The movie I shot was called *Prehistoric World.* AIP retitled it for a while but, thank goodness, they went back to the original title shortly thereafter.*

Prehistoric World was an example of my being able to work within the low-budget formula and improve upon it by using a little imagination. All American International wanted to do was film a prehistoric picture. So they said, "Make a prehistoric picture for $80,000 in ten days."

Bob Campbell, my writer, and I came up with the idea of taking the prehistoric storyline and laying it in the future after civilization had been destroyed by nuclear war. We created a religion for the cave dwellers that was based around the remnants of their previous world, our contemporary world. We placed those remnants in a radioactive area, which became a forbidden zone to these tribesmen.

What I like about *Prehistoric World* is that, for nearly the entire picture, you really think you're watching a nice little prehistoric movie about su-

---

*The 1958 film, starring Robert Vaughn as a lion-clothed kinda guy, is a television mainstay and is shown under the title of, you guessed it, *Teenage Caveman.* —E.N.

Tempers flare among the few survivors of nuclear war in both Corman's The Day the World Ended *(right, with Mike "Touch" Connors and Adele Jergens in featured roles) and* The Last Woman on Earth *(1961), with (L–R), Edward Wain, Antony Carbone, and Betsy-Jones Moreland.*

perstitious elders and a rebellious teenage warrior [Robert Vaughn]...until the last few minutes. It has an ending that is very similar to the one that was used years later in *Planet of the Apes* [1968].

I enjoyed this movie a lot more than *The Day the World Ended.* This was partially because the ideas in it were mine, but also because there were *more* ideas in it.

EN: What about *The Last Woman On Earth* [1961]?
RC: Basically, it was the story of the last three survivors on Earth following a nuclear war: two men [Antony Carbone and Edward Wain, actually writer Robert Towne] and a woman [Betsy-Jones Moreland]. Of course, a three-sided romance evolves and, of course, it does not make for a happy existence.

In Gas-s-s-s...Or, It May Be Necessary to Destroy the World in Order to Save It *(1970),* the world was inherited by the young. Left: The fine cast of essentially unknowns (L–R), Ben Vereen, Cindy Williams, Talia Coppola (Shire), Bud Cort, Elaine Giftos, and Robert Corff. Below: The good guys protect their new communal existence from marauding gang members.

The Last Woman on Earth was an offbeat little movie. I produced it for my own company, so I had total control over it. But it was never really what it could have been. We really tried to do something thought-provoking, but we were pretty much done in by our small budget. We were shooting it back to back with another film and we were so rushed that we never actually had a finished script during production. The script was written as we filmed. We got pages every day. We never knew on any given day exactly what we were going to film. We finished the whole movie in two weeks. Still, we tried our best.

My writer was Robert Towne [who later did the screenplay for *Chinatown*]. We tried to depict the aftermath of an atomic war in a realistic way. I was, and still am, very much interested in the

concept of nuclear holocaust. I think the possibility for it happening is there. Personally, I don't think it's going to occur, but I think that, through film, we should keep on cautioning and warning people that it *might*.

EN: What moved you to portray an almost existential future in the movie *Gas-s-s-s* [1970], a film that combined elements of the 1960s youth culture with germ warfare, the ghost of Edgar Allan Poe, and motorcycle gangs?

RC: *Gas-s-s-s* was a pretty personal statement. This was made towards the end of the great counter-culture cycle of the late 1960s. I had been something of a supporter of the youth culture, although I certainly was past my youth at the time. I had geared a few of my movies, such as *The Wild Angels* [1966] and *The Trip* [1967], toward a sympathetic portrayal of the counter-culture.

In *Gas-s-s-s*, it was apparent that I was beginning to get a little disillusioned. I intended that the picture be sympathetic toward our lead gang of kids yet, at the same time, I wanted to show that I was beginning to suspect that all of the ideas being spouted by the counter-culture and all of the dreams were not totally rooted in reality. In the picture, I wanted to literally *give* youth the world they desired and, then, make a cautionary statement about how youth might not be able to handle it as perfectly as they anticipated.

In the film, a cask of experimental nerve gas ruptures, and fumes spread into the atmosphere. Everyone over the age of twenty-five dies and, suddenly, the world is run by kids. Nobody knows what to do. Once I established that premise, I got pretty wild. I had Poe, Martin Luther King, Che Guevara, and even God in the movie. After I had finished it, however, American International Pictures took it and recut it. They were a little nervous about this vision of the fu-

ture and trimmed the movie pretty heavily. One of my biggest disappointments was that they cut God out of the picture. He had all the best lines.

EN: Were you more optimistic about the future then?

RC: I was most optimistic about the future during the mid-1960s. By the late 1960s, I was beginning to ease off a little. The transition for me happened about 1969–1970. I don't think I've become pessimistic since then. I've pretty much stayed on an even keel. I'm hopeful about the future but I'm not starry-eyed about it.

EN: Do you try to portray the future in terms of technology or with a more humanistic slant?

RC: I don't think you can separate the two. They interrelate. I think it's a mistake to say there's the technological world and there's the human one. They work together. They have to, don't they?

EN: What elements are necessary to interest you in a science fiction film you'd consider producing?

RC: The main idea must be interesting. Hopefully, it will be meaningful as well. Secondarily, I am concerned whether or not that idea can be told in an imaginative *visual* manner. I used to hate going to see a science fiction film and watch scene after scene of two scientists talking to one another.

EN: Do you see room for humor in futuristic editorializing?

RC: Definitely. But humor is a very tricky business. The humor in *Battle Beyond the Stars* [1980] is a good example of how I like to treat humor in science fiction. That film had a serious story, but had humorous undertones running through it. The humor was always there to underscore a statement, to further a point.

Before you can try anything else, your story has to be accepted as being realistic. The com-

edy then can be introduced to reinforce the plot. Unfortunately, many directors can't handle drama and comedy simultaneously. We had problems making that movie because there is always the tendency, when confronted with both drama and comedy, to go for the comedy. Not only that, but to go for the comedy in a broad way. It's fun to do. It's easy to do. But...it also undermines the story.

EN: Are you frustrated now, as a producer, by budgetary constraints that keep you from realizing the sprawling futures seen in, let's say, the *Star Wars* films?

RC: Yes. That's a major frustration. In one paragraph, a writer can demand $50 million worth of production costs and there's nothing you can do about it except, perhaps, weep openly. Budgetarily, you just can't film it. If you're creative, you find ways to *suggest* it but it gets very trying when you have to do that more than a few times during a picture.

Not even George Lucas's money can match the imagination that was seen in the pulp science fiction of the 1930s and 1940s: you would need an infinite budget to get all that on the screen.

EN: Why do you think it's respectable to make a science fiction film now when back in the days when you were directing, it was considered nothing more than an exercise in Saturday matinee mayhem?

RC: It's quite a legitimate genre today for several reasons. I think science fiction, as literature, is a lot more accepted today because the kids who used to read it are now adults and they *still* read it. It's been around longer so it's become more respectable. Plus, there are new generations of readers who are not ashamed to be

seen carrying science fiction books around. Science fiction literature has a much broader base of appeal today. There are more science fiction books and magazines being published today, hence, more readers.

At the same time, I think people started seeing the advantages of editorializing through science fiction films in the 1960s and 1970s. Movies like *Planet of the Apes, The Andromeda Strain* [1971], and *2001: A Space Odyssey* [1968] could not be called kid stuff by any stretch of the imagination.

George Lucas, I think, has to be considered a pivotal figure in the current science fiction boom. He made the first giant commercial success in science fiction and he made it well. That he made it well added respectability to the genre. The fact that it earned hundreds of millions of dollars didn't hurt the cause either. In Hollywood, a profitable film automatically becomes respectable.

EN: Is there any science fiction story left out there that you would like to film?

RC: The one I always wanted to do and actually tried to get an option on at one time has just been filmed...*Dune* [1984]. I even had a treatment written on my own a few years ago when I thought I could get the option. But that option never came through.

Dune, to me, is the ultimate futuristic story. It combines adventures with ideas. There are comments on society, on politics, on human relations throughout the plot. Yet, on an entertainment level it just barrels right along with space warfare and nasty villains.

If I could find a story set in the future that impresses me as much as *Dune*, I'd love to return to the genre.

The Futuristic Films of Stanley Kubrick

Richard Schickel

Life is too short."

Is it possible? Can it be? Could one reasonably, soberly, in full command of one's critical faculties and in full knowledge of one's

critical responsibilities when confronting a major portion of a major artist's work, advance the possibility that from such a commonplace, such a banality, there arose this uncommon sublimity: *Dr. Strangelove Or: How I Learned to Stop Worrying and Love the Bomb* (1964), *2001: A Space Odyssey* (1968), *A Clockwork Orange* (1971), Stanley Kubrick's marvelously varied, wonderfully ingenious, curiously gnomic contemplations of where we have arrived in the history of the human race and where we might yet be going?

"Life is too short." Surely all this virtuosity, technical and otherwise, has not been lavished on the illustration of so ordinary a cliché? And surely all the speculative frenzy, and all the outrage too, that was vented on these films when they were initially released cannot be made to dance on this pinhead phrase?

Probably not. Probably the facts of the case are more complicated than that. For Kubrick is one of the few true intellectuals (as opposed to the men who like to play that role) ever to make movies, which is to say that the range of his interests (not to mention his reading), as well as the modernist taste for ambiguity that he shares with his kind, makes one resist any attempt to understand his work too easily. Moreover, he has honed to a very high degree the intelligent artist's capacity to

cover his creative tracks with superbly misleading ex post facto rationalizations. That, too, compels a certain caution when confronting his work critically.

But still the incautious phrase, that wretched little cliché, keeps recurring: "Life is too short." It bustles back time and time again into the mind that has repeatedly banished it for the sin of oversimplification, elbowing aside all the more delicate formulations. And so in the end, however reluctantly, one grants it headway. Somehow the phrase seems to link Kubrick's three futuristic films better than any other: It directs one's attention away from the political, scientific, and social metaphors that have (in the order of their appearance) controlled the discussion of these films; it has textual support in statements Kubrick himself has made about his work; and, most useful of all, it has a double meaning that I'm convinced is crucial to our understanding of the issues with which both his art and his personal preoccupations are most centrally concerned.

Kubrick's virtuosity as a filmmaker and the range of his subjects have served to disguise his near-obsessive concern with these two matters— the brutal brevity of the individual's span on Earth and the indifference of the spheres to that span, whatever its length, whatever achievements are recorded over its course. His works, whatever their ostensible themes, must always be seen as acts of defiance against this tragic fate.

On both points he has been quite specific. Here, for example, is Kubrick on the subject of

Richard Schickel is a film critic for *Time* magazine. His books include *D. W. Griffith: An American Life, The Disney Version, His Picture in the Papers, The Men Who Made Movies,* and *Cary Grant: A Celebration.*

Dr. Strangelove, a wicked, scary, former Nazi (whose out-of-control right hand still automatically does a "Heil Hitler" salute) has become a trusted adviser of the U.S. government. He has the only survival plan in case of world destruction: live in mine shafts for a hundred years, with ten women for every man. The President (also played by Peter Sellers) has no choice but to listen.

individual mortality: "Man is the only creature aware of his own mortality and is at the same time generally incapable of coming to grips with this awareness and all its implications. Millions of people thus, to a greater or lesser degree, experience emotional anxieties, tensions, and unresolved conflicts that frequently express themselves in the form of neuroses and a general joylessness that permeates their lives with frustration and bitterness and increases as they grow older and see the grave yawning before them." It may be that this was ever thus: and certainly for any reasonably intelligent person this thought is in itself, at this late date in history, only a short crawl up from the banal. Almost every interesting sensibility must entertain it, and offer variations on it for our entertainment.

But for the modernist or postmodernist mind the gloom surrounding the contemplation of mortality is deepened by two or three other factors. The first, of course, is the loss of religious faith and the consoling promise of immortality it once offered the believer. About that also little more need be said at this late date. But as the depth and breadth of the cosmos has been made ever more evident to us by twentieth-century science, our other hope for immortality—our last hope, as it were—also diminishes. In this vastness all of our accomplishments dwindle to microscopic size; our best works, our proudest achievements become literally lost in the stars. And man, most

especially artistic man, despairs still more. Or as Kubrick once put it: "Why, he must ask himself, should he bother to write a great symphony, or strive to make a living, or even to love another, when he is no more than a momentary microbe on a dust mote whirling through the unimaginable immensity of space?" Why, indeed? Especially when it becomes more and more clear that our universe was created by chance, is ruled by chance and may well be snuffed out by chance.

It was the last of these matters that Kubrick spoke of first in his work, and it is the one (I venture to say on the basis of a certain knowledge of his way of life) that has the most effect on his day-to-day existence. About mortality and about the universal indifference one can do little except confront them with an acceptant mind. But about chance one can actually do something; one can take a few precautions that will, at least, diminish its more malevolent workings. Kubrick thus refuses to fly. Nor will he work outside the studio if he can possibly avoid it, closed environments being infinitely more controllable than open ones, especially for directors of his undisputed stature—kings in kingdoms of their own devising. He lives, too, behind gates, in well-guarded isolation—selecting those visitors he chooses to see, ordering in the books and films he omnivorously devours, reaching out by telephone and telex when he needs to get in touch with the outside world. When he sends forth his

films he does what he can to protect them from mischance. He personally inspects, for instance, every print that goes out to the first-run theaters, and he keeps a file of those houses, complete with detailed descriptions, even pictures, so he can be sure his movies are not booked into environments he regards as unhealthy for them.

In this connection one thinks of his first important picture, *The Killing* (1956), in which a perfect crime, the meticulously planned robbery of a day's takings at a race track, is undone at the last moment by chance operating at its most absurd levels. Along comes this silly woman with her stupid dog—we don't expect to encounter such creatures in heist movies; we expect to encounter them in life, where we think of them as annoyances, not as deadly dangers to our best-laid plans. For Kubrick, of course, their sudden intervention in his story, setting in train a near-comic sequence of events that results in the loot blowing away in the prop wash of what was to have been the getaway airplane, is more than an ironic coda; it is the whole point of the film, an expression of Kubrick's deepest sense of how the world works—refuses to work, actually. As he sees it, the lady and her dog, or something like them, must logically put in a blundering appearance, at some point in our venturings if, indeed, it is chance that rules our universe. What he is saying is that there is nothing chancy about chance's arrival in our affairs; the only unpredictable thing about it is the form it will take, and the precise moment of its appearance.

If this be so then obviously the prudent man, the prudent society, will take what precautions it can against the workings of omnipresent chance, try to minimize the damage it must inevitably wreak. This point is, in fact, so clear that even the dim-witted governments of the super powers have, in one instance, made such prudence into elaborate official policy, surrounding those weapons systems that have doomsday capability

and are most vulnerable to the mischief of chance—the atomic weapons—with not one but many fail-safe precautions. These are, naturally, as foolproof as the similarly elaborate fail-safe systems that surrounded *The Killing*'s robbery scheme. As a result (to borrow a subtitle) we have all "learned to stop worrying and love the bomb." Yes. Absolutely.

Dr. Strangelove is not to be read solely as a cautionary tale comically put, though it is surely a great comedy, one that we can tell, two decades after its release, is going to hold up for a very long time. That is because it is a true black comedy, a comedy that proceeds from a bleak, but deeply felt view of human nature, and is not dependent for its best thrusts on its situation—the desperate attempt by the American high command to recall an atomic strike against the Soviet Union launched by a madman—or upon its satire of the already outmoded technology of the strike and recall effort. What Kubrick is contemplating here are both the ironies of chance and the failure of rationalism to first estimate the effects of chance on human endeavors and to then build into its contingency-planning compensations for these effects.

He has clearly gone far beyond the simple statement he made about the accidental nature of existence at the end of *The Killing*. Consider just the most obvious workings of chance in *Dr. Strangelove*. There would be no film if, by chance, an unstable figure, Gen. Jack D. Ripper (Sterling Hayden), had not wormed his way into the system, and if, by chance, he had not been made C.O. of the Burpleson Air Force Base, with access to the code that can send an SAC wing on its way to Russia, and if, by chance, he had not come unglued at just the moment he did, neither sooner nor later. Certainly it is chance that sends an antiaircraft burst into the radio of one bomber (instead of destroying the plane or hitting it in a less crucial spot), so the crew cannot hear and heed the recall code when it is finally found and broadcast. It is chance, too, that dictates command of that ship rest in the hands of Major Kong (Slim Pickens), one of those otherwise good-natured souls whose only flaw is that he unquestioningly obeys orders, even ones that he is dubious about.

But the point of the exercise is not merely, or most significantly, to demonstrate how disastrously the law of unintended consequences can work out. It is rather to demonstrate the impotence of the rational in dealing with it. Reason is represented in *Dr. Strangelove* as either comically ineffectual or, when it is effective, comically perverse. In both modes, of course, it is portrayed by Peter Sellers, in his justly celebrated triple-character performance. It is interesting that as both Group Captain Lionel Mandrake, who discovers what Gen. Ripper has done and tries to undo it, and as President Muffley, who at the highest echelon must try on the Hot Line to talk his Soviet counterpart into being sensible and patient about the whole mess, Sellers adopts the wheedling tones of a parent dealing with a child caught in the grips of the Terrible Twos. Whether he speaks in the false-hearty terms of common-sensical Mandrake or the false-fatherly terms of a President who seems to be half-Eisenhower, half-Stevenson—a man of common decency—these are parodies of reasonableness, hugely comic statements of its enfeeblement when it confronts the harsh reality that rationalism must ever deny, which is that however grown-up they act, most people, including the most powerful, remain at heart children. The alternative is the one offered chillingly by Dr. Strangelove himself. Crippled in body, bent of mind, this third Sellers character—an ex-Nazi now befriended by the U.S.A.—is presented as a living critique of pure reason, calculating how to turn disaster into advantage for whoever pays his salary right up to the trump of doom. It carries no moral weight for him anyway; it has long since been drained of its human components, reduced to a set of figures in his computer's memory bank.

But whether it presents itself as hand-wringing humanism or as a set of figures on a print-out, reason, as we presently conceive it, is in Kubrick's view a poor tool with which to confront the postmodern, postatomic age. What Kubrick is saying in *Dr. Strangelove* is that though man is sufficiently advanced to imagine a rational world and to build intricately rational systems for governing it, he has not yet progressed far enough in his evolution to rid himself of his irrational impulses or rid society of those institutions and arrangements that are projections of that irrationalism. Man is, in short, incapable of building systems of governance at a level of sophistication where they will include mechanisms capable of automatically nullifying the effects of chance or the irrationally thrown monkey wrench (they

Being the adventures of a young man whose principal interests are rape, ultra-violence and Beethoven.

STANLEY KUBRICK'S

CLOCKWORK ORANGE

Poster for Kubrick's third futuristic film. Unlike Dr. Strangelove *and* 2001, *however,* A Clockwork Orange *(1971) has not achieved almost unanimous critical acceptance. The violence within the film remains a source of great debate.*

amount to the same thing, actually). He is also saying, I think, that at our present level of development we will never be able to create truly fail-safe systems; we're just not brainy enough. He may also be saying—though this point is both much more speculative and much more ironic—that it might not be such a great idea to do so because we would sacrifice something of our humanity if we managed to achieve that next evolutionary level.

But not to worry. As we said at the beginning, life is too short. Not only is it too short for any individual to achieve this higher consciousness, but also it is too short, in all probability, for the human race to achieve it, since the possibility of blowing ourselves to smithereens is now so obvious. Such hope as there is, in these circumstances, lies in the possibility of rebirth in a new form. It is the final irony of *Dr. Strangelove* that it suggests that possibility, and places the sugges-

Right: Kubrick lies on the floor with the camera, and films Malcolm McDowell during the scene in A Clockwork Orange in which Alex and his droogs rape Mrs. Alexander (Adrienne Corri) and beat up her husband. In order for Kubrick to get us to identify with Alex, he stylized such scenes in which Alex perpetrates the violence—but when Alex endures violence, scenes are realistic.

Below: Kubrick is behind the camera filming Peter Sellers (here as the President) and George C. Scott, who played General Buck Turgidson in Dr. Strangelove.

tion in the mouth of its resident mad scientist, who proposes that he and his elite colleagues retreat to deep mine shafts, there to live and procreate until the clouds (of radiation) roll by and, in a few generations, their heirs stroll forth to reclaim the Earth. Perhaps, given the elitist principles that will govern selection of the survivor population, they will be stronger and wiser than we are now. Certainly Dr. Strangelove seems to imply as much. Maybe they will be weaker—inbreeding, you know. Kubrick himself is not saying. There is just the song "We'll Meet Again" on the soundtrack. It is certain, however, that they will be different, these inheritors, in some sense reborn. And rebirth, as Kubrick sees it, is our only hope.

Vide next *2001: A Space Odyssey,* which as Andrew Sarris said, "is concerned ultimately with the inner fears of Kubrick's mind as it contemplates infinity and eternity." What Kubrick is mulling here is the reverse of what he considered in *Strangelove.* It is not the triumph of unreason, but the triumph of reason that is presented here as cause for alarm. The film's earliest futuristic passages make that painfully clear, for the everyday reality of 2001, despite the ease with which man has mastered space travel, is one in which the banalities of our own present-day everyday life are writ parodistically large. People ride from star to star eating the same plastic food, enduring the same plastic smiles from the cabin attendants, looking out the windows at space slipping by with the same bored expressions that we have when watching the land slip by beneath our jets. The people in 2001 meet with the same false cordiality, exchange the same bureaucratically flattened banalities. Even when space travelers venture deeper into the darker reaches of the galaxy on their quasi-military missions their rounds are dismally like those of today's astronauts. They tend to their physical fitness, occupy themselves with routine tasks, do everything possible to drain their adventure of a sense of adventure. Indeed, the mission of the space ship Discovery, which is to try to trace the origins of a mysterious signal-sending obelisk that was discovered on the moon (a sign that superior life forms visited us sometime in the distant past), though ostensibly commanded by Dave Bowman (Keir Dullea), is actually controlled by the talkative super-rational 9000 computer, HAL. He is, without question, by far the most interesting "character" (in the conventional sense of the term) in the film. He has wit and, it would seem, he is touched by something like original sin, which the human space travelers give no evidence of knowing about, so programmed into their routines are they.

In short, the future as Kubrick projects it from the evidence of our shared present is dismally without resonance—romantically, intellectually, culturally. It is an engineer's future, not an artist's. And 2001 is, finally, the story of a microcosmic rebellion by the one human being who survives HAL's murderous depredations on the crew. Bowman begins by lobotomizing the computer, then proceeds, in effect, to shuck off the shell in which civilization as he knows it has encased him. He exits his space ship in a smaller, auxiliary vehicle, proceeding toward Jupiter and then, when moons, planets, suns, and his ship are in alignment with a monolith that is drifting through space, he enters a "stargate," and is eventually transported into a room where the decor is half that of the eighteenth century (the Age of Reason), half modern. There he confronts his aged self, dies, and is reborn as the "starchild," a fetuslike creature with enormous brain and eyes, who is last seen whirling through space toward some new, unimaginable destiny.

For a film that was so puzzling to its initial viewers (mostly because it insisted on telling its tale imagistically rather that through dialogue) the meaning of 2001 seems in retrospect very clear—less ambiguous, perhaps, than any other work of Kubrick's maturity. It says, quite frankly, that our present "lines of play" (to borrow a chess expression Kubrick himself likes to employ when discussing his work) are used up, without creative force or possibility. Again, our opening phrase recurs to mind: "Life is too short," that is to say (in this context) the individual does not have time, in the space of a brief lifetime, to patiently await the arrival of circumstances that might be helpful in his efforts to evolve upwardly. Nor can he expect much help in that regard from society, which is bent on routinizing him. Nor, finally, can he put much faith in that old liberal hope, the idea of progress, the notion that somehow, automatically, technology and our developing social institutions are edging us upward toward a higher plane of being. No, Kubrick seems to be saying here, nothing short of the most daring rebellion, a rebellion that takes us to the threshold of the unknown, and then propels us over that threshold, will do. Somehow, like Bowman, we must will ourselves toward the higher consciousness, open ourselves to it. It is no accident that the film's principal musical theme is from *Thus Spake Zarathustra,* music inspired by Nietzsche.

But one cannot leave this remarkable movie without speaking of its history since its release in 1968. Opening to puzzlement, outrage, dismissal, and the worst kind of criticism—mystified awe—it has become, in the few years since, one of the major milestones on the postmodernist path—so far the only movie that has achieved that status. Its imagery is now burned into almost everyone's consciousness, is almost universal in its familiarity, so much so that people refer to it in the other visual media without seeming to be aware that they are quoting it. And that leads one to yet another interpretation of the film's central symbol, those monoliths scattered about the universe by the superior race on their long-ago star voyagings. The Arthur C. Clarke short story from which *2001* evolved was called "The Sentinel," and it posited the possibility that these enigmatic creations were just that, warning devices to tell the superior beings when a new race had evolved to a point where its consciousness might be of interest to them. They perhaps function similarly in the film, but I think Kubrick means us to see them in another way as well, as art objects that signal us aesthetically as well as electronically across the millennia, suggesting the possibility that there are present among us superior beings, beings capable of creating works that, even if they are buried and lost in the short term, may speak to the beings of the future and, whether or not they are shaped like men, may indeed speak more clearly to a reborn race than they speak to us. It would be characteristic of a man as oppressed as Kubrick is with time's fleeting quality and the fragility of man's works to suggest this faint hope, and to express it enigmatically, as a nonverbal sign amidst his more voluble pessimism.

Kubrick's third futuristic film, *A Clockwork Orange,* also takes up the matter of creativity, just as it takes up some of the other themes of its two immediate predecessors—the limits of rationalism, for instance, and the possibilities of rebirth. Lacking the antic spirit of *Dr. Strangelove,* or the soaring optimism of *2001,* it is a grimly comic piece, bitterly ironic in tone. It is also, in terms of sheer technique, Kubrick's most arresting work as well as his most morally ambivalent one.

Alex, its central figure (superbly played by Malcolm McDowell) is a projection into a future not much more distant than 2001, of the contemporary spirit of juvenile delinquency, amoral and anarchistic, yet with a certain cheekiness as well. His style is also a projection of the contemporary punk manner, which Kubrick presciently caught practically at the moment of its birth in London. Alex and his three droogs (friends) devote themselves almost entirely to mugging and rape and—no other way to describe it—they have a *flair* for these activities. In the dismal world of the future—all telescreens, cell-block housing developments, and a dispassionate, institutionalized, welfare-state liberalism—Alex in particular represents the life force. He has energy, a twisted creative intelligence, a strangely compelling charm. And one saving grace of a traditional kind—his obsessive passion for the music of "Ludwig Van" (Beethoven).

The scenes in which he leads his gang on their depredations—most notably the invasion of a country house where a writer is savagely beaten and his wife savagely raped (as Alex sings "Singin' in the Rain") are among the most shockingly perverse in all of cinema, for they are shot and edited and played not to stress the victim's horror but the victimizer's pleasure (more Nietzsche). They are, in short, extremely erotic—and imaginative, even darkly humorous in their savage way. Another way of putting it is that they are emotionally expressive—however unpleasant the emotions expressed are—in a way that nothing else is in the society Kubrick presents.

But, of course, that won't do. Civility, if not civilization, must be served. Apprehended for his crimes and jailed, bold Alex volunteers for a radical new re-education program being advanced by a "progressive" Minister for Home Affairs. Alex, too, believes life is too short. Society cannot afford to wait years for prison to accomplish moral regeneration of its inmates, which it mostly doesn't do anyway. In the new program drugs are used to open up the subject emotionally, so he can respond with proper loathing to brutally graphic documentary film footage recounting man's inhumanity to man. And the program works; it turns Alex into a perfect wimp—docile, passive, a good citizen. But remember, crime was his form of creativity, and when the impulse to partake in crime was programmed out of him so was his capacity to respond to any of the other higher impulses. Now he will retch when he hears his beloved Ludwig Van's music, just as he retches at the thought of committing a rape in his born-again state. The irony is superb.

And prepares the way for a new and final irony. For the re-educated Alex now becomes, in the eyes of the liberal-humanist party, a victim of the state's technocratic and bureaucratic impulse to meddle with psyche and spirit. Such an outcry is raised that the state must now agree to re-educate the re-educated, and the film ends with a close-up of Alex's wickedly glinting eyes as he contemplates a return to the life of crime.

A Clockwork Orange is obviously cautionary in the same way that Kubrick's other probes of the future are, in that it offers a radical critique of contemporary society—its politics, culture, and moral values. It also forms a coda to *2001* by making manifest the point that rebirth cannot be achieved on the cheap, through technological means or chemical means—a point that the earlier film's prime audience, Sixties youth, responding to the film through a haze of pot and self-indulgence, mostly missed.

Taken together, *Dr. Strangelove, 2001,* and *A Clockwork Orange* form a sort of intellectual trilogy. The first mourns the failure of rationalism as we have, until now, understood it. The second proposes a redemptive myth, something to live for in place of conventional rationalism and, for that matter, conventional religion. The superior beings of *2001* are superior not only intellectually, not only spiritually, but in both respects. And Kubrick is surely saying that the development of our powers in one of these areas at the expense of the other would grant us only a false and illusory power. Finally, in the last film, he is again reminding us of his main theme—that life is indeed too short, that salvation, rebirth of the kind he has proposed, is not a matter of hasty reform,

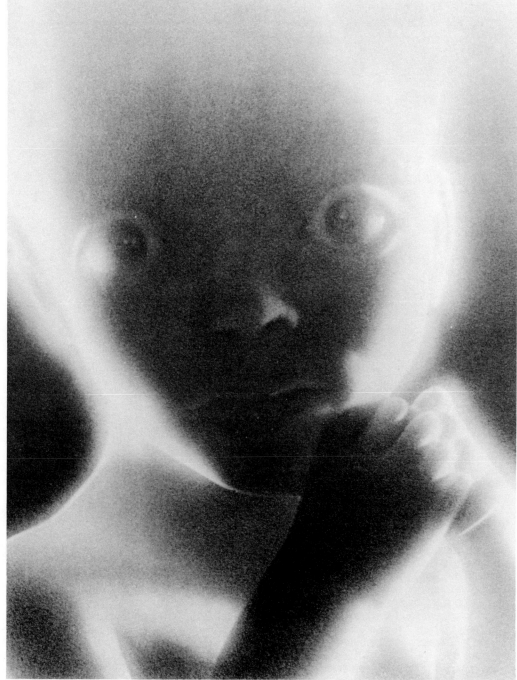

Kubrick's ultimate image of rebirth: *the starchild into whom Dave (who has died) has evolved.*

not something to be quickly and easily achieved, as our present society with its addiction to self-help books, pop psychologizing, and the quick bureaucratic fix likes to think it is. Rebirth is, to put the matter simply, a millennial matter. In the meantime, though, Kubrick is saying that short of the millennium the good society will in some measure be a violent society, if only because questing and adventuring—even when they are merely intellectual—are violent enterprises. He is also saying that only a tumultuous society is capable of leaving its mark on the centuries or, to put the matter properly, is capable of nurturing individuals who, needing to defy their mortality, must try to leave their marks on society—obelisks to guide and goad whoever, whatever, comes later, reminding them that some superior beings, an unhappy few, preceded them.

Peter Watkins:
Political and Pessimistic

Sally Hibbin

Peter Watkins's futuristic films— sharp, bleak visions of Western civilization—have, without exception, raised a storm of controversy and, on occasion, censorship.

Is it, perhaps, that Watkins's worlds come a little too close to reality, revealing the potentials of contemporary trends in a way that is sometimes beyond the bounds of acceptability for the media establishment? His films—*The War Game* (1965), with its horrific portrayal of the effects of a nuclear blast, *Privilege* (1967), with its biting attack on the machinations of big business and the hypocrisy of the church, *The Peace Game* (1968), with its satirical exposé of the causes of world war, and *Punishment Park* (1971), with its allegorical comment on the methods of law and order—are imaginative fantasies that take modern politics as their starting points. His futures suggest the ultimate in antidemocratic societies, usually conceived to protect the interests of the wealthy and the ruling classes from the challenge of individuals. They are creations where hopelessness and despondency reign, ensuring the continuation of the status quo.

But Watkins's films are not merely antiestablishment: They are strong social statements that underline the links between wealth and power, religion and law, business and government, and above all, detest the politics and brutality of war.

The War Game, made originally for the BBC, unleashed a storm of protest and discussion that, nearly twenty years later, is still unresolved. A

Sally Hibbin is a British critic who has contributed to various publications in the United States and England, including *The Movie, Magills Encyclopedia, Stills,* and *Films & Filming.*

powerful dramatized reconstruction of the effects of a nuclear blast in Kent, it has all the force of actual footage with graphic descriptions of the death and destruction following the dropping of an atomic bomb. The film begins with a possible (for the time) scenario of world war—the escalation of fighting in Southeast Asia—and is shot using documentary techniques of news announcements, narration, interviews, hand-held cameras, and nonprofessional actors. Its effect on its audience is without comparison. *The War Game* is one of those rare films that can, and does, change attitudes.

The War Game, which won an Oscar for Best Feature Documentary, has never been telecast by the BBC. While many praised its courage and outspokenness, others derided it as propaganda and blatant falsification. The BBC issued a statement that the film was "too horrifying for the medium of television" and withdrew it. Watkins resigned from his post at the BBC in anger and it took almost a year for the British Film Institute to persuade the BBC to allow them to show the film in theaters and it has since been seen by millions of people throughout the world. It remains, even today, one of the most compelling arguments against nuclear weapons that has appeared on the screen.

It has been suggested that if *The War Game* were made today, it could be shown on British television. The BBC's recent production, *Q.E.D.: A Guide to Armageddon,* and ABC's 1983 television movie *The Day After* are cited as examples of

A food riot following a nuclear catastrophe is reason for armed British police to gun down civilians in The War Game *(1967, U.S. release), the most devastating presentation of a nuclear explosion and its aftermath.*

a more relaxed attitude in broadcasting. But perhaps what makes *The War Game* quite so controversial is not its sickening close-ups of burnt flesh or the effects of radiation but its political analysis of the outcome of nuclear war. In 1965, the notion that an atomic bomb not only brought suffering in its wake but also food shortages, riots, disillusion, and the collapse of organized society was a new one. Watkins showed that, from the point of view of the authorities, law and order would be far more important than medicine and aid. Even today, it is not the horrors of the blast that shock as much as the image of (traditionally unarmed) British policemen shooting down civilians who are desperately searching for food. It is still doubtful that the BBC would ever agree to show this remarkable film.

If *The War Game* offers one possible direction for England's future, then Watkins's next film, *Privilege,* proposes an equally bleak alternative: a society "brainwashed" by a messianic pop star, who himself is manipulated by big business to reduce the masses to servility. With this film, Watkins turned away from the horrors of war toward the dangers of authoritarian control and the suppression of individual revolt. Steve Shorter (played by Paul Jones, the then lead singer of Manfred Mann, in his first film role) is far more than a rock idol—he is a public symbol, used by

the powers that be to convert his audience to whatever trend is currently thought necessary or expedient. An apple surplus is quickly solved by Shorter munching a pippin on stage; a religious revival is championed by Shorter's change of songs and image until, finally, in prison gear, surrounded by bars and sadistic wardens, Shorter's new act spearheads a fascist revival. Only a young artist (unconvincingly portrayed by top British model, Jean Shrimpton) is in a position to pull Shorter away from his admiring public and back into some kind of personal life.

As stated, *Privilege* is a story about manipulation—the manipulation of Shorter, from naive youthful star to a national figure, hero-worshipped by his adoring followers; and at the same time, the manipulation of a whole nation, the result of a conspiracy between the political, commercial, religious, and nationalistic forces of the establishment. Shorter's bid for individual freedom becomes a nation's bid to rid itself of tyranny. *Privilege* is the only one of Watkins's films to be backed by a major studio—Universal—and he forged a clever compromise to satisfy the thirst for stars: rather than compromise his own desire to use nonprofessional actors, Watkins was able to use well-known names from a different medium—the worlds of rock and fashion. Yet despite the almost prescient combination of rock and revivalism foretold in *Privilege,* it was slated by many critics and died at the box office. The result was to further reinforce Watkins's conviction that the establishment was out to suppress his radical critique of society, and he left Britain, saying he would never work there again. Watkins

joined the long list of British film directors who are unable to find either funds or enthusiasm for their projects at home. Sandrews, the Swedish production company, put up the money for Watkins's next film, *The Peace Game* (also known as *The Gladiators*). This film represents a coalition of both of Watkins's major preoccupations—a solid antiwar stance combined with a deep-seated mistrust of authority.

Like all of Watkins's films, *The Peace Game* is set in the not-too-distant future. East and West are mutually worried by the possibility of a world war and forestall the event by channeling aggressive instincts into a more controllable mode. The peace games, a violent version of the Olympics, are a series of televised competitions played to the death between soldiers of various countries. In this deadly game, two opposition players begin to ask questions about the role of the contest—they suggest that the games are not so much about maintaining world peace but more about the attempts of the superpowers to protect the status quo through fear and antagonism. The international group of officers watching the game decide that, in the interests of world stability, they must take steps to ensure the elimination of the two rebels.

The Peace Game is Watkins's most disappointing film to date. As always, he has used documentary techniques and nonprofessional actors to make the film's impact more immediate. But whereas this style is essential to *The War Game*, making the tremendous carnage seem realistic and heightening our sense of the actual potential of the events depicted, when transferred to a film like *The Peace Game* the result is a confused mixture of documentary and satire. At the level of actuality, the film fails because it is quite clearly fantasy, while at the level of satire, the documentary style turns irony into a kind of childish humor. The content, for Watkins, is also less sophisticated, for once the initial metaphor is established it leaves little room for development and the remainder of the movie is unsatisfactory.

Punishment Park is, in many ways, Watkins's most complex allegory, and chilling in its cool ability to focus on possible trends. Once again, it is the escalation of war in Indochina that sparks off the action. America has increased the draft and has to cope with the corresponding rise in mass demonstrations, pacifists, and terrorist activity, while, at the same time, the prisons are vastly overcrowded. Detention camps are set up around the country to house those charged with conspiracy. (Only a few years later the Prevention of Terrorism Act applied the same principle to Northern Ireland where, as in *Punishment Park,* the arrest and subsequent detainment assumes the guilt of the prisoner.) The detainees have a choice—they can serve out their lengthy sentence or undergo a three-day ordeal in "Punishment Park." This latter option, described as a punitive deterrent, consists of a gruelling chase across the desert, on foot and without water, pursued by members of the police and national guard. Survival is unlikely.

This time Watkins's almost immutable style works. The action is seen through the eyes of a

Left: In Privilege *(1967), rock idol Steve Shorter (Paul Jones) becomes a messiah for all people in the 1970s. It is a time when the government manipulates the masses by using such pop culture figures.*

Right: The Peace Game/The Gladiators *(1970) was about computer-directed war games between China and the West. It won the Grand Prize at the 1970 International Science Fiction Festival, but didn't do well commercially or with critics.*

Below: Political dissidents try to stay alive in Punishment Park *(1971).*

British film unit interviewing both law enforcement officers and offenders and filming "actual" events in the park. At the same time several defendants are brought before a tribunal to assess the degree of their guilt and the length of their sentence and it is here that Watkins allows a discussion of the ethics of the choice. Through the two interrelated situations, Watkins builds up a broad attack on the morals and hypocrisy of contemporary "civilized" society.

After the debacle over the showing of *The War Game* and the refusal of Universal to treat *Privilege* seriously, Watkins has had difficulty raising money for his films and has chosen to continue his work in Sweden rather than run the gauntlet of control exerted by most sections of the British film industry. In Sweden, he has more freedom to pursue his unique style of filmmaking but, in the last few years, he has again run into trouble, trying to produce a remake of *The War Game,* updated to include the latest research and politics and using local peace groups in several countries as his base. It will be fascinating to see if, after ten years of inactivity and difficulties raising capital, this innovative filmmaker can once again produce a controversial and powerful condemnation of nuclear war.

Critics of Watkins's films will argue that his view is a paranoid one—that he is apt to see conspiracy and manipulation (in his own treatment at the hands of the big media institutions as well as in the subject matter of his films) where none exists; that he suggests too high a level of complicity between the state, big business, religion, and the armed forces. But, apart from *The War Game,* whose facts and figures have proved in the light of modern research to be, if anything, an underestimation, Watkins's films are not literal visions of the future (or even, as his opponents suggest, the present). Rather they are extrapolations of contemporary political trends—warnings of a bleak tomorrow if democratic and peaceful arguments are ignored.

Watkins is, without doubt, one of the most outspoken visionaries of British cinema. If his films have not achieved a commercial success commensurate with their originality, it may be because they are a little too disturbing. The real processes and trends that his films pinpoint cannot be dismissed with the escapist ease afforded to most science fiction. Entertaining his films could not be said to be, but thought-provoking and challenging they certainly are.

SALLY HIBBIN 249

When Men and Machines Go Wrong

An Interview with Michael Crichton by Danny Peary

Danny Peary: With the exception of your historical novel and film, *The Great Train Robbery* [1979], all your fiction contains what I consider to be "futuristic" elements. Yet all but *Westworld* [1973], which is set in the not-too-distant future, are contemporary stories. Why aren't more of your works set in the future?

Michael Crichton wrote the novels *The Andromeda Strain* and *The Terminal Man,* on which films were based. He directed the adaptation of his own novel *The Great Train Robbery;* wrote the original screenplays for and directed *Westworld* and *Looker;* and directed and scripted the movie adaptation of *Coma.*

Michael Crichton: I don't think I know what's going to happen in the future. Since the future's a fantasy, futuristic stories are usually only exaggerations of present-day realities. For example, *Logan's Run* [1976] is really a statement about contemporary America's preoccupation with youth. *Westworld* is an exaggeration of the tendency to make machines that mimic human beings.

DP: Your films and novels are fairly cautionary. Perhaps if you set them in the future they'd have to be more pessimistic. . . .

MC: There are conventions in any literary or cinematic form. Detective stories are traditionally about hard-bitten, hard-driving, hard-drinking private dicks. Futuristic science fiction tends to be pessimistic. If you imagine a future that's wonderful, you don't have a story. There has to be some kind of conflict. Someone once said something I believe is true: If you live in the past, you're depressed and if you live in the future, you're anxious, so the only way to feel okay is to live in the present.

DP: I gather from your works that you think people should take more responsibility in our present time, and be watchdogs so they can see crises develop.

MC: Yes. I'm disturbed, for example, that there is so much interest in extraterrestrials and space colonies and not enough in what is really relevant to us now. I spoke to students at Swarthmore and gave them an argument on the dangers of believing too strongly in extraterrestrials, and they hated it. Because belief in extraterrestrial life is now a religious conviction with young people. My concern is that, for better or worse, we live on the only planet in the solar system that isn't barren. There is life everywhere on earth: on walls, on us, even in steaming volcanic undersea vents with incredibly high pressures and temperatures. Growing things, green things, white things, people, animals, plants— LIFE. I told the students, "I'm not saying there aren't extraterrestrials; I'm just saying let's play with the idea that *this is it, folks.* That we are the highest life form in the universe. What an arrogant thought, but suppose we are. We would behave differently, I think. We'd be very respectful of life and the miraculous series of molecular events that has led to all this proliferation of life. We certainly shouldn't blow ourselves up in a nuclear holocaust. What a stupid, irresponsible thing to do!" We just kind of think, "Oh, well . . . life's all over the place and if we wreck this planet, there are plenty of other planets."

Director-writer Michael Crichton on the set of Looker *(1981), with leading lady Susan Dey.*

But where are they? How, exactly, will we get there? You think of establishing space colonies? Try using a zero-gravity toilet and then let's talk about it. . . .

DP: Do you agree with the Russians who believe that the purpose of our space missions is not exploration and eventual space colonization but attaining military superiority in space? That's a great fear that seems to have validity because of all the expensive research being done in the field of space weaponry.

MC: Of course, they're right. One of the great hypes of the last fifteen-twenty years has to do with our space program. When John Kennedy said we're going to the moon, that was a noble quest. It really was. But slowly and surely our space goals have changed. The space shuttle is essentially a military effort. Most of its payloads are military. We pretend that it's not, but it is. And that's too bad. The Russians have a good beef. And by the same token, Americans have legitimate gripes with them. Nobody has a claim on nobility.

DP: In *The Andromeda Strain,* you begin with the premise that government-connected scientists are searching for deadly bacteria in near space, presumedly to be used as a weapon by the military. Is this actually going on?

MC: I have no idea. But I think right now, which is fifteen years since I wrote the novel, it would be much easier to create a nasty organism with genetic engineering done in a laboratory.

DP: In the book, you refer to a government document that sets up a scary scenario: if an American satellite carrying back a deadly bacteria from space accidentally comes down in the Soviet Union, America would not inform the Russians of the danger because it would reveal our work in biological warfare. Does this have any basis in fact?

MC: There have been analogous situations. . . . But if you're asking "Do I know of any program or document that states we won't tell if a U.S. satellite with deadly bacteria lands in Russia?" the answer is no. I've never seen a classified document in my life. I don't know what they look like. I've never been in the military. I don't know anything about that stuff. I made it all up.

DP: You're very convincing.

MC: It's my job to be.

DP: Nothing you write about seems preposterous to me. It all makes sense, even the most inhumane acts perpetrated. Do you leave room for a viewer's/reader's "suspension of belief" or is everything set up to be believed?

MC: *The Terminal Man* was a fictional book about a specific surgery that was being done. I felt it was being done recklessly and unwisely and wanted to write a book that opposed it. I was very interested in the kinds of reactions it caused. It was the first set of reviews I'd gotten where critics said "this is absurd and impossible. Atomic pacemakers—ridiculous!" And yet I knew they were already putting atomic pacemakers in dogs; in fact, atomic pacemakers were put in people within a year or two of publication. In the same way, a lot of reviewers of *Congo* argued that the book was unbelievable in ways that demonstrated their own ignorance. *Congo* sort of swings between what's now the "Star Wars" view of the military uses of space and studies of language acquisition in primates—both touchy areas. *It's fiction but I know perfectly well it's not wrong.*

With *Congo* I was interested in seeing to what degree the general shape of the story could be real, while the specific details, the things most authors use to bolster their credibility, were all made wrong. So in almost every instance where I could, I would alter the factual detail and make

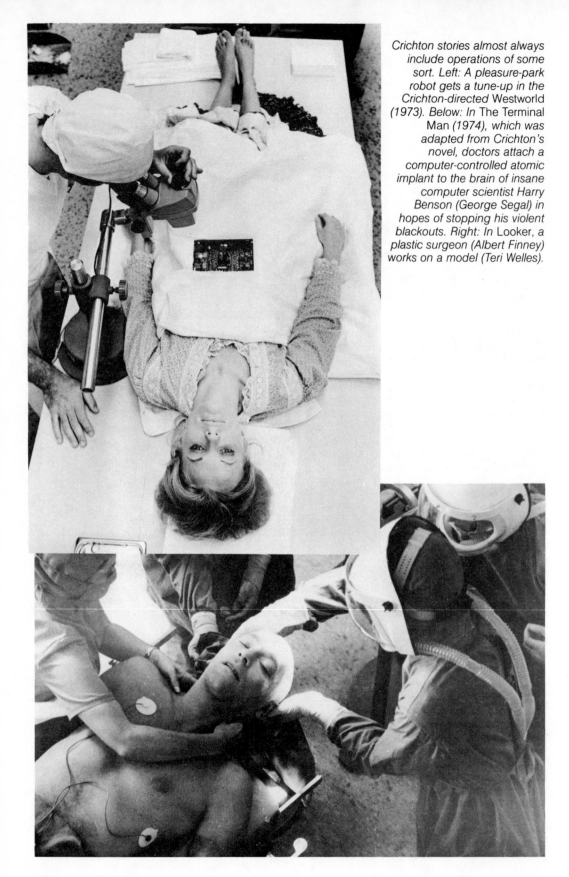

Crichton stories almost always include operations of some sort. Left: A pleasure-park robot gets a tune-up in the Crichton-directed Westworld (1973). Below: In The Terminal Man (1974), which was adapted from Crichton's novel, doctors attach a computer-controlled atomic implant to the brain of insane computer scientist Harry Benson (George Segal) in hopes of stopping his violent blackouts. Right: In Looker, a plastic surgeon (Albert Finney) works on a model (Teri Welles).

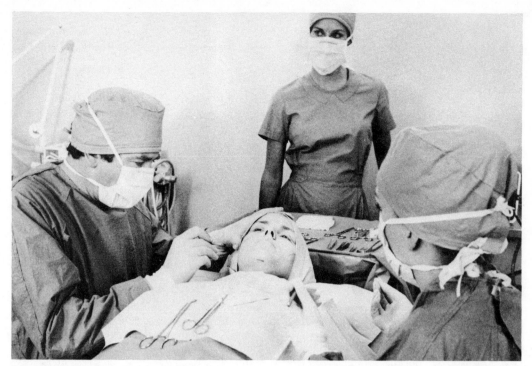

it incorrect. My idea was to make a fictional environment like Rousseau's jungles, where you see palm trees that look like palm trees but not like any specific palm trees. I imagined people would see it for what it was. What happened was that people with great expertise in electronics or satellite communications would jump in and say "this is wrong!" *Congo* is basically accurate overall but in its specifics it's wrong. It was an experiment, but nobody seemed to understand what I was doing. So I won't do it anymore.

DP: When I read your books I sort of take for granted they're scientifically correct.

MC: I think most people do. And they want to do that. It's exasperating to feel, "Well, *maybe* this isn't right...."

DP: Although *The Terminal Man* is fiction, did it have any effect on halting experimentation with atomic pacemakers?

MC: The research has stopped to a large extent. I don't know what impact the book had. I tend to discount the practical effects of what I do. Because they're stories, there's a level where I don't take them seriously. And I discount their impact on both sides, good and bad. When people asked how I could make a movie like *Coma* [1978] and "interfere with organ donor programs," I didn't know what to say. I think people understand it's just a movie, a story, and that Richard Widmark and Genevieve Bujold are just actors. So I don't believe it had a deleterious effect. Conversely, I don't think *The Terminal Man* had a positive effect in stopping the experimentation I opposed. There were other, more important factors, including the recognition that

using atomic pacemakers was very expensive and not very effective.

DP: In some ways, there are similarities between *The Terminal Man* and Stanley Kubrick's *A Clockwork Orange* [1971]. In both there is the idea of mind control and behavior modification. Both present a man with an uncontrollable murderous-violent nature, who has his thought processes tampered with by doctors who don't fully comprehend what they're doing. In neither case does the new, revolutionary treatment work.

MC: *A Clockwork Orange* is almost a parable. I think it deals with very difficult issues. I'd say the major difference between the two is that *A Clockwork Orange* is about the victim while *The Terminal Man* is about the perpetrators, the irresponsible doctors who use Benson as a guinea pig.

DP: What do you think could, alternatively, have been done with Benson [played by George Segal in the Michael Hodges-directed 1974 film] in his extreme mental state? Should he be left alone?

MC: I'm quite comfortable with the idea that certain mental conditions are insoluble. I think there are large categories of phenomena, from environmental to personal, that are virtually uncontrollable. We're very distressed to learn that events can't be controlled. But there are limits to our knowledge. And, personally, I feel there's security in recognizing the limits. Psychiatrists can't really predict when a patient like Benson will become violent. Psychiatry doesn't know much, and that terrifies us.

DP: We are resistant to behavior modification,

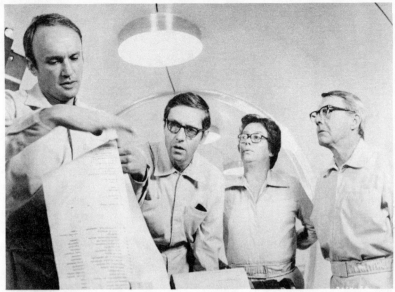

Left: In The Andromeda Strain (1971), which Robert Wise directed from Crichton's novel, mistakes by man and machine happen by the minute. Here scientists discover a computer error that may prove to be catastrophic. The Wildfire team: (L–R) Mark Hall (James Olson), Jeremy Stone (Arthur Hill), Ruth Leavitt (Kate Reid), and Charles Dutton (David Wayne).

Right: Hall races against time to stop a bomb from detonating.

and there are all types of it. That by scientific means, education, child rearing, even Christian learning...

MC: Let's face it: We are all subjected to behavior modification. I'm not actually opposed to the technique as a technique. I took it to quit smoking. It worked great for a while. I think it is great for changing some forms of behavior. But, it's my prejudice, you can't use it to change a killer like Benson.

DP: There are strong philosophic differences, we must remember, between the implantation of a pacemaker in the heart and in the brain, which is what is done to Benson. Especially considering that you describe him as "the man with two brains."

MC: Yes. I think the doctors' way of treating mental disorder in The Terminal Man is mechanical and extremely simplistic. The Terminal Man was intended to be a story about arrogance. It is about people who didn't really think through the consequences of what they were doing. It shows a group of scientists who were not very psychologically aware who perform a procedure on a disturbed man that in some ways makes him much worse. They did not recognize this. They did not anticipate the consequences of their behavior.

DP: Would it be fair to characterize your works as being about mistakes like that made by the scientists in The Terminal Man; malfunctions—I immediately think of the robots going haywire in Westworld; oversights—I think of the scary line in the book The Andromeda Strain, "neither man nor machine could pick up the mistake"; and bad or even evil decisions like that made in Coma whereupon hospital patients are murdered for their high-priced organs?

MC: Yes, I think so. I'm interested in how mistakes happen. How does it go wrong? Nothing is mistake-proof. I wrote The Andromeda Strain

to try and create a situation that characterizes what I think is generally true of certain kinds of situations: They're best handled by not allowing them to happen in the first place. For instance, the best way to deal with an oil spill is to not let it happen. Once it has occurred, everything you do to fix it has its own cascading ramifications.

DP: There are "heroic" actions in The Andromeda Strain, particularly in the final sequence where Hall [James Olson in the film] climbs up ladders and gets shot with drug-filled darts [laser beams in the film] while trying to stop an atomic bomb from detonating. But what's fascinating, which many people may fail to notice because of the excitement of this scene, is that in reality the Wildfire group that's brought together to do something about the deadly bacteria need never have been brought together. They accomplish nothing. Regardless of their actions, the bacteria would have mutated into a benign form at the end.

MC: That's exactly right. A sixth grade girl wrote me a letter and said exactly that. And I wrote back and said, "My goodness, you're the only person who's worked this out." I mean, they're doing this and that, using all their machines, yet in the broadest view, all their efforts come out to nothing. They don't fix it. It's interesting that so many people fail to notice that. From my point of view, it's a book about powerlessness. And that's in keeping with my intention to write a story about something that should never have been done. They never should have made that satellite, they never should have tried to find the organisms. It was an incredibly thoughtless undertaking from the beginning. And however likeable the people are who try to clean up the mess, the Wildfire team, they fail to clean it up and cause major new problems. In fact, what becomes the suspense part of the story is really their effort to turn off this clockwork mechanism,

the bomb, which, again, somebody else has made.

DP: It's man and machine taking turns putting the world in jeopardy.

MC: Yes. In that way it's fairly pessimistic.

DP: Despite the new problems that result from their misguided, mistake-filled actions, I think you believe that the Wildfire scientists, being who they are, had to try something. Luckily they don't entirely blow it, as the scientists do in *The Terminal Man.*

MC: There's a difference. The Wildfire group, the scientists we're paying attention to in *The Andromeda Strain,* didn't cause the initial problem. In *The Terminal Man,* they are responsible.

DP: In *The Andromeda Strain,* after the accident at Piedmont that wiped out the town, the scientists looking through the giant microscope discover the organism. Stone [Arthur Hill in the film] is so excited, as if he has forgotten that this organism can mean countless deaths in little time. That I find really scary.

MC: Yes, but it's his job to find it. Having established that such a bacteria exists out there, I think anyone would be glad to find it.

DP: I just worry that the scientists seem to enjoy having a problem to solve, rather than wishing that there was no need to bring them together.

MC: I don't think the people in *The Andromeda Strain* are happy about it. The people in *The Terminal Man* are.

DP: What Stanley Kubrick seems to respect most about man, and this is a theme of *2001: A Space Odyssey* [1968], is his willingness to explore until he finds something, even if it creates culture shock. I think this is the only thing Kubrick likes about man. Some of your scientists seem to like making discoveries just to make discoveries, whether they're harmful or not. I would guess that you respect research, but you also fear it.

MC: I'm not a very fearful person. I don't fear the research, I fear certain people. My sense is that many people proceed in a misguided way. But I don't fear research as research.

DP: But if a scientist is unchecked...

MC: *Some* scientists. There are many examples of appalling things done in the name of research. The CIA's LSD research in the Fifties was unspeakable. And what about the black people who were kept as untreated syphilitics, supposedly so doctors could study the progress of the disease. That's a *major* scandal. I can't imagine who could have thought that was okay except Adolf Hitler. And it happened in the United States.

DP: Are some scientists so detached, so isolated, so intent on discovery that they forget which country they represent?

MC: No, I don't think so. First of all, it's wrong to lump together somebody who's doing medical transplantation with somebody who's doing work on radar detection systems with somebody who's figuring out how to design comfortable chairs, and to say these are all scientists. As a group, I'd say scientists are like everyone else.

Left: In the computer-run futuristic Westworld amusement park, where everyone plays out their fantasies, timid Peter Martin (Richard Benjamin) can outdraw this gunslinger robot (Yul Brynner). John Blane (James Brolin) watches his friend act tough.

Right: In Coma *(1978), a doctor (Genevieve Bujold) discovers a devious plot in the hospital to kill patients in order to get their organs for expensive transplants. Crichton directed from Robin Cook's bestseller.*

There are some extraordinary, wonderful people; there are some sick people; there are some neurotic people. You'll see a spectrum of work coming from these people that ranges from some of the most noble things possible to some pretty base things.

We imagine the scientist in his lab coat and his round-the-clock research, his mechanized view of the world, his reductionist philosophy, his whole sterile way of being. That's our stereotype of the *scientist.* And we imagine the *artist* as being full of life, the ultimate humanist. Well, I know plenty of artists who are pretty callous in their treatment of other people and who are intensely focused on their work to the exclusion of all else. In truth, science and art are very, very similar activities. I don't think there's anything inherent in science, in doing scientific research, that would make you into an inhuman person. I think that's a twentieth-century belief. It comes out of some areas we don't often look at—academic specialization for one thing. Nobody's a plain physicist anymore: you're a high-energy physicist, a plasma physicist, etc. People have very narrow interests and they exclude all else. And when knowledge becomes so fragmented it becomes very easy to say "this group is the humanist group and those others over there are inhuman because I have no idea what they're doing—it's all mathematics, a mysterious language to me and whatever it is, it's very abstract and has nothing to do with life." When Darwin presented his theory, the last major convulsion in thought in my opinion, it set forth a debate throughout the breadth of civilized society. Everyone discussed it on some level. Yet today nobody but the specialists discuss quantum mechanics. In my day, cosmology—quasars, black holes, pulsars—became a topic of heated scientific debate, but it's never been accessible to the entire society. People just don't know, don't care, don't understand. It's sad, because this work is very interesting.

DP: In *The Andromeda Strain,* the novel and the film, lab animals are killed repeatedly. I thought you were trying to make a point about some scientists having no respect for life. . . .

MC: Animal research is an area of great controversy. To argue that all animal research is really fine and humane and that these animals are as happy as can be undergoing experiments is a lie. And to argue that it should all be stopped, that the people doing this work are hideous human beings, and that there are no benefits to man coming from all this is equally ridiculous. The truth is somewhere in the middle. The truth is *always* somewhere in the middle. I have seen people do research in which animals die and they conducted it with what I'd say was great respect. And I've seen people who didn't seem to care for the animals. And I think—this gets to be religious, you know—we all tend to have more feeling when it's a dog than a rat. When I get into my feelings about the sanctity of life, very soon after I'll swat the mosquito on my arm. I think these are ambiguous areas. If there were an easy answer, we would have resolved it by now.

DP: I get a different impression now, having spoken to you, but I had believed your works were trying to emphasize the *dehumanization* of scientists and doctors. Like David Cronenberg, you create tension and terror within environments that theoretically should be warm. Such as a hospital, where people come for help. But your settings are sterile, lifeless, scary.

MC: I certainly believe medicine is dehumanizing to some degree. It is necessary to have some dehumanization. To do his job, the doctor has to remain objective, to keep his distance.

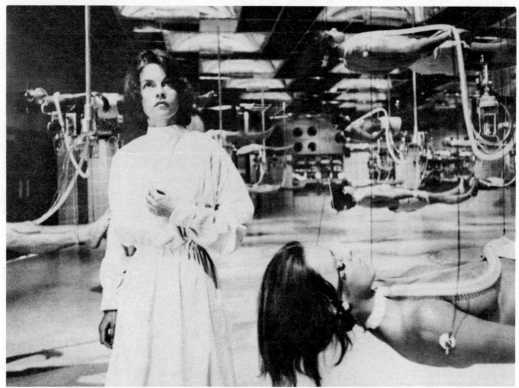

The complaint is about doctors who become *too* distant. But it's difficult to maintain your human empathy without getting so caught up that you're of no use to the person who needs your help.

DP: In *Coma,* those scenes of the masked doctors having conversations while in the operating room were quite unnerving. And *too* realistic.

MC: Whatever people thought about it, it was just reportage. That's really what happens. I don't think it's bad. To take such scenes as evidence that these doctors don't care is incorrect.

DP: How do you think scientists have been portrayed in films in general?

MC: You have to realize that films about science have traditionally been B-movies. Horror movies, sci-fi movies, Karloff films. The sophistication of the characterization is not very great. People tend to be cardboard signposts that *stand* for something. There's no subtlety. Cops and military men are also cardboard cut-outs. And again, since the twentieth century is increasingly treating science as some mysterious undertaking, it becomes possible to make all scientists some variation on Dr. Zarkoff from *Flash Gordon.* How many variations are there on the self-centered scientist, the mad-bomber scientist, the sterile unfeeling scientist, the scientist who wants to make discoveries whatever it costs, etc.? I find movie characterizations quite boring.

DP: What about films like *WarGames* [1983] and *Colossus: The Forbin Project* [1970], where scientists have created computers capable of taking over?

MC: *WarGames* is a very significant picture in that its hero is somebody who uses these machines. And we've never had that. It was always some outsider who brings wisdom to the loonies at the helm. And that's still the basic structure in *WarGames,* but the hero is a computer-competent person. And we, the audience, are expected to identify with him. And I think with good reason—there's five million of these machines out there. An awful lot of people have them, whether they use them or not.

DP: Why are we so resistant to the computers?

MC: It's a new machine, it's difficult to learn, it's time-consuming, and it makes you feel stupid while you're trying to learn it. I think until computers become a lot easier, which I hope will be in the next five years, we'll be in a transitional period where there's no getting around how difficult they are. I was very good at BASIC so I decided to learn a new language; and it was right back to ground zero. I was exhausted trying to get my head into it. In some ways it didn't get any easier.

DP: From films like *WarGames* and *Colossus: The Forbin Project,* we even have become frightened of computers. We fear they are becoming too big, we don't understand their capabilities, we don't know who is using them. I assume that you consider Benson's view in *The Terminal Man* that machines are *competing* with man to be an exaggeration?

MC: That's a psychotic's view. My book *Electronic Life* deals with this area of Benson's thinking. It's about how to find the middle view toward computers. How not to fear them, hate them, or reject them, because I think that increasingly society has made a decision to adopt these machines.

DP: In *The Terminal Man* one of the scientist's viewpoints is that we shouldn't fear computers because they're only machines.

MC: I think there's a new equally dangerous tendency to accept them with an excess of enthusiasm. All I say over and over again is that you must always carry in your mind the possibility that they will stop or malfunction in some way. They're probably right, but they could be wrong. I think we should have the same tentative attitude toward computers that we have for a watch or car. We think of computers being infallible—but they're not.

DP: Another of your themes: computers should be conceived to be aids, not to take over. Can computers help us? Will they change *our* functions?

MC: Yes. Now we're making increasingly sophisticated machines and we're afraid they will take away everything we have. I don't think that's true. I think that by giving the machine a lot of our present-day functions, we'll just move up to some other function. I don't know what that is but I think it'll be a new consciousness. We now only use four percent of our brain capacity: we have a great deal of exploration to do inside our own heads. I think man promotes his own psychic evolution.

DP: Isn't the speed of change alarming to you? It becomes scarier and scarier to me that we're now capable of blowing ourselves up. It wasn't that way back in 1920.

MC: No. It doesn't scare me. Computers haven't taken over, have they? And I don't think they ever will. And I don't think we will do something foolish. But people won't change without being provoked.

DP: What does frighten you? In *The Terminal Man,* Benson has blackouts, in *The Andromeda Strain* a scientist [Kate Reid in the film] has epileptic seizures and loses track of time, in *Looker* [1981], characters are victims of a hypnotic gun that causes them to black out.

MC: It's interesting that you would pick up on that. There are two things that I'm aware of that frighten me that I use as themes. One has to do with heights, either up above ground or way below ground-level. Altitude seems to be a recurring theme. And I always return to blackouts. I'm haunted by what we don't know. When you've blacked out you've missed something. You're not aware. I'm terrified of not being aware. That's what frightens me most.

DP: The early scenes in *Looker* are creepy: a flash of light, then the character looks at a clock and discovers that several minutes have disappeared.

MC: The general subject is scary. As in life, to

become inattentive is scary. But in the film, I think it was more confusing than frightening. The audience found it hard to accept the time change.

DP: Because of its television commercial theme, *Looker* always makes me think of a *Mad* magazine strip years ago on subliminal advertising. . . .

MC: Let me stop you now. *Looker* was originally written to be a comedy. It should have stayed a comedy. It was supposed to all be funny—the material was too fluffy to be taken seriously. Somehow it ended up that the studio wanted to make a suspense melodrama. I still remember the phone call. I should have said no, but I didn't. It just got ponderous. It was certainly the most difficult film experience I've had. I'm not happy with it at all, which says something.

DP: How come you didn't adapt *The Andromeda Strain* or *The Terminal Man*?

MC: I was still in medical school when *The Andromeda Strain* was made. I did write a screenplay for *The Terminal Man* and I wanted to direct it. But at the last minute they didn't want me to. And I thought I'd given them a terrific script and they hired another director. I was very disappointed not to direct.

Something always goes terribly wrong. Left: In the midst of a violent blackout induced by his computer implant, Benson murders his girl friend (Jill Clayburgh). Above: The gunslinger robot refuses to stay "dead," no matter how many times he is killed. It keeps coming back, intending to kill Peter Martin. Meanwhile the other robots have killed all the other guests.

DP: How were the results?

MC: I've never seen it all the way through....

DP: It's slow, which isn't so bad because your novels are very deliberately paced. The pacing of Robert Wise's *The Andromeda Strain* is almost exactly that of your book.

MC: That's funny because I thought they could have edited a little more. It's slow in the middle. That was Robert Wise's decision. It was his movie, and he made a good movie out of it, so I should shut up.

DP: Your directional pacing is faster than in your books.

MC: *The Great Train Robbery*'s slow, but in general, with film, I'm very interested in how rapidly I can go. On *Coma,* for example, we accelerated the pace and dialogue. The actors would come in and rehearse a scene—if they took a minute to say some lines, I'd say "Okay, now do it in forty seconds." They'd complain, "We can't, we have to have our dramatic pauses...." And I'd say "No. Forty seconds. Do it again." And they'd do it. And the whole movie is paced like

that. It doesn't seem they're talking fast—the whole movie is at that pace so you accept it. Old-time directors used that trick.

DP: You wrote the screenplay for a very obscure low-budget film called *Extreme Close-up* [1973]. As I recall, it was an R-rated film having to do with a guy trying out various superpowered cameras to spy on beautiful women having sex. It wasn't particularly good, but it had an oddly fascinating last shot: The guy has become such a voyeur that when he makes love himself he looks at the images in his mirror.

MC: I can't remember the ending. I thought I'd written a very good screenplay but the people I'd written it for didn't trust me to direct it. I was directing a TV-movie at the time it was shot, so I couldn't have directed it anyway. All I can tell you about it was that I intended it to be an X-rated film, a voyeuristic movie that was meant to make viewers uncomfortable. But the final movie doesn't make any sense because it's not tough enough. It was an R-rated nothing.

DP: *Westworld,* your first feature film as director, was the surprise hit of the summer of 1973.

MC: It turned out very well. It was my first directing job and there was no money for anything and I couldn't get a cast, but it turned out well. It was great fun to do. It was shot in six weeks. It was virtually camera cut because I was very worried about the studio making changes.

DP: What do you think is the scariest thing about *Westworld*? I think it's that such amusement parks with human-like robots fulfilling our fantasies are inevitable.

MC: They're coming...they're coming. For me the scariest thing in *Westworld* is that this robot, played by Yul Brynner, just kept coming back from the dead. You just couldn't get rid of him no matter how many different ways you killed him. It was that *idea* more than any specific incident that I found frightening.

DP: What are your feelings about the creation of artificial life; for instance, the robots in *Westworld* that are fake human beings?

MC: There is a profound human fascination with the imitation of human behavior by mechanical things. It's in the Nutcracker ballet, it's in Frankenstein. I don't quite know what the fascination is.

DP: Cloning has an evil connotation. Why would anyone want to create something exactly like something else?

MC: It's odd. But I don't know if it's evil. Anyway, I don't think it's around the corner. I wouldn't lose sleep over it. I mean, what are our real risks? Our real risks are that we're going to wreck the environment...that we're going to acid rain ourselves to death. That is a real risk, but we don't think about that. Instead we think about these elusive, fantastic things. I agree that they are fun to think about, but it's wrong to take them seriously. Very wrong.

The Inner Search for Spock

An Interview with Leonard Nimoy by Ed Naha

In the history of science fiction film, very few characters have had the cultural impact of Star Trek's resident Vulcan, Mr. Spock. In the seventeen years since the show's inception, the superlogical alien has become a role model for countless fans of all ages and the object of an equal number of video-spawned crushes.

Spock's "death" in Star Trek II: The Wrath of Khan (1982) caused quite a furor in science fiction fan circles, leading to the release of Star Trek III: The Search for Spock (1984).

At the center of the hurricane is actor Leonard Nimoy, who, over the years, has had to grapple with the Spock persona both on and off screen. As the director of Star Trek III: The Search for Spock, Nimoy had a chance to cinematically express his feelings about the entire Star Trek phenomenon: In the following interview he reflects on his alien status verbally.

Ed Naha: Rather than discuss the specifics of the three *Star Trek* movies, I'd like to concentrate on you and your character. I'll begin with two interrelated questions that will require lengthy responses: Who is Mr. Spock and what is it about him that people find appealing?

Leonard Nimoy: Remember *The Day the Earth Stood Still* [1951]?. Michael Rennie's character comes from a planet where people have superior intelligence and superior scientific knowledge, and he in effect says, "You Earth people are getting into trouble. Trouble for you means trouble for others as well. You must stop the dangerous things you're doing." In a sense, Mr. Spock is that same character: *He's an emissary from the future, from another time, another world.*

You may recall that Rennie provides an amazing demonstration of his power to prove that he is indeed what he presents himself to be. However, Mr. Spock doesn't have to prove himself. He's not on trial. The Earthlings of the future, who work and live with him, know he is from this *other* place and has a super-logical approach to problems, a superior scientific knowledge, whatever.

Although Spock is accepted as one of the crew, he *still* is a spokesperson for another philosophy. He represents a philosophy that is different from the philosophies of the various Earth people including Kirk [William Shatner], McCoy [DeForest Kelley], and Sulu [George Takei]. In this sense, his relationship to his crew members is similar to Michael Rennie's relationship to his Earth people; and to the scientist Sam Jaffe played, the Einstein character who first recognizes Rennie for what he is: an outside commentator on Earth life.

I think there are a lot of other characters like this in fiction, in science fiction particularly. They present an opportunity for us, contemporary people, to see ourselves in a somewhat different

Ed Naha is the West Coast film correspondent to the New York *Post.* A former coeditor of *Future Life,* he has contributed to such publications as *Science Digest, The Village Voice, The Toronto Star, The Twilight Zone, Starlog,* and *Heavy Metal.* In 1976, he produced the album *Gene Roddenberry: Inside Star Trek.*

Leonard Nimoy played Mr. Spock on the television series *Star Trek,* and continued the role in the *Star Trek* feature films. He directed *Star Trek III: The Search for Spock.* He is the host of the syndicated television series *In Search of...,* and is author of the book *I Am Not Spock.*

Leonard Nimoy as Mr. Spock in Star Trek.

and *hopeful* light. These characters are compassionate and understanding. They praise us for what we have done right but show us where we are going wrong. To a certain extent, they are father figures, security blankets.

Isaac Asimov described Spock as a "security blanket with sexual overtones." That's a pretty concise and accurate description. The sexuality of Spock has to do with a lot of factors. He is a father figure, compassionate and understanding, yet he is also the mysterious dark stranger. Who knows what could happen should his hidden passions become unleashed? There's a devilish side of the character that is attractive to females. They are curious about him.

Above all, though, I think people see Spock as a hopeful individual. He's good to have around. He can be extraordinarily helpful when humans get into trouble.

People tend to project certain capabilities onto him. If you ever get into serious trouble, Spock will fix it, Spock will help us. He'll find a way. Everyone else will be running around behaving like humans do: screaming and fighting and punch-

ing and kicking and shoving, and Spock will calmly walk over, and press the right button and say, "Relax, it's all taken care of."

In a sense he's a deus ex machina. He's a device that a writer can use to make the proper move at the proper time and save the situation.

In *Star Trek II,* Spock gives his own life to make the proper move at the proper time. With all the yelling and carrying on that was taking place at the end of that movie, he still managed to save the day.

"The device is going to blow up in four minutes!"

Kirk turns to his son, David. "Well, reprogram it!"

David yells, "We *can't!*"

Kirk yells to Scotty, "I've got to have warp speed in three minutes or we're all dead!"

What does Spock do? He gets up and leaves the bridge and decides to solve the problem himself. He fights his way past McCoy and gets the job done. The price that he pays is his life. So? He views the situation logically. He sees the turmoil, figures that it's silly and does what has to be done.

He represents a solution to problems in that sense. He is also a role model for young people who admire his sense of personal worth, of dignity. He's not a perfect person. He has flaws. A lot of people sense that. A lot of people feel, and perhaps rightly so, that Spock would be much "happier" if he could allow himself to have feelings. They believe he's unhappy because of that. Spock would deny this, of course. He would say "I am insulted by the concept that humans feel that their happiness is something everyone must strive for and achieve. I don't have the need for your kind of happiness. I am, if you will, *happy* without being what your concept of *happy* is."

In a sense, Spock has made a conscious decision to deprive himself of certain pleasures in order to be the kind of person he desires to be. While a lot of people sympathize or even empathize with him for making his decision, they realize that the result of his paying the price is that he remains different. He retains his own sense of identity. So we have a role model to study and to reflect against. I don't think he's necessarily the kind of person that we all would like to be but it's nice to know that there is a person around like that when we need him.

Spock's "outsider" image is what many people find most intriguing about him. The alien aspect of him is something that a lot of people can identify with. I've written about this and talked about this before but, let's face it, we all feel like an alien at some point of our lives. Some of us feel like that for our entire lives. You know; "I am different from everyone else. Why? Why can't I just be like the rest of the people around me? Why can't I be the life of the party? Why am I shy? Why am I nervous when other people are relaxed? Why do I always feel that I have to dress like everyone else in order to be accepted? Why do I smell worse than other people?"

Spock has found a way, the writers tell us, not only to live with his difference but to be proud of it. He is not inclined to be like everyone else, although other people try to make him part of the herd. Humans do tend to want to make other people just like themselves. It makes them feel better. The person who says "I won't walk your road" makes a lot of us uncomfortable. You immediately start thinking "Does he know something I don't?"

McCoy, in a sense, is always trying to humanize him. Spock's attitude is "The poor doctor. He doesn't realize that I am quite comfortable being who I am. Being like him would not necessarily make me a better person. I am me."

Finally: People also like the magic of the character. Spock is magic. He *can* do things that humans cannot. He has mental powers. He can mind-meld. He can pinch you unconscious. He's a pretty cool character and somewhat unpredictable in that sense. You're never quite aware of what a Vulcan is capable of. I think that one of the wisest things we've done with the character is to never really clearly define his limits. Occasionally he'll do something that will cause an audience to gasp and say, "Wow! Spock can do that, too! I didn't know that." Somewhere, there's an editor's note about Spock's character that says "And that's not *all* . . ." Nobody knows *all* the talents that Spock has.

EN: In spite of all these attributes, Spock could have turned out to be just another science fiction cliché. What did you bring to the role? What part of Leonard Nimoy is now part of Mr. Spock?

LN: As important as anything else, I think, are my instincts as an actor to go for the dimensional being. I try to flesh out my characters. I think that had an impact on Spock.

There's also something about me, which a studio head pointed out to me one day. Every actor projects something. I was told that I project intelligence. This doesn't mean that I'm smart in real life. But people see me and expect me to say something intelligent.

Some of the things I say as the Spock character might not go over successfully if another actor was saying them. I manage to ring the right bell when I say the lines. I can make scientific pronouncements and people will say, "Oh, yeah. He really knows." Someone else might say them and sound like an idiot.

I feel comfortable with Spock's persona. Spock brings me back to the very strong feelings of alienation I had as a kid. I've played alienated characters since I was a teenager. There have been a string of them, starting with Ralphie, a character in Odets's *Awake and Sing.* He's a teenager who is totally uncomfortable with his family and surroundings. The first major film role I played was *Kid Monk Baroni,* the story of a kid with a scarred face. He looks different than his peers.

Spock is clearly one of the most successful alien characters in history. Yet, a very good friend of mine, the late director Boris Sagal, commented when he first saw the show, "You clever devil. You're playing the most *human* character on the series." I didn't set out to do that. But he perceived that way back then.

In *Star Trek II,* Bill Shatner, during Spock's funeral, says in his eulogy that "of all the souls I have ever known, his was the most human."

Now Spock might say "Hey, now wait a minute. Stop insulting me! This is my eulogy here. Don't try to make me one of you!"

But some people consider Spock the perfect *human* from the future: intelligent, cool, and mysterious.

EN: If we do see Spock as being the most hu-

Star Trek—The Motion Picture *(1979). Ilia (Persis Khambatta) leads the Enterprise's (L–R) Spock, Decker (Stephen Collins), Kirk (William Shatner), and McCoy (DeForest Kelly) across a pathway to a rendezvous with a mysterious alien force.*

man of all that crew, what does that say about the rest of human society in that future?

LN: I don't think Spock's status makes any of his crew members *less* than human, if that's what you mean. Every character aboard that ship has a function. And, each, in a wonderful way, works as a foil for the others . . . particularly in the trio of Kirk, Spock, and McCoy.

Kirk is an archetypal character. He is the dashing hero. A classic. Sometimes you don't take him too seriously. Sometimes you enjoy him. Sometimes you vicariously get off on him. He's Errol Flynn. He's the guy who will leap over the chasm rather than find a logical way to engineer a crossing.

McCoy, of course, is the arch-humanist. He's emotional to the point of being on the edge of irrationality *all* the time. He and Spock serve as good foils for one another. We both serve as two sides of the brain, if you will, for Kirk.

I remember talking with Gene Roddenberry [the creator of *Star Trek* and the producer of the original TV series] at a story conference and saying "It's getting to the point where the dialogue should have McCoy saying 'To be,' Spock saying 'or not to be,' and Kirk concluding 'That is the question!' "

It's the perfect symbiotic relationship.

EN: How has Spock evolved over the years?

LN: He has probably allowed some human elements to *invade* his personality. He hasn't kept his guard up. I think he's mellowing. I'm not really sure if it's for better or worse. I take responsibility for his state as much as anyone else. It's a curious situation.

Obviously, we are essentially in an entertainment business. One of the questions I'm always putting to myself is, "What is the most interesting and entertaining way to direct Spock's character in the future?"

Sometimes I wonder if we've allowed him to slip into an easier mold by making him more human. Easier to write for. Easier to act in. Thereby allowing him to become mellow. Thereby allowing him to become less interesting.

I'm curious about that. Time will tell if we're pushing Spock in the right direction or not.

At the end of *Star Trek II,* a lot of people were particularly moved at Spock's death because they felt, "Gee. He was just on the verge of a personal breakthrough that would have been more comfortable for everyone and, then, he had to go and die on us!"

EN: And yet, when audiences saw Spock's coffin at the end of the film, they breathed a sigh of relief. They figured he'd be back. Spock seems to have a Houdini side to him that humans long for, the ability to get out of *any* tight situation, including death.

LN: Nothing is impossible for Spock. Do you see the parallels between him and E.T.?

I think both are viewed as the perfect beings and emissaries from the future. What does that mean? It means that somewhere there is another place, another time, where someone exists that is all-knowing, powerful, magical, compassionate, and a *friend.*

A friend.

If you had one choice to decide who was to visit Earth and to deal with the President or the Russian leaders or the leaders of the U.N. . . . you probably wouldn't choose a Klingon. You'd choose a friend.

E.T., in that sense, is similar to Spock. He is the children's secret friend. He's the pal they have hidden in a closet upstairs who has all these magical powers. He can do things that no human can do. He's not very good at talking but, boy, is he magical.

When I was a kid, *I* fantasized about having a secret little friend who would only talk to me and that no one would know about. He was so small that I could even carry him around in my pocket. A person from another place and another time. He'd help me when I was stuck.

I think Spock and E.T. are simply an extension of that idea. They are our secret friends. Someone who will *always* be there for us when we need them.

EN: Do you think Spock is E.T. for an older crowd?

LN: Not necessarily. I think that Spock is just another way of stating the case.

EN: When the space shuttle was christened "The Enterprise" honoring *Star Trek,* suddenly your fictitious existence was intertwined with real life. Members of the *Trek* cast were suddenly popping up at NASA functions. Has that science fiction/science fact overlap ever intimidated you?

LN: The first time I ever was shaken by it was during the night of the moon landing. When that happened and you could walk out of your house that night, as I did, and look up at the moon and say, "There are really humans stand-

ing on that body right now." When that happened, *Star Trek* took on a new meaning for me. You know, we weren't just kidding around anymore. Science fiction was serious business.

That's when it hit me.

Now, we have a President talking about space stations and *Star Wars* defense systems. There's a certain amount of déjà vu there for me.

EN: Are you optimistic or pessimistic about the future?

LN: I prefer to think of myself as a survivor. I have hopes that the human race will be around for a while.

I'm not a religious person. But the more complicated the international situation becomes, the more complex are the problems of power struggles and political and military gamesmanship; and the more I hear of these complex problems, the more I find it necessary to draw upon religious beliefs. I believe that mankind will not do right by itself. I deeply hope that there is something out there larger than mankind that will save us.

EN: Have you ever been tempted to use your Spock persona to drumbeat your own political or religious beliefs? You know, if Spock says don't kill the whales, we'd better not because Spock *knows.* . . .

LN: No. I couldn't do that. I have always felt very uncomfortable bringing Spock into a contemporary situation . . . except when I do one or two lines as a joke during a convention appearance or something. I have never tried to present myself as Spock-like.

There are potential benefits in lending Spock to a cause, I suppose, but there are also potentially terrible drawbacks. Can you just see the press with that? Spock's presence also might undermine a cause. I wouldn't want to find that out.

Spock has taken part in some heavy editorializing but only in the context of the TV shows. During the late 1960s, a lot of the *Star Trek* shows got involved in topical subjects—racism, militarism—in a black-and-white way. There were good guys and bad guys. Period.

During the late 1960s, I thought in black-and-white terms, as well. There was a wrong way and a right way and the right way was mine. There was only one possible person to be President and that was my guy.

I've gone beyond that.

Star Trek III went beyond that as well. I suspect I might get a nasty letter from the Klingon Empire about how they were depicted . . . although I think we managed to capture a couple of Klingon concepts that gave them a little more dimension than they had in the past. Maybe we understand them a little better because of this movie.

But, Klingons aside, this movie wasn't about black ideas and white ideas. What I tried to do

Nimoy picks up some directorial tips from Nicholas Meyer, the director of Star Trek II: The Wrath of Khan *(1982). William Shatner and the film crew looks on.*

with the project was demonstrate a thematic idea that examines the idea of friendship, of family relationships. I didn't have to set up a straw enemy to knock down so that I could prove a point.

The Klingons were a useful device as the antagonists of our story but they were not at the heart of the story. They were part of the adventure aspect, they were obstacles. But they were not essential to the thematic line. Basically, we wanted to look at this terrific family unit aboard the Enterprise. How do they interact with each other? How do they feel about each other? What are they prepared to do for each other? What price are they are willing to pay for this friendship? If I had to sum up the film's theme in one word, it would be *friendship.*

It was a challenge directing the movie. *Star Treks* had been directed by a number of directors: the TV directors, as well as Robert Wise and Nick Meyer in the first two films. But this was the first time it has been directed by an *insider,* by one of the family.

Therefore, I, coming from within the family, had to find richer and better ways to use these characters as a family. Because I had been privy to the development of this family over the years I thought I'd be able to present the members in a more fully realized way. I knew the little touches that bring the characters to life. I knew the details of their lives. That's what I was after in doing the movie. The actors have all told me that they felt wonderfully comfortable in *Star Trek III: The Search for Spock.*

EN: People have written about *Star Trek* as the single most phenomenal example of popular culture in history. . . .

LN: Yeah, but there's something equally amazing to me. We've had reams and reams of print put out telling us how wide-reaching the popularity of this show is, what a wide variety of fans it has from teenagers to philosophers and space scientists and sociologists. On the other hand, what has not been explored and what, to me, is an intriguing question is: Who are all the people who don't care about the show at all? There's a wide variety of people in that group too, from school kids to educators. They sit there and say,

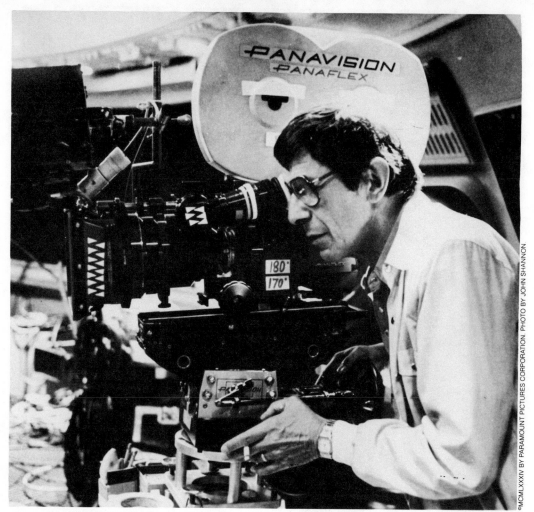

"I don't know what they see in this show!"

A study on that aspect of the show would fascinate me. I know *Star Trek* has developed an intense following but it's never been in the numbers that would have allowed a network to keep the show on the air for ten or twelve years. Who are all those people out there who could care less about it? Who are those people out there who are ridiculing us?

Maybe the whole phenomenon tells us something about science fiction today. We all know that poor science fiction has always been kicked around as a bastard child of literature. It's only been in the past few years that it has been studied seriously as literature. In film, it's only recently that science fiction has been considered a mainstream, commercial type of film. For years it was considered to be kid stuff.

For some odd reason, I've always been drawn to it. Not as an avid reader or viewer but as sort of an "understander" of it. I've always felt comfortable acting in science fiction projects. Before *Star Trek* I did *Satan's Satellites* [1958] and *The Twilight Zone, Night Gallery* and *The Outer Limits.*

Star Trek III: The Search for Spock (1984) found Nimoy behind the camera for the first time, working as director.

EN: The behind-the-scenes stories concerning the making of *Star Trek* films have always been intriguing—the security involved in keeping the scripts out of the hands of thieves, keeping the actors from talking with fans about the plot, etc. How did it feel, as a director, to be a security chief as well?

LN: I tried to be as loose about it as possible. In a sense, it's flattering that so many people would care about the movie to want to try to steal the scripts and props. But we had tremendous security problems. We tried to learn from other filmmakers what security measures worked and which ones didn't.

On the one hand, it's a pain to worry about security; on the other hand, it's great that the fans *care*. Here we were working very, very hard at something and the fact that these people are interested in it, even in this bizarre way, is like someone saying "thank you." They care. It's flattering.

A funny thing about directing this movie was how people, during production, kept on trying to find out the answer to...THE QUESTION! Everyone wanted to know if Spock was back in this movie but everyone knew that they just couldn't come out and ask me that. So, I frequently got asked things like, "What was it like directing yourself?" Or, "Have you ever directed yourself *before*?"

I laughed. I thought it was terrific that people would be interested enough to be Machiavellian in their questioning.

One of the most interesting aspects of the last two *Star Trek* films is that they seem to elicit a response from moviegoers that goes against the normal concept of movie viewing.

For instance, if you hear two people talking about a movie and one has seen it while the other hasn't, the one who has seen it might begin describing the film to his friend and then stop, saying, "I don't want to spoil it for you." Or the person he's talking to might interrupt him, saying, "Hey, don't tell me the ending. I want to see it myself." But, with *Star Trek,* it's the exact opposite. You have all these people yelling, "Come on! Spoil it for me! Tell me what's going to happen!" My attitude on the *The Search for Spock* was, "I don't want to spoil it for you." So, I smiled a lot and kept my mouth shut.

EN: Would you like to direct *Star Trek IV* ?

LN: Oh, yeah. I had a great time on *Star Trek III.* It's common knowledge that the *Star Trek* connection has presented me with some frustrations over the past seventeen years but I must say that I never had a more wonderful time in my life.

A lot of people have thoughts on my relationship with *Star Trek* but I don't think anyone has it down right. There are some who know everything that has happened and misinterpret it and there are some who know nothing.

I wrote a book that tried to examine what it is like being constantly identified with Spock: *I Am Not Spock.* That turned out to be a terrible title. People who have read the book have some insight as to what my attitude is but there are a lot of people who have only read the title of the book and have perceived it as a negative comment. I considered it a declarative sentence, a statement of fact.

I find it very frustrating that I am still being cornered by professional journalists who say things like, "Well, you wrote a book called *I Am Not Spock* that shows how much you hate the character." As recently as two weeks ago, I went through this. I asked the reporter if he had read the book. He said "No." How can I answer questions about a book when he hasn't read it?

Well, the point is: There have been frustrations and they have been dealt with. My frustrations were rather overexaggerated by certain individuals for various reasons. During the early 1970s there was a really nasty movement in fan circles singling me out as someone to hate. "He is denying us *Star Trek.*"

I couldn't figure that out. A lot of people were going through *Star Trek* withdrawal, I suppose, since there weren't any new episodes being filmed, and they focused their anger on me. I was somehow blamed for the show's going off the air and never returning. What could I say? No one approached me during those six or seven years and asked me if I wanted to do more *Star Treks.*

It wasn't until 1979 that people got serious and actually asked me. There has never been a *Star Trek* made that I have refused to appear in.

Yet, somehow, that whole sense of deprivation was focused on me. It's another fascinating aspect of the Spock phenomenon. You tear down the people you build up. The flipside of love is hate. Look what our society did to Ingrid Bergman, to Charlie Chaplin. I'm not putting myself in those categories but just look at what happened.

Leonard Nimoy, the actor who plays Mr. Spock, somehow became a villain. Perhaps it's because, since Spock often stands apart from the crew, I was seen as doing the same in terms of my costars, thus hurting the series.

When we were doing *Star Trek II,* a story was published saying that Spock died at my insistence, that I would agree to do the second movie *only* if Spock was killed. It got so crazy that, at one point, when I was talking to the head of Paramount Pictures about directing *Star Trek III,* he said, "Leonard. Why would you want to do that? *You* are the one who wanted Spock dead in the last movie!" The president of this company said that! He said "You insisted on having that in your contract, right?"

I said, "No."

He said, "Come on, don't kid me. It's in your contract!"

I told him to check the contract. Anyhow, we proceeded from there and I directed it. Everyone had a great time. I'd love to do another *Star Trek.*

I mentioned Spock as a father figure before. Some of this recent rejection is similar to the type of thing we do to our parents. First you love them and think they're wise. Then you leave home and dismiss everything they say. It's like Mark Twain's experience. He said when he left home he thought his father was the most ignorant man he ever knew and when he returned, as an adult, he was amazed at how much his father had learned during his absence.

After a while, you just learn to laugh about it all. I don't mind it. I've been involved in a really phenomenal experience. A seventeen-year experience. It's been an interesting ride.

I would love to continue it.

Mathemagicians: Computer Moviemakers of the 1980s and Beyond

Tim Onosko

Far apart from the notorious glitter and deal-making of Hollywood, the movies are being reinvented. It is happening, not on sound stages or noisy locations, but in tiny offices and cubicles. For the most part, there are no actors, no gaffers or key grips, and, sometimes, no cameras. Yet, the dreams that are being spun are as impressive as any studio fantasy of the past.

Imagine creating a motion picture with a computer—a motion picture, in some cases, indistinguishable from a photographic image of real life. Imagine creating ancient cities, exotic locations, even other worlds. Imagine creating not only spaceships, but steamships. And, one day, perhaps, even people.

The prime movers of this quiet revolution are diligent men and women who are both artists and technicians, and whose creativity is exercised both in the creation of images and the mathematical expressions and equations that yield those pictures. Their chief tool is, of course, the computer. And their arena is the world as seen on a video screen.

Computer filmmaking is, like traditional animation, a difficult and complex task. Because the powerful computers necessary to create complicated pictures have been extremely expensive, the art has been restricted to a few groups. Today, however, computer prices are falling as rapidly as their power is increasing. New talent is being attracted to the field, and programming

Tim Onosko is an author and journalist with a special interest in technology and popular culture. His books include *Wasn't the Future Wonderful?* and *Funland, U.S.A.* He is a regular contributor to *Omni* and is a contributing editor to *Video Magazine.*

tools that make the process of creation easier are rapidly being developed.

Here's how a computer can make movies: Everything a computer does must be reduced to numbers, and the computer's principal activity can be reduced to manipulating "bits" of memory. (A bit is the most elementary unit of information, essentially a switch that can be either "on" or "off.") A group of hundreds of thousands, even millions, of bits, can represent a picture, much like the dots you see when you look closely at photographs in newspapers and magazines. Electronic circuitry scans the memory and converts it to an image on a video screen. Each dot on the screen, called a "pixel" (for picture element) is represented by one bit in a black-and-white picture, and as many as twenty-four where color is used.

As in film, a motion sequence requires multiple images to be generated—twenty-four per second for film, thirty for video. Since conventional television screens are too coarse to be used for motion pictures, special display screens that rival the resolution of film are used instead, then photographed on film. In the near future, electron beams or possibly lasers will be used to "paint" directly onto the film.

Computer pictures themselves originate in a variety of ways. Some are scanned—that is, they are photographs or drawings that are first captured by a video camera or some other electronic means—and are converted automatically into computer code. Others are digitilized by drawing

or tracing on the surface of an electronic tablet. Still others (some of the most exciting) are mathematically described as a series of complicated formulae, or algorithms. Much of the "number crunching" that computer filmmaking requires demands giant, high-speed computers, and, except for the simplest and crudest of pictures, a motion sequence is not generated in "real time." That is, frames are produced one at a time and individually recorded on film or video tape. A complicated frame, one approaching photographic realism, for instance, can take hours to produce.

As complex as all of this may seem, it is beginning to attract Hollywood's attention. Digital film techniques offer the possibility of not only giving movies a new look, but of replacing or enhancing many traditional crafts, including setmaking and special effects. *Tron,* a milestone film that utilized both special optical effects as well as computer-generated objects and backgrounds, was released in 1982. Almost simultaneously came Nicholas Meyer's *Star Trek II: The Wrath of Khan* (1982), which featured the first digitally produced sequence from the computer graphics unit set up by George Lucas.

Among the antecedents of computer movies were examples of the automated art created by such experimental filmmakers as Oskar Fischinger and John Whitney, Sr. Machines held a fascination for both men. Fischinger's experiments in Germany during the 1920s and 1930s ranged from attempts at synthetic soundtracks (which were calculated and mechanically drawn with pen and paper and photographed on movie film) to a unique machine that sliced multicolored wax molds to produce hypnotic swirling patterns onscreen. Whitney's work with pattern-producing

One of the most stunning visual sequences in the history of motion pictures is the "trip" by astronaut Dave Bowman (Keir Dullea) through a stargate in 2001: A Space Odyssey *(1968). Director Stanley Kubrick and special effects supervisor Doug Trumbull employed slit-scan photography to give the impression of real movement. The use of a computer-controlled animation stand to provide the precise degree of streaking necessary was the first application of the computer to special effects.*

machines directly inspired the famous "slit scan" techniques used in the "stargate" sequence of Stanley Kubrick's *2001: A Space Odyssey* (1968). Alfred Hitchcock, too, utilized Whitney's mandala-like designs for the opening titles of *Vertigo* in 1958. Both Fischinger and Whitney recognized the artistic potential of machines.

Some of the first computer-generated images in modern films were those included in Michael Crichton's science fiction story *Westworld* (1973), directed by Crichton, and its sequel, *Futureworld* (1976), directed by Richard T. Heffron. For both films, Information International, Incorporated (known as "Triple-I"), a Los Angeles firm specializing in computer-imaging, was employed to produce new imagery. The company's designer in charge of those sequences was John Whitney, Jr. Since *Westworld,* director Crichton's interest in computers has continued. His 1982 film, *Looker,* had as a premise the complete synthesis of the human image. As an author, Crichton's fascination with computers surfaced in a 1983 treatise on living with machines, called *Electronic Life.*

Triple-I is no longer in the computer-filmmaking

business. Its equipment was put up for sale shortly after the completion of its work on various projects at Walt Disney Productions, including *Tron*. Among Information International's last computer work for Disney was a contribution to Murray Lerner's "Magic Journeys," a three-dimensional film exhibited at Walt Disney World's EPCOT Center. The use of computer graphics and animation is particularly well-suited to 3-D movies, since it is relatively easy for the computer to generate pairs of pictures encoded with the proper depth information. For "Magic Journeys," Triple-I developed several impressive images, including the film's titles, which spiral off the screen and into the audience, and a synthesized close-up of a human eye. Save for one or two obvious computer effects (a moving, multilayered mandala), it's probable that only a few in the audience at EPCOT recognize the use of a computer in the film.

Though *Tron* was received poorly by critics (mainly for its sketchy plot, but also because it was expected to be another *Star Wars,* which it certainly wasn't), it represented the first major attempt at integrating computer techniques into a Hollywood film on a major scale. It also served to pull together creative personnel in the field of computer graphics.

Both John Whitney, Jr., and Gary Demos (Whitney's partner and associate at Triple-I) contributed to *Tron*. The film's creative supervisor and a major contributor to its look and feel, Richard Taylor, had been associated with Triple-I as well. Robert Abel, whose visual effects shop became known for its work on a series of stunning television commercials for 7-Up and Levi's, offered a sequence to the film, too. For "Bit," a minor character who makes a brief appearance in *Tron,* another pioneer, Judson Rosebush of New York's Digital Effects, was called to the film.

Much of *Tron*'s visual appeal is established early in the film, in a sequence that features a chase involving computer-generated Lightcycles, motorcyclelike vehicles that, in the story, are part of a video game. Those vehicles, as well as futuristic-looking tanks and a kind of flying arch called a "recognizer," were all created by MAGI—Mathematics Application Group, Incorporated, a company that began creating digital images under contract to the United States military in the 1960s. With MAGI's process, called Synthavision, solid geometric "primitives" (simple shapes) are created by the computer, then "glued" together to form more complex objects. MAGI's work is earmarked by its geometric appearance and illusion of solidity. For MAGI, Larry Elin worked with Disney designers and animators to choreograph the film's sequences, which were created in California at a terminal linked by telephone to the company's computers in Elmsford, New York.

Disney Studio's interest in computer animation and effects comes, at least in part, from its interest in staying in the forefront of film technology and in restoring some of the graphic excellence of animation's "golden age." Traditional animation is incredibly labor-intensive as well, and the potential of the computer to eliminate much of the drudgery of cartooning (and thereby increase production output) isn't lost on the studio either.

With MAGI, Disney has experimented with a new animation process named "Synthamation." Briefly, this is the way it works. In place of conventional, flat backgrounds, an actual environment that the cartoon will be played within is modeled on the computer. Lighting and camera moves can be simulated within the scene. Finally, a simple shape—the approximate size of a character and the equivalent of a "stick figure"—is placed into the picture and moved. Isolating the figure from this environment, film is shot of the character, its relative size and limited movements, as a guide for hand animators, who will draw the character as usual, with pen and paper. The animators' drawings are then scanned and entered into the computer, where "in betweening"—making those drawings in between the principal cartoonist's key poses—is accomplished. Working with the hues assigned to the drawing by the animator, the computer can also color the drawings, just as teams of artists assigned to paint the traditional "cels" would do.

For study purposes, Disney animators produced a 50-second scene from Maurice Sendak's famous children's fantasy *Where the Wild Things Are,* using Synthamation. At various times, the process (or one like it) has also been mentioned in conjunction with a new Wizard of Oz film and with an adaptation of a modern fantasy, *The Brave Little Toaster.*

The approach at the Disney studio is, of course, oriented toward classical screen animation. At Lucasfilm, Ltd., however, programmers and artists are working toward designing Pixar, a computer system that will produce scenes with the kind of realism required by the types of fantasies that the group, which produced the *Star Wars* and Indiana Jones films, is noted for.

The Lucasfilm computer group has already begun to explore the possibilities in its scene for *Star Trek II.* In the sequence the "Genesis Effect," a fictitious process used in the plot to foliate barren planets is demonstrated. Probably few moviegoers recognized that the sequence was chiefly computer-generated. (In its final form, it was embellished with traditional animation and other optical effects.) This flight through space, then over the planet's mountainous surface and back again, was startlingly realistic. The landscape, looking like any other aerial footage (save for the dramatic descent from space to the surface) was actually mathematically described by a series of formulae known as "fractals."

Although the Genesis Effect sequence hints at

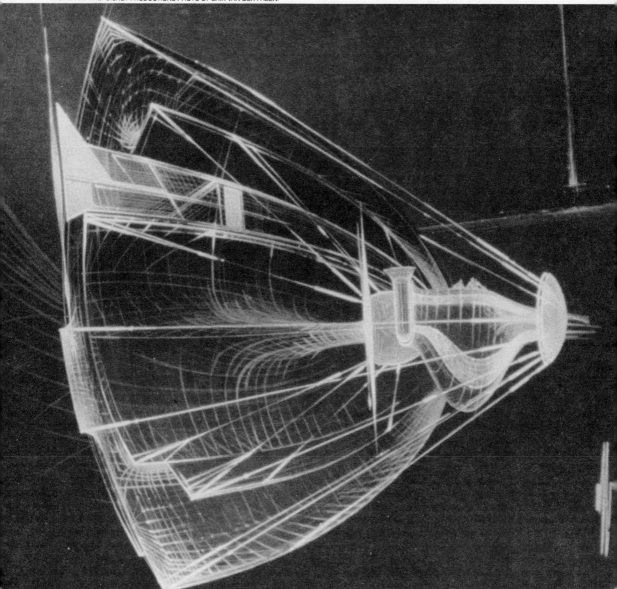

A solar sailor, conceived by Syd Mead for
Tron (1982), but not used.

computer filmmaking's promise, Alvy Ray Smith, a principal computer animator and developer with Lucasfilm, cautions about wanting too much too soon. "Computer pictures," says Smith, "are single-frame movies." By this, he means that each single scene is an effort requiring dozens of programmers, each of whom has developed various mathematical descriptions of lighting effects, optical characteristics, brush strokes, etc.

Pixar, the Lucasfilm system-in-development, may one day become a standard in the film industry. With it, images will be created, manipulated, even combined with film in a digital/laser optical printer, a machine as important to the creation of movie effects and the illusion of life as the first optical printers of the 1930s were. The system will display up to 16 million colors simultaneously on a grid of 16,777,216 individual pixels.

As successful as George Lucas's computer project may eventually be, it is unlikely that any single individual or group will dominate computer filmmaking. The base of knowledge in the field is already enormous and grows with each new project, each new objective. Consider the efforts of Digital Productions, Inc., the company devoted to computer imagery and founded by John Whitney, Jr., and his associate, Gary Demos. Whitney, who calls as much on his experiences with his experimental filmmaker father as his previous work with Information International, and Demos, a software specialist, head a group trying to convince Hollywood that the day when computers can replace certain traditional special effects

Michael Crichton (R) has written about computers and has made movies that are about computers and also use computer-generated images. Computer moviemakers hope someday to create exact images of people; indeed Looker *deals with the computer synthesis of models and politicians in order to sell products and political platforms to television watchers. Above: The body on the table is real but the mother and two children are computer-generated images. Far right: The subject of computer synthesis is a pretty model (Susan Dey).*

such as matte painting, model building and motion-control photography is here.

Their computer technique, which they call "digital scene simulation," is meant to produce objects with photographic realism, as has already been demonstrated by the group's work for various television commercials. Digital Productions' first feature film contribution, appropriately, was for a science fiction film, *The Last Starfighter* (1984), for whch it created twenty-seven minutes of footage ranging from battles in outer space, to asteroids and planetary landscapes. The very method of producing the film pointed up some of the new opportunities that computer filmmaking offers.

Digital Production's noted production designer, art director, and cartoonist Ron Cobb, was called

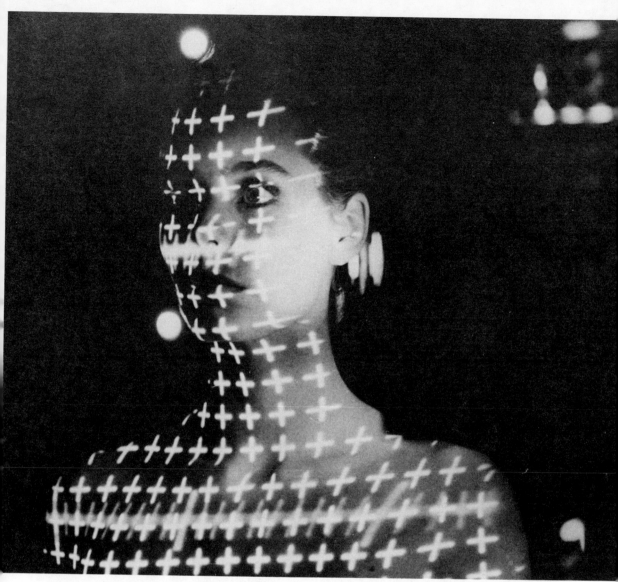

upon to design a futuristic auto to be used in the story. After sketching the car on paper, the final design was done using the company's computer system. Three-dimensional models were built, not by hand in wood, plaster, and clay, but in the computer's memory, and these images were actually used to generate certain sequences. It became obvious, however, that a full-size prop vehicle would be necessary during live-action filming, so one was built to match the computer-aided design that would be seen in the actual movie. In the old days, on studio backlots, effects technicians would have worked in the opposite direction, building models for effects sequences, from full-sized props and sets.

Photographic computer effects come about at the expense of both human effort—programming, designing, and entering graphic information into the computer—and machine "horsepower." After calculating the requirements for producing ultra-high-quality images in a short enough time to assure commercial viability, Whitney and Demos selected the world's most powerful computer, the Cray-1, a supercomputer designed by Seymour Cray, a reclusive and legendary engineer who builds his machines in the woods of northern Wisconsin. After taking delivery of their Cray computer, Whitney and Demos thought again and decided that one of these beasts was not enough, and placed an order for the machine's successor, the even more powerful Cray-XMP. Together, the two computers now form the core of Digital Productions' "studio."

The Cray computers, it should be noted, are truly special objects. The XMP weighs over eight tons, and occupies 120 square feet of space, and is capable of roughly a billion computations per second. The Cray 1, holder of the title "most powerful" until the introduction of the XMP, is a million or so times faster than a typical Radio Shack home computer. In all, fewer than sixty Cray computers are installed worldwide. And of those, most are usually dedicated to more mundane tasks, like running mega-corporations or governments. Digital Productions' Crays are the only ones given solely to making pictures.

John Whitney, Jr., sees a bright future for his Digital Scene Simulation, that may one day extend to synthesizing the human form and face, which he refers to as "the ultimate surface." He is already talking about synthesizing humans in the very near future, but only in noncritical long and medium shots, possibly replacing or augmenting crowds of extras. Though the art has a long way to go before a human face is synthesized with the kind of detail necessary to fool an audience, Whitney believes it will someday happen. "And when it does," he says, "it will be necessary to legislate against abuse of the technique." He cites, for instance, the possibility of synthesizing the persona of a national leader, who would appear on television and urge the country to war.

Whitney, Demos, and company have chosen a difficult task in trying to move Hollywood into the twenty-first century. Another group of computer filmmakers toil far from lotus land and instead concentrate on research, development, and a better understanding of how artists will actually use this new medium.

Yet the pictures coming from the Computer Graphics Laboratory of the New York Institute of Technology in Old Westbury, New York, are no less impressive. NYIT has demonstrated its prowess in computer imagery and has emerged as the leader in the field. Like many of the computer-effects houses, New York Tech is most recognized for its work in television commercials and other TV work. (Among its credits is the impressive opening for Public Television's "Nova" series.) But the group has also developed important new computer systems for computer animation, and has long been involved with several major projects, including a surrealistic animated fantasy, "The Mouse's Ear," "3DV" (described as the world's first computer-generated television program), and The Works, a feature film with a cast comprised of photo-realistic robots—characters far easier to describe and imagine with a computer than in real life.

"3DV," which was produced as a ten-minute pilot incorporating many of the group's important images and techniques, is a staggering short reel. Its two main players, the mistress and master of ceremonies, are "Dot Matrix" and "User Friendly," a robotic pair as entertaining as any pair in the history of cartoons, and almost as expressive as most human actors. Together, they introduce a mythical all-digital television channel, complete with children's programs, film classics (one of which is the yet-to-be-completed The Works), an advertisement for a robot company

called "Helping Handroids," cultural programs, sporting events, and video games. It is a tour-de-force of computer graphics and animation.

"The Works" remains one of the most talked-about, yet least-seen pieces of computer animation. A small group within NYIT devotes its efforts to the film in their spare time, between developing new animation techniques and other projects, and creates a few new characters every year. The present cast of robots includes the film's most amazing character, a giant automated ant (with an android who "drives" it like an earth mover), and various worker machines involved in building a world in which computers rule (and from which humans, presumably, have been banished).

But "3DV" and The Works are much more than just pretty-looking exercises in computer art. Both are sharpest in their demonstration of the kind of illusion of life that can be bestowed on computer creations. The characters in these films are real and uncannily vivid. Very wisely, their creators have also given them a keen sense of humor. What has been produced of "3DV" and The Works clearly puts them in the category of contemporary satire—commentary on our own fascination with computers and machines. Lucky thing, too. If not for the films' funny side, we might mistake their characters for escapees from technology's dark side—machines smarter than we are.

Sadly, the reality of computer filmmaking has meant that work on The Works is moving slowly. So slowly, in fact, that "3DV" pokes fun at the project, calling it the "Best Film of 1992," and NYIT animators have taken to wearing T-shirts that prematurely (and cynically) announce the sequel, "Works II." Computer animation, at least for now, has progressed, but only to the point where the elaborate art that The Works relies on still requires a kind of hand-crafting that rivals traditional film animation.

A sadder reality is that Hollywood may not be ready for The Works. MAGI's Larry Elin points out that if Disney's Tron had been a commercial hit, the film studios would have embraced computer animators as the new saviors of the movies. Since it wasn't, the moguls are taking a wait-and-see attitude, looking for the next round of breakthroughs in the art. As a result, audiences may first see The Works, not in movie theaters, but in video arcades. NYIT has been contemplating producing a laser-videodisc-based game using characters originally developed for the feature film in an interactive "mini-movie."

The only thing certain about the future of computer filmmaking is that it is inevitable. But the artists and technicians working to nurture the medium today are proving more than the viability of production techniques. They are demonstrating that the computer—considered the very antithesis of creativity in the recent past—can be the tool that will show us futures not yet imagined.

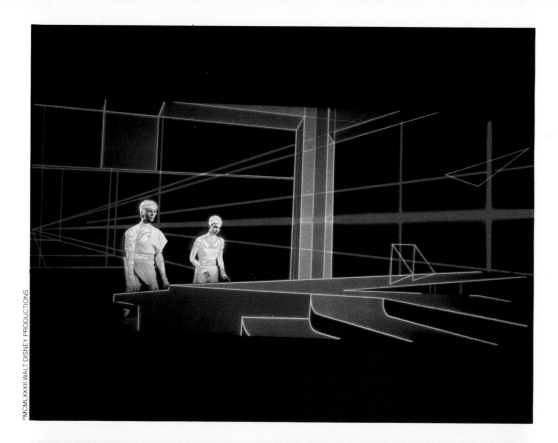

Top: In Tron, actors Jeff Bridges and Cindy Morgan stand within a computer-generated setting. Above: Another striking computer-generated visual from Tron.

Digital Productions, a Los Angeles-based firm that employs sophisticated Cray computers, has risen to the top of the computer-image field. Its services are increasingly in demand in Hollywood; it was recently commissioned by Universal Studios to do its lengthy computer sequence in *The Last Starfighter* (1984). Shown here are three examples of Digital's striking computer imagery.

"Moonscape." The planet in the background is artistically manifested with soft colors blended together in a rainbow effect to represent clouds. The terrain was created by using a propriety fractal package that produces random surface textures.

"Devo Hat." A simulated plastic hat tumbling forward; it was used as a backdrop for the rock group Devo, which has employed computer images in their musical videos. The surface is comprised of cubes; note the highlighting and shadowing.

"Star Frontiers Game." This stylized fantasy town incorporates real architectural structures (colorful umbrellas, reflective facades) that zoom into a textured, tiled fantasy toy store with a door opening (as a transition to the live action shot of the actual commercial product).

George Miller's The Road Warrior *(1982), a postapocalyptic film with medieval elements. Top: A warrior woman of the future (Virginia Hey), who will die bravely fighting brutal marauders who are after her people's oil supply. Above: The Humungus (Kiell Nilson), the leader of the marauders, keeps a chain on his brutal henchman, Wez (Vernon Wells). In the* Mad Max *films, most everything the villains do is ritualistic—they, more than the good people, revert back to the Dark Ages.*

Directing
Mad Max
and
The Road Warrior

An Interview with George Miller by Danny Peary

Danny Peary: Did the fact that *On the Beach* [1959], the most famous antinuclear film, was filmed in Australia leave any lasting impression on your country?

George Miller: I was a kid at the time, and I remember only two things about it being made, the first being that for one Sunday morning they cleared the streets of Melbourne, a southern city, which has a population of three million. The city was deserted. I think a lot more people remember leading lady Ava Gardner's remark that Melbourne is a great place to make a picture about the end of the world. She was alluding to the rather staid, boring quality of the city. I'm afraid Melbourne, one of Australia's older and more established cities, has never been able to live down her comment.

I didn't actually see *On the Beach* until many years later. I was very impressed with the film and I think it's great that one of the first nuclear films was made in Australia. But I'd say it wasn't one of those pivotal films in Australian society. It didn't have an enormous effect as far as I can tell.

DP: How do Australians regard the nuclear issue?

GM: There is a fairly large antinuclear movement here among those who are politically committed, yet in general Australians tend to have a fairly relaxed political nature. Australia's often called "The Lucky Country" because we have a very small population on a continent that has a great deal of abundance, and we don't seem to have the more obvious problems of many other nations. Australians view the nuclear question in the same way people do in other countries but, I'd say, with a little less sense of urgency than they have in America or Europe. Of course, we're down on the other side of the Earth, so I don't think the question surfaces as acutely in Australia—I guess somehow people here feel we're too far away. . . . Even when I'm overseas I tend to find people who talk of coming to Australia as a kind of refuge from an eventual nuclear war. I think it's a fairly forlorn hope. I'm one of those people who believes that a nuclear war will be total and contaminate the atmosphere everywhere. Anyway, we have American tracking stations here, which "current wisdom" says will be targets in case of war.

DP: Do Australians better understand your *Mad Max* films than people from other countries?

GM: Not really. Because the films are set in some nonspecific future, they tend to be fairly universal. I think Australians would be more familiar with the accents, locations, the cars driving on the right side of the road, and things like the boomerang that the Feral Kid [Emil Minty] uses as a weapon in *The Road Warrior*. Even so,

George Miller is the Australian director of *Mad Max, Mad Max 2/The Road Warrior, Mad Max 3*, and the "Nightmare at 20,000 Feet" segment of *Twilight Zone—The Movie*.

Mel Gibson is Mad Max, the road warrior, a violent, self-torturing hero, who has caught the fancy of moviegoers worldwide. The Mad Max *films were influenced less by "hero" pictures than chase films, including Buster Keaton and Harold Lloyd silent comedies.*

I don't think there is anything in the *Mad Max* films that is specifically Australian.

I should point out, however, that it was an interest that Byron Kennedy* and I had in Australia's car culture that, coupled with our obsession for the pure kinetics of chase movies, led us to make *Mad Max*. We have a vast country and a small population, and so we have a large network of nearly deserted rural roads. When I was growing up in the Sixties, these roads were used as sporting arenas as much as they were used for transportation. During that period there was a disproportionate number of highway casualties. It seems as if in the absence of a gun culture—we don't have handguns—we express our violence through cars.

DP: The most devastating moment in *Mad Max* happens on the highway. Max's [Mel Gibson] wife Jessie [Joanne Samuel] and their baby are struck down by the Glory Riders. Afterward, hospital doctors discuss Jessie's grave injuries as if she were a wrecked car. Was this scene influenced by your having been a doctor in a hospital?

GM: After getting out of medical school, I interned for two years, and spent a good six months in the casualty ward of a major city hospital. That's where I was exposed to an enormous amount of road trauma. That, of course,

---

*Byron Kennedy was the producer of *Mad Max* and *The Road Warrior* and George Miller's partner. He was killed in a helicopter crash in July 1983.—D. P.

was one of the germinating influences of the *Mad Max* films.

DP: How far into the future does *Mad Max* and *The Road Warrior* take place?

GM: I think of the films taking place about fifteen years from now. But we were deliberately vague about the time frame. The only reference to time is at the very beginning of *Mad Max,* when a title reads "A FEW YEARS FROM NOW..." *The Road Warrior* makes no reference to when this future is; the Narrator simply states that a great war over oil has taken place.

DP: Your use of a narrator at the beginning and end of *The Road Warrior* is quite interesting and, in a *good* sense, disorienting. When he turns out to be the Feral Kid, grown up, the film suddenly turns out to be a futuristic tale that was told as if it were already history. So time is completely out of whack.

GM: We were attracted to the notion of using a narrator for *The Road Warrior* because it said very clearly that this is *storytelling, fable, mythology*. It also served to move the film yet another degree into another time. And it has just occurred to me from your suggestion that the time frame is out of whack, that the story is indeed really told many years down the line—so it is removed once again in time and fits into a mythological framework even more than I realized until now. In fact, one of the early cuts of the film, which didn't have the narration, didn't play well, so it's interesting how its addition did have such an impact on the film.

At the beginning of Mad Max *(1979), Max leads a fairly normal family life, despite living in a postapocalyptic age. His happy relationship with his wife Jessie (Joanne Samuel)—an extremely likable character—is one any man could envy. But when Max loses her and their baby, all he has to live for is revenge.*

DP: *Mad Max* and *The Road Warrior* seem to be set in a postnuclear age. But why does no one, including the Narrator, mention the Bomb?

GM: I think that the two films fall into the category of postapocalyptic storytelling—but they are *not* postnuclear. When we discussed the kinds of events that might have led to this primitive world we depict, including the global war that the Narrator alludes to, the nuclear question was avoided entirely. That's because I firmly believe that a nuclear winter would at best leave a world of insects and grass. Even if we were to include human beings, they'd all have to be suffering enormous problems from radiation; perhaps they'd all be mutants. If we had wanted to *accurately* depict a postnuclear future, we'd have made entirely different films.

DP: Nevertheless, are the films meant to be speculative? Or are they allegorical?

GM: They definitely weren't intended to be speculative; we didn't show what I believe to be a true vision of a postapocalyptic future. I think that the films are somewhat allegorical in nature. The function of a storyteller should be to reveal truths about human nature through the depiction of people and their problems in a particular place and time. The reason we told these postapocalyptic stories was to show some of the more primitive impulses that drive human beings. I think both films have value in that they help us explore the darker, more unthinkable side of ourselves. They serve as warning fables. It's very difficult to tell these kinds of stories in contemporary, naturalistic formats, so we set them in heightened, caricaturized futuristic worlds.

What triggered off the *Mad Max* stories was in fact the petrol rationing we had in Australia in the late Seventies, just as you had in the United States. I was really stunned by how readily the

normal fabric of society can start to disintegrate when you remove something that is as essential as gas. Australia is not a violent society, at least not overtly violent, but it took only a week or so for this severe rationing to have people trying to jump queues, resorting to violence, and going at each other with guns—just to get enough gas to go to work that week. So when we started thinking of our back story to *Mad Max,* we simply postulated the kind of events that would result from removing one of the fossil fuels from the Earth. I mean, if we learned today that there was going to be very little energy generated from now on, a lot of things would happen suddenly.

DP: Did you have a detailed pre-film scenario all worked out?

GM: We could have told our stories without trying to define for ourselves what the rest of the world, the world off-screen, was like. But we made sure that everyone involved with the films had some knowledge of our back story. So we told the actors and the extras, and the art department and those in wardrobe, and the construction people how the world as we know it had disintegrated, and had become primitive and medieval. We said that there'd been a massive energy shortage in the world. Nothing is manufactured anymore, so everything must be found—things can only be made from the debris of the old, decaying world.

It occurred to us sometime after we completed the films that they are more medieval than futuristic. The time is the future, yet it is a very regressed world, where the ground rules that hold society together are quite rudimentary. The normal interractive society has given way, and you have a much more futile, scavenging, hierarchical society. And we're dealing with a Darwinian survival-of-the-fittest world: Survival is

not just a matter of "making a living," as it is today, but actually refers to preserving one's life on a day-to-day basis. So I guess one of the things these films do is suggest that in any post-apocalyptic world people will revert, at best, back to a fairly medieval hierarchy and social order.

I see the world breaking up into three types of people. First, there are those who try to maintain the status quo. In *Mad Max,* this group is represented by the Bronze, policemen like Max and the Goose [Steve Bisley]. These men are remnants of the old small-city police forces that existed prior to the apocalypse, and they naively believe they can maintain law and order as they had in the past. Max realizes the futility of it after the Goose is killed, and he and Jessie go away. But events catch up with him.

The second group of people are those who realize that the normal bonds that keep society together have broken down completely. Their concern is to survive at all costs. Necessity unites people into unholy alliances and these people join together because of their common need for mobility in the vast landscape. They realize that the best way to survive is by organizing into cooperative, efficient gangs. They neither want to maintain the status quo nor look forward to any kind of future or for any kind of rebirth to come out of the fragmented society.

Then there are those people who say things can't go on this way forever and try to change things. They want to stay alive and eventually move toward the organization of a new society. This third group is represented by the people inside the compound in *The Road Warrior.*

DP: Do you like the members of this tribe?
GM: I kind of like their ideals, but they're also the most boring characters in the film—which is probably an index to our limitations as storytellers. Of course, I'm also aware of the cynical way they use Max by having him be their unsuspecting decoy: He drives their tanker, which both he and the marauders assume is filled with gas—later he discovers that it is filled with sand.
DP: In *Mad Max,* the highway is territory, a metaphor for power; in *The Road Warrior,* gasoline serves the same function.
GM: One of the problems when you have a regressed world is that people become territorial in the sense that they believe in a kind of sovereignty, either of a little patch of earth or an ideology. And it's that kind of ignorance and rather limited view of the universe that is, I'll be presumptuous enough to say, at the heart of all evil, of all the warmongering that goes on—in the film and in actuality. We'll be able to breathe a sigh of relief only when the sovereignty of the planet Earth overrides all other sovereignties, be they ideological, national, or geographical.
DP: One of the most striking features of your future world is the wild costuming and hairstyles, which are part punkish, part medieval. Wez (Vernon Wells) looks scary with his Mohawk cut, but the chief marauder, The Humungus [Kiell Nilson], in his spooky mask, is truly terrifying.
GM: We invented a back story for every character. We imagined that The Humungus had been some kind of military man who'd been in a severe accident or explosion and suffered facial or head burns. He wore that mystifying mask as a

The villains fight for control of the road and fuel in the Mad Max *films. Left: In* Mad Max, *the Glory Riders line up like the cycle gang in the Brando classic* The Wild One. *Right: In* The Road Warrior, *the villains ride in souped-up racing cars—chariots suitable for their knight personas. "Oddly, I'm not that interested in cars and bikes," says Miller, "just in the potential of filming them for the screen. If one of the bikes I owned had broken down, I wouldn't have known how to fix it."*

form of intimidation and sign of authority.

All the warrior types had to resort to an enormous amount of pageantry, because that helped them establish a hierarchical order; moreover, there's an efficiency attained if everyone looks alike, warriorlike. The marauders, in particular, had to look as formidable as possible. If you look scary enough, half the battle is won.

DP: What about sex in your world? Obviously there is much homosexuality, particularly among the bikers.

GM: We repeatedly asked ourselves what price sexuality would pay in this kind of medieval world. It certainly couldn't function as it does in our contemporary society. People wouldn't have time for recreational sex. There's no time for a woman to have a baby, to nurse infants, etc. It's very unlikely that a pregnant woman or a woman with a child could survive. This could be one of the things that resulted in homosexual relationships in both stories. One of the other things, however, was that we changed a lot of the sexes of characters without changing their roles. The Warrior Woman (Virginia Hey), for instance, was originally to be a man; the blond youth on the back of Wez's cycle was originally a woman. So the women and men and their sexual roles are not as defined in this primitive world as they are in our society. Men and women are simply interchangeable.

DP: Do young Australian audiences identify with the good guys or the fancier-dressed bikers?

GM: I would hope, as a storyteller, that there is identification with both sides. I think a well-told story gives one insights into all the forces that in-

teract in any conflict. I really think it's important. I find that in both *Mad Max* films, the bad guys are more interesting than the good guys. On a pragmatic level, it's more fun for the actors and designers to be working with the marauder, bad guy types than the good guys, who I'm afraid can be rather boring. If I had a chance to do the films again, I think I'd give a bit more insight into both sides. Then hopefully the audience would be able to see that those people with the broader knowledge, who are prepared to make broader connections, should be classified as "good guys." I think the "bad guys" in *Mad Max* and *The Road Warrior* are designated "bad" because basically they have chosen to limit their perspective. They are people who say, "There's no hope, there's no chance for rebirth, so our goal is to merely survive, which we'll do by taking what's left." And really that's all that differentiates them from the "good guys." Max is only marginally better than The Humungus; although he is as committed as the marauders to survival at all costs, he hasn't the total amorality of the marauders.

DP: Is the "Mad" in *Mad Max* meant to imply he is angry or batty?

GM: It stands for both. *Mad Max* is essentially a vengeance fable in which Max kills those responsible for killing his baby and turning his wife into a vegetable. The "mad" means angry up to a point in the film, but at the end—in spite of his earlier attempts to prevent himself from being dehumanized by his profession—events also force on him a rather beastlike state. He really ends up quite insane. In times of great turmoil,

people tend to resort to the more reptilian parts of the brain. There's an argument, which the films adhere to, that to some degree a lot of people need to be a little "batty," as you say, in order to survive this world. The normal morality and the normal rituals no longer apply, and people like Max resort, in both stories, to a primitive state that reflects the brutal times.

DP: Would you say *Mad Max* is more pessimistic than *The Road Warrior*?

GM: That's *definitely* the case. *Mad Max* is a very dark film. We begin with an admittedly harsh world, but Max is a fairly normal man, working a day job, and having a wife and baby at home. He begins to understand through the death of his friend and the kinds of things he's been forced to do as a highway policeman the kind of world he's living in. So he quits his job and tries to get away. But the world catches up to him and his family is decimated; and he descends into the dark side. By the end of the film, mad, angry, crazy Max has become a full monster, the avenging demon. His last killing, of Johnny the Boy [Tim Burns], is a physical death combined with psychological torture [Johnny can *possibly* save himself by sawing through his ankle] and was meant to be more horrible than the quick, purely physical death of Toe-Cutter [Hugh Keays-Byrne], the leader of the Glory Riders, who was run over by a large truck. It leaves Max in the most pessimistic situation I'd like to leave any character. We must question whether he's redeemable.

Mad Max concludes with Max's killing of Johnny the Boy (Tim Burns), the last, and most pathetic, of the Glory Riders. The sadism evident signifies that good Max's descent into madness is complete.

On the other hand, *The Road Warrior* starts off with a pessimistic world and ends with there being the possibility of rebirth, no matter how dark the order of the day is. Max spends most of the film attempting to deny his humanity. Mel Gibson called his character a "closet human being" who doesn't want to be involved with other human beings because he believes an emotional investment will be too painful and also compromise his chances for survival. He can barely bring himself to have contact with his dog. By the end of the film however, he realizes—perhaps entirely *unconsciously*—that he can't live that way any longer, and that his life must have some greater purpose. He realizes that he has no choice but to drive the oil tanker for the people of the compound and be the one who is attacked by the marauders. It turns out that he was just a pawn of the collective, but even as a decoy he was responsible for the people's gaining freedom and a new order emerging from the chaos. He begins to see that he's part of the collective, like it or not. It's a much more optimistic outlook than we have in *Mad Max*.

DP: Why doesn't Max go with the tribe north to "paradise"?

GM: It would be completely unnatural, too much

of a turnaround, if he'd suddenly embrace the
value system of these people who want to escape to the relative safety of the north. He isn't
one of them, and he's served his purpose as far
as they are concerned. He is destined to roam
the wilderness alone because he is still tortured
by demons of the past. If there is a time for him,
it is yet to come. The jury is still out on Max.
He's ripe for change, but the change must come
slowly for him.

DP: How was Mel Gibson cast as Max? And do
you think he has influenced the character?

GM: We knew we wanted to cast someone relatively young. At the time, Mel was graduating
from the National Drama School. We went to see
him there, and then he came in for a screen
test. I recognized what a fine actor he was already. I think he did change the character to
some degree. If actors do have personas, then
Mel has a quality of "goodness" to him. A
"good core," for want of a better term, is
present in him. And I think this did come across
a fair bit in his character. Not so much in *Mad
Max,* but in *The Road Warrior.* You knew Max
was a character who is essentially ripe for
change. Even though he denies the humanity in
himself, you recognize that he's really ready to
rekindle the spark of compassion within him.
And that's best characterized by his friendship
with The Gyro Captain [Bruce Spence] and his
regard for the boy, the Feral Kid.

DP: It's interesting that we're won over by The
Gyro Captain, who also has potential for brutality, when we see how disgusted he becomes
while watching the marauders commit a rape-
murder of a captive female.

GM: He probably has the most important function in *The Road Warrior.* He's a fairly venal
character but at this horrendous moment he reveals himself, showing us much earlier than Max
does that he has compassion. So we suspect
that he is going to be more generous, more
open, and will be able, one hopes, to tip Max
back into his humanity. We particularly liked The
Gyro Captain because, apart from all else, he
gave us a lot of humor that fitted quite naturally
into the film. I'd have liked to have done more
comedy in *Mad Max,* but it just didn't fit comfortably into that film; also I was not as confident
then as a director of comedy.

DP: As befitting the world you show, there is
much violence in your films and much dying. Yet
importantly one never becomes desensitized.
We are particularly affected by the single
deaths. Still I'm sure that you get criticized for
the violence in your films. How do you respond?

GM: I had censorship problems with the two
films in certain countries because of the violence. And it was extremely difficult to make any
cuts because, as you'd see if you looked at
them frame by frame or sequence by sequence,
there's not much violence on the screen. They

*Wez is the fiercest, most deadly of the
wasteland's marauding horde in* The Road
Warrior. *Even The Humungus seems to have
a conscience. "This world is not meant to be
inviting. It is brutal, scary, and forbidding."—G.M.*

appear to be more violent than they are. That
was deliberate. I think it's always more effective
when you're able to keep the monster offscreen.
Because the audience's imagination can be a
powerful ally of the director.

The question of how to use violence in films,
or whether to use it at all, is very difficult to answer. I do know that there's an impulse in filmmakers and other storytellers to try and confront
both violence and death and shed some light on
each. Of course there is a very fine line between
exploiting these subjects and *examining* them.
And I'm not sure quite where the *Mad Max* films
fall.

One thing that has helped me try to put everything into context is the notion that movies are
really public dreams. For me, it's almost the best
definition I've heard of movies. They're dreams
we share collectively in darkened theaters. And
just as all dreams have functions, *nightmares*
help us confront our dark sides. I think Stephen
King wrote very well on it once, when he called
horror stories and other stories of great terror
"dress rehearsals for termination." These dress
rehearsals for our own deaths help us experience that part of ourselves which we are unable
to deal with in normal, conscious, everyday living. And I think that's the kind of impulse that
gives rise to the violence in our storytelling.
There's obviously a need for violence in stories,
as it has always been present in them, whether
we're talking about biblical stories or children's
fairy tales.

DP: Although not particularly moral, Max is certainly a hero-type—but he'd be the last to admit
it. Did the scene in *Mad Max* in which Fifi [Roger
Ward], the police captain, tries to get Max to
recognize his heroic capabilities have any special significance?

GM: If Max is grand enough to be designated a

The Road Warrior. *The Gyro Captain (Bruce Spence) traps Max with the old hidden-pet-snake trick. Friendships have begun in stranger ways.*

hero, he would of course deny it. Heroes, I guess, are fairly ordinary people with extraordinary potential—and one of their common traits is that they are often reluctant to assume the status of hero.

Your question interests me because when we wrote the scene, I don't think we thought very much in terms of heroes—it really came out of Fifi, and he had the right idea. It was only a lot later that we began to analyze Max's popularity in countries as diverse as Japan, Switzerland, Australia, France, the United States, and the South American countries, that I could see that *Mad Max* was a rather corrupted version of hero mythology. The film enjoyed success way beyond normal, exploitation car films because we had unwittingly, unconsciously, been "servants" of a collective unconsciousness: *Mad Max* was in fact another story about a lone outlaw hero who wandered through a dark wasteland—similar stories had been told over and over again, across all space and time, with the hero being a Japanese samurai, or an American gunslinger, or a wandering Viking, etc.

The truth is that I had a tough time making *Mad Max*. I was dissatisfied with the film and felt that we had been constrained by my inexperience and our small budget, and for a long time when I was cutting it, I honestly felt it was unreleasable. When the film succeeded financially, I thought it would give me the chance to go off and do something quieter. We didn't imagine that there would ever be a sequel. But the whole mythological question in regard to our hero made us want to do the first film *again,* to push the character a little further. Somehow it seemed that we didn't have a choice. I think the only way we'll ever be able to get rid of Max is to kill him off. These stories just plop out of the unconsciousness, which is how I think *Mad Max 3* came about. Now I'm looking forward to taking

a crack at that. Perhaps it will bring Max closer to going full circle.

DP: Compare your vision of the future to what we see in your *Mad Max* films.

GM: One of the most exciting things about being a human being and having some curiosity is to speculate about the future. I think in a crazy sort of way, the thing I most regret about dying sooner or later is that I won't be around to see what extraordinary things lie ahead. I don't mean only the technological advances, but also human advances—though quite often it takes longer to recognize them. I'm someone who is optimistic about technology. I think John Naisbitt was correct in *Megatrends* when he stated that with high technological advances you also will get "high touch," or a great need for human interaction. And I think that those artists and communicators who are best in touch with technology are going to contribute a lot more than those who feel reactionary toward it. Essentially, what our computer microchip technology is doing is freeing us from our fairly mundane, left brain functions and forcing us to come to terms with our more creative right brain functions. The more spiritual we'll become, the more connections we'll be forced to make, and the more we'll see ourselves in the broadest possible context. We'll have a more realistic view of our place in the universe, a view afforded us by the knowledge we'll gain from our advanced technology.

For that reason I'm optimistic about the future—assuming of course that we can overcome the threat of total extinction through a nuclear holocaust. If I had to make a film about a postnuclear world it would be about a barren planet. But if I did a story about a true future in which there had been no holocaust, it would be of an extraordinary world, in which human potential—or collective human potential—would be breathtaking.

Andrei Tarkovsky:
Russia's Science Fiction Poet

Michael Wilmington

A world slow, stately, and eerily beautiful, glowing with pale greens and silvery grays; a world of silences, which stretch along inexorably, of empty streets, barren fields that pulse with a peculiar threat; of clouds billowing upon clouds, mist on mist, shattered mirrors; a world of water in all its variegated forms—drops and trickles, rivulets, pools, streams, lakes, and finally oceans that have swallowed land, swallowed whole planets; water vaporized into pearly mists, crystallized into spears of ice...Eyes watching this world, full of liquid anxiety, tension, eyes like pools, like mirrors—*eyes that have seen the horror, or expect it imminently,* or that gaze into some unfathomable distance (the eyes of the dreamer); a world of artifacts and treasures; and, beyond it, a charnel house, cathedral steps swimming in blood, corpses in a foggy, twilit swamp—corridors, tunnels, concrete sewers, a world of mazes and traps...The sound of a bell and its resonating chime, the crack of gunfire, the sound of thrumming starship engines, of wind kissing the wheat and the grass, the sound of hoofs clopping, glass breaking, the rush of water, and the incessant hushed hymn of human breathing, infinitely small, infinitely precious, the chime and engine of life under an eternal sky, stretching out toward vastness, blackness, sunlight, and infinity...This is the world (but only part of it, that part I've seen, remembered, or distorted) of Andrei Tarkovsky and his films.

Tarkovsky is relatively little-known in the United States—and perhaps even less-known in the subculture of science fiction, though he and Stanley Kubrick are its two greatest cinematic practitioners. But his international credentials are prodigious: three grand prizes at major film festivals for his debut film, *Ivan's Childhood* (shot before he was thirty); three more major awards at Cannes (including the Grand Prize, Critics Prize and Directors Prize) split among his next five; and for his 1966 classic *Andrei Rublev,* a ranking of twelfth on *Sight and Sound*'s Critics Directors Poll of the all-time best films. By any standards Tarkovsky is a remarkable talent, distinctive and unusual. But, perhaps even more impressively, he accumulated his many awards and honors for only six films spread over two decades—and despite the virtually consistent disfavor of his own government (the U.S.S.R.), which shelved three of his movies for up to five years each (the worst penalty was for *Rublev*), refused all of his projects for another six, and once turned down a request by the Cannes Film Festival to submit his 1974 *The Mirror,* though they were informed *in advance* that it was the likely Grand Prize winner.

Tarkovsky's tribulations (not quite as severe as those of his great colleague, Serge Paradjenov—who endured a long prison term for "homosexuality") are striking. It may be tempting to see him as a sort of cinematic Solzhenitsyn—but he himself rejects any role of martyrdom, pointing out that he was able to make five of his films inside the Soviet Union exactly as he wanted to, with no

Michael Wilmington is the movie editor for the *L.A. Weekly* and *High Times,* and is the film critic for *Milwaukee Magazine.* He has also contributed to *Film Comment, The Real Paper,* and the *Velvet Light Trap.* He is the co-author of *John Ford.*

Left: Solaris (1972). On a space station above Solaris, a strange, hypnotic, fantasy-inducing planet, Christ Kelvin (Donatis Banionis) is joined by the image of his dead wife Hari (Natalya Bandarchuk). This meeting forces him to face up to past events in his life, including their relationship. Is "Hari" an instrument by which some alien force can study him?

Right: Christ Kelvin must suffer the repeated deaths and resurrections of "Hari." Over and over again, he must deal with the guilt he felt when the real Hari died.

commercial or ideological constraints...until *afterwards.* In fact, his masterpiece, *Andrei Rublev,* nearly destroyed his directorial career, after government censors objected to "violence," "sexuality," and "historical falsifications"—all in an obviously fictionalized portrayal of a legendary Russian medieval icon painter, about whom next to nothing is actually known.

He is, in the end, exactly what his numerous awards and citations would imply: one of the finest of all contemporary film directors—the legitimate heir (along with Paradjenov) of that great Russian film tradition that runs through Pudovkin, Eisenstein, Dovzhenko, Vertov, and Kozintsev: that tradition at times mystical, at times lucid and "pragmatic," fervent, stirring, roaring along like some turbulent Asian cataract battering down dams and boundaries...that great tradition of the Twenties and early Thirties (of *Earth,* of *October,* of *The New Babylon*), later dismantled and destroyed by Stalin in the name of "socialist realism." (A movement, as we now see, neither inherently "socialist" nor remotely "real.") He is a director of power, and high passions, with per-

haps the finest eye for composition of any of his contemporaries.

What interests us here is that Tarkovsky is one of a handful of great directors who have specialized, and returned repeatedly, to science fiction. Two of his movies, *Solaris* (1972) and *Stalker* (1981)—from genre novels by Stanislaw Lem and the Strugatsky brothers, respectively—are "hard" science fiction, with plots based on extraterrestrial exploration or "alien invasion." And two others, *The Mirror* and *Nostalghia* (1983), have a sort of extrapolative or fantastical patina; they play with time and consciousness, suggest the weird or inexplicable, fragment memory or shatter it altogether. Even *Andrei Rublev* and *Ivan's Childhood,* set recognizably in the past (medieval Russia and World War II), have a kind of alien, otherworldly atmosphere—"flying" sequences, a nightmarish intensity. Only Kubrick has shown so consistent or deep a fascination with the genre (at least in its "adult" forms)—and like Kubrick, like Lang, like (to a lesser degree) Buñuel, Tarkovsky has become a fantasist and moralist, spinning apocalyptic fables, myths of the mechanical age,

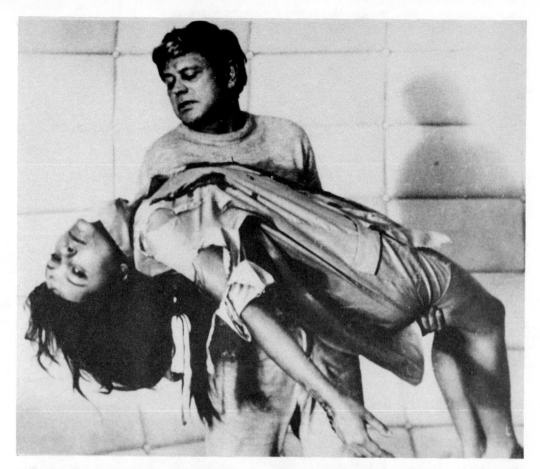

"cosmic" adventures of the body and spirit.

Solaris and Stalker have different backdrops—the first is set in a space station circling a distant planet; the second in a mysterious "Zone" on Earth. But their basic themes are identical: the deadly search, through an alien landscape, for personal or spiritual realization. In Solaris, this theme is slightly more opaque; it was Tarkovsky's first work after the six-year-long period of "disgrace" that followed Andrei Rublev, and he was additionally hindered by a troubled collaboration with Polish science fiction novelist Stanislaw Lem.

We are presented with a situation that seems vaguely Twilight Zone-ish. Astronauts and scientists on a space station have been gradually cracking up. A man (Donatis Banionis) sent to investigate discovers that the planet which the station has under surveillance is covered by a mysterious, sentient "Ocean" that reproduces images and people from their past—in his case, the image of his dead wife. The conflict is a simple one: reality and illusion, desire and "truth" . . . with the protagonist gradually slipping into the feverish world of his own memory. But this bald statement of the theme can hardly prepare you for the experience of the film itself—its almost mystical, rapt slowness; its hypnotic rhythms—or the bewitching images. The film has been called "Russia's 2001," and Tarkovsky—like Kubrick, and

perhaps like David Lynch (of Eraserhead [1978] and Dune [1984])—does not want to deal with the elements of "space opera," but with philosophical science fiction—stories that have a psychological or metaphysical edge; where exploration is always inward.

In Stalker, an eerie masterpiece (and I think, along with 2001, the best science fiction film of our era), the deadly search theme becomes fully fleshed, lucidly stated. The story—taken from another well-known novel, this time by Russia's Strugatsky brothers, Arkady and Boris—follows three men, the "Stalker" (Alexander Kaidanovsky), the "Writer" (Anatoli Solonitsin), and the "Scientist" (Nikolai Grinko), into the Zone: an utterly mysterious, desolate region on the outskirts of the city that has been hollowed out by some distant, unexplained explosion (possibly by a meteorite, possibly by an extraterrestrial ship crash). The government forbids entrance into this Zone, where everything is deadly, inexplicable, barren. It is a maze where death is omnipresent, and where all the trails and tunnels double back on themselves—and where travellers can lose themselves with one false step. But at the center of the maze lies a Wishing Room—a curious dank cell in which, it is said, one's "heart's desire" can be achieved if only one asks properly; if only, indeed, one knows what it is (one seeker, who

Left: The Stalker (Alexander Kaidanovsky) walks through the vegetation of the mysterious Zone. The color scenes in the Zone, and the fact one enters it to search for one's heart's desire, leads one to consider that Stalker may be the Russian, adult version of The Wizard of Oz.

Right: The Stalker, the Scientist (Nikolai Grinko, with the hat), and the Writer (Anatoli Solonitsin) gaze though a sewer tunnel on their way to the central wishing room.

Below: Perhaps the key to the story is the Stalker's oldest daughter, a girl whose special talents are revealed at the end. As in The Wizard of Oz, one's heart's desire can be found right at home.

achieved the limitless wealth he desired, killed himself within weeks). The Writer, the Scientist, and the Stalker all have different, conflicting motives for seeking the Room: The Scientist wants to destroy it, to keep it from being reached by more evil destroyers; the Writer wants simply to observe and describe it (he is afraid that the achievement of his heart's desire will result in the ruin of his willingness to search for answers or create); and the Stalker himself is simply a medium; a guide. He is willing to lead people to the center; toward this sacred, apocalyptic temple—but he never attempts to use it to benefit himself. Always at the brink of Heart's Desire, he draws back and returns to his real world of misery and depredation.

The Search through the Zone lasts a good three hours of screen time. The movie begins as the Stalker himself awakes—in a powerful sequence full of huge intense monochrome close-ups; a sequence (in his house, with his family) resonant with despair, and dull, aching defeat. Gradually, as the characters meet, converse tersely, and as their movements begin to take on an almost drugged heaviness—a lethargy that is always impregnated with tension and anxiety—our sense of time begins to alter. Every incident is stretched out; Time itself seems to be idling toward stasis—and the movie begins to achieve an alternate world: a world so hypnotic and strange, that it seems (although the movie is shot mostly in a barren field, a railroad trestle, and in a variety of concrete buildings and, apparently, sewers) pregnant with some otherworldly "presence." The means in *Stalker* are so simple (compared with the lavish art direction in Lucas's space operas or, to give two better examples, Ridley Scott's *Alien* [1979] and *Blade Runner* [1982]) that the *intensity* of this world within the Zone comes as something of a shock. Very simply, this is a film that completely alters and reshapes your impressions as you watch it—film poetics of a very high order.

Both *Solaris and Stalker* are only superficially about *external* explorations: either on distant planets or in the danger-laden "Zone." Actually, of course, their gaze turns inward: they are about the spelunking of the individual soul. In each of them, Tarkovsky's methods—subtle, allusive, cryptic, and beautiful—stand out rather shockingly, not only from other science fiction films but, with a handful of exceptions, from most of the other films of our time. He is a genuine original, a director of almost frightening power and intensity—and, even more than that, of an unusual, and admirable spiritual and moral integrity. The clouds that boil off Solaris's sentient ocean, the bleak skies above the grayish-green fields of the Zone—they both disclose landscapes of the mind, regions of the soul, regions that inspire even as they terrify, exalt even as they mesmerize.

Ciel Reisner and I interviewed Tarkovsky during his brief visit to the United States in 1983. We found him to be a short man, slender, bearded at the time, and, as you might expect, extremely intense: an intellectual, an idealist, a man possessing both an assurance that borders on arrogance and a true spiritual humility. The following is excerpted from our discussion:

Question: What about the whole question of poetry in filmmaking—imparting personal images and feelings in a work intended for a mass audience?

Tarkovsky: All real film artists—or "auteurs"—are really poets. It's not enough just to direct a performance. The author of a film is really always a poet. Directors can be divided into two kinds. There are those who attempt to present the world that surrounds them—the real actual world that you see with your eyes. And then there are those who are concerned with presenting their *internal* selves.... These are the poets: Dovzhenko, of course; Bergman, Buñuel, Mizoguchi, Kurosawa, Vigo, Bresson. When they make films, they express themselves internally. No one else could make that particular film....

But you must understand that artists really never talk about themselves directly. No real artist does. Even when he *talks* about himself, he *doesn't* talk about himself—or he wouldn't be a great poet. A great poet, whether he's talking about himself, or talking about the community, is always talking about larger questions....

Q: You often deal—in *Andrei Rublev, The Mirror, Stalker,* and *Nostalghia*—with the problems of the artist in society. To what extent do you view these problems as local; and to what extent are they universal, or spiritual, problems?

Tarkovsky: I can't really say. All I can talk about is from my own world. I wish I *could* talk about the world in general, and its problems. I really only have this personal perception: a personal statement to make. The critic—you and others—must make the judgment as to whether this statement is in a purely local context, or whether it applies to other cultures, elsewhere.

Q: I think your films are very universal....

Tarkovsky: Of course, it's said that movies and the theater itself are international. *I don't really think so.* Art, in its best form, is a *national* form; you see that always. Even music, which is sort of international, has the same problem as film: people elsewhere perceive it quite differently than the composer's own contemporaries in his own world. Art can have a national meaning, and an international, or "transnational", meaning and context; they're not necessarily the same. An illustration of this is that American and Russian film versions of *Crime and Punishment* are totally different. If you read Faulkner, in translation, in Russian, he *is* different than when he is read in

English. I'm not trying to say whether a book is good or bad, but it's something that belongs in the possession of a given culture. Your own spiritual values belong to you, and you alone: to your own eye, your own self. Their only assessment can be from my *own* point of view. I can like, I can respect, your spiritual being—but I cannot receive it, and sense it, as you can. You simply cannot translate culture adequately; it is always perceived differently. It is *never* the same.

Q: Isn't that just a general problem among human beings: the difficulty of seeing through someone else's eyes?

Tarkovsky: Of course, that's the sad thing. . . . It's the meaning of our personality, our freedom of will.

Q: What do you feel, realistically, of the spiritual crisis of contemporary times . . . and art's role in ameliorating it?

Tarkovsky: Man's spiritual world and his physical world—the one that he creates—have been separating from each other, going in different directions, for a long time. And the problem is to bring them together. Here is an example: When—in a physical-scientific-technological sense—we achieve such a thing as atomic energy, what we use it for is to make weapons. What a disparity between our spiritual needs and our technical accomplishments!

Q: Could you talk about your collaboration with Stanislaw Lem on *Solaris*.

Tarkovsky: It was very *difficult* to work with him. He did not write the scenario, and, in fact, had nothing to do with it, but he rejected everything that was done to his book. He didn't like the film very much. He insisted: "You must follow each detail: exactly what was in the book." He did not understand that working that way, you don't get a movie.

Q: Are you disturbed, as Herman Melville was concerning his works, at the overly allegorical interpretations made of films like *Solaris* and *Stalker*?

Tarkovsky: I don't see the symbols others see in my films. I don't see the allegorical significance some people say is present. I reject such interpretations totally. A symbol, after all, has an elliptic significance. As soon as a viewer perceives the meaning of a symbol, he stops being interested in what's going on. What I'm interested in is not "symbols," but "images." An image has an *unlimited* number of possible interpretations . . . precisely as in Zen culture.

Q: It's interesting, following that line of thought, that most of your films are set in the past, or the future, and yet all of them have striking applications to the present. To a certain extent, it's a way of speaking indirectly. Or is it?

Tarkovsky: No artist can get away from himself, or from his times. No one can do an exact retrospective, or repetition, of the past. You just can't do it. Whether you're talking about the past, or about the future, the only thing you can *really* talk about is yourself. You cannot re-create the past, or create the future. Either way, the meaning of what you're talking about lies in yourself.

Q: Well, maybe I'm just sneaking up on this question. I'll ask it directly. Would there be any problem in applying your methods—which are very subtle, allusive, poetic and critical—to a story set in the contemporary Soviet Union? Is there an external or political reason for choosing subjects set in the distant past or future?

Tarkovsky: *The Mirror, Solaris, Stalker,* and *Nostalghia* were really all films about today. They're not "past," "present," or "future" films: I don't see a great deal of difference between the past and the future. I have not chosen the past or the future as a means for *invading* the problems of the present.

Q: What is your own personal search? What is your point of view?

Tarkovsky: We don't know what love is. Love is a gift . . . to you, and to the person who is giving it to you. And that is what we can't understand. We try to defend ourselves from life, protect ourselves, guard ourselves, and not to give anything. We want to be paid, somehow, for each spiritual movement that we make. We want to be thanked. We don't know what "selflessness" means. That's one of the problems: We don't know how to sacrifice. If our neighbor comes to us with his hand out . . . all we can think of is how to strike out, how to defend ourselves.

Q: What hope do you have then for humankind?

Tarkovsky: Hope lies within. The tragedy is that people are prevented from doing what they want. . . .

Andrei Tarkovsky, Russia's most famous director.

Directing
Alien and
Blade Runner

An Interview
with
Ridley Scott
by Danny Peary

Danny Peary: Prior to directing *Alien* [1979], had you a strong interest in science fiction?
Ridley Scott: I had virtually *no* interest in science fiction until I saw *Star Wars* in 1977, other than having been tremendously impressed by *2001* [1968]. Fantasies don't work unless they quickly take on a reality of their own, and the sci-fi films I'd seen always contained silly, utopian ideas or tended to take the more extraordinary dilemmas of the day and assume they'd develop in nonlogical, unbelievable ways. The people who made sci-fi films didn't understand what they were doing.

After the completion of my first film, *The Duellists* [1977], I prepared to do another period piece, "Tristan and Iseult." While this was in progress, I was in the United States and saw the opening of *Star Wars*. It impressed me so much! It was innovative, sensitive, courageous—I saw it on three consecutive days and it didn't diminish at all. I consider it to be a milestone film—one of the ten best I've ever seen. I was most struck by how Lucas took what is essentially a fairy tale and made it seem totally real. The combination of *2001*—a threshold film that presented science fiction as I thought it should—and *Star Wars*

convinced me that there was a great future in science fiction films (which may sound naive in hindsight). So I decided to terminate my development of "Tristan and Iseult."

Coincidentally, at that time I received the script of *Alien*. In my work on "Tristan and Iseult," I had used *Heavy Metal* magazine as a reference. While I was absorbing the sorcery side of that magazine, I also looked with great interest at its visions of the future. So when I read the *Alien* script, not only was I fascinated by the marvelous, strong, simple narrative, but also I realized that because of my brief education reading *Heavy Metal,* I knew how to do the film. I accepted *Alien* almost immediately.
DP: Was it essential for those involved in *Alien* to have scientific knowledge or at least insight into how a believable futuristic film should be made?
RS: When I came onto the project, there were already people involved who did have scientific knowledge. My first in-depth meetings about how sci-fi should be and how it should look were with Dan O'Bannon, who'd written the original screenplay with Ron Shusett. O'Bannon introduced me to Ron Cobb, a brilliant visualizer of the genre with whom he'd worked on *Dark Star* [1975]. Cobb seemed to have very realistic visions of both the far and near future, so I quickly decided that he would take a very important part in the making of the film. In fact, I brought both him and O'Bannon to England during the making of *Alien,* and he became a very important member of the art department [as a conceptual artist]. We based a lot of our interiors of the Nostromo on Cobb's visuals.
DP: You were a designer yourself. . . .
RS: I was a painter and then a designer in art school, which totaled a period of seven years' training. I eventually ended up at the BBC as a set designer. I was a set designer for a number of years, so whatever film I do, I always have great input into the decision on how the sets and the atmosphere will be. This also means that my selection of a production designer is a painstak-

Ridley Scott is the British director of *Alien, Blade Runner, The Duellists,* and *Legend.*

ing process. I consider myself a good designer, therefore I require an extremely good designer because I push him all the time. It's fairly easy to find a production designer who can cope with contemporary environments or period pieces for which there are paintings or photographs to use as visual references, but production designers who are "into" visualizing future environments are few and far between. I believe I have a good take on the future and it's vital for the production designer I choose—be he Michael Seymour on *Alien* or Lawrence G. Paull on *Blade Runner* [1982]—to be in total sympathy with what I'm doing.

DP: In *Alien,* everything *looks* old, uninviting, bleak, disheveled. What was the look you wanted for your major set, the starship Nostromo?

RS: The look really was meant to reflect the crew members who, I felt, should be like truck drivers in space. Their jobs, which took them on several-year journeys through space, were to them a normal state of affairs. Therein lies the fantasy. The reality would not be like this for maybe a thousand years—but in our tongue-in-cheek fantasy we project a not-too-distant future in which there are many vehicles tramping around the universe, on mining expeditions, erecting military installations, or whatever. At the culmination of many long voyages, each covering many years, these ships—no doubt part of armadas owned by private corporations—look used, beat-up, covered with graffiti, and uncomfortable. We certainly didn't design the Nostromo to look like a hotel.

DP: The characters in *Alien* seem more spirited than those in *Blade Runner.* But there is also a strong sense of melancholia, claustrophobia (which you've been quoted as saying frightens you most), and irritation. What personal views on space travel were you trying to get across? What about sex among crew members?—I know you cut out a sex scene involving Ripley [Sigourney Weaver] and Dallas [Tom Skerritt].

RS: I think the crew members of the Nostromo seem spirited only because of their argumentative nature, which is due to the fact they probably can no longer stand the sight of each other. It wouldn't matter how it was worked out in the prevoyage stage, when a computer probably determined the compatibility of the unit; like all crews in confined spaces, they'd get on one another's nerves and would be cutting each other's throats in six months' time. I tried to glean as much as I could from the problems that present-day astronauts go through preparing for prolonged periods in space. I then factored in ten years in space and tried to envision how a character would react to going off for that kind of period. Obviously it would raise all sorts of psychological problems, above and beyond claustrophobia and melancholia. The idea of spending *really* prolonged periods in space—say, of up to three years—is inconceivable and at the moment only exists in fantasies such as *Alien.*

We took out the scene where Dallas and Ripley discuss sexual "relief," because after the scene in which Kane [John Hurt] is killed when the alien bursts through him from the inside, it just seemed out of place. That scene proved much more powerful, *and* successful, than I expected, and for the sex to follow would have seemed totally gratuitous. The "relief" scene

Left: On the Nostromo in Alien *(1979): Captain Dallas (Tom Skerritt), second-in-command Ripley (Sigourney Weaver), and science officer Ash (Ian Holm), who turns out to be a robot. According to Ridley Scott, it is "because Ash is an unfeeling scientist, not that he is Nazilike," that he admires the alien's "purity."*

Right: Dallas, Kane (John Hurt), and Lambert (Veronica Cartwright) discover it was a long-dead space jockey that had sent the radio transmissions. Was he transmitting a warning?

was to be our token attempt to answer the question about sex in space. If you think about it logically, the only way that mixed crews could work out on long missions is by neutralizing everyone and forbidding sex entirely, or by having free "open sex" for whoever wants it. Close relationships in tightly closed ships with small crews would certainly have to be discouraged. The problems that would result from some men and women pairing off and leaving other crew members on their own is obvious.

DP: *Alien* is the first space film, I believe, that features working-class characters rather than a crew of scientists, military men, or astronauts.

RS: That's absolutely accurate. At this point in time, I believe everyone in a crew can be a working-type. The Nostromo is driven by Mother, a computer, and, as far as running the ship goes, the crew is secondary. Once on the ship, their function is minimal. They need know only how to work the ship's basic equipment. That equipment can start itself, repair itself, think for itself, and act as its own monitoring system.

DP: At this point in time, has the value of humans diminished even further than today as far as the military-industrial complex is concerned? I

am struck by the opening scene in which the ship's computers and machinery "come to life" before the humans are revived from their suspended-animation state.

RS: It's possible that the value of humans could have diminished. I'm now thinking on the level of the Big Brother idea of a lifeless megastructure and its attitude toward human employees, who are considered expendable. In this instance, the machinery, information data, and cargo are of more importance to corporations than the individuals on their ships. I certainly think this situation has parallels today. But the fact that computers can run the ship before the humans are revived is meant to be logical and not, as you suggest, antihuman—it really has nothing to do with Big Brother and an unfeeling company. Ships will be run by computers specifically for efficiency reasons.

DP: I see the corporation, even more than the alien, as being the villain of the film. Its top priority becomes the alien, and it could care less about the danger that this causes its crew.

RS: The industrial-government complex is responsible for the attitude that allows such an alien to be brought on board the Nostromo. In fact, it is already responsible for the paranoia prevalent on all the ships because of its insistence on placing a company man on each vehicle. In this case, he takes the form of a robot, Ash [Ian Holm]. This would seem to be the normal development of a huge corporation trying to protect its interests. In this particular future, it would be very easy for "pirating" to exist. Corporations will have to find ways to assure that vehicles carrying minerals or vital information will not be hijacked.

DP: Was it the intention of the corporation that owns the Nostromo to bring back an alien, any alien? And for what reason?

RS: I think any corporation that sends probes into unknown territory is going to think of the possibility of finding something *new*. I'm sure that the crew members on all its ships would have been briefed to bring back anything of interest. It would be part of one's job to bring it back. An alien would, of course, be of top priority. This particular corporation didn't have a preconceived notion that an alien would be found on this mission, much less the particular alien that is brought onto the ship. The idea of bringing it back alive would not have been on the minds of the corporation executives when they first received the alien transmission. They just had high expectations when they ordered the Nostromo to investigate—it was purely out of curiosity.

DP: Yet the film seems to express a "topical" theme: For selfish reasons, our leaders in government and business will side with "aliens" who have no regard for humanity, at the expense of the people who trust them.

RS: Although I didn't set out to make such a statement, the parallels on both a political and company level are quite obvious.

DP: What is the nature of the alien? Is it vulnerable? Does it fear anything? Is it interested in the crew members for any reason other than food? Is it male or female?

RS: In relation to humans, the alien does seem to be indestructible. It does *not* fear anything. In fact, it is a supreme being. The kind of creature we came up with emerged from the logic of how it could reproduce itself and, in fact, what its development or life cycle would be: Therefore, I guess, the alien is a hermaphrodite.

DP: In the film, Dallas seems to be killed instantly, but originally there was a shot of him trapped in the alien's cocoon....

RS: That was simply a visualization of the alien's life cycle. What gave us the cocoon concept was that insects will utilize others' bodies to be the hosts of their eggs. That's how the alien would use Dallas and each of the crew members it kills. This explains why the alien doesn't kill everybody at once, but rather kills them off one by one: It wants to use each person as a separate host each time it has new eggs.

COPYRIGHT© TWENTIETH CENTURY FOX FILM CORP.

DP: Would the alien have killed Ash?

RS: Probably not. We theorized that the alien would feel or understand that Ash was a construction of robotics, however complex and strange. Because Ash wasn't human, he'd have been no use as a host for its eggs. The biological makeup of humans was useful, however, for the alien eggs to feed on—a revolting explanation!

DP: The alien is obviously intelligent and crafty. Does it sneak into the shuttle at the film's end because it knows the main ship is about to blow up, because it expects Ripley to go there, or...

RS: ...because we needed an end to the picture....

DP: Sigourney Weaver told me that she believed the alien looked at Ripley in the final scene with curiosity and perhaps sexual interest.

RS: I never thought about it that way. I find that her comment is... certainly odd. Perhaps Sigourney has a touch of sympathy for the creature because she looks at it from the viewpoint of her character. Ripley was part crew member and part scientist, someone who thought in logical terms. Maybe at that moment her scientist side emerged and she began to study the creature like a scientist would and started to get a perspective on what it may have been thinking. Previous to this scene, remember, there had been absolutely no communication between the alien and the crew members, other than the violent experiences.

DP: Ripley is one of the bravest, smartest, toughest women in science fiction. Veronica Cartwright's Lambert character is also quite

Left: One of the screen's scariest moments: Kane (with all the forethought of an Inspector Clouseau) bends over to peer into a quivering pod he discovers in the hatchery on the space jockey's derelict ship.

Right: Parker (Yaphet Kotto) and Lambert hope to flee the Nostromo in the shuttle. But the alien will prevent it.

strong and capable. Are these two women such strong characters because today's audience demands such women in scripts or because that's how you expect women will be in the future?

RS: My film has strong women simply because I like strong women. It's a personal choice. I'm in no way a male chauvinist, nor do I understand female chauvinsim—I just believe in the equalilty of men and women. It's as simple as that.

DP: Because the alien was not killed in *Alien,* but was merely blown into space, there may some day be a sequel. What should it be about?

RS: It certainly should explain what the alien is and where it comes from. That will be tough because it will require dealing with other planets, worlds, civilizations. Because obviously the alien did come from some sort of civilization. The alien was presented, really, as one of the last survivors of Mars—a planet named after the god of war. The alien may be one of the last descendants of some long-lost self-destructed group of beings.

DP: In *Alien,* you built suspense by having characters talking in hushed tones, smoking incessantly, drinking coffee, pacing nervously, sweating . . . . In *Blade Runner,* you emphasize characters' eyes to create tension, paranoia, mystery. Did you learn how to effectively manipulate an audience back when you made commercials?

RS: My training in commercials was really my film school. It helped build my awareness of how to present suspense and—"manipulate" is a bad word—*fascinate* the audience and hold it in

a kind of dramatic suspension. I learned how to communicate immediately, to use every conceivable visual and aural device to work on the senses and grab the viewer's attention for a particular time-span.

The emphasis I placed on characters' eyes in *Blade Runner* was just my playing games with the audience. Obviously if every replicant in the film had glowing eyes, then there would have been no need for the Voight-Kampff machine to detect them. We went through a little tap-dance argument as to whether or not I should present something different about their eyes. I decided to take a middle line on this, to be deliberately intriguing and confusing rather than specific. So it varies throughout.

DP: In *Blade Runner,* the head of an enormous business conglomerate, Tyrell [Joe Turkel], is also the man responsible for the replicants' existence. Does he represent *science* to you? If so, do you believe this direction science is taking—its becoming part of private enterprise—is scary?

RS: Tyrell represents the ultimate in science and industry, or scientific-industrial development. Here you see a large corporation that specializes in one area buying up another corporation that does something in an entirely different field. Obviously two separate sides of the conglomerate world—perhaps genetic engineering and biochemistry—will eventually merge; just as I think industries will develop their own independent space programs. It's bound to happen and, yes, it is scary.

AN INTERVIEW WITH RIDLEY SCOTT BY DANNY PEARY **297**

DP: How does your vision of the future compare to what you present in *Blade Runner*?

RS: Much of what I envisage for the year 2019 is reflected in the look of the streets and the attitudes of the people in *Blade Runner*. The viewpoint speaks for itself. I thought about it very carefully. I presented a future world that I believe would come close to being a totalitarian society—if not quite 1984, then one step from it. It *is* 1984, in the sense that the world is controlled by perhaps only four major corporations, of which the Tyrell Corporation is one, and the people exist in what is almost a Kafkaesque or Orwellian environment. To cope with the anarchy in the streets there is a sort of a paramilitary-police group, by which Deckard [Harrison Ford] is employed as a replicant exterminator. It's a world where the poor get poorer, and the wealthy get wealthier and think it chic to protect themselves even more than they do in America today. Even Deckard lives in a condominium with electric gates. It looks rather like a fortress and one only gets access to his floor by undergoing a voice-pattern check-out system in the elevator—otherwise it won't move. It's a time of self-protection and of paranoia.

DP: In the city of Philip K. Dick's novel *Do Androids Dream of Electric Sheep?*, on which *Blade Runner* is based, there are no murders, no abortions. . . .

RS: In the city of the film, I imagine everything would be done, from abortions to murders. In a city where only the wealthy can afford to protect themselves, and there is chaos on the streets, surely anything goes.

DP: The *look* of the city in *Blade Runner* is spectacular. Discuss your work with Syd Mead, the film's conceptual designer, specifically on the architecture.

In Blade Runner *(1982), detective Rick Deckard chases replicant Zhora through the crowded, cluttered streets of downtown L.A. in 2019. "I wanted this to be a curious world where people would have the choice of staying or leaving. If you went off-Earth you were rewarded, but obviously people like Deckard didn't want to leave their familiar home environment."—R.S.*

RS: *Blade Runner* was a difficult project to conceive because it is set only about thirty-five years from now, in a "tangible" future rather than in the obscure future of *Alien*. It was essential not to go wrong or everyone would realize it. So it made sense to ask an industrial designer who is also a futurist, like Syd Mead, to design the film's hardware. We worked very closely on the vehicles and he proved so prolific that I had him branch out and help us envision what would happen architecturally to existing cities.

I think that the mistake a lot of futuristic films make when they attempt short leaps forward in time is that they devastate whole cities and erect hokey-looking utopias. Things wouldn't work that way. Look at New York or Chicago. They have their business centers, middle-class areas, ghettoes, and central areas of development. One wouldn't possibly flatten it all. In today's cities there is already the practice of taking existing architecture and making applications to the outside of buildings—for example, because of cost factors, it's preferable to apply an air-conditioning or communication system to the outside than to rip the whole building apart to make it function. We took that line of thought further: As we move farther and farther into the future, the probability is that the construction of new buildings will diminish, except in certain areas of the city, and the constant repairing, shoring up, and modernization of older architecture will begin to take on a rather retrofitted look.

Our vision was really of a clogged world, where you get the sense of a city on overload, where things may stop at any time. Services may give out—in fact, they already have ceased in at least some parts of the city. Everything is old or badly serviced, and the bureaucratic system running the city is totally disorganized. One of the few things in fine order is advertising. I expect that by this time, billboards and electric signs will be everywhere. There will be an even bigger media explosion than there is today.

DP: One of the most intriguing features of your city is the constant rain and haze. I get the feeling that everything is contaminated and everyone will soon die from radiation poisoning. Has World War III occurred? Judging by all the Orientals in the streets, could China have defeated America?

RS: I think the Cold War is still going on. If there had been a third world war, the world would not have been in the state we presented it—it wouldn't exist. Again, we were working in the context of a fantasy, so I don't necessarily believe there will be a future in which the air is *so* contaminated—at least I hope that at some point we'll actually do something about the way things have been going. The idea of a world filled with radiation is abhorrent. It was only presented that way as a dramatic device. The constant rain was "dramatic glue," if you like. It also amused me to think that it was taking place in Los Angeles, meaning the whole weather pattern would have changed by 2019. If L.A. gets all the rain, then maybe New York would get the sunshine.

DP: You switched the book's setting of San Francisco to Los Angeles.

RS: Originally we were going to begin the film with a title that read "San Angeles." Our idea was that San Francisco and Los Angeles would become one city and cover the entire western seaboard.

DP: What does your city smell like?

RS: New York City.

DP: Is there religion in this world?

RS: That's something I never really came to terms with. That is difficult to speculate about. But it may be stronger than it is today, when it seems to be on the wane in certain areas. Maybe the governments will have become the religions—then you've gone one step closer to 1984.

DP: In the novel Rachael and Pris look exactly alike—they are the same model of replicant. Why did you have two actresses—Sean Young, a brunette, and Daryl Hannah, a blond—play the two roles? And why was Rachael's last name changed from Rosen to Tyrell?

RS: It would have been confusing and not

Replicant Roy Batty (Rutger Hauer)—until the end, the picture's villain—has come to Earth to see if his brief life span can be increased. If not, he'll kill his creator, Tyrell.

worked dramatically to have had Rachael and Pris played by the same actress. The name change was just a matter of us preferring Tyrell.

DP: Dick died before the release of the film. Did you have a chance to meet him?

RS: Only once. I showed him the special effects I'd just completed with Doug Trumbull's EEG [Entertainment Effects Group]. He was more than delighted—I think he was stunned by the look of our environment: He said it was exactly how he had envisioned the world with which we were dealing.

DP: Except for the fact that he tracks down renegade replicants rather than standard criminals, our hero Deckard is in many ways like the classic disillusioned, morally ambivalent detective—which is fitting considering the other noir elements found in the film, including his hard-edged narration.

RS: When we first meet Deckard, he is already thinking of giving up his job as professional exterminator. The job was in fact getting to him, as it did to, say, Philip Marlowe. His attitude toward his profession had already discolored his vision of the world and affected his attitude toward himself. As in classic detective stories, his background is not central to the film and is suggested by innuendo rather than fact; but what I wanted to do at the beginning was show a man who wanted to change his whole way of life and was in a way trying to find some kind of absolution or, maybe, a conscience.

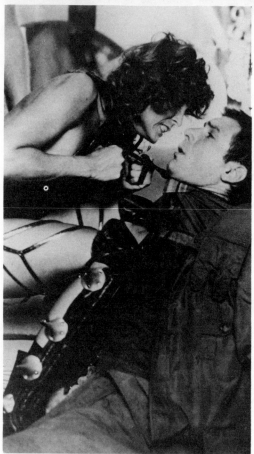

Above: Ridley Scott works with Joanna Cassidy, who plays Zhora, and Harrison Ford, whose blade runner character is on her trail. Left: In the scene as filmed, Zhora proves to have more physical strength than Deckard.

DP: Deckard's romantic involvement with a replicant, Rachael, humanizes him to a certain degree—at least it causes him to release some of his pent-up "human" emotions and gives his personal life meaning. On the other hand, do you see his line of work, killing replicants, as being dehumanizing?

RS: I think Deckard is simply doing a job within his futuristic time slot. Therefore he should be unemotional about his work. I don't really believe that the nature of his job must necessarily dehumanize him. What he does is act as a garbage disposal—it's rather like getting rid of industrial waste. Certainly because the replicants are highly sophisticated machines one starts to relate to them as human beings. But one must remember that they are *not* human beings.

DP: But when Deckard murders replicant Zhora [Joanna Cassidy], by shooting her in the back, you certainly intended viewers to not only find his brutal method devastating but also cowardly and upsetting.

RS: The audience reaction to Zhora's death is how you describe it. Of course, one was meant to feel sympathy and possible sadness for some of the replicants. But I must remind you that Deckard is just doing his job and following

through on what he set out to do. Zhora could have come quietly but she decided she had to have freedom and she ran. So he did what he was there to do. The scene ends with Deckard looking down at this "woman" he has just killed and we get one more facet of the reason he wants to quit his profession. For we're now dealing with a man who is guilt-ridden.

DP: How do you see the relationships between the replicants? I find them to be a bit schizophrenic. Sometimes they're loyal to one another. When Batty [Rutger Hauer] kisses the dead Pris, it indicates he loved her. Yet Rachael kills the replicant Leon [Brion James] in order to save Deckard, a human.

RS: To me, the way replicants relate to each other and to humans is one of the points of the story. Batty kisses Pris with affection and love. It demonstrates that even replicants can have those kinds of feelings. If you create a machine through genetic engineering, biochemistry, or whatever, the very fact that it has been created by a human being indicates to me that when it becomes truly sophisticated it will ultimately be free-thinking. I'm sure that in the near future, computers will start to think for themselves and develop at least a limited set of emotions, and make their own decisions. The same goes for the replicant that is so sophisticated that it's on par with the human being—in fact, in some ways it may even be superior. The replicants

Deckard tracks Batty through an abandoned building. White pigeons, the only animals shown in the film, fly about—"symbols of peace and life," according to director Scott.

that Tyrell designed were the first of his "master race," which he planned to unleash to develop his interests on other planets, but within the context of this film, the replicants are more "human" than humans *or* "more equal" than humans. They are superior—they make their own choices.

DP: Aside from Rachael falling in love with Deckard, how do replicants feel toward human beings? With pity? With hatred?

RS: Certainly not with pity. The replicants would regard their human creators very much as a slave would a master he despises. Also I think they'd fear humans. And in some ways they'd empathize or want to identify with them.

DP: The female replicants, at least, are capable of having sex. Do you think they have the capabilities of enjoying sex and actually having orgasms?

RS: I never went into this in much detail, either. But I guess that if Tyrell went to the trouble of making *perfect* replicants, then he'd have taken into account their sexual capabilities. For obvious reasons. Maybe some female replicants like Pris were employed in military camps on space

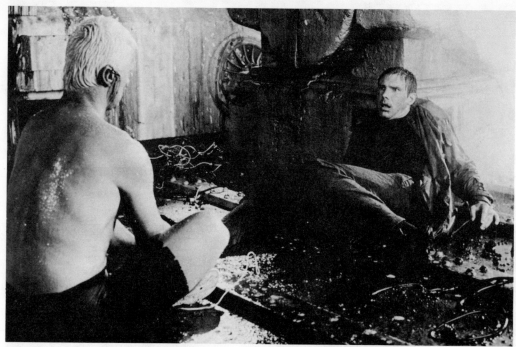

The dying Batty allows Deckard to live. This is the ultimate peaceful gesture in sf cinema between man and machine. It gives us hope that we can live in harmony.

bases and were constructed for specific sexual purposes.... That's a very fascistic viewpoint, a very sick one, and I don't really like discussing it.

DP: Deckard finds himself sexually attracted to Rachael. Was it your intention to have male viewers find themselves attracted to the three female replicants in order to further diminish the distinction between humans and androids?

RS: No. I just happened to cast three actresses who are rather beautiful. Anyway, if you're going to make female replicants, why would you want them to be ugly?

DP: Comment on the climactic scene in which Batty saves Deckard. Batty's own death (with slow-motion employed) is quite stirring and dignified.

RS: Batty's death scene is in a way the final demonstration of his superiority over Deckard and the replicants' superiority over human beings. He could have taken Deckard's life—Deckard had just killed Pris—but decided as a gift to let him live. The white pigeon that he sets into the sky is, of course, a symbol of peace and life.

DP: In the novel, Deckard constantly worries he will mistakenly kill a human he thinks is a replicant. In fact, he constantly worries that he, himself, is a replicant.

RS: At one stage, we considered having Deckard turn out to be, ironically, a replicant. In fact, if you look at the film closely, especially the ending, you may get some clues—some by slight innuendo—that Deckard is indeed a replicant. At the end there's a kind of confirmation that he is—at least that he believes it possible. Within the context of the overall story, whether it's true

or not in the book, having Deckard be a replicant is the *only* reasonable solution.

DP: I see this film as possibly being about several endangered species, namely the human beings who roam the contaminated world, animals which, except for the pigeons, are no longer part of this world, and replicants, who have only a brief life span.

RS: I don't see the film as being this serious. I make films to entertain and this was really meant to be a "heavy metal" comic strip about a future society and a character who just happens to be a replicant detective. I don't think the film is about several types of endangered species. It's a film about some goodies and some baddies. The baddies are presented as replicants who, we discover eventually, are like all good antiheroes in that they have sympathetic streaks. At this point the balance of the drama changes—but this film does not have any deep messages.

DP: Yet wouldn't you consider *Blade Runner* to be cautionary?

RS: It doesn't say "watch out for this!" or "watch out for that!" It simply presents the kind of world I see in 2019. However, if you do take it seriously, then there are cautionary notes in regard to future environments and the way people relate to one another in them. Admittedly, the vision in *Blade Runner* isn't very promising, but unless we do something drastic to change the flow of things I don't think the world will be a very pleasant place in the future.

Checklist
of Futuristic Films

☐ *Abbott and Costello Go to Mars* (1953) d: Charles Lamont
☐ *Absent-Minded Professor, The* (1961) d: Robert Stevenson
☐ *Aëlita/Revolt of the Robots, The* (1924–Russian) d: Yakov Protazanov
☐ *Aerial Anarchists, The* (1911–British) D: Walter Booth
☐ *Aerial Submarine, The* (1910) d: Walter Booth
☐ *Airplane II: The Sequel* (1982) d: Ken Finkleman
☐ *Airship/100 Years Hence* (1908) d: J. Stuart Blackton
☐ *Airship Destroyer, The* (1909–British) d: Walter Booth
☐ *Algol* (1920–German) d: Hans Werkmeister
☐ *Alien* (1979) d: Ridley Scott w: Dan O'Bannon
☐ *Alien Contamination* (1981–Italian) d: Lewis Coates
☐ *Alpha Incident, The* (1977) d: Bill Rebane
☐ *Alphaville* (1965–French) d: Jean-Luc Godard
☐ *Alruane* (1918–Hungarian) d: Michael Curtiz
☐ *Alruane* (1918–German)
☐ *Alruane/Unholy Love* (1928–German) d: Henrik Galeen
☐ *Alruane/Daughter of Evil* (1930–German) d: Richard Oswald
☐ *Alruane/Unnatural* (1952–German) d: Arthur Maria Rabenalt
☐ *Amazing Dr. G, The* (1965–Italian-Spanish) d: G. Simonelli
☐ *Amazing Transplant, The* (1971) d: Louis Silverman
☐ *Americathon* (1979) d: Neil Israel
☐ *Android* (1982) d: Aaron Lipstadt
☐ *Andromeda Strain, The* (1971) d: Robert Wise
☐ *Andy Warhol's Frankenstein* (1974–Italian-German-French) d: Paul Morrissey
☐ *Angel of H.E.A.T.* (1982) d: Myril A. Schreibman
☐ *Animated Doll, The* (1908)
☐ *Anna to the Infinite Power* (1982) d: Robert Wiemer
☐ *Apple, The* (1980) d: Menahem Golan
☐ *April 1, 2000* (1953–Austrian) d: Wolfgang Libeneiner
☐ *Are We Civilized?* (1934) d: George Carewe
☐ *Around the World Under the Sea* (1966) d: Andrew Marton
☐ *Assignment Outer Space/Spacemen* (1962–German) d: Antonio Margheriti
☐ *Astro-Zombies, The* (1969) d: Ted V. Mikels
☐ *At the Edge of the World* (1927–German) d: Karl Grune
☐ *Atomic Brain, The/Monstrosity* (1963) d: Joseph V. Mascelli
☐ *Atomic Kid, The* (1954) d: Leslie Martinson
☐ *Atomic War Bride* (1966)
☐ *Attack of the Robots* (1962–French-Spanish) d: Jesus Franco
☐ *Automatic Monkey, The* (1909–French-British)
☐ *Automatic Motorist, The* (1911–British) d: Walter Booth
☐ *Automatic Servant, The* (1908–British) d: Walter Booth

☐ *Barbarella* (1968–French-Italian) d: Roger Vadim
☐ *Battle Beneath the Earth* (1968) d: Montgomery Tully
☐ *Battle Beyond the Stars* (1980) d: Jimmy T. Murakami w: John Sayles
☐ *Battle Beyond the Sun* (1963) d: Thomas Colchart
☐ *Battle for the Planet of the Apes* (1973) d: J. Lee Thompson
☐ *Battle in Outer Space* (1960–Japanese) d: Inoshiro Honda
☐ *Battle of the Worlds* (1960–Italian) d: Anthony Dawson
☐ *Bed Sitting Room, The* (1969–British) d: Richard Lester
☐ *Bedford Incident, The* (1965) d: James B. Harris

☐ *Beneath the Planet of the Apes* (1970) d: Ted Post
☐ *Beyond the Time Barrier* (1960) d: Edgar G. Ulmer
☐ *Black Box, The* (1915; serial)
☐ *Black Friday* (1940) d: Arthur Lubin
☐ *Blackenstein* (1972) d: William A. Levy
☐ *Blade Runner* (1982) d: Ridley Scott
☐ *Boogie Man Will Get You, The* (1942) d: Lew Landers
☐ *Born in Flames* (1983) d: Lizzie Borden
☐ *Boy and His Dog, A* (1975) d: L.Q. Jones
☐ *Boys from Brazil, The* (1978) d: Franklin Schaffner
☐ *Brain, The* (1965–German-British) d: Freddie Francis
☐ *Brain of Blood* (1971) d: Al Adamson
☐ *Brain Machine, The* (1956–British) d: Ken Hughes
☐ *Brain That Wouldn't Die, The* (1963) d: Jason Evers
☐ *Brain Waves* (1982) d: Ulli Lommell
☐ *Brainstorm* (1983) d: Douglas Trumbull
☐ *Bride, The* (1985) d: Franc Roddam
☐ *Bride of Frankenstein* (1935) d: James Whale
☐ *Bride of the Monster* (1956) d: Edward D. Wood, Jr.
☐ *Britannia Hospital* (1983–British) d: Lindsay Anderson
☐ *Buck Rogers (serial)/Destination Moon* (feature) (1939) d: Ford Beebe
☐ *Buck Rogers in the 25th Century* (1979) d: Daniel Haller

☐ *Cafe Flesh* (1982) d: Rinse Dream w: Dream and Herbert W. Day (Jerry Stahl)
☐ *Captain America* (1944; serial) d: John English and Elmer Clifton
☐ *Captain Nemo and the Underwater City* (1969) d: James Hill
☐ *Captain Video* (1951; serial) d: Spencer Gordon Bennet and Wallace A. Grissell
☐ *Captive Women/1,000 Years from Now* (1952) d: Stuart Gilmore
☐ *Casino Royale* (1967–British) d: John Huston, Ken Hughes, Robert Parrish, Joe McGrath, and Val Guest
☐ *Castle of Evil* (1966) d: Francis D. Lyon
☐ *Cat Women of the Moon* (1954) d: Arthur Hilton
☐ *Chairman, The/Most Dangerous Man in the World, The* (1969) d: J. Lee Thompson
☐ *Change of Mind* (1969) d: Robert Stevens
☐ *Charly* (1968) d: Ralph Nelson
☐ *Chess Player, The* (1927–French) d: Raymond Bernard
☐ *Chitty Chitty Bang Bang* (1968) d: Ken Hughes
☐ *Chosen Survivors* (1974) d: Sutton Roley
☐ *City Limits* (1984) d: Aaron Lipstadt
☐ *Clockwork Orange, A* (1971–British) d: Stanley Kubrick
☐ *Clones, The* (1973) d: Paul Hunt and Lamar Card
☐ *Clown and the Automation, The* (1897–French) d; Georges Méliès
☐ *Code of the Air* (1928) d: James P. Hogan
☐ *Colossus of New York, The* (1958) d: Eugene Lourie
☐ *Colossus: The Forbin Project/Forbin Project, The* (1970) d: Joseph Sargent
☐ *Coma* (1978) d: Michael Crichton
☐ *Computer Wore Tennis Shoes, The* (1970) d: Robert Butler
☐ *Conquest of Space* (1955) d: Byron Haskin

- Conquest of the Planet of the Apes (1972) d: J. Lee Thompson
- Coppelia (1912–Danish)
- Cosmos—War of the Planets (1978)
- Countdown (1968) d: Robert Altman
- Counterblast (1948–British) d: Paul L. Stein
- Crack in the World (1965) d: Andrew Marton
- Creation of the Humanoids (1962) d: Wesley E. Barry
- Creature Wasn't Nice, The (1981) d: Bruce Kimmel
- Creature with the Atom Brain (1955) d: Edward L. Cahn
- Crimes of the Future (1970–Canadian) d: David Cronenberg
- Curious Female, The (1969) d: Paul Rapp
- Curse of Frankenstein, The (1957–British) d: Terence Fisher
- Cyborg 2087 (1966) d: Frank Adreon
- Cyborg 009—Legend of Super Galaxy (1981–Japanese) d: Masayuki Akehi and Yasuhiro Yamaguchi
- Cyclotrode "X" (1946, serial) d: William Witney and Fred C. Bannon
- Daleks—Invasion Earth 2150 A.D. (1966–British) d: Gordon Flemyng
- Damnation Alley (1977) d: Jack Smight
- Damned, The/These Are the Damned (1962–British) d: Joseph Losey
- Dancing Doll, The (1915)
- Dark Star (1975) d: John Carpenter w: Carpenter and Dan O'Bannon
- Day After, The (1983-TVM; 1984 theatrical release in Europe) d: Nicholas Meyer
- Day the Earth Caught Fire, The (1962–British) d: Val Guest
- Day the Fish Came Out, The (1967–Greek) d: Michael Cacoyannis
- Day the Sky Exploded, The (1958–German) Paolo Heusch
- Day the World Ended, The (1955) d: Roger Corman
- Dead Man's Eyes (1944) d: Reginald LeBorg
- Death Race 2000 (1975) d: Paul Bartel
- Death Ray, The (1924–Russian) d: Lev Kuleshov
- Death Watch (1980–French) d: Bertrand Tavernier
- Deathsport (1978) d: Henry Suso
- Deluge (1933) d: Felix E. Feist
- Demon Seed (1977) d: Donald Cammell
- Der Tunnel (1933–German) d: Curtis Bernhardt
- Destination Moon (1950) d: Irving Pichel
- Diamonds Are Forever (1971–British) d: Guy Hamilton
- Doctor Blood's Coffin (1961–British) d: Sidney J. Furie
- Dr. Coppellius (1966–Spanish) d: Ted Kneeland
- Dr. Frankenstein on Campus (1970–Canadian) d: Gil Taylor
- Dr. Goldfoot and the Bikini Machines (1965) d: Norman Taurog
- Dr. Goldfoot and the Girl Bombs (1966–Italian-American) d: Mario Bava
- Dr. No (1963) d: Terence Young
- Doctor of Doom (1962–Mexican) d: Rene Cardona
- Dr. Strangelove Or: How I Learned to Stop Worrying and Love the Bomb (1964–British) d: Stanley Kubrick
- Dr. Who and the Daleks (1965–British) d: Gordon Flemying
- Dr. X (1932) d: Michael Curtiz
- Dog, A Mouse and a Sputnik, A/Sputnik (1958–French) d: Jean Dreville
- Doll's Revenge, The (1911–Great Britain) d: Percy Stow
- Doomsday Machine, The (1972) d: Lee Sholem
- Doomwatch (1972–British) d: Peter Sasdy
- Dreamscape (1984) d: Joe Rubin
- Earthquake (1974) d: Mark Robson
- Egghead's Robot (1970) d: Milo Lewis
- Electric Dreams (1984) d: Steve Barron
- Electric Servant, The (1909–British) d: Walter Booth
- Electric Doll, The (1914–British) d: Edwin J. Collins
- Electronic Monster, The/Escapement (1958–British) d: Montgomery Tully
- Embryo (1976) d: Ralph Nelson
- End of August at the Hotel Ozone (1965–Czech) d: Jan Schmidt
- End of the World, The (1916–Danish) d: August Blom
- Endgame (1984) d: Steven Benson
- Enemy Mine (1985) d: Wolfgang Petersen
- Eraserhead (1978) d: David Lynch
- Escape from New York (1981) d: John Carpenter
- Escape 2000 (1983–Australian) d: Brian Trenchard-Smith
- Evil of Frankenstein (1964–British) d: Freddie Francis
- Exterminators, The (1965–French-Italian) d: Riccardo Freda
- F.P.I. Does Not Answer (1932–German) d: Karl Hartl
- Fabulous World of Jules Verne, The (1961–Czech) d: Karel Zeman
- Fahrenheit 451 (1966–British) d: François Truffaut
- Fail-Safe (1964) d: Sidney Lumet
- Falling, The (1984) d: Deran Sarafian
- Fantastic Voyage (1966) d: Richard Fleischer
- Fearless Frank (1967) d: Philip Kaufman
- Final War, The (1960–Japanese)
- Fire of Life, The (1912–Danish) d: Schedler Sorenson
- Firefox (1982) d: Clint Eastwood
- Fire-Maidens of Outer Space (1955–British) d: Cy Roth
- First Man into Space (1959–British) d: Robert Day
- First Men in the Moon (1919–British) d: J.V. Leigh
- First Men "in" the Moon (1964–British) d: Nathan Juran
- First Spaceship on Venus (1962–German-Polish) d: Kurt Maetzig
- Five (1951) d: Arch Oboler
- Flash Gordon (serial)/Spaceship to the Unknown (feature edited from serial's first half) and Perils from the Planet Mongo (feature edited from serial's second half) (1936) d: Frederick Stephani
- Flash Gordon (1980) d: Mike Hodges
- Flash Gordon Conquers the Universe (serial)/Purple Death from Outer Space (feature) (1940) d: Ford Beebe and Ray Taylor
- Flash Gordon's Trip to Mars (serial)/Deadly Ray from Mars (feature) (1938) d: Ford Beebe and Robert Hill
- Flesh Gordon (1974) d: Howard Ziehm and Michael Benveniste
- Flight That Disappeared, The (1961) d: Reginald LeBorg
- Flight to Mars (1951) d: Lesley Salander
- Flying Saucers, The (1955–Mexican) d: Julian Soler
- Flying Torpedo, The (1916)
- For Your Eyes Only (1981–British) d: John Glen
- Forbidden Planet (1956) d: Fred McLeod Wilcox
- Forbidden World/Mutant (1982) d: Alan Holtzman
- Four-Sided Triangle, The (1953–British) d: Terence Fisher
- Frankenstein (1910) d: J. Searle Dawley
- Frankenstein (1931) d: James Whale
- Frankenstein and the Monster from Green Hell (1974–British) d: Terence Fisher
- Frankenstein Must Be Destroyed (1969–British) d: Terence Fisher
- Frankenstein—1970 (1958) d: Howard W. Koch
- Frankenstein's Daughter (1959) d: Richard Cunha
- From a View to a Kill (1985–British) d: John Glen
- From Russia with Love (1963–British) d: Terence Young
- From the Earth to the Moon (1958) d: Byron Haskin
- Future War 198X (1983–Japanese) d: Tomoharu Katsumata and Toshio Masuda
- Futureworld (1976) d: Richard T. Heffron
- Galaxina (1980) d: William Sachs
- Galaxy Express (1979–Japanese) d: Taro Rin
- Galaxy of Terror (1981) d: B. D. Clark
- Gas-s-s-s (1970) d: Roger Corman
- Girl of Tin, The (1970–Italian) d: Marcello Aliprandi
- Give Us the Moon (1944–British) d: Val Guest
- Gladiators, The/Peace Game, The (1970–Swedish) d: Peter Watkins
- Glen and Randa (1971) d: Jim McBride
- Gog (1954) d: Herbert L. Strock
- Goldengirl (1979) d: Joseph Sargent
- Goldfinger (1964–British) d: Guy Hamilton
- Greatest Power, The (1971) d: Edwin Carewe
- Green Slime, The (1969–Japanese-American) d: Kenji Fukasaku
- Green Terror, The (1919–British) d: Will P. Kelling
- Gulliver's Travels Beyond the Moon (1966–Japanese) d: Yoshio Kuroda
- Halloween III: Season of the Witch (1982) d: Tommy Lee Wallace
- Hands of a Stranger (1962) d: Newton Arnold

☐ *Hands of Orlac, The* (1925–Austrian) d: Robert Weine
☐ *Hands of Orlac, The* (1960–British-French) d: Edmond T. Greville
☐ *Have Rocket, Will Travel* (1959) d: David Lowell Rich
☐ *Heartbeeps* (1981) d: Allen Arkush
☐ *Heaven Ship* (1917–Danish) d: Forest Holger-Madsen
☐ *Heavy Metal* (1981–Canadian; segments) d: Gerald Potterton
☐ *High Treason* (1929–British) d: Maurice Elvey
☐ *Homunculus/Homunculus der Führer* (1915–German; serial) d: Otto Rippert
☐ *Horror Hospital* (1973–British) d: Anthony Balch
☐ *Horror of Frankenstein, The* (1970–British) d: Jimmy Sangster
☐ *How They Work in Cinema* (1911–French)
☐ *How to Make a Doll* (1967) d: Herschell Gordon Lewis
☐ *Hu-Man, The* (1976–French) d: Jerome Laperrousaz

☐ *I Eat Your Skin/Voodoo Blood Bath* (1964) d: Del Tenney
☐ *I Love You, I Kill You* (1972–German)
☐ *I Was A Teenage Frankenstein* (1957) d: Herbert Strock
☐ *Illustrated Man, The* (1969; segments) d: Jack Smight
☐ *Impossible Voyage, The (An)* (1904–French) d: Georges Méliès
☐ *In Like Flint* (1967) d: Gordon Douglas
☐ *In the Year 2889* (1965) d: Larry Buchanan
☐ *In the Year 2000* (1912) d: Alice Guy-Blaché
☐ *In the Year 2014* (1914)
☐ *Incredible Melting Man, The* (1978) d: William Sachs
☐ *Inseminoid/Horror Planet* (1981–British) d: Norman J. Warren
☐ *Invasion U.S.A.* (1952) d: Alfred E. Green
☐ *Inventor Crazybrains and His Wonderful Airship* (1906–French) d: Georges Méliès
☐ *Invisible Boy, The* (1957) d: Herman Hoffman
☐ *It Happened Here* (1966) d: Kevin Brownlow and Andrew Mollo
☐ *It! The Terror from Beyond Space* (1958) d: Edward L. Cahn
☐ *It's Great to Be Alive* (1933) d: Alfred Werker

☐ *Jesse James Meets Frankenstein's Daughter* (1965) d: William Beaudine
☐ *Journey to the Center of Time* (1967) d: D. L. Hewitt
☐ *Journey to the Far Side of the Sun/Doppelganger* (1969–British) d: Robert Parrish
☐ *Journey to the Seventh Planet* (1962) d: Sidney Pink
☐ *Just Imagine* (1930) d: David Butler

☐ *Kamikaze 1989* (1982–German) d: Wolf Gremm
☐ *King Dinosaur* (1955) d: Bert I. Gordon
☐ *King of the Rocket Men* (1949; serial) d: Fred C. Bannon
☐ *Kiss Me Deadly* (1955) d: Robert Aldrich
☐ *Kiss the Girls and Make Them Die* (1966–Italian-American) d: Henry Levin and Dino Maiuri
☐ *Krakatit* (1948–Czech) d: Otakar Vávra

☐ *La Fin du Monde* (1930–French) d: Abel Gance
☐ *La Folie du Dr. Tube* (1915–French) d: Abel Gance
☐ *La Jetée* (1962–French; short) d: Chris Marker
☐ *Lady and the Monster, The* (1944) d; George Sherman
☐ *Lady Frankenstein* (1971–Italian) d: Mel Welles
☐ *L'Alliance* (1971–French) d: Christian de Challonge
☐ *Last Chase, The* (1981) d: Martyn Burke
☐ *Last Days of Man on Earth, The/Final Programme, The* (1973–British) d: Robert Fuest
☐ *Last Days of Planet Earth, The* (1974–Japanese) d: Toshio Masuda
☐ *Last Generation, The* (1971) d: William Graham
☐ *Last Man on Earth, The* (1924) d: John D. Swain
☐ *Last Man on Earth, The* (1964–Italian-American) d: Sidney Salkow
☐ *Last War, The* (1961–Japanese) d: Shue Matsubayashi
☐ *Last Woman on Earth, The* (1961) d: Roger Corman
☐ *Latitude Zero* (1970–Japanese) d: Inoshiro Honda
☐ *L'Homme au Cerveau Greffe* (1972–French) d: Jacques Doniol Valcroze
☐ *Life Without Soul* (1915) d: Joseph W. Smiley
☐ *Light Years Away* (1981–Swiss) d: Alain Tanner
☐ *Lightning Bolt* (1966–Italian-Spanish) d: Antonio Margheriti

☐ *L'Inhumaine* (1924–French) d: Marcel L'Herbier
☐ *Live and Let Die* (1973–British) d: Guy Hamilton
☐ *Logan's Run* (1976) d: Michael Anderson
☐ *Looker* (1981) d: Michael Crichton
☐ *Lost Missile, The (1958) d: Lester Berke*

☐ *Mad Doctor of Market Street, The* (1942) d: Joseph H. Lewis
☐ *Mad Love* (1935) d: Karl Freund
☐ *Mad Max* (1979–Australian) d: George Miller
☐ *Mad Max 2/Road Warrior, The* (1982–Australian) d: George Miller
☐ *Mad Max 3* (1985–Australian) d: George Miller
☐ *Madrid en el Ano* (1925–Spanish) d: Manuel Noriega
☐ *Magnetic Monster, The* (1953) d: Curt Siodmak
☐ *Man in the Half-Moon Street, The* (1944) d: Ralph Murphy
☐ *Man in Outer Space, The* (1961–Czech) d: Oldrich Lipsky
☐ *Man in the Moon* (1961–British) d: Basil Dearden
☐ *Man in the White Suit, The* (1952–British) d: Alexander Mackendrick
☐ *Man They Could Not Arrest, The* (1933–British) d: T. Hays Hunter
☐ *Man They Could Not Hang, The* (1939) d: Nick Grinde
☐ *Man Who Could Cheat Death, The* (1959–British) d: Terence Fisher
☐ *Man Who Lived Again, The/Man Who Changed His Mind, The* (1936–British) d: Robert Stevenson
☐ *Man With Nine Lives, The* (1940) d: Nick Grinde
☐ *Man With the Golden Gun, The* (1974–British) d: Guy Hamilton
☐ *Man with Two Brains, The* (1983) d: Carl Reiner
☐ *Manhunt of Mystery Island* (1945; serial) d: Spencer Bennet, Wallace Grissell, and Yakima Canutt
☐ *Marooned* (1969) d: John Sturges
☐ *Master Mystery, The* (1918; serial) d: Burton King
☐ *Master of the World* (1934–German) d: Harry Piel
☐ *Master of the World* (1961) d: William Witney
☐ *Mechanical Husband, A* (1910–British) d: S. Wormwald
☐ *Mechanical Man, The* (1915) d: Allen Curtis
☐ *Mechanical Mary Anne, The* (1910–British) d: Lewis Fitzhamon
☐ *Megaforce* (1982) d: Hal Needham
☐ *Men Must Fight* (1933)
☐ *Metropolis* (1926–German) d: Fritz Lang
☐ *Mind of Mr. Soames, The* (1970–British) d: Alan Cooke
☐ *Mind Benders, The* (1961–British) d: Basil Dearden
☐ *Mind Snatchers, The* (1972) d: Bernard Girard
☐ *Miracle of Tomorrow, The* (1923–German) d: Harry Piel
☐ *Miss Muerte/Diabolical Dr. Z, The* (1966–Spanish-French) d: Jesus Franco
☐ *Missile to the Moon* (1959) d: Richard Cunha
☐ *Mission Mars* (1968) d: Nick Webster
☐ *Mission Stardust* (1968–Italian) d: Primo Zeglio
☐ *Mister Freedom* (1969–French) d: William Klein
☐ *Mister, Are You a Widow?* (1972–Czech)
☐ *Monitors, The* (1969) d: Jack Shea
☐ *Monster and the Ape, The* (1945; serial) d: Howard Bretherton
☐ *Monsters* (1984) d: Stephen Marra
☐ *Moon Mask Rider, The* (1981–Japanese) d: Yukihiro Sawada
☐ *Moon Pilot* (1962) d: James Neilson
☐ *Moon Zero Two* (1970–British) d: Roy Ward Baker
☐ *Moonraker* (1979–British) d: Lewis Gilbert
☐ *Motor Valet, The* (1906–British) d: Arthur Cooper
☐ *"?" Motorist, The* (1905–British) d: Robert Paul
☐ *Mouse on the Moon, The* (1963–British) d: Richard Lester
☐ *Mouse That Roared, The* (1959–British) d: Jack Arnold
☐ *Murder By Phone* (1980–Canadian) d: Michael Anderson
☐ *Murder By Television* (1935) d: Clifford Sandforth
☐ *Mutiny in Outer Space* (1965) d: Hugo Grimaldi
☐ *Mysteries of Myra, The (1916; serial)*
☐ *Mysterious Dr. Satan, The* (1940; serial) d: William Witney and John English

☐ *N.P.* (1971–Italian) d: Silvano Agosti
☐ *Neutron Against the Death Robots* (1961–Mexican) d: Luis Garcia de Leon
☐ *Never Say Never Again* (1983–British) d: Irvin Kershner
☐ *Night Key* (1937) d: Lloyd Corrigan

☐ *Night of the Blood Beast* (1958) d: Bernard Kowalski
☐ *Nine Days in One Year* (1961–Russian) d: Mikhail Romm
☐ *1984* (1956–British) d: Michael Anderson
☐ *1984* (1984–British) d: Michael Radford
☐ *1990: The Bronx Warriors* (1983) d: Enzo Castellari
☐ *No Blade of Grass* (1970) d: Cornel Wilde
☐ *Noah's Ark Principle, The* (1984–German) d: Roland Emmerich
☐ *Non-Stop New York* (1937–British) d: Robert Stevenson

☐ *O Lucky Man* (1973–British) d: Lindsay Anderson
☐ *Octopussy* (1983–British) d: John Glen
☐ *Omega Man, The* (1971) d: Boris Sagal
☐ *On Her Majesty's Secret Service* (1969–British) d: Peter Hunt
☐ *On the Beach* (1959) d: Stanley Kramer
☐ *On the Threshold of Space* (1956) d: Robert D. Webb
☐ *Our Man Flint* (1966) d: Daniel Mann
☐ *Outland* (1981) d: Peter Hyams

☐ *Panic in the City* (1967) d: Eddie Davis
☐ *Panic in the Year Zero* (1962) d: Ray Milland
☐ *Parasite* (1982) d: Charles Band
☐ *Paris Qui Dort/Crazy Ray, The* (1923–French) d: Rene Clair
☐ *Parts: The Clonus Horror/Clonus Horror, The* (1978) d: Robert S. Fiveson
☐ *People Who Own the Dark* (1975–Spanish) d: Armando de Ossario
☐ *Percy* (1971–British) d: Ralph Thomas
☐ *Perfect Woman, The* (1949–British) d: Bernard Knowles
☐ *Phantastic World of Matthew Madson, The* (1974–German)
☐ *Phantom Creeps, The* (1939; serial) d: Ford Beebe and Saul A. Goodkind
☐ *Phantom Planet, The* (1961) d: William Marshall
☐ *Pirates of 1920, The* (1911–British) d: A.E. Coleby and Dave Aylott
☐ *Plague/Plague-M3: The Gemini Strain* (1978–Canadian) d: Ed Hunt
☐ *Planet of Blood/Queen of Blood* (1966) d: Curtis Harrington
☐ *Planet of Storms* (1962–Russian) d: Pavel Klushantsev
☐ *Planet of the Apes* (1968) d: Franklin Schaffner
☐ *Planet of the Vampires/Demon Planet, The* (1965–Italian) d: Mario Bava
☐ *Planet on the Prowl/War Between the Planets* (1970–Italian) d: Anthony Dawson
☐ *Pleasure Machines, The/Love Machines, The* (1969–Italian) d: Ron Garcia
☐ *President's Analyst, The* (1967) d: Theodore J. Flicker
☐ *Privilege* (1967–British) d: Peter Watkins
☐ *Project Moonbase* (1953) d: Richard Talmadge
☐ *Project X* (1968) d: William Castle
☐ *Punishment Park* (1971–British) d: Peter Watkins

☐ *Queen of Outer Space* (1958) d: Edward Bernds
☐ *Quintet* (1979) d: Robert Altman

☐ *Radioactive Dreams* (1984) d: Albert Pyun
☐ *Rataplan* (1980–Italian) d: Maurizio Nichetti
☐ *Ravagers* (1979) d: Richard Compton
☐ *Reluctant Astronaut, The* (1967) d: Edward Montagne
☐ *Return of Dr. X, The* (1939) d: Vincent Sherman
☐ *Revenge of Frankenstein, The* (1958–British) d: Terence Fisher
☐ *Riders to the Stars* (1954) d: Richard Carlson
☐ *Robinson Crusoe on Mars* (1964) d: Byron Haskin
☐ *Robots* (1932–French) d: Eugene Deslaw
☐ *Rocket Attack, U.S.A.* (1960) d: Barry Mahan
☐ *Rocketship X-M* (1950) d: Kurt Neumann
☐ *Rollerball* (1975) d: Norman Jewison
☐ *Rollover* (1981) d: Alan J. Pakula
☐ *Rome 2023: Fighter Centurians* (1984–Italian) d: Lucio Fulchi

☐ *Satan Bug, The (1965) d: John Sturges*
☐ *Satisfiers of Alpha Blue, The* (1981) d: Gerard Damiano
☐ *Satellite in the Sky* (1956) d: Paul Dickson
☐ *Saturn 3* (1980–British) d: Stanley Donen
☐ *Scream and Scream Again* (1970–British) d: Gordon Hessler
☐ *Seconds* (1966) d: John Frankenheimer
☐ *Secret of the Submarine, The* (1916; serial) d: George Sargent

☐ *Secret Room, The* (1915) d: Tom Moore
☐ *Seven Days in May* (1964) d: John Frankenheimer
☐ *Seven Days to Noon* (1950–British) d: John and Roy Boulting
☐ *Sex Machine, The* (1976–Italian) d: Pasquale Festa Campanile
☐ *Sh! The Octopus* (1937) d: William McGann
☐ *Shadow, The* (1940; serial) d: James W. Horne
☐ *Shanks* (1974) d: William Castle
☐ *Shape of Things to Come* (1979–Canadian) d: George McCowan
☐ *Shielding Shadow, The* (1916; serial)
☐ *Silent Rage* (1982) d: Michael Miller
☐ *Silent Running* (1971) d: Douglas Trumbull
☐ *Sins of the Fleshapoids* (1965) d: Mike Kuchar
☐ *Sky Bandits* (1940; serial) d: Ralph Staub
☐ *Sky Bike, The* (1967–British) d: Charles Frend
☐ *Sky Parade, The* (1936) d: Otto Lovering
☐ *Sky Pirates* (1939) d: George Waggner
☐ *Sky Ship* (1917–Danish) d: Holger Madsen
☐ *Sky Skidder, The* (1929) d: Bruce Mitchell
☐ *Sky Splitter* (1922) d: John R. Bray
☐ *Sleeper* (1973) d: Woody Allen
☐ *Solaris* (1972–Russian) d: Andrei Tarkovsky
☐ *Some Girls Do* (1969–British) d: Ralph Thomas
☐ *Someone Behind the Door* (1971) d: Nicolas Gessner
☐ *Son of Flubber* (1963) d: Robert Stevenson
☐ *Son of Frankenstein* (1939) d: Rowland V. Lee
☐ *Sorcerers, The* (1967–British) d: Michael Reeves
☐ *Soylent Green* (1973) d: Richard Flesicher
☐ *Space Cruiser Yamato* (1977–Japanese) d: Yoshinabu Nishizaki
☐ *Space Master X-7* (1957) d: Edward Bernds
☐ *Space Monster* (1965) d: Leonard Katzman
☐ *Space Vampires, The* (1984) d: Tobe Hooper w: Dan O'Bannon and Don Jakoby
☐ *Space Raiders/Star-Child* (1983) d: Herman Cohen
☐ *Spaced Out/Outer Touch* (1979–British) d: Norman J. Warren
☐ *Spaceflight IC-1* (1965–British) d: Bernard Knowles
☐ *Spacehunter: Adventures in the Forbidden Zone* (1983) d: Lamont Johnson
☐ *Space-Watch Murders, The* (1978)
☐ *Spaceways* (1953–British) d: Terence Fisher
☐ *Splatter* (1984) d: Ronald Moore
☐ *Spy in Your Eye* (1966–Italian) d: Vittorio Sala
☐ *Spy Who Loved Me, The* (1977–British) d: Lewis Gilbert
☐ *Stalker* (1981–Russian) d: Andrei Tarkovsky
☐ *Star Trek—The Motion Picture* (1979) d: Robert Wise
☐ *Star Trek II: The Wrath of Khan* (1982) d: Nicholas Meyer
☐ *Star Trek III: The Search for Spock* (1984) d: Leonard Nimoy
☐ *Stepford Wives, The* (1975) d: Bryan Forbes
☐ *Strange Behavior* (1980) d: Michael Laughlin
☐ *Stranger, The* (1973) d: Lee Katzin
☐ *Streets of Fire* (1984) d: Walter Hill
☐ *Submersion of Japan* (1974–Japanese) d: Shiro Moriana
☐ *Sun Never Sets, The* (1939) d: Rowland V. Lee

☐ *Teenage Caveman/Prehistoric Planet* (1958) d: Roger Corman
☐ *10th Victim, The* (1965–Italian) d: Elio Petri
☐ *Terminal Island* (1973) d: Stephanie Rothman
☐ *Terminal Man, The* (1974) d: Michael Hodges
☐ *Terror Beneath the Sea* (1966–Japanese) d: Hajimoto Sato
☐ *Terror from the Year 5000* (1958) d: Robert Gurney, Jr.
☐ *Testament* (1983) d: Lynne Littman
☐ *Things to Come* (1936–British) d: William Cameron Menzies
☐ *This Is Not a Test* (1962) d: Frederic Gadette
☐ *Those Fantastic Flying Fools/Blast Off* (1967–British) d: Don Sharp
☐ *Threshold* (1983) d: Richard Pearce
☐ *Thunderball* (1965–British) d: Terence Young
☐ *THX 1138* (1971) d: George Lucas
☐ *Tidal Wave* (1975–Japanese-American) d: Shiro Moriani and Andrew Mayer
☐ *Time Machine, The* (1960) d: George Pal
☐ *Time Travelers, The* (1964) d: Ib Melchior
☐ *Tobor the Great* (1954) d: Lee Sholem

☐ *Torture Garden* (1968–British; segment) d: Freddie Francis w: Robert Bloch
☐ *Transplant* (1970–Italian-Spanish) d: Stefano Steno
☐ *Transatlantic Tunnel/Tunnel, The* (1935–British) d: Maurice Elvey
☐ *Trip to Mars, A* (1910)
☐ *Trip to Mars, A* (1920–Italy)
☐ *Trip to the Moon, A* (1902–French) d: Georges Méliès
☐ *Trip to the Moon, A* (1914)
☐ *Tunneling the English Channel* (1907–French) d: Georges Méliès
☐ *Tunnelvision* (1976) d: Neal Israel
☐ *12 to the Moon* (1960) d: David Bradley
☐ *20 Million Miles to Earth* (1957) d: Nathan Juran
☐ *2084* (1985–British) d: Roger Christian
☐ *2069 A.D.—A Sex Odyssey* (1969) d: Cam Sopetsky
☐ *Twenty Thousand Leagues Under the Sea* (1907–French) d: Georges Méliès
☐ *20,000 Leagues Under the Sea* (1916) d: Stuart Paton
☐ *20,000 Leagues Under the Sea* (1954) d: Richard Fleischer
☐ *2020 Texas Gladiators* (1984) d: Kevin Mancuso
☐ *Twilight's Last Gleaming* (1977–German-American) d: Robert Aldrich
☐ *2001: A Space Odyssey* (1968) d: Stanley Kubrick
☐ *2010: Odyssey Two* (1984) d: Peter Hyams
☐ *Twonky, The* (1953) d: Arch Oboler

☐ *Ultimate Warrior, The* (1975) d: Robert Clouse
☐ *Underwater City, The* (1962) d: Frank McDonald
☐ *Unknown World* (1951) d: Terrell O. Morse

☐ *Vampire Men of the Lost Planet/Horror of the Blood Monster* (1970) d: Al Adamson
☐ *Vanishing Shadow, The* (1934; serial) d: Louis Friedlander
☐ *Victor Frankenstein* (1975–Swedish-Irish) d: Calvin Floyd
☐ *Videodrome* (1983–Canadian) d: David Cronenberg
☐ *Virus* (1982–Japanese) d: Kenji Fukasaku
☐ *Vortex* (1982) d: Scott B and Beth B
☐ *Voyage into Space* (1968–Japanese)
☐ *Voyage to the Bottom of the Sea* (1961) d: Irwin Allen w: Allen and Charles Bennett

☐ *Voyage to the End of the Universe/Ikarie XB 1* (1963–Czech) d: Jindrich Polak
☐ *Voyage to the Planet of Prehistoric Women* (1968–Russian-American) d: Derek Thomas (Peter Bogdanovich)
☐ *Voyage to the Prehistoric Planet* (1965–Russian-American) d: John Sebastion (Curtis Harrington)

☐ *War Game, The* (1965–British TV; 1967 theatrical release in U.S.) d: Peter Watkins
☐ *WarGames* (1983) d: John Badham
☐ *Warlords of the 21st Century/Battletruck* (1982–New Zealand) d: Harley Cokliss
☐ *Warriors of the Wasteland* (1984–Italian) d: Enzo Castellari
☐ *Water Cyborgs/Terror Beneath the Sea* (1966–Japanese) d: Hajime Soto
☐ *Way . . . Way Out* (1966) d: Gordon Douglas
☐ *Welcome to Blood City* (1977–British-Canadian) d: Peter Sasdy
☐ *Westworld* (1983) d: Michael Crichton
☐ *When Worlds Collide* (1951) d: Rudolph Maté
☐ *Who?* (1974–British) d: Jack Gold
☐ *Whoops Apocalypse* (1981–British) d: John Reardon
☐ *Wild in the Sky/Black Jack* (1972) d: William T. Naud
☐ *Wild in the Streets* (1968) d: Barry Shear
☐ *Wizard of Mars* (1964) d: David L. Hewitt
☐ *Woman in the Moon/Frau Im Mond* (1928–German) d: Fritz Lang
☐ *Women of the Prehistoric Planet* (1966) d: Arthur C. Pierce
☐ *World, The Flesh, and the Devil, The* (1959) d: Ranald MacDougall
☐ *World Without End* (1956) d: Edward Bernds

☐ *The X From Outer Space* (1967–Japanese) d: Nazui Nihomatsu

☐ *Year of the Cannibal* (1971)
☐ *Yellow Cab Man, The* (1950) d: Jack Donahue
☐ *Yor, the Hunter from the Future* (1983) d: Anthony Dawson
☐ *You Only Live Twice* (1967–British) d: Lewis Gilbert

☐ *Z.P.G.* (1972–British) d: Michael Campus
☐ *Zardoz* (1974–British) d: John Boorman

The Women of the Prehistoric Planet *look toward the future.*

Index